RHETORIC
IN THE
EUROPEAN
TRADITION

RHETORIC
—IN THE—
EUROPEAN
TRADITION

THOMAS M. CONLEY

The University of Chicago Press
Chicago and London

The University of Chicago Press, Chicago 60637
The University of Chicago Press, Ltd., London

All rights reserved. Originally published 1990
University of Chicago Press Edition 1994
Printed in the United States of America
12 11 10 09 08   6 7 8 9 10

ISBN-13: 978-0-226-11489-7
ISBN-10: 0-226-11489-9

Library of Congress Cataloging-in-Publication Data

Conley, Thomas M., 1941–
    Rhetoric in the European tradition / Thomas M. Conley.
        p.   cm.
    Includes bibliographical references (p.) and index.
    1. Rhetoric.   I. Title.
    [PN175.C55   1994]
    808—dc20   93-32600
                                                                      CIP

⊗ The paper used in this publication meets the minimum requirements of the American National Standard for Information Sciences—Permanence of Paper for Printed Library Materials, ANSI Z39.48-1992.

Contents

130 067

Preface

Most teachers of courses in the history of rhetoric have heard complaints from their students about the lack of a good, comprehensive text that would give them both an overview of the subject and some detailed information about particular authors and texts. During some 20 years of teaching, I myself have heard such complaints repeatedly from students, quite literally, from coast to coast. And I have heard similar complaints from colleagues and students in departments of English, Romance languages, even Classics. My own solution to this has been to assign only primary texts, trusting that my students' stenographic abilities would enable them to record most of what I gave them in background lectures. But that led me to see that it was not only the students who could use a good survey/reference text but also the teacher who must sacrifice valuable time better spent in explicating those primary texts than in supplying information that students could simply "look up" if there were some place to do the looking. As it is, most of the available secondary literature is scattered widely in books and journal articles that tend to be either too specialized or too superficial to be very useful, much less convenient. This book is meant to change all that, at least until another, better one comes along.

On a train platform in Tours in the summer of 1987, George Kennedy warned me that this book, then only in the planning stage, would probably please no one completely, no matter what I did. Everyone would find something wrong—a favorite writer missing, a topic overdone. With that warning in mind, I have tried to be both prudent and fair in allocating room to various periods and authors. This process has involved decisions that Kennedy told me that morning would be "agonizing." How right he was! It did not take me long to discover that I had to compromise occasionally between the demands of exhaustive treatment and the preservation of a coherent line of exposition. The basic criterion I have used in deciding which authors to discuss, and at what length, is the degree of actual influence they exercised on their contemporaries and on succeeding generations. Accordingly, some authors whose importance is recognized today—Aristotle, for instance, or Vico—are not treated at length because they had no visible impact on the rhetoric of their times and little or no influence on later thinkers. And by the same token, I have taken opportunities where I saw them to dwell on some areas or authors I think have been unjustifiably ignored in most histories— Keckermann and Lamy, for instance. I expect that some instructors who use this book may wish to correct what they see as deficiencies or exaggerations in my version of the rhetorical tradition and present their own versions to their students. But I hope such responses will stimulate not confusion but debate. After all, rhetoric is about nothing if it is not about controversy.

In what I have done, I have been guided by two thematic principles. First, I see rhetoric, historically, as becoming particularly important to people during times of strife and crisis, political or intellectual. Accordingly, I have tried to locate the texts I discuss in that context, even when doing so has required highly compressed reference to those conditions. Second, I see various perennial responses to such crises productive of distinctive views of what rhetoric is, or ought to be, or should do; and not of a single, unitary art or discipline called "Rhetoric." Thus the "story" here tracks different responses, some of which dominate in one period, others in another, within the European tradition.

In the interests of pedagogy, I have added brief summaries to each chapter, as well as bibliographical notes indicating useful further reading, both for general background and for more detailed accounts of the texts or authors discussed in the chapter. I have also included outlines and tables of contents of some important works (marked with an asterisk at their first mention in the text), particularly of works not easily accessible. Much can be learned from merely scanning the contents and proportions of these works— sometimes, even, about one work's relationships to another. Students will also find a brief table putting the works discussed in this book in chronological perspective and a short glossary of (mainly) technical terms that appear relatively frequently.

My correspondence and conversation with fellow members of the International Society for the History of Rhetoric have provided me with a scholarly perspective I would not otherwise have acquired and without which this book could not have been written. I have been greatly helped in assembling the materials for this book by the staff of the Rare Book Room at the University of Illinois Library. To my colleagues here also, particularly Joe Wenzel, I owe thanks for support and advice.

All translations, unless otherwise noted, are my own. Any errors, of course, are my own, too. *Lectori benevolo.*

Abbreviations

ADB	*Allgemeine Deutsche Biographie*
ANRW	*Aufstieg und Niedergang der Römischen Welt*
BU	*Biographie Universale*
CM	*Communication Monographs*
DNB	*Dictionary of National Biography*
GRBS	*Greek, Roman, and Byzantine Studies*
JHI	*Journal of the History of Ideas*
OCT	Oxford Classical Texts
PG	*Patrologia Graeca*
PL	*Patrologia Latina*
QJS	*Quarterly Journal of Speech*
SM	*Speech Monographs*
TAPA	*Transactions of the American Philological Association*
WSJ	*Western Speech Journal*

CHAPTER 1

Classical Greek Rhetorics

At the beginning of Book Two of the *Iliad*, Zeus sends a dream to Agamemnon, first among Greek kings in the campaign against the Trojans. The dream, in the guise of the old wise man Nestor, tells Agamemnon that the gods have become impatient with the lack of progress in bringing the war, by now nine years in the waging, to an end. "Do something," the dream says in effect, "to rouse your troops and take the city" (2.23–34). Agamemnon, after consultation, conceives of a strategy for doing that. Rather than giving yet another stirring speech to his fellow Greeks, he will urge them to give up the battle, counting on their sense of honor and of the warrior's *aretē* (often translated "virtue") to result in precisely the opposite reaction, arousing in them "the heat of the hero."

The speech fails to do that, and instead the troops begin preparing their ships for the journey home. Odysseus, admired by all for his courage and shrewdness, intervenes and tries with only partial success to stem the flight. At this point, as the Greeks have been gathered, one Thersites, "the ugliest man beneath the walls of Troy," the poet remarks (2.216), rises up and gives a sharp speech counseling his fellows to take to the ships after all, since the only profit to be made from continuing the campaign would accrue to Agamemnon and the other kings (2.229ff.). On hearing this speech by Thersites, Odysseus berates him and thrashes him about the back and shoulders until Thersites begins to weep. The assembled Greeks, on seeing this, laugh heartily and congratulate Odysseus for keeping "this thrower of words, this braggart, out of assembly" (275f.).[1]

This brief episode is perhaps more instructive about rhetoric in ancient Greece, and indeed about rhetoric in general, than it might at first appear to be. It teaches us something, to begin with, about the way Greeks, from Homer's time onward, conducted public assemblies. To be sure, the Homeric

1

assembly, presided over by a king, was not exactly a showcase for participatory democracy. But it is important to note that public discussion, where options were debated and consensus sought, was evidently the traditional way in which decisions were reached. Second, while the actions of Odysseus may seem at variance with our idea of public discussion—particularly when it is clear that what Thersites says is what Agamemnon had said just before—they were not perceived that way by Homer. The reason is that in the resolution of problems of action, it is not only the argument that counts. In Homeric assemblies particularly, the status of the speaker who presents the argument is all-important. Thersites, being ugly and undistinguished in battle, has no *aretē* and consequently no right to take the floor, so to speak, ahead of the likes of Agamemnon and Odysseus, who do. Yet, Thersites counseled the same course of action that Agamemnon did.

The tension that appears here is the tension between being right and having the social right to participate in public discussion. Homer's warriors were of course very clear on what gave one the social right: basically, health, wealth, and good looks. But it is odd that Agamemnon, in trying to obey the injunction of Zeus, failed and that only after listening to a speaker who said the same thing he did, but out of turn, did the Greeks come around to a renewed desire to fight. That is, the "right" speaker goes wrong, and the "wrong" speaker makes things right. Is this merely a coincidence? Or does it tell us something about why rhetoric was of such enormous interest to the Greeks?

In Thucydides' *History of the Peloponnesian War* we read of other rhetorical episodes that bring out even more tensions evident in the way ancient Greeks thought about the role of discourse in the consideration and resolution of disagreements. In Book Five, for instance, Thucydides relates the so-called Melian Dialogue (5.85ff.). The Melians had gotten on the bad side of Athens because they wanted to remain neutral in the war between the Athenians and the Spartans, which had been going on intermittently for over a decade. Athens insisted on some commitment to their side by the Melians, and the Melians refused. Athens sent a delegation to "negotiate." Their "argument" is summed up pretty well in what they say at 5.89:

> You know as well as we that what is just is arrived at by human arguments (*tōi anthropeiōi logōi*) only when the necessity [for doing so] on both sides is equal; but that the powerful do whatever they want, while the weak yield.

When the Melians object that the threats against them are unjust and impious, the Athenians counter with an argument (5.105) to the effect that the record of divine relations with humans actually supports their side. In the end, the Melians were besieged, starved out, and reduced: the men were killed, the women and children sold into slavery, and the city repopulated by less intransigent folk.

Here we have a classic instance in which having might is equated with being right. Discourse is placed at the service of brute power. There is, in truth, no argument; only threats cast in argumentative terms. And the threats in this case are far more serious than those of social disgrace. Of course, the Athenians had few reservations about acting this way, since, after all, the Melians were originally a Spartan colony. Yet they are careful to present their case as though they were truly interested in debating the issue, and the language throughout is the language of persuasion, not the language of physical threat. Thucydides' account, then, becomes a sort of commentary on the uses of language for the sake of appearance when the reality is quite different, and about language as an instrument of power. This, too, is a virtual preoccupation of Greeks who wrote on rhetoric in the Classical period.

Another example from Thucydides is provided by his account, in Book Six, of the debate in the Athenian assembly over the question of who should lead the expedition against Sicily and how it should be conducted. The assembly had already voted (in March, 415 BC) to mount the expedition; the question on this occasion had to do with who would be in charge. One candidate was Alcibiades, who makes his case at 6.16ff. Since Alcibiades was so prominent and had been elected one of the generals (*strategoi*), there was no problem with his "right" to take to the floor, and clearly there was no possibility of his achieving his goal by threats to the gathered assembly. Alcibiades, therefore, draws attention to his accomplishments and contributions to the City and then invokes the ideals of the Athenian "spirit," scoffing at the moderation of his rival Nikias and applauding the courage and ingenuity of his fellow Athenians (see 6.16.2, 17.2f, 18.1f.). The Athenians vote him in as commander, and the expedition is later sent off.

The Sicilian Expedition, as it happened, failed disastrously. Athens suffered a defeat from which it never recovered, and eventually lost the war with Sparta. Thucydides' readers knew this, perhaps only too well. And so there is in his story another sort of tension evident in his account of the debate. It is true that Alcibiades possessed a sort of representative authority and the right to speak. In fact, at the time, he really was qualified to command. It is not so much that he was wrong about the advisability of going off to conquer Sicily—a decision the Athenians were to regret (8.1.1)—that concerns us here. It is, rather, the fact that he was able to urge successfully what was wrong because the audience thought it right, and probably also because they appreciated his implicit praise of them in his speech. But they confounded having authority with being right, which is to say that Alcibiades' success was a function of their ignorance and vanity, and so voted in the majority to mandate as right what was, at the very least, unwise.

We see in these rhetorical situations "representative anecdotes"[2] of the tensions between privilege and correctness, right and might, power and persuasion, and persuasion and ignorance that pervade Greek thinking—and perhaps all thinking—about rhetoric. It is just such tensions—all of them social in nature and not just philosophical—that lie behind the various accounts and analyses of rhetoric that begin to appear in the late fifth and early fourth centuries before the common era. In this chapter, we shall be concerned to sketch the outlines of four quite different responses to those tensions, which center on the role of discourse in the resolution of problems, the sources and criteria of authority, and the proper activities of those practicing what is generally referred to as "the art of persuasion." Obviously, we cannot cover this subject in any great detail in a single chapter, so we need to concentrate on the basic principles underlying the various conceptions of rhetoric as something systematic and of its duties and ends. At the same time, it is important that we keep in view the very real political conditions that gave rise to speculation about the nature of rhetoric—variously defined as it was—and to the attempts to systematize it.

THE TEACHINGS OF THE "SOPHISTS"

There is an old story that tells us the first "course" in rhetoric was taught by one Corax in response to a surge of litigation in Sicily over confiscated plots of land. It may be true, but it is probably just another of those stories about "first discoveries" Greeks were so fond of.[3] The true birthplace of rhetorical instruction was Athens, and the first instructors were those itinerant teachers who flocked there in the mid-fifth century, the so-called sophists.

It is no accident that the sophists should have been drawn to Athens. These teachers (sophos, in Greek, means "wise") found there a ready market for their wares, particularly for what they had to offer in terms of rhetorical instruction. Two sorts of political reform had been instituted in Athens by 450: the reforms of Kleisthenes, which established a form of democratic government, and the reform of the court system in Athens by Ephialtes in 462. Kleisthenes eliminated the traditional political structure built around clan and family ties and replaced it with a system of representative government that cut across the old boundaries of influence. Two new basic principles were inaugurated: (1) that power should reside in the people as a whole, and not in an elite few, and (2) that high offices should be entrusted by lot to those among the citizens who were perceived as best fitted for them. The reforms of Ephialtes resulted in the diminution of the importance of the board of magistrates, which convened at the Areopagus, and the institution of a system of common courts, the "Heliastic courts," where decisions were rendered by juries chosen by lot from the citizenry.

The reforms of Kleisthenes opened up Athenian politics. As all citizens, at least in principle, were eligible to become members of the assembly, to vote on public issues, and to hold administrative offices, an unprecedented social mobility became possible. Any citizen could, by law, aspire to a career in politics or civil service. The reforms of Ephialtes made it possible for any citizen to bring suit against any other and mandated that such cases, with the exception of suits over sacrilege or certain kinds of homicide that fell under the jurisdiction of the Areopagus, should be decided by a Heliastic jury. Two features of this new court system need to be kept in mind. First, every citizen involved in a lawsuit had to argue his own case. There were no lawyers in the modern sense. Second, these juries consisted of upward of two hundred members; so the deliberations were considerably more public than the jury deliberations of today.

In both arenas of public action, the assembly and the courts, a measure of eloquence was greatly to be desired; thus, among the many things the sophists claimed to be able to teach, a facility in public speaking was the most sought after. This was especially true because the political and legal reforms did not succeed in eliminating entirely the privileges of status and bloodline, privileges that could potentially be neutralized by the power of public influence a skillful speaker might possess. In view of this, it is no small irony that, because the fees charged by the sophists for their instruction were so large, only the wealthy could afford the sort of training a sophist might provide.

There is no single set of principles on which that training was based that can be characterized as "sophistic." While the methods of instruction they used were probably common to all of them—and indeed to all teachers in fifth-century Athens—we can discern at least two quite different lines of thinking about rhetoric in the rather sketchy evidence we have for what the sophists were telling their followers. One of these we will characterize as "Protagorean" and the other as "Gorgianic."

Protagoras (c. 490–c. 400) came to Athens before 450, possibly about the time of Ephialtes' reforms. We know at least that he was commissioned by the Athenian government to compose a constitution for the colony set down by it at Thurii in 444, which would suggest that he was already by that time known and respected in Athens. We have only fragments of his writings and Plato's accounts of his theories to go on, but one feature of his approach to rhetoric seems beyond question. Ancient testimony points to a basic belief in the centrality of debate to Protagoras' thinking. Our authorities are almost unanimous in ascribing to Protagoras the "invention" of "antilogic"—that is, the method of resolving disputes by examining the arguments on both sides of the question, without recourse to some objective criterion of truth or to some traditional standard of behavior. The truth, for all practical purposes, was held by Protagoras to be inaccessible; and matters of prudence, virtue, and honor were all contestable. Thus, only by examining the arguments for and against a given proposition can one come to some determination as to which side is to be believed and acted upon.[4]

Gorgias, some ten years younger than Protagoras, came to Athens as part of a delegation from Leontini, in Sicily, in 427. Once there, he became quite famous as an orator able to speak eloquently and at length on any topic proposed to him and offered instruction in the arts of persuasion. Aside from the rather negative picture of Gorgias Plato gives in his *Gorgias** (which we shall look at later), we have a number of fragments of works he composed, including two declamations, the *Encomium to Helen* and the *Palamedes*. Whether or not the *Encomium to Helen* can be taken as truly representative of Gorgias' thinking, the observations on the power of discourse he makes in it reveal an interesting view of persuasion, one that is with us to this day.

In his speech on Helen's behalf, Gorgias seeks to absolve her of any blame for the Trojan War as "the face that launched a thousand ships" by arguing that the most likely explanation for her deserting her husband and going off with Paris is that she was "struck out of her wits" by Paris' beauty and eloquence. The power of speech (*logos*) cannot be overestimated. "Speech is a powerful lord." Gorgias says (*Helen* 8), "which by means of the finest and most invisible body [sound] had effects that are almost divine." Indeed,

> the effect of speech upon the condition of the soul is comparable to the power of drugs over the nature of bodies. For just as different drugs dispel different secretions from the body, and some bring an end to disease and others to life, so also in the case of speeches, some distress, others delight, some cause fear, others make the hearers bold, and some drug and bewitch the soul with a kind of evil persuasion (*peithō*) (*Helen* 14).[5]

Like Protagoras, Gorgias rejected claims to knowledge and held that opinion (*doxa*) was the only guide to action. Both, then, implicitly rejected the criteria of "truth," on the one hand, and tradition on the other, at least insofar as tradition was held to provide unquestionable standards of good behavior. These implications were taken seriously by their Athenian audiences and explain much of the opprobrium heaped upon them by satirists like Aristophanes and philosophers like Plato. Protagoras was accused of teaching his students how to "make the worse case appear the better" and Gorgias of providing his with a power equivalent to "putting a knife in the hands of a madman in a crowd."[6] It is unlikely that these charges reflect an accurate picture of their teachings, but it is not hard to understand why such charges might have been laid against them. They were, after all, outsiders. Like all of the sophists we know of, they came to Athens from some other place and were therefore suspect. More important, their teachings had a destabilizing effect, or so conservative Athenians thought, on traditional social and political institutions. Nevertheless, they both enjoyed a measure of respect and even power, though neither was a citizen; and both were to continue to be influential for some time to come, as we shall see.

The positions we have called "Protagorean" and "Gorgianic" are quite different from one another, and the differences are fundamental. Since it will be difficult to understand the positions developed later by Plato, Aristotle, and Isocrates on the subject of rhetoric without reference to these two positions, it will be useful to summarize those differences here. In the Gorgianic view, rhetoric is a unilateral transaction between an active speaker and a passive audience. A skillful orator can influence the audience, delighting them, making them bold or fearful, or indeed bewitching them with "evil persuasion," as is clear from the *Encomium to Helen*. Thus, the relationship between speaker and audience is, so to speak, "asymmetric," as it is the speaker who casts a spell over the audience, and not the other way around. The Protagorean view, by contrast, appears to be bilateral, in that the two sides of a question must be brought to bear on each other to effect some resolution of the issue at hand. Since neither side is privileged *a priori* over the other, and both are founded on the hearer's *doxa*, we may characterize the relationship between speaker and audience as "symmetric." The two positions are as different as the ones propounded by, on the one hand, the behaviorist, who sees persuasion as a simple matter of stimulus and response—a sort of sublimated coercion—and, on the other, by a pragmatist, who sees controversy and debate as the only reasonable alternative to force and deception.

Both positions have strengths and weaknesses. The speaker of the *Helen*, for instance, can point to actual examples of the power of discourse to sway listeners to act against even the most strongly held convictions (see *Helen* 15ff.). The Protagorean emphasis on debate appears to have been encouraged by the actual workings of the Athenian assembly and courts. On the other hand, the reliance of both on *doxa* alone deprives them of any objective criterion by which to distinguish between what is true or false or between what is right or wrong. Protagorean debate, in other words, could easily degenerate to a dialogue between two equally ignorant and misguided parties, and Gorgianic persuasion could easily become a cynical exercise in manipulation by one who had mastered the techniques of charming one's listeners. In short, if it is true that Gorgias and Protagoras could supply their students with instruction that would guarantee them the ability to function in public life as effective speakers, it is also true that their teachings could serve to exacerbate the tensions inherent in rhetorical activity instead of resolving them.

It is precisely these possibilities that explain the responses to the sophists' teachings by Plato and Aristotle in the generations after Gorgias and Protagoras, as we shall see later. Here, however, we should mention another important aspect of rhetoric as it was taught and practiced in fifth-century Athens. The establishment of popular courts resulted in opportunities for litigation that, in turn, resulted in the emergence of a class of professional speechwriters and consultants (*logographoi*), of whom the most famous is Lysias (d. circa 375). These *logographoi* supplied to their clients speeches or advice on what to say in civil or criminal suits, and evidently charged large fees (which were paid) for their services. Their craft is visible both in the speeches of Lysias, most of which were composed for his clients, and in the existence of handbooks containing sample speeches or parts of speeches. These handbooks include the *Tetralogies* composed by Antiphon (d. circa 400?), four sets of speeches containing arguments for and against various charges, and, for instance, the collection of speech openings (*prooimia*) attributed to Demosthenes (384–322). They may perhaps be most accurately characterized as compendia of commonplaces and lines of argument (*topoi*) general enough to be applied in a variety of cases and based on the soundest of accepted opinion. As such, they give us a unique picture of the conventional ethics and standards of reasonability current in fifth- and fourth-century Athens. They also constitute the literary background of the formulations of rhetoric we find in Plato, Aristotle, and Isocrates, to which we now turn.[7]

PLATO

Born in Athens to a wealthy family with aristocratic connections in 427, Plato grew up during the darkest and most turbulent years of Athenian history. By the time he reached 25, Plato and his fellow Athenians had seen military disaster and demoralization as a result of the decision to send the expedition to Sicily, an oligarchic *coup d'état* followed by savage retributions, and the final defeat of Athens and the destruction of her Long Walls by the victorious Spartan forces. As a young man, moreover, he had become part of the circle around his revered Socrates, who became in Plato's eyes a kind of martyr after his trial and execution in 399 and who would be the inspiration for the central character in Plato's dialogues. Plato must have felt, at that time, like the man described in the *Republic* (6.486D) who, "standing aside, as it were, under the shelter of a wall in a storm of dust and sleet and seeing others filled with lawlessness, is content if in some way he may keep himself free from iniquity."

Plato's recollections of political and personal misfortune and loss may explain his turn to two sorts of idealism, one political and the other philosophical. Deeply troubled by the events in his home city, he came to be convinced that there had to be a better way to conduct one's personal and political life than that of the Athens he knew. There was, in his view, something wrong with a society like that. Indeed, he writes in one of his extant letters:

> I decided at last that *all* existing forms of society are wrong: their institutions are just about past remedy, unless some uncanny force should intervene at just the right time. I was thus moved to give my attention to a true philosophy and say that only from the standpoint of such a philosophy could one get a comprehensive view of what is right, for the social order as well as for the individual. Mankind would never get rid of its miseries until philosophers, in the true sense of the term [i.e., as "lovers of wisdom"], gained political power, or else, by some stroke of fate, the ruling classes took to that true philosophy (*Ep.* 7, 326 A).[8]

Athens, it was clear to him, had fallen because of the ineptitude and ignorance of its democratic leaders and, in no small measure, the teachings of the likes of Gorgias and Protagoras. Plato's alternative was founded on the other sort of idealism, philosophical idealism.

Plato's "true philosophy" begins with the conviction that only genuine knowledge of the eternal and immutable essences of things (the so-called ideas) can supply a firm basis for making true statements about them. Such essences are not grasped by experience but by the mind alone, and only by the lover of wisdom who apprehends them as a result of divine inspiration or by recollection (*anamnesis*) of them as they were viewed by the soul before birth or by the process of dialectic. Only the true philosopher, moreover, really knows how to lead a virtuous life, for only he is free from the vagaries of pleasure and the deceptions of mere *doxa*.

On both practical and philosophic grounds, therefore, Plato had nothing good to say about rhetoric or its practitioners. Rhetoricians dealt in mere *doxa*, denying or ignoring truth, and worked their wiles by appealing to the appetites of their audiences. Plato's estimation of rhetoric is expressed in many places, but nowhere more clearly than in two of his dialogues, the *Gorgias* and the *Phaedrus*. The *Gorgias* is a scathing attack on the art and the artists alike. The argument of the *Phaedrus* seems more accommodating to a version of rhetoric that is legitimate but, as we shall see, is by no means inconsistent with the attacks in the *Gorgias*.

The *Gorgias*, subtitled "On Rhetoric" in many manuscripts, is divided into three parts, as Socrates engages in dialectical interrogation of Gorgias, Gorgias' pupil Polus, and Kallikles, in turn. In the first two parts, Socrates is able to get Gorgias to see that his claims to be able to teach the art of persuasion are both confused and dangerous (449C–461B) and to get his student to admit that his brand of rhetoric is not conducive to the good life (461B–481B). In the third part, the longest (481C–527E), Socrates tries and fails in a difficult and occasionally nasty exchange to get Kallikles, in whom one modern scholar has detected resemblances to Nietzsche's *Übermensch*, to admit that rhetoric and the sort of power it has are quite corrupt. When it becomes clear that his methods of interrogation are not succeeding with him, Socrates carries the dialogue to a different level in the "myth" describing the judgment of souls that will occur in everyone's afterlife.[9]

The theme of the relation between rhetoric and the good life (*eudaimonia*) runs through the entire dialogue. In demonstrating that Gorgias' claims on behalf of rhetoric are without foundation, Plato's Socrates shows that rhetoric has nothing to do with justice or virtue, and certainly does not endow the *rhētōr* with the sort of power Gorgias claims it does. He then proceeds to get Polus to admit that rhetoric is not truly useful, but dangerous, and lays it down that since rhetoric is simply a form of flattery (*kolakeia*), a rhetorician is little more than a lickspittle bent on ingratiating himself to his audience. Both of these exchanges cast Athens' democratic system in an ugly light, characterizing Gorgias' students as unscrupulous seekers after political power, and both Gorgias and his students as catering to the base pleasures of "juries and other mobs" (458B), for instance. In his exchange with Kallikles, the scathing tenor of the attack on democracy becomes more severe, with Socrates condemning the actions of all the notable democratic leaders from Themistokles to Perikles (515D), both of whom "compelled" the ignorant and, instead of educating them, corrupted them utterly (517B–519A). Thus, it is not only rhetoric but democracy itself that is unable to foster *eudaimonia*.

Socrates' "arguments" have been subjected to considerable scrutiny by scholars concerned either to expose the fallacies they involve or, more positively, to defend rhetoric against its detractors.[10] But most readers would have a hard time resisting the conclusions Socrates is able to force from his interlocutors. One reason for this is that Plato's Socrates is a master at the technique of dialectic. An understanding of that technique will help us to see why Socrates' arguments seem so compelling and will help us to detect the basic strategy of the *Phaedrus*, at which we also need to look in this discussion of Plato's views on rhetoric.

Dialectic has a game-like quality to it. Two people are needed to engage in dialectic, one of whom is the questioner and the other the answerer. The questioner seeks to get the answerer either to agree to a position or to contradict an answer previously given. The answerer must respond with "Yes" or "No" to the questions put by the questioner. Refusal to answer is "against the rules," for it halts the interchange. A parodic example can be found at *Euthydemus* 298DE (here, in an abridged version):

Q: Have you a dog?

A: Yes

Q: Has he got puppies?

A: Yes.

Q: Then your dog is a father?

A: Yes.

Q: Now, is the dog yours?

A: Of course.

Q: Then being a father he is yours, so the dog becomes your father and you the puppies' brother.

This exchange might perhaps more accurately be called an example of *eristic*, but eristic and dialectic differ only in that the eristic is not serious and dialectic is. Thus, at *Theaetetus* 189A, in the middle of a discussion of the question whether believing something false is thinking "that which is not," we see this exchange between Theaetetus and Socrates:

SOC: If one thinks, he thinks something, doesn't he?

THE: Necessarily.

SOC: And when one thinks something, he thinks a thing that is?

THE: Yes.

SOC: So to think what is not is to think nothing?

THE: Clearly.

SOC: But surely to think nothing is the same as not thinking at all, isn't it?

THE: That seems plain.

SOC: If so, it is impossible to think what is not, either about anything that is, or absolutely.

THE: Evidently.

SOC: Then thinking falsely must be something different from thinking what is not!

The lines of questioning in these two exchanges work by establishing equivalences and adding them together, so to speak. Clearly, the progression in the *Euthydemus* from "dog" = "father" + "your" to "the dog is your father" works by reassigning "your" from "dog" to "father,"—that is, by means of equivocation. So, in fact, does the exchange from the *Theaetetus*.

Another device is the use of alternatives derived through the process of division (*diaeresis*), which requires that the answerer pick one of two possibilities. This technique is very common in Plato's dialogues. Consider another exchange in the *Euthydemus* (at 277C), for instance:

Q: Are those who get anything those who have it already or those who have not?

A: Those who have not.

Q: Do those who do not know belong to the class of those who have not?

A: Yes.

Q: Are learners of the class of those who get or those who have?

A: Those who get.

Q: Then those who do not know, learn, not those who do.

We shall see some other variations of this sort of strategy later. For now, we need to realize that much of what Socrates, as questioner, does with Gorgias, the answerer, follows these lines (at 453Cff., for instance); that Polus is unable to play the game very well, allowing Socrates to put questions in his mouth (as he does at 462CD); and that Kallikles sometimes simply refuses to answer, not wanting to play Socrates' game (see 490Cff.)—whence Socrates' frustration. Outside the context of the set of rules governing the dialectical exchange, it might be possible to imagine Gorgias, for instance, giving rather different answers from those he gives; within it, it is not. In short, it is Socrates' skillful play as questioner (even when he is, presumably, the answerer) that explains his success in *Gorgias*.

The *Gorgias* is an example of what is called an "elenchic" dialogue, in which Socrates attempts to catch out his interlocutors in contradictions or to bring them around to his way of thinking. The *Phaedrus* is not that kind of dialogue. Nevertheless, the same sort of strategies are at work there, only they are Plato's strategies, not Socrates'. Let us first summarize briefly what occurs in the *Phaedrus* and then make a few observations on its argument.

The dialogue begins with young Phaedrus telling Socrates about a perfectly wonderful speech he has heard Lysias give. After Socrates asks repeatedly to hear it, Phaedrus begins reading it. The speech (almost certainly not by Lysias, but a parody) argues that the object of erotic attention should give his favors not to the lover but to the nonlover. Socrates is greatly taken with the speech at first, but soon lets Phaedrus know that he is not at all happy about it.

Phaedrus challenges Socrates to do better, and Socrates reluctantly agrees to try. Socrates' speech (237Bff.) attempts to argue Lysias' point better than Lysias had. But Socrates ends his speech abruptly, just as he is "beginning to utter epic verses" (241E), and offers to try again.

His second speech (at 244Aff), often seen as the bearer of the true meaning of the dialogue, argues that love is a good kind of madness, akin to the possession experienced by the soul when it beholds the ideas of truth and beauty in "the place above the heavens" (*hyperouranios topos*, 247C) in its state as unencumbered by the "oystershell of the body." He then develops the image (*eikos*) of the soul as a charioteer controlling two steeds, one obedient and the other unruly (253Cff.).

This summary does not do justice to the considerable literary merits of the dialogue, particularly those of Socrates' second speech, which has long been recognized as a masterpiece. But it is important to notice here what Plato has done up to this point. The technical term that best describes the strategy of the dialogue thus far is *expeditio*, what is sometimes called in English the argument "from residuals." There is no technical term for this in Greek, but it is recognized as a variation on the technique of *diaeresis* that we saw before: "It must be A or B or C; it is not A, nor B; so it must be C." In this case, "C," Socrates' second speech, seems to be presented as an example of speaking "well" (*kalōs*) by elimination, as it were. The speech is, to be sure, much more eloquent than the others; but Socrates says (265CD) that the only serious point of the speech was as a demonstration of his powers of division and merger, the rest being "really playfully done." In other words, Plato's Socrates employs the same strategy within his speech as Plato himself had used as the principal strategy of the dialogue up to this point.

Here, Socrates abruptly turns the discussion in a different direction. In what follows, briefly, Socrates reverts to his customary tactic of the leading question. "Would you say, Phaedrus, that rhetoricians deal with the true or with that which is merely probable?" "Well, Socrates, they say that they have to deal only with what is probable." "But," says Socrates, this is nonsense, because...Don't you agree?" "I most certainly do." "So rhetoric must of necessity deal with the true!" (259Eff.). Notice that we are once again in the realm of *diaeresis*: "A" or "B"; but not "A"; therefore "*of necessity*" "B"! The "necessity" is of course a function here (as it is everywhere in Plato) of the agreement of Socrates' interlocutor, not of any real necessity, nor even a logical one; and that agreement is achieved by virtue of the answers he knows his interlocutor will give.

By means of this dialectical technique, Socrates establishes a model of an apparently legitimate kind of rhetoric. Unlike that professed by Gorgias in the dialogue of that name, the rhetoric Socrates describes is a true "art" (*technē*) involving knowledge of reality (262Aff.), of the forms of discourse, and of the corresponding kinds of souls (271Aff.). This rhetoric, moreover, does not corrupt, as Gorgias' did. The true rhetorician will adapt his discourse to the type of soul being addressed, proceeding by way of *diaeresis* to "carve up (*diatemnein*) the subject at the joints" (see 265E), thus communicating the truth effectively. This "rhetoric" is dialectical in character, then; and it is the role of dialectic in it that guarantees its legitimacy (277B–278B).

Without going into the question of whether the notion of rhetoric Socrates develops in the last sections of *Phaedrus* can resist being assimilated altogether into Socratic dialectic, we can see that what is presented in that dialogue is a conception of rhetoric that is quite different from the Gorgianic and Protagorean rhetorics we spoke of before. It is different in its intolerance of *doxa*, to begin with. This rhetoric is grounded in the truth, which means in turn that this is no debater's rhetoric, weighing both sides of a dispute to see which is preferable or more probable. Persuasion is not a matter of bewitching the hearer's soul or knocking it out of its wits, but of leading the soul to truth—a process of *psychagōgia* (see 261A, 271C). At the same time, it will be noticed that Plato's rhetoric is in one respect like the one we called Gorgianic. Both are "unilateral" and "asymmetric." The difference, of course, is in Plato's insistence that his rhetoric, unlike the Gorgianic, is grounded on truth as it is known by the philosopher.

In this chapter, so far, we have identified three different conceptions of rhetoric generated in the atmosphere of fifth-century Athens, although, strictly speaking, Plato's belongs to the fourth. Two are "sophistic," the third that of Plato. All three, as we have suggested, may be seen as responses to the social and political conditions current in Athens. For the sophists, Athenian reforms presented an occasion for systematic thinking about rhetoric. Thus, Protagorean rhetoric supplies a rationale for the resolution of problems by means of public discussion in the absence of political or ethical absolutes. 'Gorgianic' rhetoric likewise rejects claims to absolute knowledge of what is true and good, but offers a set of instructions that would make it possible for an orator to prevail in the current system, rather than a rationale for the system itself. Plato's response, as we have seen, is negative, denying the legitimacy both of rhetoric as it was taught and practiced and of the democratic system that made it possible.

There remain two figures of paramount importance for the history of rhetoric in ancient Greece, Aristotle and Isocrates. Aristotle is important, for our immediate purposes, because he developed a rhetoric different from the three we have seen. In our remarks on his *Rhetoric*, we shall be concerned to sketch the outlines of that rhetoric. Isocrates is doubly important, for he was important in his own time as one who was able to rehabilitate one sort of "sophistic" rhetoric; and he was vitally important to succeeding generations, particularly that of the Roman orator Cicero. Since Cicero was such an important authority until the modern era, it might be said that Isocrates, of all the Greeks, was the greatest. Our discussion of Isocrates will, accordingly, attempt to explain why Isocrates exercised so much influence over Hellenistic and Roman rhetoricians.

ARISTOTLE

Aristotle was born in Stagira, in the North of Greece, in 384 BC. In 367, he traveled to Athens to study in Plato's Academy and stayed there until Plato's death in 347. Tensions between Athens and Macedon, with which, as a northerner, he might have been associated, made it wise for Aristotle to leave Athens about then. What he did for the next dozen years or so is unknown. The story that he spent two years as tutor to Alexander, son of Philip of Macedon, is probably a canard. But it is clear at any rate that he returned in 335 to Athens, where he set up his own school, the Lyceum, in the covered walk (*peripatos*, whence "Peripatetic" philosophy) of a public gymnasium. He taught there until he retired in 323, a year before his death.[11]

Aristotle's 20-year association with Plato certainly had an effect on his intellectual formation, but Aristotle differed with his master on several crucial issues. One of these was the question of what constitutes knowledge. Plato's conception of what constitutes knowledge is univocal and absolute. Knowledge claims are for him valid only if they are made by one who has grasped the immutable essences of things, the "ideas." Aristotle's conception is more catholic, allowing for a plurality of kinds of knowledge. "Knowledge" can be distributed in a number of ways. Experience, for instance, is a kind of knowledge, that of particulars. Knowledge of universals (*epistēmē*) is another kind of knowledge. And between those two, there is an intermediate level of knowledge, that of what is generally the case, but not always. Again, we can distinguish, according to Aristotle, between "theoretical," "practical," and "productive" knowledge. The important point to be observed here is that all of these can legitimately be called "knowledge" without reducing all to a single criterion. "We cannot expect of ethics," he says in his *Nicomachean Ethics*, "the same rigor we would expect from geometry."[12]

A second area in which Aristotle differed from Plato is that of "art" (*technē*). "Art," for Plato, involves knowledge (*epistēmē*) of the "ideas." Aristotle saw (correctly)[13] that this notion conflated two different kinds of knowledge, and in doing so limited the range of intellectual activity that could legitimately be called a *technē*. One who claimed to be in possession of a *technē* did not have to have knowledge of universals, only of what is generally the case, "what happens for the most part."

In consequence of these distinctions, Aristotle took a different view of the relationship between rhetoric and dialectic from what Plato had taken. Both, for Aristotle, are universal verbal arts, not limited to any specific subject matter, by which one could generate discourse and demonstrations on any question that might arise. The demonstrations, or arguments, of dialectic differ from those of rhetoric in that dialectic derives its arguments from premises (*protaseis*) founded on universal opinion and rhetoric from particular opinions. "Sophistic" is different from both in that it is not concerned with argument but only with manipulating words, usually for some not very respectable reason.

Rhetoric, therefore, was for Aristotle a legitimate "artistic" pursuit involving the knowledge of general principles and in some respects very like dialectic. Indeed, the opening words of his treatise on rhetoric, *Technē rhetorikē*, draw attention to that connection: "Rhetoric is the counterpart (*antistrophē*) of dialectic" (1.1, 1354al).[14] Aristotle's *Rhetoric** is a highly systematic treatise on the art in which he works out a conception of it different not only from Plato's but from the two "sophistic" rhetorics we saw before. For that reason, we need to get some idea of what is in it and how it is put together.

Aristotle defines rhetoric not as "the art of persuasion" but as "the power of perceiving the available persuasives (*pisteis*)" (1.2, 1355b26ff.). One is persuaded when one has become convinced of something—i.e., when something is perceived to have been demonstrated. Persuasion, then, is a kind of demonstration (see 1356b28ff.), in rhetoric, concerning matters that are contingent (see 1357al4ff.), based on "probabilities," "things that happen," Aristotle says (1357a34), "usually." As in dialectic, the instruments of demonstration are the syllogism and induction (*epagogē*); in rhetoric they are the *enthymēma*—the "rhetorical syllogism"—and example. Other notions of rhetoric, insofar as they ignore this fact, neglect the "body" of the art. Thus, right at the outset, Aristotle has distinguished his notion of rhetoric both from those contained in the handbooks composed by sophists and from that of Plato, who exhibits no interest in argumentation as such. Furthermore, Aristotle has made it possible to defend rhetoric as useful, as he does at 1355b36ff., and to clarify its relations with dialectic, on the one hand, and politics and ethics on the other (1356a25ff.).

Pisteis are either "artistic" or "nonartistic," and it is the former that are able to be treated systematically. The three sources of persuasion that fall within the purview of the art of rhetoric are the character of the speaker as it comes across in the speech (*ēthos*), the disposition of the audience toward the speaker and the matter at hand (*pathos*), and the speech (*logos*) itself "when we have demonstrated a truth or an apparent truth by means of the persuasive arguments suitable to the case in question" (1356a1–21). These are at all times coordinate and interact mutually, distinguishable but not separable from one another, although one may occasionally take precedence over the others (3.12, 1413b3ff.).

The systematic discovery of such persuasive arguments, in rhetoric as in dialectic (compare *Topics* 1.14), is constructed around the available "places" (*topoi*) (1358a14ff.; 2.22, 1396b3ff.). *Topoi* may be limited in scope to particular subject matters or not, and those that are not are the ones most properly said to be "rhetorical." There is a good deal of scholarly disagreement about just what a *topos* is and how it functions, but it is clear that before anyone can support a thesis or claim by means of an enthymeme, it is necessary (as Aristotle points out repeatedly, and as any debater knows) to have a grasp of the facts of the case (*hyparchonta*, 1396a6), to have a store of *protaseis* understood by and acceptable to one's audience (see 1355a17, 1402a34, etc.), and to be able to reason "logically" (1355a15f.). That ability requires that one should be able to distinguish between mere evidence and the sort of "premises" (a rough translation of *protaseis*) that can supply argumentative links between one's claims and the available data. This triad of claim, evidence, and *protaseis* is an argument only when the statements of them are put into the proper relationship to one another; and the proper relationship seems to be (1) the claim being made by the orator; (2) the evidence cited in support of it; and (3) the *protasis* that links them together. A *topos*, whether limited to a particular subject matter or not, is just such a *protasis*.[15]

If this is correct, then the structure and contents of *Rhetoric* 1.4 up to 2.26 become clear. Thus, 1.4 through 1.14 lay out systematically the available *topoi* a *rhētōr* can call upon in the three basic kinds of rhetorical situation (see 1358b7ff.): the deliberative (ch. 5–8, with chapter 4 outlining the *hyparchonta* of political speeches), ceremonial or epideictic (ch. 9), and legal (ch.

10–14, with chapter 15 being devoted to the nontechnical means of persuasion). Book 2.2–11 lay out systematically the *topoi* concerning emotions and 12–17 those concerning the "ages and fortunes" of the three kinds of men. As these matters cut across all three "genres" of rhetoric, they can be seen to have broader application than the *topoi* discussed in Book 1. At 2.18, Aristotle takes up the most general, and therefore most properly rhetorical, *topoi* ("the more and the less," "the possible and the impossible," etc.) and in 2.23ff. provides a list of the best-known *topoi* used by *rhētores*, along with a discussion of refutative *topoi* and fallacious enthymemes. By 2.26, in short, Aristotle has provided his reader with a huge, and elegantly economical, storehouse of the sorts of *protaseis* speakers can use in constructing enthymemes, the same sort of thing he did for dialectic in his *Topics* (cf. *Rhetoric* 1.2.1358a27f.).[16]

Book 3 is devoted to a lengthy and sophisticated discussion of style and arrangement. His discussion of style (ch. 1–8) and composition (9–12) lays down the doctrine of the three virtues of style (clarity, propriety, and correctness), the importance of metaphor in rhetorical discourse, and the differences between "periodic" (compact) and "free-running" (loose) forms of sentence composition. These analyses were to exercise enormous influence over subsequent treatments of style by both Greek and Latin authors. As for the arrangement of the parts of a speech (see 3.13–19), Aristotle makes the observation that, strictly speaking, only two parts are necessary: an introductory statement and the argument proper. In this, he rejects in principle the current teaching, which called for at least four parts: prologue, narration, argument, and epilogue (1414b8ff.). At the same time, he devotes considerable attention to those four parts and to the recommended conduct of one's argument in each. What ties all of these subjects together is Aristotle's constant insistence on the connections between stylistic, compositional, and strategic matters alike with "the body of the art"—the enthymeme generated by means of *topoi*—that he had worked out in Books 1 and 2.

This brief sketch cannot adequately convey the precision and rigor of Aristotle's thinking on the art of rhetoric, but it should provide some idea of how significantly his notion differs from the platonic and sophistic notions alike. On epistemological matters, about the only conviction common to Aristotle and his master is the idea that good rhetoric is based on objective truth; only for Aristotle, that includes "what happens usually." Opinions concerning what is probable held by particular audiences tend to be on the mark, as the same faculty allows one to grasp that which is merely apparent as to grasp the true (1355a14f.). Whereas legitimate rhetoric in Plato is derivative of dialectic, in Aristotle rhetoric and dialectic are coequal and coordinate verbal arts. And while Aristotle may be said to share Plato's distaste for the teachings of the sophists, he objects to them on quite different grounds. He is opposed, on the one hand, to manipulation and to the notion that ethics is irrelevant and, on the other, to the idea that a question can rightly be debated in the absence of some rigorous criterion of persuasiveness—namely, the canons of enthymematic reasoning. While the sort of rhetoric envisioned by

Plato may be characterized as dialectical in nature, and Gorgianic rhetoric as operational, Aristotle's may not be characterized as either of those. As criteria for determining what is true or right differ according to the type of problem one is trying to solve, we might call Aristotle's rhetoric "problematic" in nature. In short, we have in Aristotle a notion of rhetoric distinct in principle from those of his master and of those his master did so much to villify.

For all of the ingenuity—indeed genius—shown in it, the *Rhetoric* failed to exercise much influence in the centuries after Aristotle's death. For one thing, his entire corpus of writings was lost, not to be found again for many centuries. In fact, it is arguable that the *Rhetoric* was first perceived as a truly significant contribution to rhetoric in the nineteenth century, although many writers before then mention it, virtually in passing. The reasons for this have yet to be sorted out in detail.[17] But it is clear that one important reason is to be found in the success of Aristotle's older contemporary, Isocrates, in capturing the imagination of the Greek world both by what he had to say and how he said it. It is to Isocrates that we now turn.

ISOCRATES AND THE PRIMACY OF ELOQUENCE

Isocrates was born in Athens in 436 and remained there until his death at the age of 97, in 338. Thus his career spans that of Plato and of the great Athenian orators of the late fifth and most of the fourth centuries, including the conservative patriot Demosthenes and his own student Isaeus, among others. In the 390s, Isocrates abandoned a career as a *logographos* and opened a small school, which counted among its students, in addition to Isaeus, the great general Timotheus and the historian Theopompus. When Aristotle opened his school at the Lyceum, he found himself in competition with Isocrates for the best minds of Athenian youth, and there is evidence that he was acutely conscious of that fact.[18]

Isocrates has been dismissed by some scholars as politically unimportant and as a base opportunist. Nevertheless, he was famous in his own day, and for many centuries to come, for his program of education (*paideia*), which stressed above all the teaching of eloquence. His own works, which are actually political pamphlets composed in the form of orations, are examples of Attic prose in its most elaborate form and were clearly intended to provide a model of the eloquence he held to be so crucial in the conduct of public affairs. More than that, they were the vehicles for his notion of the true "philosophy," for him a wisdom in civic affairs emphasizing moral responsibility and equated with mastery of rhetorical technique. In what follows, we shall try to summarize briefly the position he took and sought to communicate to his contemporaries.

To begin with, it is clear that Isocrates must be viewed in the context of the "sophistic" strain in rhetorical thinking. Like Protagoras and Gorgias, with whom he is rumored to have studied, Isocrates believed that human knowledge is limited and that knowing the right course of action in every case is "one of the impossibilities of life" (*Against the Sophists* 2). "It is not in the nature of man," he says in his *Antidosis*,

> to attain exact knowledge (*epistēmē*) by which, having it, we can discern clearly what we should do or say. From what is left, I would say that those who are wise are those who are able by opinion (*doxa*) to hit upon what is for the most part the best course of action (271).

Isocrates set himself against the "philosophizing" of the Socratics and Cynics of his day, dismissing it as idle speculation and vain quibbling: "It is much better to form probable opinions about useful things than to have exact knowledge of useless things" (*Helen* 5). At the same time, he differentiated his own view from that of the sophists, whom he saw as responsible for the bad reputation of rhetoric, calling for a rhetoric that was more than a mere technique for winning lawsuits, of "making the worse case appear the better."

Isocrates tried to bridge the gap between morality and technical skill that had been created by his sophistic predecessors and Plato alike. The ability to speak well (*eu legein*) was, for him, the surest sign of sound understanding (*eu phronein*: cf. *Antid.* 86,255f.). Familiarity with noble themes and models and a sense of appropriateness, of the right word at the right time (*kairos*), assist the *rhētōr* not only in the artful composition of discourse but also in right reason and good thinking. The ability to speak well and to think well go hand in hand, and it is style that links the two. The ideal speech will be composed in a lofty style, which enhances the moral character of the speaker, will deal with a worthy subject, and will benefit the city by creating in the audience a likemindedness (*homonoia*) as regards virtue and justice (*Antid.* 67). In short, Isocrates tried to combine rhetoric, ethics, and political action in a literary form suitable for both private study and public discussion.

What is this "lofty style" that Isocrates calls for and himself strives to attain? The general effect of Isocrates' style derives from its ornateness—particularly in the construction of periods and in the modes of amplification (*makrologia*) he employs. Periodic composition, which we have had occasion to mention in connection with Aristotle's *Rhetoric*, is characterized by its finiteness. A good period is so constructed, as one later Greek critic was to explain,[19] so that the hearer, like a runner on a circular race track (*periodos*), can see the end ahead and thus derive satisfaction when the end of the thought around which the sentence is constructed has been reached. Balance and a rounded-off quality are achieved chiefly by Isocrates' ample use of parallelism and antithesis at every level from that of diction to that of larger units of composition. The techniques of amplification involve the prolongation of sentences by the use of synonyms and antonyms to amplify single words, by the expression of the same thought twice in different words, and by the opposition of two or more ideas where a single statement might have conveyed the basic idea more briefly. These devices give Isocrates' prose a distinctive, indeed almost unmistakable, ring, and force the hearer to dwell upon each idea, to follow its development and augmentation, and to arrive with Isocrates at the completion of its expression. At times, the experience of Isocratean style is, as Isocrates meant it to be, almost hypnotic.[20]

It is difficult to convey in English the plasticity of syntax and the resources of assonance and alliteration possible in the Greek. But it is impossible to comprehend what periodic composition is capable of without seeing it in action. A sentence from Isocrates' *Letter to Archidamus* provides a reasonably good illustration of his style:[21]

> I might have spoken passably about even these matters
>> since I knew, in the first place
>>> that it is easier to treat copiously in cursory
>>> fashion occurrences of the past
>>>> than intelligently to discuss the future
>> and, in the second place
>>> that all men are more grateful to those who praise
>>>> than to those who advise them—
>>>>> for the former they approve as being
>>>>> well-disposed,
>>>>> but the latter,
>>>>>> if the advice comes unbidden,
>>>>> they look upon as officious—
> nevertheless,
>> although I was already fully aware of all these considerations
> I have refrained from topics which would surely be flattering and
> now I propose to speak of such matters as no one else dares to discuss
>> because I believe that those who make pretensions to fairness
>> and practical wisdom should choose
>>> not the easiest subjects, but the most arduous,
>>> nor yet those which are sweetest to the ears of the
>>> listeners, but such as will avail to benefit
>>>> not only our own states,
>>>> but also all the other Greeks;
> and such is the subject, in fact, on which I have fixed my attention at the present time.

This is a rather long sentence by English standards, indeed even by Greek standards; but for all its length, it is carefully constructed and possesses considerable vitality. In the first section, Isocrates tells us what he is not going to talk about; in the middle section, what he refuses to talk about and what he feels he has to say; and in the final section, he tells us what he needs to talk about. There is a clear plan guiding what appears to be a rather meandering thought, in other words; and a carefully modulated tone of urgency that is enhanced, not obscured, by the artistry of the speaker. "I have not come here to tell you what you want to hear," Isocrates is saying. "I have come to tell you what you must do to save ourselves"; and then, at the very end, a note of emphasis capping the climax of the "not...not...but..." structure of the sentence up to that point. The structure of expectation and fulfillment demanded of good periodic composition and helped along by the balance of the sentence's elements is almost that of a well-made play.

If it is true that Isocrates sometimes appears to overdo what he usually does well, it is equally true that for him such devices were required of one who would raise his fellow citizens to a new political and moral consciousness. The main constraint on the orator was not a set of rules about how speeches ought to be put together, but that of *kairos*. The ability to perceive the demands of the occasion and exploit them, in turn, was not something one could be taught by handbooks alone. Technical instruction must be supplemented by the speaker's own good moral character and by constant involvement in public affairs, as befits the good citizen who possesses civic virtue (*aretē*). What seems to us overdone or even monotonous, in fact, was for Isocrates a mark of deep commitment and a sense of moral urgency that demanded forceful expression.

The irony, of course, is that for all of Isocrates' celebration of the old ideal of the "speaker of words and the doer of deeds," in the Homeric phrase, he himself never actively participated in politics. He did his civic duty, as he saw it, through his students. And indeed, aside from the fact that he was able to provide solutions to at least two significant problems of his day—the discord within the city due to poverty and that between cities due to petty ambition—there is little evidence that his calls were heeded by his contemporaries. Certainly, the continuation of turmoil in Athens and the eventual reduction of the city by Philip of Macedon were nothing to be very optimistic about. Yet, as we shall see in the next chapter, his program of rhetorical study and the ideals it represented would continue to be influential for centuries to come, as the ideal of "the good man skilled in speaking" would continue to be the goal to which generations of students aspired.

RHETORIC AND POLITICS

We suggested earlier that the rhetorics of Plato and the sophists might be viewed as responses to political conditions in the Athens of their time. In the present, and concluding, section of this chapter, we will try to see if the rhetorics propounded by Aristotle and Isocrates might be similarly viewed. In some ways, it is obvious that they can, but a closer look at this aspect of their respective views seems in order. After that, we will turn to the other side of this question, exploring the rhetorics of this period not just as responses to but as having implications for the realities of political life.

In contrast to Plato and Isocrates, both Athenians and both quite clearly concerned with Athenian politics, Aristotle was not an Athenian but an outsider who exhibited little interest in the problems of Athens itself, even though those problems affected his life and career significantly. By the time he set about composing his *Rhetoric*, he had completed his survey of dialectical arguments in the *Topics*, worked out his analytic theory of the syllogism, developed a broad comparative view of political systems, and had written at least one treatise laying out the questions and methods proper to ethics. At the end of the *Nicomachean Ethics*, in a chapter marking the transition to the *Politics*, Aristotle contests the claims of "the sophists"—among whom he clearly counts Isocrates—to be able to teach the art of politics. Similarly, in the *Rhetoric* he is critical not only of the authors of the handbooks that ignore "the body of the art" (the rhetorical syllogism) but also the idea that rhetoric can do anything more than "masquerade" as politics, although rhetoric has clear ties to ethics and therefore to politics. In general, Aristotle sees the answers to political questions as best handled not by orators but by the intelligentsia, men of reason and a deep commitment to rationality. That most people do not act rationally is no argument that they shouldn't or don't need to. /

At the same time, there is a need for an art like rhetoric—a genuine art—for men often deliberate about matters without systems to guide them, and before hearers who cannot "take in at a glance a complicated argument or follow a long chain of reasoning" (*Rhetoric* 1.2, 1357a1ff.). Rhetoric is, moreover, useful (*chrēsimos*), for reasons he points out in the first chapter of the *Rhetoric*, at 1355b36ff., which we cited earlier. Yet the final appeal must be made not to success in achieving consensus or in raising the moral sensibilities of one's fellow citizens but to the court of reason: "Persuasion is a sort of demonstration, for we are most fully persuaded when we consider a thing to have been demonstrated" (1355a4f.). Thus, rhetoric is only grudgingly accepted, and only with the proviso that it adhere to the standards of dialectical coherence. It is, therefore, a rhetoric with appeal to the philosopher who is more interested in determining the status of rhetoric as a systematic inquiry into how persuasives can be discerned than in the resolution of actual, pressing, and complex problems. It is the rhetoric of the outsider.

Isocrates, of course, was an insider unable to attain the level of detachment of an Aristotle. There is a consequent sense of urgency in Isocrates' responses to the crises that afflicted Athens, from the "innumerable evils" caused by poverty, which polarized Athenian society in the 380s (*Paneg.* 114ff., 172ff.), to the Social War of the 350s, to the threat of Macedonian domination in the 340s.[22] If, for Aristotle, politics is to be governed by reason, for Isocrates it must be guided by eloquence. That eloquence, based not on Aristotle's "probabilities" (what happens for the most part) but on opinions (*doxai*), aims at creating *homonoia* and good counsel (*euboulia*) among Athens' citizens in the process of public deliberation (*Paneg.* 3, *Antid.* 255ff., etc.) and debate. "With this faculty," he says, "we contend against others in matters open to debate (*amphisbetesimon*) and seek light on those things we don't clearly know...we regard as sage (*euboulous*) those who most skillfully debate (*dialechthōsin*) their problems" (*Antid.* 256). If Aristotle was critical of politicians in general, so too was Isocrates; but to him, it was "philosophizers" like Aristotle who were responsible for the politicians' inability to deal effectively with the problems that faced the city. Only the eloquence of the "good man skilled in speaking" could save Athens and restore her to her former glories; only that eloquence, Isocrates argued, could bring about Panhellenic unity and the defeat of the barbarian enemies of the Greeks. Rhetoric approached with "a love of wisdom and a love of honor" (*Antid.* 277), not idle philosophy, was the instrument of salvation.

Thus it is possible to see the notions of rhetoric shaped by Aristotle and Isocrates as two very different responses to fourth–century political events. But these notions also have implications for politics, for the political ideals entertained by them and by their rivals. Both Aristotle and Plato place a premium on reason as the principle behind the ideal constitution (*politeia*). Given Plato's demands, as is clear from his *Republic* and his *Laws*, the ideal city (*polis*) has a distinctly vertical structure, with the philosophers at the top, which some of his critics have characterized as "totalitarian."[23] Aristotle does not go that far, but still maintains that in any well-run *polis* the philosophers must have an important voice. If there is *technē*, a true art, of politics, it is that *technē* that must guide the governors and governed alike. Thus Aristotle's politics, no matter what the exact nature of the *politeia* in question, will be a "technocracy."

Neither Plato nor Aristotle took a particularly favorable view of rhetoric, especially the rhetoric practiced by their contemporaries. The sophists and Isocrates did, but with mixed implications for politics. On the one hand, the Gorgianic *rhētōr* could exercise enormous influence over others. But the resulting *politeia*, in view of the nature of the relation between speakers and their audiences, would under the best of circumstances involve considerable instability. People are fickle and do not always agree with one another. An orator who knows the art of manipulating hearers may eventually rule over them, as Socrates charged in the *Gorgias*, like a master over slaves. Thus we have another highly vertical political structure, only this one is, by comparison with Plato's ideal, unprincipled. The Gorgianic *politeia* would not in fact be democratic but Machiavellian, with the *rhētōr* playing the part of the prince. On the other hand, to the extent that debate in democratic assembly could, in the Protagorean version of things, offer the way toward resolution of problems, we can see a very different political vision, one that might be characterized as "horizontal" and founded on the premiss that all questions are debatable by equals, as long as they have representative authority. In passing, we note that the praise of the *logos* so often seen in Isocrates echoes the sentiments attributed to Protagoras by Plato in his *Protagoras* (322Bff.).

Isocrates' ideals, as we have noted, did not have much of an impact on the practical politics of his day and were not to crystalize into a political philosophy until they were rearticulated by Cicero. There is a hint of frustration in Isocrates' later works, as in his speech addressed to Philip of Macedon, where, while defending his educational program, he calls for the invasion of Persia as the surest way of bringing about *homonoia* among the Greeks. Persia would be attacked by Philip's son, Alexander; but there is no evidence that it was Isocrates who gave him the idea to do that. But the ideal of the statesman-orator and the commitment to eloquence as the key to social redemption continued to grip the imaginations of philosophers and rhetoricians for centuries to come.

The different rhetorics defined and developed by the Greeks we have looked at can, in short, be seen both as responses to political conditions and as having implications for political institutions. Plato, the sophists, Aristotle, and Isocrates—as different as they were—all grappled with the same questions of authority, right, power, and the place of persuasion in public affairs, each offering a different account of the role of rhetoric in the resolution of moral and political questions. In subsequent eras in the history of rhetoric, we shall see, versions of these different rhetorics reassert themselves, take hold, and wane as cultural and political conditions evolve and shift. In the chapters that follow, we shall be concerned to trace the traditions defined by the four Greek models we have discerned in this one. As the story is long and complex, we need to turn at this point to the examination of such developments as occurred in the centuries after Aristotle's death.

SUMMARY

Greek literature from Homer on shows a virtual preoccupation with the role of discourse in the resolution of public problems. A survey of Classical Greek rhetorics shows that there is no one, single notion of rhetoric that can be called typical or dominant in the period. We see, in fact, at least four different models, each with its own fundamental commitments and each with its own view of the nature and ends of rhetoric. Two are "sophistic," the Gorgianic and the Protagorean, with the latter achieving its fullest expression in the works of Isocrates. Plato's objections to the rhetorics being taught by the sophists are embodied in his *Gorgias*, in which Socrates' dialectic forces the conclusion that rhetoric is neither an art nor a means of achieving *eudaimonia* (the good life). In the *Phaedrus*, Plato has Socrates lay out a vision of a legitimate rhetoric, founded on dialectical reasoning, as a way of communicating the Truth effectively. Aristotle, for his part, takes exception to the limitations placed by his teacher on what counts as knowledge and develops a rhetoric based on opinion and probability with the enthymeme at its core.

The rhetoric we have called Gorgianic may be characterized as "motivistic," in that its chief concern is with the manipulation of the audience by means of a process that resembles modern behavioral conditioning by stimulus and response. The Protagorean-Isocratean rhetoric may be called "controversial," as it seeks consensus (*homonoia*) arrived at by debate and eloquence—a notion that we will see again in Cicero's rhetorical works. Platonic rhetoric is "dialectical," with dialectic being understood as both the means of arriving at the Truth and as the method of discovering the means of communicating that truth effectively. Aristotle's rhetoric we have called "problematic," since the available "persuasives" will vary according to the nature of the problem being addressed in a rhetorical situation. These four models seem to exhaust the possibilities as regards rhetorical theories; all persist throughout the history of rhetoric, some achieving dominance at one time, others at another. In very broad terms, that is to say, the history of rhetoric may be seen as the story of the elaboration and rearticulation through the ages of the four basic models we have been able to identify in classical Greek thinking about the nature and function of persuasive discourse.

FURTHER READING

The bibliography on Classical Greek rhetorics is immense. A basic list of works may be found in R. Enos, "The Classical Period," in *The Present State of Scholarship in Historical and Contemporary Rhetoric*, ed. W. Horner (Columbia, MO, 1983). Although G. Kennedy's views differ from those expressed here, *The Art of Persuasion in Greece* (Princeton, 1963) is still the best comprehensive treatment of the subject available.

On Homeric society, see M. Finley's *The World of Odysseus* (New York, 1959) and A. Adkins, *Merit and Responsibility* (Oxford, 1969). K. Dover's *Greek Popular Morality* (Berkeley, 1974) contains much that is illuminating about Athenian moral standards; and W. Connor's *The New Politicians of Fifth Century Athens* (Princeton, 1971) is good on the democracy in that city. On Thucydides and Plato, the essays in D. Grene, *Greek Political Theory* (Chicago, 1965) are to be recommended. G. Kerferd presents a useful survey of the sophists in *The Sophistic Movement* (Cambridge, 1983), although it is unclear whether there really was such a "movement." The fragments of the works of the sophists can be had in translation in R. Sprague (ed.), *The Older Sophists* (Columbia, SC, 1972).

The bibliography on Plato and Aristotle is also immense. There is a sensible introduction to Plato's thought in C. Rowe's *Plato* (Brighton, 1984) and an excellent discussion of his attacks on rhetoric in B. Vickers, *In Defence of Rhetoric* (Oxford, 1987). Although it needs to be brought up to date, K. Erickson's *Aristotle's "Rhetoric": Five Centuries of Philological Research* (Metuchen, NJ, 1975) is the most complete bibliography on the subject. The second volume of W. Grimaldi's commentary on the *Rhetoric* has, at this writing, just come out. This, together with vol. 1 (both published by Fordham University Press, NY), is indispensable to the serious student. See also his *Studies in the Philosophy of Aristotle's Rhetoric, Hermes Einzelschriften 25* (Wiesbaden, 1972), which is very useful, although Grimaldi's reading differs from the one presented here.

On Isocrates, see for example, D. Gillis, "The Ethical Basis of Isocratean Rhetoric," *Parola del Passato* 128 (1969), pp. 321–348; and S. Usher, "The Style of Isocrates," *Bulletin of the Institute of Classical Studies* (London) 20 (1973), pp. 39–67.

The works of Plato, Aristotle, and Isocrates are all available in various translations, including those in the Loeb Classical Library series.

NOTES

1. Unless otherwise noted, the texts used are the Oxford Classical Texts and all translations are my own.
2. The phrase is Kenneth Burke's in his *Grammar of Motives*.
3. The classic treatment of this subject is G. Kleingünther's *Protos Heuretes, Philologus*, Suppl. Bd. 26 (Leipzig, 1933); see also A.T. Cole, *Democritus and the Sources of Greek Anthropology* (Chapel Hill, 1967).
4. Cf. the fragments in H. Diels *Fragmente der Vorsokratiker*[7] (Berlin, 1954), 80 A1 (Diogenes Laertius 9.51). See also Seneca *Ep.* 88.43; Cicero *Brutus* 12.46.
5. These texts can be found in Sprague, cited in Further Reading.
6. On making the worse case appear the better, cf. Aristophanes, *Clouds* vv. 112f.; on the madman in a crowd, see Plato's *Gorgias* 469C 8ff.
7. There is a good account of the activities of the *logographoi* in K. Dover, *Lysias and the "Corpus Lysiacum"* (Berkeley, 1968), pp. 148ff.. Demosthenes' *Prooimia* are collected in the Loeb series, ed. N. De Witt. I have deliberately left out mention of the so-called *Dissoi Logoi* since I am not convinced that they were composed in Classical times. See *Ancient Philosophy* 5 (1986), pp. 59–65.
8. The standard references to Plato's works are to the "Stephanus numbers" usually found in the margins (e.g., 467C).
9. The comparison was noted by E. R. Dodds in his annotated edition of the *Gorgias* (Oxford, 1959); see pp. 387–391 especially.
10. The "fallacies" in Socrates' arguments have been discussed extensively by T. Irwin in his translation and commentary on the *Gorgias* (Oxford, 1979).
11. The story that Aristotle tutored Alexander was neatly disposed of by Anton Chroust in "Was Aristotle Actually the Chief Preceptor of Alexander the Great?" in *Aristotle*, vol. 1 (Notre Dame, IN, 1973), pp. 125–132.
12. See *EN* 1.3, 1094b11ff.
13. See the observations of H. Marrou in "Les arts libéraux dans l'antiquité classique," in *Arts libéraux et philosophie au moyen âge* (Montreal/Paris, 1969), pp. 5–27.
14. I have used R. Kassel's edition (Berlin, 1976). References are to the so-called Bekker numbers in the margins of the text.
15. On this interpretation of *topos*, see W. DePater, *Les topiques d'Aristote et la dialectique platonicienne* (Fribourg, 1965); O. Bird, "The Re-discovery of the Topics: Professor Toulmin's Inference Warrants," *Mind* 70 (1961), pp. 543ff.
16. That this is the case is evident from 1360b1f., 1378a28ff. (Kassel's reading), etc.
17. The nineteenth century saw two full-scale commentaries, one by L.Spengel, the other by E. M. Cope—the first since Vettore's in the Renaissance. There is no visible Aristotelian influence in Byzantine rhetoric.
18. In what follows, I have used Norlin's Loeb texts of Isocrates' *Antidosis, Against the Sophists, On the Peace, Helen,* and *Panegyricus*.
19. See Demetrius *On Expression* 11, obviously with Aristotle *Rhet.* 3.9, 1409b35ff. in mind.
20. Isocrates' style is often denigrated, especially by nineteenth-century German

philologists and their followers, as monotonous. That is their problem, not his.
21. I have tried to indicate subordination of thought and parallelism by means of indentation.
22. See especially A. Fuks in his *Social Conflict in Ancient Greece* (Leiden, 1984), pp. 52–79.
23. I would not go quite as far as Karl Popper did in *The Open Society and Its Enemies*, in which Plato's ideal republic is portrayed as a prototype of modern totalitarian states; but see Vickers (cited in Further Reading), pp. 140f.

PLATO, *GORGIAS*

I. Introductory scene (447A–449B)	Topic discussed
II. Socrates and Gorgias (449C–461B)	
Art and knowledge (449C–451D)	A(B)*
Power and the Good (452A–455C)	A(B)
Power and knowledge (456C–461B)	A(B)
III. Socrates and Polus (461B–481B)	
Analogy with cookery, etc. (461B–466A)	A
Power and happiness (466A–480A)	B
True utility of rhetoric (480A–481B)	A
IV. Socrates and Kallikles (418C–527E)	
Nature and convention (482C–486D)	B + A
Power and happiness (486D–500A)	B
Rhetoric and pleasure (500A–503D)	A
Doing/suffering evil (503D–515B)	B
Rhetoric and statesmanship (515B–521A)	A
Judgment of souls ("myth") (521A–526D)	B
Conclusion (526D–527E)	A + B

ARISTOTLE, *RHETORIC*

(References are to Bekker numbers; edition used is that of R. Kassel, Berlin/New York, 1976.)

Book One (1354a1–1377b11)
   I. Chapters 1–3 (1354a1–1359a29) General observations, rhetoric, the nature of rhetorical argument, and the kinds of rhetoric defined
   II. Chapters 4–14 (1359a30–1375a21) The *topoi* peculiar to the different kinds of rhetoric
      A. Ch. 4–8 (1359a30–1366a22) Symbouleutic (political) rhetoric
      B. Ch. 9 (1366a23–1368a37) Epideictic rhetoric
      C. Ch. 10–14 (1368b1–1375a21) Courtroom rhetoric
      D. Ch. 15 (1375a22–1377b11) The "nonartistic proofs"

* A = What rhetors do; B = *eudaimonia*.

CHAPTER 2

Hellenistic and Roman Rhetorics

In just over a decade, Alexander the Great and his armies conquered most of the known world. At the time of Alexander's premature death, in 323, the Macedonian Empire extended over a million square miles, stretching from Sicily to the Punjab. Alexander's death was followed by 20 years of internal strife, betrayals, and assassinations until, finally, the shape of the Hellenistic world began to appear. The empire was divided into three parts. Western Asia and Asia Minor were held by Antigonus, the one-eyed veteran of Alexander's campaigns. Egypt and the southeast Aegean region were ruled by Ptolemy and his successors. The territories from Syria to the Hindu Kush fell under the rule of Seléucus. In all these areas, colonies of Greeks were established and Greek culture imposed on the native peoples, the *barbaroi*, with astonishing speed and efficiency. An idea of just how pervasive Greek became can be gathered from the fact that the Buddhist decrees of the Indian monarch Akosa were published in Greek in the mid-third century BC.

ENKYKLIOS PAIDEIA

The military and cultural achievements of Alexander, who is said to have slept with a dagger and a copy of the *Iliad* beneath his pillow, were to persevere for centuries to come, persisting even after the rise of the other great power of this post-Classical period, Rome. He and his successors carried out a hellenizing policy by establishing urban centers on the Greek model, each with its own bureaucracy administering the affairs of the surrounding countryside. The Greek colonists, isolated in foreign lands and surrounded by alien cultures, built temples, gymnasia, and theaters in older cities, such as Babylon and Susa, and in the string of Alexandrias set down by the Greeks, extending from the Nile Delta to the Himalayas, where, in the north of Afghanistan, the ruins of Alexandria Eschate—" Alexandria the Furthest"—were recently discovered by Russian archeologists.[1]

In the effort to realize the Panhellenic program of Alexander, the Greeks also established in these places schools where Greek letters and science were taught, the latter greatly enriched by the accomplishments of Egyptian and Babylonian astronomers and mathematicians. The new Greek world assimilated many foreign elements—Persian, Semitic, Egyptian, even Indian—mainly by promoting as the common bond uniting all of them the Greek language and cultural heritage, or *paideia*. A new program of education came into being that had as its goal the initiation of young men into the Greek way of life.

This program eventually became rather standardized throughout the Greek world as the *enkyklios paideia*, roughly, "the rounded education," which consisted of instruction in grammar, rhetoric, logic, arithmetic, geometry, music, and, in most cases, astronomy.[2] "Encyclical" studies would continue to be pursued by Romans and, centuries later, by all European students under the rubric of the *trivium* (grammar, rhetoric, and logic) and *quadrivium* (the other four subjects) during the Middle Ages and Renaissance.

During the Hellenistic period, the teaching of grammar and rhetoric as part of the *enkyklios paideia* created demands for systematic rigor that had a permanent effect on the shape and contents of those arts, on the way they were taught, and on what was taught. Grammar included what would today be called literary criticism as well as orthography, syntax, and composition; and it was in the course of their grammatical studies that students would be taught to read and understand the classics of Greek literature—Homer, the tragedians, and the canon of Attic orators that was recognized by the schoolmasters. Here, too, the study of style was in order, usually structured around various analyses of types of style, such as those in Theophrastus' *On Style*, which set out the classic three levels of style (high, low, and mixed), or Demetrius' *On Expression* (*Peri hermeneias*), where the plain, the elevated, the elegant, and the forceful styles are distinguished and discussed.[3]

The teaching of rhetoric centered on an analysis of the art into five component parts: invention, the modes of discovering arguments; arrangement; expression, which included the study of style in argumentation; memory; and delivery, including both pronunciation and gesture. This five-part analysis persists throughout the history of rhetoric into the eighteenth century. Similarly, the analysis of the parts of a speech into five (sometimes six) parts became a pedagogical commonplace. Every speech, students were taught, had to include a prologue (*prooimion* in Greek, *exordium* in Latin); narration (*diēgesis, narratio*); argument (*pistis, confirmatio*); rebuttal (*lysis, reprehensio*); and conclusion (*epilogos, peroratio*). This format, too, persists into the eighteenth century.[4]

Another pedagogical innovation that became common to all the schools of rhetoric in the Greco-Roman world was the set of elementary exercises known as *progymnasmata.* These are first referred to in the *Rhetorica ad Alexandrum,* a fourth-century BC treatise probably composed by one of Alexander's tutors, Anaximenes of Lampaskos; by the first century AD they had become standard components of the rhetoric curriculum. The textbooks of progymnasmata present a graded series of patterns for students to follow in writing and speaking on assigned themes, each building on what the student should have learned from the previous exercise and adding something new. The first two, in the standard collections, are exercises in retelling fables and tales from poetry and history. Next came the *chreia* and proverb, in which students amplified on sayings by paraphrase, illustration, comparison, and citation of other authorities. Refutation and confirmation were argumentative exercises designed to demonstrate that a given story was, or was not, incredible, inconsistent, or inexpedient. The exercise of the commonplace (*koinos topos*) required the student to enlarge on a stock theme; those of encomium and vituperation, to praise a person or thing for being virtuous or to blame a person or thing for being wicked. Comparison went one step forward in requiring the student to show which of two persons or things was better or worse. Next came exercises in impersonation (*prosopopoeia*), where the student composed a monologue in the character of a historical or fictional character; description (*ekphrasis*), designed to train the student to present a vivid verbal picture of some thing; the *thesis,* an exercise in arguing a general claim such as "Should anyone marry?"; and, finally, an exercise in which the student was asked to argue for or against a law, real or imaginary. The tradition of teaching rhetoric in this way also extends to relatively modern times.[5]

More advanced students were required by their teachers to compose rather substantial speeches, declamations on deliberative or forensic themes. These exercises probably go back to the school of Isocrates and seem to have been a permanent feature of rhetorical education in both Greek and Roman schools. The third-century BC papyrus fragments found at el-Hibeh in Egypt contain an early example of such a school declamation, and we have both the *Controversiae* and *Suasoriae*—forensic and deliberative declamations—of Seneca the Elder and a collection of declamations from the first century AD attributed to Quintilian. Since declamatory exercises also continue to be part of the curriculum in rhetoric up to modern times, it is clear that Hellenistic school reforms and innovations set the agenda for rhetorical education for a very long time to come.[6]

The reason so much attention was paid to the dvelopment of methods for teaching rhetoric in the schools had a great deal to do, clearly, with the bureaucratic needs of Hellenistic governments. But there is a deeper reason as well, one that harkens back to the vision of Isocrates and that is nicely summed up in an observation made by the first-century AD historian Diodorus Siculus. Diodorus writes in the introduction to his *History*:

> History also contributes to the power of speech, than which no nobler thing may easily be found. For it is speech (*logos*) which makes the Greeks

superior to the barbarians, the educated (*pepaideumenoi*) to the uneducated; and, more, it is by means of speech alone that one man is able to prevail over many. On the whole, the impression made by any proposal corresponds to the power (*dynamis*) of the speaker who proposes it; and we call great and virtuous men "worthy of speech," as though in that they had won the greatest prize of virtue (*aretē*) (1.2.6).

That the goal of *paideia* was nothing less than eloquence was one of the most deeply held convictions of the entire age. Thus, however artificial these various distinctions and exercises might seem, their development in Hellenistic schools set not only a pedagogical but a cultural agenda for rhetorical education in the European tradition.

"STASIS" IN RHETORICAL INVENTION

None of those curricular innovations is quite as significant as the introduction of stasis theory, credited to Hermagoras of Temnos, who wrote some time around 150 BC. Hermagoras' treatise is not extant, but its main outlines can be reconstructed from such works as Cicero's *De inventione** and the pseudo-Ciceronian *Rhetorica ad Herennium*,* both composed about 85 BC. This method of rhetorical invention dominated in rhetorical teaching up to the seventeenth century, so it is important that we get some idea of what it is.[7]

Stasis, in Greek, may be translated either as "strife" or as "immobility," as in the English *static*. Both senses are operative in the context of stasis theory, since *stasis* in that context refers to the basic issue in dispute resulting from the positions taken by adversaries in a debate. Stasis theory was designed to enable one both to locate the relevant points at issue in a dispute and to discover applicable arguments drawn from the appropriate "places" (*loci*, the Latin equivalent of the Greek *topoi*). This concept has been traced variously to the so-called scientific questions of Aristotle's *Posterior Analytics* and to pretrial procedures in Roman legal practice. Whatever its origin, stasis theory is most easily explained, and is so explained in classic treatments of it, in terms of a case at law.[8]

Suppose a man is discovered burying a corpse in an isolated place and is accused of murder. The first question at issue in his trial will be a question of fact—Did he do it?—which falls under the heading of the "conjectural stasis" (*I* 2.15). If this is the point at issue, one side will argue that he did and the other that he did not, appealing to particulars of the man's character or to the nature of the deed itself for arguments that will establish the probability one way or the other (*I* 2.16–51; *H* 2.3f.). If it is certain that the defendant did kill the victim, we must ask whether his action falls under the accepted definition of *murder*, as not every taking of life can be so defined. This question falls under the heading of the "definitive stasis"; and for arguments about the definition of a thing or an act, one must turn to the accepted definition or attempt to establish a definition by appeal to such things as synonyms, etymologies, or genus-species relationships (*I* 2.52ff.; *H* 2.17). If it is admitted that the right name for the act is *murder*, we must ask about the quality of the act: was it just, or expedient, or honorable, in fact—that is, are there any mitigating aspects to it? This question falls under the heading of the "qualitative stasis." The relevant arguments here will turn on whether a defendant denies any wrongdoing or admits, but attempts to justify, his act by attempting, for instance, to shift the blame to some other party or to claim that some significant benefit resulted from the act (*I* 2.64–115; *H* 2.19ff.). If the charge of wrongdoing still sticks, the issue in the last resort becomes whether the court is competent or not. This is the "translative stasis," or issue of transference (*I* 2.57–64; *H* 2.18).

Along with such questions of fact, definition, quality, and jurisdiction, there are other questions for debate in a trial that center on the interpretation of written documents such as contracts, wills, or, indeed, the wording of the law. Thus, stasis theory extends beyond the so-called rational questions resolvable by establishing the probability of one's contentions to legal questions resolvable by arguments about proper interpretation: how to resolve questions concerning the letter vs. the spirit of a given document, conflicting laws, ambiguities, and allowable inferences from what is expressed to what is not (*I* 2.116ff.; *H* 2.13ff.). Consideration of such questions invariably involves questions of fact and definition—that is, "legal" questions are, in the last analysis, resolvable only by appeal to the methods for dealing with "rational" questions. It is in this way that stasis theory provides the means of discovering arguments on almost any question whatsoever. And once one understands that, it becomes possible to see why stasis theory was as pervasively influential, even outside the boundaries of specifically rhetorical concerns (in philosophy, for instance), as it was for so many generations of writers on rhetoric.

The foregoing account is based largely on Cicero's *De inventione*, a work he composed not long after completing his school studies and before he began his career as an advocate and politician. This early work, which Cicero himself was to disparage later in life, is restricted to the study of the rhetorical lore on invention that was structured around the stasis questions, as the outline appended to this chapter will show. The *Rhetorica ad Herennium*, written about the same time as the *De inventione*, contains a briefer, yet no less complete, discussion of stasis theory that is so similar to Cicero's that there can be no doubt that both drew on the same source—namely, Hermagoras. But the the *Rhetorica ad Herennium* is rather more complete in its treatment of rhetoric, as it includes the current doctrines concerning the other parts of the art: arrangement, expression (treated at great length), memory, and delivery. This book, which was long thought to have been written by Cicero, continued to be used along with Cicero's *De inventione* until the end of the Middle Ages. Stasis theory also survived and, indeed, dominated, in the Greek tradition that runs down through to the end of the Byzantine Empire in the fifteenth century.

CICERO AND THE IDEAL ORATOR

Having looked briefly at the products of Hellenistic rhetorical education, we need now to turn to one who received that education and went on to be the most famous orator of his time, a successful politician, and one of the greatest proponents in history of the relation between eloquence and wisdom, Marcus Tullius Cicero. Cicero's impact on subsequent generations of rhetoricians and, eventually, on the entire tradition of rhetoric in Europe is hard to overstate. In fact, although he was by no means the most original thinker in Classical antiquity, one could say without much fear of contradiction that he was and remains the most prominent figure in the history of rhetoric. So broad is the scope of his achievement and so immense the body of critical literature that has been devoted to his works that we can hope here to give only the briefest of accounts. Accordingly, we shall restrict our discussion in what follows, treating in any detail only the masterpiece of his mature period, the *De oratore* (composed 55 BC) and leaving aside consideration of such works as the *Brutus* and *Orator*, which he wrote just before his death.[9]

Cicero was born on January 3, 106 BC, on his family's estate near Arpinum, about 60 miles southeast of Rome. When he was still a boy, his family moved to Rome, partly to ensure that he would receive a good education; and there he completed the *enkyklios paideia*, which at that time demanded mastery of Greek as well as Latin. After the age of 15 or so, when he was presented with his man's *toga,* he went on to pursue a career in the courts and the Roman senate, rising up through the ranks to the highest office of *consul* and gaining a reputation for the eloquence he exhibited in the law court and in the assembly.

Cicero's lifetime was marked by enormous turmoil in Roman politics, turmoil which by the 50s BC degenerated into virtual gang warfare. He was always at the center of these political storms, forming alliances and, of course, making enemies. Perhaps the most significant constant in Cicero's career was his opposition to those of the nobility who tried to impose their will on the Roman political apparatus by force and threats. At various times, the political ferment forced him into temporary retirement from public affairs and even exile from the city; and it was during these times of enforced leisure that he composed most of his many philosophical and rhetorical works. During the last of such periods, Cicero's enemies undertook a scheme to eliminate him from the picture altogether and assassinated him in 43 BC, the year after they had murdered his archrival, Julius Caesar.

At about age 50, with almost 30 years of public life behind him, Cicero composed his *De re publica* and *De oratore,* the former outlining the ideal structure within which ideal republican politics could be practiced, the latter a portrait of the ideal statesman, who, it happens, is the *orator perfectus.* As we have noted, Cicero had written his handbook on invention, the *De inventione,* while still quite young. With age and experience he came to rhetoric with a rather less scholastic attitude, arguing through the characters who talk about it in *De oratore* that the rhetoric of the schools means nothing in itself. It cannot, so to say, make swans of geese, nor can it justify itself in the face of political reality unless it is practiced by the "good man." the *vir bonus*.[10]

Most of the dialogue in *De oratore* is put in the mouths of L. Crassus and M. Antonius, both real orator-statesmen from the generation just before Cicero's, with a few contributions made by other figures from that generation, among them Q. Scaevola, C. Julius Caesar Strabo Vopiscus, and P. Sulpitius. The dramatic date of the dialogue is some time in fall 91 BC, at a time that Cicero saw as a high point in the republic that was, in his view, so thoroughly undermined by his own contemporaries. The discussion—Cicero calls it a *disputatio*—covers a three-day period. The first day, reported in Book 1, is occupied with the conversation between Crassus and Antonius, with Crassus doing most of the talking, on the nature and scope of oratory and what a truly eloquent orator needs to know. Crassus holds that while the school rhetorics might produce competent (*disertes*) speakers, real eloquence presupposes wide learning, particularly in philosophy and the law. Rules (*praecepta*) are not enough, as they cannot make up for deficiencies in natural talent (*ingenium*) and cannot make one virtuous as well as good at speaking (1.95ff.).

Book 2 reports the conversation on the second day, most of which is dominated by Antonius. Antonius, like Crassus in Book 1, claims that he has not bothered himself with the teachings of the school rhetorics and is critical of the "theorizers." And, like Crassus, he shows himself to be remarkably well informed about their teachings, as well as about the history of philosophy, of history itself, and of Greek and Roman oratory (see 2.55ff., 75ff., 92ff.). His is the voice of experience, he says as he begins to explain how he would go about putting a speech together. His subsequent account moves, however, in a direction that is in fact not much different from that in the *Ad Herennium*, with 2.114 taking up the distinctions of stasis questions and the materials of proof; 162ff. dealing with *loci*, 185ff., with emotion and wit; 291ff., with the principles of arrangement; at the end of his account, he discusses memory, which he regards as a virtual subdivision of invention.

In Book 3, the conversation is once again dominated by Crassus, who gives a detailed account of the nature and significance of style in true eloquence. Here again, the treatment is quite similar in content and structure to that found in the handbooks. But like Antonius on invention, arrangement, and memory, Crassus embeds his discussion of style firmly in the realm of practice, not just theory. Moreover, the actual discussion of style is preceded by two long digressions on the relation of wisdom to eloquence (3.55–82) and the necessity of a firm foundation in general culture and learning (109–143). Thus Crassus places his observations on the four basic requisites of a good style, on diction and composition, on prose rhythm, and on amplification and embellishment (see 3.37–51; 148–209) in a broad context of right reason and virtuous action. Crassus ends his discourse on expression with some observations on enunciation and gesture, thus finishing a treatment of the art that is structured around the standard five-part model familiar from the handbooks.

This brief sketch of the *De oratore* will give a rough idea of its contents, but we must not imagine that this work is essentially a handbook, though written in a lively dramatic style more conducive to an evening's entertainment than a dry didactic style. It is true that in the *De oratore* Cicero succeeds in conveying all the material taught in the schools, and more; and that by weaving digressions on history and philosophy into the expositions of such things as the principles of good style, he is perhaps able to make those lessons more interesting. But there is more than that going on in this work, as the brief prologues at the beginning of each of the books that comprise *De oratore* make plain to even the most casual reader.

To begin with, it is clear that Quintus, Cicero's brother, who is the putative audience, is not the only one for whom *De oratore* was intended. Like the *De re publica*, a dialogue composed a little later and also with a dramatic date set in the heyday of the republic, the *De oratore* was addressed to the wider audience of Cicero's contemporaries and designed to influence them. Far from a work of retirement, it is meant both as a call for a return to an earlier republican ideology and as an apologia of sorts for Cicero himself. The problems addressed in *De oratore* are not just the scholastic quibbles about, say, whether rhetoric is really an art, but the more real political problems of the mid-50s. Cicero's choice of speakers in his dialogue was quite deliberate, meant to provide a clear contrast with the politicians of his own time. In this connection, there is no small irony in the fact that two of the speakers, M. Antonius and J. Caesar Strabo Vopiscus, had namesakes who were politically active in the 50s—M. Antonius (Mark Antony), the grandson of the Antonius of the 90s, and Julius Caesar, Cicero's rival and eventual bitter enemy. Neither could fare well by comparison to their forebears.

Moreover, Cicero's choice of speakers was a choice of his own candidates for the distinction of being the ideal republican orators. He clearly intended to identify his own thinking with theirs, as in the *De re publica* he was to identify with Scipio and his circle, and theirs with his. This comes out clearly in the prologue to Book 3 (3.13f.), but it also emerges in Crassus' defense of all styles in 3.28ff, for instance, and in the long passages on the relation of wisdom and eloquence that echo similar ideas from Cicero's youth in the *De inventione* and adult career in his extant correspondence. Read in the context of Cicero's career, that is to say, the *De oratore* can be seen as both apology and manifesto.[11]

As has been noted by other scholars, Cicero's political ideology was not altogether Roman, but greatly influenced by his familiarity with the ideas of Isocrates. That influence is frequently evident in *De oratore*, in the passages that argue, for instance, that the supreme end of education is its application to the practical affairs of daily life (see 3.23f., 86ff.), and the passage in which the loss of the the old union between statesmanship, eloquence, and philosophy is deplored (as at 3.59ff.). Indeed, in a letter to a friend (*Fam.* 1.9), he states explicitly that *De oratore* was written with Isocrates in mind. To the influence of Isocrates we must add that of the philosopher Carneades: eloquence is the supreme achievement, but a crucial element of true eloquence is the ability to argue *in utramque partem*—that is, in the absence of certain knowledge, to argue both sides of any issue, as Carneades had taught. Given the enormous importance of Greek writers in Cicero's intellectual formation, it is no wonder that his contemporaries referred to him (contemptuously, as it happens) as "The Greek."

The principle of *in utramque partem* supplies a philosophical base for the Isocratean-Ciceronian emphasis on the vital importance of eloquence to the state and is, indeed, at the heart of Cicero's rhetorical and philosophical methods as well. It is a *multiplex ratio disputandi*, a multivoiced method, which begets *controversia*, a dialogue in which practical or philosophical formulations are situated in divergent frames of reference, brought into conflict in debate, and tested for their respective claims of *probabilitas*. *Controversia* requires that both sides of any question be heard, thus creating the conditions necessary for arriving at decisions and negotiating differences in a reasonable way in both politics and philosophy. This necessity, in turn, arises from the Carneadean doctrine that there are no absolute certainties from which one can deduce or extrapolate conclusions as to right actions or ideas. Rhetorical invention and philosophical inquiry alike are activities in which *loci*, the "seats of argument" (*sedes argumentorum*), which constitute our common store of facts and the evidence associated with them, are primary. *Controversia*, that is, does not move platonically from universals and differences to assimilate "lesser" truths to "greater" truths; it is resolved only insofar as one decides to adopt one of the positions in conflict or to modify it or to formulate a new position within the body of *loci* that will allow one to discover new interpretations of facts or statements. It is precisely this method that Cicero uses in *De oratore* and such philosophical works as *De natura deorum* or the *Tusculan Disputations*, which Cicero wrote shortly before he was murdered.[12]

The *De oratore*, then, is far more than a treatise on the art of rhetoric alone. It is a work in which oratory, philosophy, and statesmanship are bound together as a single whole and in which the true dimensions of the notion of the "good man skilled in speaking" (*vir bonus dicendi peritus*) are, as it were, mapped and measured. In it, Cicero reveals himself as an engaged writer and thinker who, even when it was dangerous for him to appear in the Forum, did not hesitate to broadcast his ideas to his contemporaries. Eventually, those ideas would appear so dangerous to his rivals that they sought to cut them off at the source by killing him. The dangers that Cicero's eloquence represented to them is perhaps nowhere more evident than in the account of his assassination in Dio's *Roman History*. After they had slain him, Dio tells us (47.8.3f.), his murderers brought his head to Marcus Antonius, who ordered it to be displayed in the Forum, where Cicero had so often spoken against him. Then Fulvia, wife of Antonius' ally Octavian, got hold of it,

> took the head in her hands...and after abusing it and spitting on it out of spite, set it on her knees and opened the mouth, and pulled out the tongue, and pierced it with hairpins while muttering many brutal insults over it.

This story is probably apocryphal, but it is nonetheless symbolic of the respect with which Cicero's eloquence was regarded, even by his most ferocious enemies.

THE SURVIVAL OF CICERONIAN IDEALS

For over a century after Cicero's death, Rome was wracked by political turmoil and radical change in the transformation of the republic into an empire whose rulers claimed, in imitation of Alexander the Great, to be divine. Two of Rome's emperors in this period were notoriously insane— Caligula in particular, but with Nero running a close second. By the time Vespasian was able to gain control, in AD 69, the Roman treasury had been depleted by civil strife and irresponsible administration.

Vespasian's general policy was one of rigorous fiscal control coupled with a strong public works program that, in addition to its obvious propaganda advantages, had beneficial effects on employment rates and the circulation of currency. In the midst of his frugality, however, Vespasian ordered two surprising expenditures. The first was to impoverished senators, whom he presented with substantial sums of money to prevent them from losing their qualifications for seats in the senate. Such an action was not unprecedented (see Tacitus *Annals* 1.75) and is understandable as a measure taken to stabilize the government. The second expenditure took the form of grants from the public treasury, the *fiscus*, to artists and teachers of grammar and rhetoric. The grants to artists were apparently meant to stimulate the recovery of traditional values and thereby to restore public confidence. The grants to grammarians and rhetoricians also had a practical aim: the restoration of education at the high level required to prepare young men for civil service.[13]

One of the rhetoricians—in fact, the only documented one—to receive an imperial grant was Marcus Fabius Quintilianus, who had come to Rome from his native Spain and made a reputation both as an advocate and as a teacher of rhetoric. After his retirement from active teaching, at age 50, in AD 90, Quintilian set about composing his *De institutione oratoria** (*On the Education of the Orator*), a compendium of theories of rhetoric discussed in the context of the production of the perfect orator. The *Institutes,* as we shall call it for the sake of brevity, is one of the fullest records of rhetorical lore in the Isocratean-Ciceronian tradition ever written, as it covers in 12 books a program of education from the cradle to the grave.[14]

All of Book One is devoted to general considerations of early childhood education, principles of pedagogy, and the shape of the ideal "encyclical" curriculum. In Books Two and Three, he turns more directly to the teaching of elementary lessons in rhetoric and to the basic principles of the art, including (at 3.6) a long discussion of stasis theory. Books Four through Six are on invention, arranged according to the standard divisions of a speech (exordium, narration, etc.), including a detailed treatment of the nature of argument in Book Five. Book Seven is about arrangement in relation to both rational questions and legal questions. Style is the subject of Books Eight and Nine; the importance of imitation of the right authors that of Book Ten; and memory and delivery, along with some observations on decorum, that of Eleven. Book Twelve is devoted to a discussion of the character of the perfect orator and his activities upon retirement from active practice.

Quintilian's dedication to the Ciceronian ideal of the *orator perfectus* is obvious. What is perhaps less obvious is the place of "controversial" thinking in the *Institutes*. In the *De Oratore, controversia* is dramatized in the exchanges between the characters who speak in the dialogue. In Quintilian, it is of course not presented in such a form, but it is there nonetheless. His procedure in setting up a definition of rhetoric provides a good example. He begins at 2.15.2 by observing that some have defined the art as "the power of persuasion." But money also has the power to persuade, he argues; hence such a definition is not satisfactory (2.15.9). Then there are those who define it as "the power of persuading by speech." This seems a bit closer to the mark; but since prostitutes and seducers also persuade by what they say, this is not satisfactory, either. And so he proceeds, building up by accumulation to "oratory is the power of judging and discoursing on such civil matters that are put before it with a certain persuasiveness, action of the body, and delivery" (2.15.22). By taking up successive definitions offered by his predecessors and arguing against them, one by one, Quintilian is clearly engaged in a sort of *controversia*, and this method eventually brings him to what he considers the most "probable" definition: "the art of speaking well (*bene dicendi*)" (2.15.38). Quintilian works this way throughout the *Institutes*, whether he is examining the matter of stasis (as at 3.6.1ff.), the meaning of "argument" (5.10.3ff.), or the status of various figures and tropes (in Books Eight and Nine *passim*).

Quintilian's adherence to Cicero's ideals is most striking not in his account of the general shape of the art, however, nor even in his use of the method of controversy, but in his insistence that the art is pointless unless applied in practical affairs. He stresses this in the preface to the work:

> I cannot admit that the principles of right and honorable action are...to be left to the philosophers; for the man who can maintain his role as citizen, who is qualified for the management of affairs both private and public, and who can govern communities by his advice, settle them by means of laws, and improve them by legislative actions can most certainly be no other than the orator. (Pref. 10)

Likewise, at the end of the *Institutes*, in discussing the character of the ideal orator, Quintilian catalogues the orator's duties: to protect the innocent, defend the truth, deter criminal behavior, inspire the military, and in general inspire the citizen body (12.1.26–28). The entire educational program so painstakingly laid out by Quintilian, in other words, is ultimately practical in orientation.

Such an orientation may seem strange in a milieu that many have seen as hostile to rhetorical practice. The consolidation of imperial rule in Rome, with its increasing concentration of power in the person of the emperor and its diminution of senatorial influence, would seem to make the Ciceronian ideal irrelevant, conceived as it was in the context of the republic. It seems equally clear, however, that Quintilian thought that ideal the most compelling and the most likely to achieve his imperial patrons' aim of "stabilizing and enhancing"—as Suetonius put it in his *Life* of Vespasian—the Roman people.[15] To be sure, ideals seldom match realities. Quintilian completed the *Institutes* during the regin of Domitian, whose arrogation of the title *dominus et deus* to himself is reminiscent of the excesses of Nero and Caligula before him. Hence, perhaps, Quintilian's praise of the emperor's poetry at the beginning of Book Four in a passage that some scholars have characterized as abject flattery, but that may just as easily be seen as an assurance that his true attachment was not to republicanism as such but to traditional Roman values. Whatever our assessment of Quintilian himself, his *Institutes* show very clearly that those values still found an eloquent spokesman in Cicero even in times of rigid imperial control.

Evidence of the persistence of Cicero's ideal can be found also in the works of Quintilian's younger contemporaries, Tacitus and the younger Pliny. We do not of course see anything like a direct application of Cicero to current conditions. But in Tacitus' *Dialogue on Oratory* and Pliny's *Panegyric*, addressed to the emperor Trajan, we can see that Cicero's ideas continue to inform both literary production and concrete political action. Moreover, to the extent that Pliny's *Panegyric* influenced later orators at the imperial court—as indeed it did well into the fifth century—those ideas can be said to have persisted almost to the threshold of the Middle Ages.

P. Cornelius Tacitus (55–c. 115) was a successful public figure under Vespasian, Titus, and Domitian. He was famous for his eloquence, but gave up his political career in 100 and turned his hand to history, for which he is most famous. His *Dialogus de oratoribus* suggests Tacitus' reasons for abandoning rhetoric, so to speak, and taking up the task of recording the growth of tyranny as an important theme in Roman politics from Augustus on.[16]

The *Dialogue* is, first of all, consciously Ciceronian, both in its form, reminiscent of the *De oratore*, and in the style Tacitus' interlocutors speak in, a style strikingly different from that of his historical works. But the leading question in the *Dialogue* is not "What is oratory?" but "Why is oratory dead?" The question is prompted by the discovery by M. Aper, one of the main characters, that the famous orator C. Maternus has retired from public life and taken up writing tragedies instead. Maternus explains that he is ashamed to participate in an art that has so decayed. Aper contests this view, and attacks Maternus' abandonment of oratory, vaunting its greatness (5–10). After Maternus has amplified on his fatigue with public affairs, he and Aper debate the relative merits of the old orators as compared to the new (11–16). In his second speech (16–23), Aper defends contemporary rhetoric as clearer and more graceful than the old. At this point, V. Messala, a late arrival (at 14) to the conversation, holds forth on the virtues of the old rhetoric and explains why the art has fallen into disrepute: these new orators are lazy and soft, he says, and spend most of their time, for lack of any great subjects to address in their speeches, simply declaiming school themes (25–35). After a lacuna in the text, we find Maternus speaking again, explaining that, during the republic, strife gave rise to eloquence as a response. In their own time (the dramatic date is 75 AD), the order and stability under the emperor remove the necessity for the sort of genuine eloquence that republican orators practiced, and hence that eloquence has died out. The most eloquent speakers in the city are not public leaders but informers (36–42). The conversation ends here, with Maternus promising to discuss any point the others may want elucidated at some other time. As Aper rises to leave, Maternus puts his arm around him and says:

"We shall both denounce you—I to the poets and Messala to the ancients."

And Aper replies, jokingly, "I shall denounce you two to the teachers of rhetoric and the professors."

The good humor the characters in the *Dialogue* exhibit toward one another while discussing such a serious issue conceals the bitterness of its author, but not very successfully. Like Maternus, Tacitus can neither abide the new rhetoric nor satisfy himself with looking nostalgically to the past. Nor can he tolerate the professors, including, it seems, Quintilian. But in rejecting the likes of Quintilian, Tacitus does not, as some have argued, reject the Ciceronian ideal. It is, rather, unfortunate that conditions have rendered that ideal so irrelevant, conditions whose origins and developments he traces in his great historical work, the *Annals*. In short, if it cannot be said that Cicero was an inspiration to Tacitus, it can be said that Tacitus was haunted by his achievement.

Tacitus' good friend, the younger Pliny, took a less gloomy view of his times and of the opportunities available to the orator. Born in AD 62 in northern Italy, Pliny enjoyed success in public life, rising through a succession of government offices climaxed by his appointment late in his life as imperial ambassador to Bithynia, in the East. Pliny is perhaps most famous for his letters, but what interests us here is rather the speech he composed on the occasion of his appointment as consul in 100. In this, the famous—or infamous, depending on one's point of view—*Panegyricus* addressed to the emperor Trajan, Pliny demonstrates that eloquence of public importance was not dead. The Ciceronian ideal orator is, in this speech, directed toward a different task using different tactics more suited to the times.[17]

The most obvious faults of the speech are its length and its occasional overdevelopment of topics to the point of obscurity. The version we have, however, was not the version he delivered, but a revised version meant for the edification of a small group of fellow senators. In one of his letters, Pliny tells his friend Vibius Severus that he read the *Panegyricus* to them in separate installments over a three-day period. This revised version, he says, was written in a fit of exuberance, which explains why the style he adopted was so florid, which is another aspect of the speech faulted by modern critics. Still, this speech came to be regarded in late antiquity as a virtual prototype for imperial prose panegyrics, not only for its literary qualities but for its political strategy.[18]

The speech is built around the development of standard *loci* of military and political achievements and personal qualities. Thus, after a brief exordium, Pliny treats in detail Trajan's career before, in 100, he became consul for the third time (4–23), including his adoption by the emperor Nerva and his arrival in Rome. In the second major part (24–55), Pliny relates a long list of Trajan's accomplishments as emperor; and in the third his achievements as consul (55–80). After a brief but thorough account of his personal virtues in private life (81–89), Pliny offers elaborate thanks, as the convention evidently demanded, for Trajan's generosity. All six parts were doubtless included in the original version, but in a less highly amplified form.

It is impossible to tell how much the *Panegyricus* resembles or differs from previous speeches given on such occasions, since no trace of those speeches survives. But it is clear that this speech was no piece of abject flattery in conventional form; for it is in fact a sort of manifesto, as many historians have recognized, of the Senate's ideal of a good ruler. Such a manifesto is unlikely to have been tolerated by most of Trajan's predecessors. Indeed, Pliny is quite specific in contrasting Trajan's rule as the *princeps optimus*—"the best possible leader"—with the despotic behavior of those who came before him; and he repeatedly predicts that Trajan will serve as a model for all rulers to come. Pliny's subtle way of mixing fact with ideal is, in the end, a skillful way of telling Trajan what his subjects expect of him, not just an encomium designed to win the emperor's favor.

What is particularly striking about Pliny's speech, aside from its elaborate development of the *loci* of praise, is its assimilation of Ciceronian themes and even of his language in its conscious echoes of Cicero's *Pro Marcello* and *De lege Manilia*.[19] These echoes cannot have failed to impress his audience with their relevance to the very un-Republican occasion for which the speech was composed. If the *Panegyricus* could be read as a "Mirror for Princes," it could also be seen as evidence that eloquence still had an important function—a social and political function—in an imperial setting. This speech of praise summarizes those values around which good government must be built, values that need to be attended to by the ruler and the ruled alike. Thus the orator in Pliny, like the orator in Cicero and, before him, Isocrates, is the creator of consensus, of *homonoia*. This role for rhetoric would continue to be recognized by later emperors and assumed by their panegyrists down to the end of the fourth century.[20]

Cicero's influence, in short, continued to be felt as long as there was a Latin Empire in the West, at least, that is, up to the sack of Rome by Alaric, king of the Visigoths, in AD 410. Indeed, as we shall see, it was felt long after that momentous event. It was not, of course, the republican ideal of *De oratore* and *De re publica* that survived, but the ideal of the *vir bonus dicendi peritus* adapted to the new circumstances created by a new form of government. Contrary to the belief implicit in Tacitus that rhetoric had decayed and that such education as one might receive from a Quintilian was for naught, there was still a role for the eloquent orator, and therefore also for rhetorical training, in society. Rhetoric did not wither under the emperors, it just changed tactics.

GREEKS IN THE ROMAN WORLD

Greek teachers of rhetoric began to appear in Rome toward the end of the second century BC and were sought after by those wealthy enough, like Cicero's parents, to send their sons to study with them. The official response to their presence in the city was rather less than enthusiastic, however, as can be seen by a decree from 92 BC preserved for us by Suetonius:

> It has been reported to us that there are some who have introduced a new form of teaching and that our youth are attending their schools; that these youngsters have adopted the name "Latin rhetoricians"; and that they spend whole days in idleness [in the schools]...We deem it appropriate to make it clear to those who conduct those schools and those who attend them that we do not approve.[21]

As the Athenians mistrusted the traveling sophists, so conservative Romans were wary of these Greeks. In this case, it is perhaps noteworthy that one of the censors who published the above decree was L. Crassus, the same Crassus we saw in Cicero's *De oratore*.

In spite of the suspicion with which they were viewed, Greek teachers of grammar and rhetoric continued to enjoy a measure of hospitality in Rome, particularly in the salons of wealthy familes such as the Pisones and the house of the patron of poets, Mycenas, in the first century BC. Under the emperors from Claudius to Theodosius, at the end of the fourth century, Greek teachers and orators were cultivated eagerly. Since some of these Greeks became as influential in later centuries as they were in the Roman literary circles that patronized them, we should include here a brief account of a few of the more prominent ones and what they did.

The first was Philodemus of Gadara (c. 110–35 BC), who came to Rome around 75 BC under the sponsorship of the Pisones. He eventually took up residence in Herculaneum and probably died there. That he was well known and admired in Rome in the 50s is clear from Cicero's *Ad Pisonem* (28.68f.). He was the author of numerous works on virtually every subject, including poetry and rhetoric. While those works were known to his contemporaries, they survive today only in the form of the fragments discovered in the eighteenth century in the ruins of the library in Piso's villa in Herculaneum, which was destroyed by the same eruption of Mount Vesuvius that buried Pompeii in AD 79.

One set of fragments contains parts of Philodemus' *Peri rhetorikēs* (*On*

Rhetoric). Most of what we have of this treatise is taken up with discussion of rival notions of rhetoric, and not much about Philodemus' own concept of the art. That has pretty much to be inferred from his criticisms of others' ideas. The main theme of the surviving fragments is the question of whether rhetoric can legitimately be called an art; and on this subject Philodemus takes the position that one kind of rhetoric, "sophistic" (display rhetoric) may qualify, but not others, such as courtroom or political rhetoric. They are based sheerly on trial and error. On the whole, however, rhetoric must be avoided by the philosopher and scientist, since it tries to establish true propositions without using rigorous empirical methods and enchants its hearers by emotional appeal. Rhetoric as practiced has less to do with content (*dianoia*) than with form (*synthesis*), which works its effects on the ear, not on the mind. This critique of rhetoric is rooted in the tradition of the philosopher Epicurus, although on the surface it sounds platonic. It should be noted, too, that Philodemus' version of rhetoric is close to the Gorgianic version we saw in Chapter 1.[22]

The concern with questions about the artistic status of rhetoric and how rhetoric works its effects was common among the Greek writers in Rome in the generation after Philodemus. Dionysius of Halicarnassus, who taught in Rome between 30 and 8 BC, for instance, wrestled with the problem of how rhetoric works, both in his treatise *On Composition* and in the set of critical essays he composed on the speeches of the great Attic orators.[23] In some respects, Dionysius seems to agree with the view of rhetoric that Philodemus had criticized when he held that the value of a rhetorical composition is defined primarily by its effects on the ear. At the same time, Dionysius finds that appeal to what is, in the final analysis, an irrational criterion unsatisfactory. True eloquence must, like that of Isocrates, make of men "not only clever speakers but men of good moral character" (*Isocrates* 4), and will convey *dianoia* that is "useful" (*chrēsimon*). In short, while Dionysius writes mainly about the beauties of word choice and composition, his basic concern, like that of the Isocrates he so admired, is with the social function of rhetoric.

By contrast, the debate between two younger contemporaries of Dionysius, Caecilius of Calacte and "Longinus," does not not appear to reveal much interest in the social issue. Caecilius, a Hellenized Jew who taught in Rome, and one Longinus (whose true identity we do not know) were concerned to explain the key to the sort of style that sweeps one off one's feet. Hence the treatise by Longinus *On the Sublime*, in which he tries to determine the sources in nature and in art of that style. The work by Caecilius to which *On the Sublime* was a response is lost.[24]

Longinus' work is more, however, than a merely literary essay. It is, to be sure, structured loosely around the five sources of "sublimity." Thus sections 9–15 discuss the nature of the ability to conceive impressive thoughts and the role of emotion (*pathos*); in 16–29, Longinus treats of various kinds of figures and tropes that lend sublimity to expression. In 30–38, he discusses nobility of diction; and at 39–42 elevated *synthesis*, including consideration of word order, rhythm, and euphony. All combine to produce not just a special style but a special effect. Longinus displays his admiration for both pungent gravity and rich solemnity, but he goes further to unite such stylistic qualities under a moral, not just a literary, ideal. On the one hand, therefore, we see in his discussion of techniques a constant emphasis on the presence of *pathos* and the importance of occasion (*kairos*) as conditions of success, but he balances this potentially irrationalist approach—reminiscent of Gorgianic rhetoric—with the insistence that, in effect, the true source of sublimity is in the character of "the good man skilled in speaking." Like Dionysius of Halicarnassus, in other words, Longinus struggles to maintain a political ethic in what could easily be an amoral, or perhaps immoral, rhetorical enterprise.

Neither Dionysius nor Longinus had much influence in their own day outside of the professorial circles in which they were active. As far as we know, their activities were restricted to the study and classroom. Later in the empire, however, we see the emergence of a class of professional orators who not only taught rhetoric but practiced it. Some of these self-proclaimed "sophists" were patronized by the emperor himself. Polemon, for example, was sponsored by both Trajan and his successor, Hadrian. Marcus Aurelius bestowed imperial favors on Herodes Atticus and on a young prodigy whose career we will survey in the next chapter, Hermogenes.[25]

In short, a fairly large number of Greeks found hospitality in Rome from the second century BC to the end of the fourth century of the common era, when the empire was officially divided into two separate administrative units, the West and the East, and the official residence of the emperor was transferred to the "New Rome," founded by the Emperor Constantine in 330 and called by him Constantinople. The influence of these writers on the Latin West was negligible, but their works continued to be copied and read by the scholars of the Greek East. Having looked at the main outlines of the developments in rhetoric in Rome, then, we must continue by looking at the continuation of those developments in later Classical and medieval settings.

SUMMARY

The conquests of Alexander the Great resulted in the hellenization of a vast region extending from Sicily to the Himalayas. An essential feature of that cultural imposition was the development of a standard system of education, the *enkyklios paideia*, an important part of which was rhetorical training. By the second century BC, the rhetoric curriculum had been standardized to include the five-part analysis of the art itself, the elementary exercises known as *progymnasmata*, training in declamation on stock themes, and the method of invention based on what was called *stasis*. All these were to continue to define the curriculum well past the Renaissance in European rhetorical education.

The Greek *paideia* eventually made its way to Rome, where, despite initial reservations on the part of conservative leaders, it became the norm. The Latin version of the Hellenistic rhetoric curriculum can be seen in the pseudo-Ciceronian *Rhetorica ad Herennium* and in Cicero's *De inventione* and *De oratore*. In both of the latter, it is clear that it was not only the curriculum that was absorbed but the cultural and social values that the curriculum was intended to foster as well. Thus there is a strong strain of Isocratean influence in those works, the ideal of the eloquent speaker who plays the role of educator and leader of society.

Cicero's eminence in Roman rhetoric and politics, both in his own time and for centuries to come, is hard to overstate. To the Isocratean conception of the orator's place in the community, Cicero added a philosophical dimension, the method of *controversia*, which he appropriated from philosophers such as Carneades. This method was, in Cicero's view, particularly suited to the sort of ideal republic he envisioned as well as to effective rhetorical invention. The Isocratean ideal and the method of *controversia* would continue to influence his successors up to the end of the Western Empire and beyond—in fact, until the end of the Renaissance.

The persistence of Ciceronianism is apparent in the *Institutes* of Quintilian, which lays out in detail both an elaboration of the Hellenistic rhetoric curriculum and a portrait of the orator as a *vir bonus* skilled in speaking. It should also be noted that Quintilian's method of exposition and criticism is based upon the method of *controversia*. In Tacitus' *Dialogue*, and Pliny's *Panegyricus*, too, we see the lingering influence of Cicero as the norm for politically significant eloquence. Indeed, that influence continues in Roman rhetoric until the fall of Rome. Rhetoric does not wither under the empire; it simply changes tactics from those of the courtroom to those of the court.

Greek teachers and critics found a measure of hospitality in Rome despite the suspicion with which they were viewed. In the period of the republic, in the principate under Augustus, and in imperial Rome alike, Greek teachers were patronized by the rich and powerful. Philodemus, Dionysius of Halicarnassus, and Longinus can all be seen to have grappled with the questions of, on the one hand, how rhetoric works its effects and, on the other, what bearing that has on the ethical mission of the ideal orator, recapitulating the tensions between Gorgianic and Isocratean rhetorics that manifest themselves in fourth-century Athens.

On the whole, the history of rhetoric in Hellenistic Greek and Roman settings is the history of the continuing influence of Isocrates. The method of controversy that Cicero incorporated into that tradition loses much of its political relevance at the collapse of the republic, surviving only in the encyclopedic method of the schoolmaster Quintilian and in the literary conventions of the dialogue, as in Tacitus. But the ideal of the eloquent orator survives, in revised form, until the beginning of the Middle Ages in the Latin West—and beyond.

FURTHER READING

A most comprehensive survey of this period can be found in G. Kennedy's *The Art of Rhetoric in the Roman World* (Princeton, 1972). Also very useful for the study of this period are H. Marrou, *A History of Education in*

Antiquity (New York, 1956) and F. Walbank, *The Hellenistic World* (Cambridge, MA, 1982). See also A. Leeman, *Orationis Ratio: The Stylistic Theories and Practice of the Roman Orators, Historians, and Philosophers* (Amsterdam, 1963), which is particularly useful to students who have no Latin, since Leeman translates the Latin texts he discusses into English.

A good idea of the nature of the progymnasmata can be gotten from the translation of the treatise of Aphthonius' *Progymnasmata* by R. Nadeau, *SM* 19 (1952), pp. 264–85. On stasis, see Nadeau's "Classical Systems of Stases in Greek: Hermagoras to Hermogenes," *GRBS* 1 (1959), pp. 28–52. On Theophrastus, see D. Innes, "Theophrastus and the Theory of Style," in *Theophrastus of Erisos* (ed. W. Fortenbaugh) (New Brunswick, NJ, 1985), pp. 251–267. For Demetrius, see G. Grube, *A Greek Critic: Demetrius on Style, Phoenix* suppl., vol. 4 (Toronto, 1961). On declamation, with specific attention to the *Suasoriae* and *Controversiae* of Seneca the Elder, see J. Fairweather, *Seneca the Elder* (Cambridge, 1981). These are now available in the Loeb series (ed. M. Winterbottom, 1974).

There is a useful bibliography on Cicero's rhetorical works appended to A. Douglas' "The Intellectual Background of Cicero's *Rhetorica*," in *ANRW* III:1 (Berlin/New York, 1973), pp. 95–138. For a good brief biography of Cicero, see W. Lacey, *Cicero and the End of the Roman Republic* (London/ Sydney, 1978). R. McKeon's "Introduction to the Philosophy of Cicero," in H. Poteat's translations of Cicero's *Brutus, On the Nature of the Gods, On Divination,* and *On Duties* (Chicago, 1950) remains one of the best treatments of that subject. On the influence of Isocrates on Cicero, see S. Smethurst, "Cicero and Isocrates," *TAPA* 84 (1953), pp. 262–320. All of Cicero's rhetorical works can be obtained in Loeb Classical Library editions with facing translations.

A good survey of the literary production after Cicero's generation can be found in *Empire and Aftermath*, ed. T. Dorey (London, 1975). On Quintilian, see G. Kennedy, *Quintilian* (New York, 1969). The *Institutes* is also available in the Loeb series (ed. H. Butler), as are the *Dialogue* of Tacitus (ed. W. Peterson) and Pliny's *Panegyric* (ed. B. Radice). On Latin panegyric under the empire, see S. MacCormack's admirable essay in *Empire and Aftermath*, pp. 143–205.

The literature on the Greek teachers and sophists in Rome is rather extensive. A paraphrase of Philodemus' *On Rhetoric* by H. Hubbell can be found in *Transactions of the Connecticut Academy of Arts and Sciences* 23 (1920). An improved text has recently been published by F. Longo Auricchio in *Ricerche sui Papiri Ercolanesi* 3 (Naples, 1977) with an Italian translation. R. Gaines' "Philodemus on the Three Activities of Rhetorical Invention," *Rhetorica* 3 (1985), pp. 155–164 offers an interesting interpretation of Philodemus. In addition to the references on Greeks in Rome in Kennedy (*The Art of Rhetoric in the Roman World,* cited above), see also A. Podlecki, "The Peripatetics as Literary Critics," *Phoenix* 23 (1969), pp. 114–37; D. Russell, "Rhetoric and Criticism," *Greece and Rome* 14 (1967, pp. 130–44; D. Schenkeveld, "Theories of Evaluation in the Rhetorical Treatises of Diony-

sius of Halicarnassus," *Museum Philologicum Londoniense* 1 (1975), pp.
93–107; D. Russell, "Longinus Revisited," *Mnemosyne* 34 (1981), pp. 72–
84. The "critical essays" of Dionysius of Halicarnassus are available in a Loeb
edition by S. Usher (vol. 1, 1974; vol. 2, 1985).

NOTES

1. On Alexander the Great and his hellenizing mission, see Walbank (cited in
   Further Reading) and R. Fox, *The Search for Alexander* (Boston, 1980).
2. On the *enkyklios paideia*, see the article "Enkyklios Paideia" by H. Fuchs,
   Reallexicon für Antike und Christentum 5.365–398, with bibliography; Marrou
   (see Further Reading), pp. 142–204.
3. The best treatment of the ancient grammar curriculum is still W. Rutherford's in
   Scholia Aristophanica. III: A Chapter in the History of Annotation (London,
   1905). See also M. Clarke, *Higher Education in the Ancient World* (Albuquerque,
   1971), pp. 11–28. For Theophrastus, see Innes (cited in Further Reading). The
   dates for Demetrius have been the subject of continuing debate. Grube's arguments (see *A Greek Critic*, cited in Further Reading, pp. 39ff.) for an early
   date—c. 275 BC—are hard to refute. The most thorough examination of *On
   Expression* is D. Schenkeveld's *Studies in Demetrius' "On Style"* (Amsterdam,
   1964).
4. The list of parts in the *Rhetorica ad Herennium* 1.4 is clearly in line with
   Hellenistic school teaching. For full documentation of the treatment of the parts
   of a speech in the handbooks, see J. Martin, *Antike Rhetorik, Handbuch der
   Altertumswissenschaft* II:3 (Munich, 1974), pp. 52–166.
5. The *Rhetorica ad Alexandrum* was, for centuries, wrongly attributed to Aristotle,
   partly on the basis of the belief that Aristotle had served as Alexander's tutor.
   Although there are superficial resemblances to Aristotle's *Rhetoric*, the orientation of the *Ad Alexandrum* is quite different, reflecting a spirit, rather, of the
   Gorgianic rhetoric we saw in Chapter 1.
6. The early rhetorical exercise from el-Hibeh can be found in *The Hibeh Papyrus*,
   part I (ed. B. Grenfell and A. Hunt) (London, 1906), pp. 55–61. It is not very
   interesting except as an example of what was done in third-century BC schools.
7. On Hermagoras, see Kennedy, *The Art of Persuasion in Greece* (see Further
   Reading for chapter 1), pp. 303–326. On the *Ad Herennium*, see H. Caplan's
   excellent introduction to the Loeb edition (Cambridge, MA/London, 1954). See
   the outline appended to this chapter.
8. The following is based on the *Ad Herennium* (*H*) and Cicero's *De inventione* (*I*),
   references to which appear in parentheses.
9. Lacey's book, cited in Further Reading, puts Cicero's works into their biographical context.
10. *Vir bonus* can be translated "good man," but the English misses the connotations
    in Latin of these words. Thus *vir* is not simply "man," but something rather
    stronger—*hombre* or *Mensch*, for instance. It is, after all, the root of our *virile* and
    has similar connotations. As for *bonus*, we must not forget that "good" in this
    sense does not refer to some interior state of grace but to an exterior sort of virtue
    (again, from *vir*). Hence, "good man" might be understood to convey what we
    mean in English when we say, "What we need around here is a good man" or

"He's a good man for the job." The sexism of Classical Rome, unfortunately, is hard to get around.

11. Some idea of Cicero's anguish caused by contemporary political events can be gathered from his letters. See for instance, *To Atticus* 4.19.1 (written in November 54 BC): "Come and look at the empty husks of the real old Roman Republic... get the smell of a Dictatorship in your nostrils." See also, for instance, 2.1.18; 2.9.2; 2.21.1; 4.18.1. Cicero's letters to Atticus have been ably edited by D. Shackleton-Bailey: vol. 1 (Cambridge, 1965), vol. 2 (Cambridge, 1970).
12. M. Buckley's "Philosophic Method in Cicero," *Journal of the History of Philosophy* 8 (1970), pp. 143–154, is essential reading on this matter.
13. On Vespasian's reforms, see M. Woodside, "Vespasian's Patronage of Education and the Arts," *TAPA* 73 (1942), pp. 123–129. On the general background, consult the first chapter in Kennedy's *Quintilian* (Further Reading).
14. A brief outline of Quintilian's *Institutes* can be found at the end of this chapter.
15. Suetonius, *Vespasian* 8.1.
16. R. Syme, in *Tacitus* (2 vols.: Oxford, 1958) vol. 2 p. 673, suggests that the *Dialogue* can in fact be seen as a byproduct of Tacitus' *Histories*.
17. This reading of the *Panegyricus* owes much to the observations of B. Radice in "Pliny and the *Panegyricus*," *Greece and Rome* n.s. 15 (1968), pp. 166–171.
18. For Pliny's accounts of his reading of the speech, see *Ep.* 3.13.3.18. On *Panegyricus* as a prototype, see MacCormack (in Further Reading).
19. Echoes of Cicero are noted in the apparatus of Schuster's 1958 Teubner edition *passim*. The rhetorical influence of Cicero on Pliny is discussed in detail by G. Picone, *L'eloquenza di Plinio* (Palermo, 1978).
20. On the influence of Cicero and Pliny on later panegyrists, see MacCormack and R. Klotz in *Rheinisches Museum* 66 (1911), pp. 531ff.
21. Suetonius *De rhetoribus* 1.1.
22. In addition to the works cited in Further Reading, see P. and E. DeLacey, *Philodemus: On Methods of Inference* (Philadelphia, 1941), pp. 127ff.
23. The text of *On Composition* can be found in volume 2 of Usher's Loeb edition of Dionysius' "Critical Essays," pages 14–242.
24. I have used D. Russell's 1965 Oxford edition of Longinus, which contains a useful introduction and notes. The fragments of Caecilius were collected in an ambitious, but not very reliable, Teubner volume, ed. C. Ofenlach (Leipzig, 1907).
25. On the lionized "Sophists" of the later empire, see G. Bowersock, *Greek Sophists in the Roman Empire* (Oxford, 1969).

[CICERO], *RHETORICA AD HERENNIUM*

(Section numbers follow the Caplan edition; page numbers correspond to the edition of F. Marx, Leipzig, 1894.)

CICERO, DE INVENTIONE

(Section numbers are from Strobel's 1915 Teubner text.)

1. Forensic speeches (*genus iudicale*)
   a. Cases involving general reasoning
      i. Issue of fact (14–51)
      ii. Issue of definition (52–56)
      iii. Issue of competence (57–61)
      iv. Issue of quality (62–115)
   b. Cases involving interpretation of a document
      i. Ambiguity (116–120)
      ii. Letter and intent (121–143)
      iii. Conflict of laws (144–147)
      iv. Reasoning by analogy (148–153)
      v. Definition (153–154)
   2. Political speeches (*genus deliberativum*) (155–176)
   3. Epideictic speeches (*genus demonstrativum*) (176–177)
   C. Conclusion (178)

QUINTILIAN, *DE INSTITUTIONE ORATORIA*

(Page numbers are from Winterbottom edition [OCT], Oxford, 1970.)

Preface: The object of the book and its parts (pp. 3–7)
Book 1. The early education of the orator
     ch. 1– 3. General considerations on pedagogy (7–22)
          4– 9. Grammar curriculum (22–58)
          10–12. Other "encyclical" studies (58–73)
Book 2. Early education (contd.); the nature of rhetoric
     ch. 1–10. Elementary exercises (73–98)
          11–21. The nature of the art of rhetoric (98–128)
Book 3. Origins and divisions of the art; stasis theory
     ch. 1– 5. Branches and precepts of rhetoric (129–142)
          6. Stasis questions: their nature and number (142–160)
          7–11. Panegyric, deliberative, and judicial oratory (160–184)
Book 4. The parts of a speech
     [Proem] (185f.)
     ch.   1. The exordium (186–200)
              2. Narration (200–225)
          3– 5. *Excursus, propositio, partitio* (225–236)
Book 5. The *confirmatio*
     [Proem] (237f.)
     ch. 1– 7. Nonartistic "proofs" (238–249)
          8–12. Artistic proofs
          8– 9. General considerations (249–253)
             10. Nature of *argumentum* (253–279)
          11–12. Argument from example; order (279–293)
          13–14. Refutation; enthymemes (293–314)

CHAPTER 3

Late Classical and Medieval Greek Rhetorics

The entry on Hermogenes of Tarsus (155–225) found in the *Suda*, an encyclopedia of sorts composed in Constantinople in the tenth century, gives us a hint of the fascination of later generations with his life and career. Hermogenes was a child prodigy, the *Suda* informs us, who at the age of 15 so impressed the emperor Marcus Aurelius with his oratorical skills that he was showered with gifts and endowed with an imperial sinecure. At the age of 19 or 20, he wrote his *Technē*, consisting of a book on stasis and two on the forms of style. Tradition also ascribes to him a volume of *Progymnasmata*, a treatise on invention, and a work called *On the Method of Forcefulness* (*Deinotēs*). At the age of 24, he "took leave of his senses," as the *Suda* puts it, lost his intellectual powers, and "as an old man became like a child." On his death, an autopsy was performed and his heart was found to be much larger than usual "and covered with hair." This account, fanciful as it might seem, tells us something both about the stature of Hermogenes in the rhetorical tradition and about the sort of world in which he lived, that of the so-called Second Sophistic, to which we shall turn in due course.

Hermogenes' works dominated in a rhetorical tradition that lasted well into the sixteenth century. This tradition, the Greek rhetorical tradition in the East, is one that not many aside from specialists know much about.[1] Since it persisted for so long, however, and was responsible for the conservation of most of what we know and possess of Classical Greek literature, and since it so clearly shaped the cultural identity of the epoch ordinarily referred to as the *Byzantine Age*, the topic obviously needs to be included in any history of rhetoric.

The important status accorded to Hermogenes' works can perhaps be measured by the huge number of manuscripts that survive, only a fraction, of course, of the actual number of copies that circulated in the late Greek educational milieu. But the real importance of Hermogenes lies in the scope and theoretical elegance of his vision of rhetoric, of the interrelations between the discovery of "heads," as treated in his *On Staseis*; the resources for discovering things to say, dealt with in *On Invention*; and the kinds of style, their discursive features and psychological effects, as discussed in *On Qualities of Style*. That vision, rivaled in comprehensiveness only by that of Quintilian in the West, may justly be described as amounting to a watershed in rhetorical theory.

HERMOGENES' WORKS

The *Progymnasmata* attributed to Hermogenes (perhaps incorrectly) resembles many that were current in antiquity—that of Theon, for instance. Hermogenes' treatise is at once more compact and more exhaustive, however, and aims at a rather more expansive sort of eloquence than that in the comparable treatises by his predecessors. An example can be seen in his treatment of the exercise called the *chreia*. In addition to the standard definition, classification, and examples found in the other progymnasmata, Hermogenes prescribes a pattern for the *ergasia*, "working up," of the *chreia*. After the statement of the *chreia*, Hermogenes says, must come some words of praise for it (*enkomion*), a paraphrase (*paraphrasis*), a rationale (*aitia*), a statement "from the opposite" (*kata to enantion*), one from analogy (*ek parabolēs*), an example (*ek paradeigmatos*), a citation of some authority, and, finally, an exhortation (*paraklesis*). These modes of *ergasia*, one notices, would yield quite a long and complete speech, developed systematically using commonplaces (*kata to enantion, ek parabolēs*, for instance), which would be appropriate not only in a schoolroom but in a deliberative or, as later writers were to find, a homiletic setting.

On Staseis consists of an introduction, a section on how to determine whether a question is accessible to stasis treatment, and an extended account of the *diaireseis*, or divisions, of staseis ("points at issue") into "headings" (*kephalaia*). In many ways, Hermogenes' treatment resembles earlier ones such as that in the *Rhetorica ad Herennium*, and much of his technical vocabulary is consistent with that in earlier Greek accounts. But Hermogenes is able to achieve a level of theoretical elegance not to be found in earlier treatments, possibly because the matter of staseis, for Hermogenes, was not so closely tied to forensic considerations but conceived more broadly in the context of rhetorical declamations on assigned topics or questions.

Disputes arise, Hermogenes explains, either about persons or things (deeds). Questions are open to stasis treatment when there are disputed claims about them for which plausible arguments can be adduced when the decision in a given case is uncertain. Otherwise, the case does not involve stasis—it is *asystaton*. This is hardly novel, for it was always recognized that if the deed was admitted, for instance, no stasis of fact arose; the question then becomes one of definition, and so on, as we saw in Chapter 2. But Hermogenes adds to the traditional material an enumeration of eight types of cases that are *asystata*: for instance, cases in which the evidence on one side is overwhelming, cases that are utterly implausible, or that are purely arbitrary. He also fills out the traditional list of the three or four kinds of persons to seven and introduces a classification of deeds that is theoretically exhaustive: (1) deeds done by the accused; (2) deeds not done by the accused but by another party that ipso facto may result in the indictment of the accused; and (3) deeds done by both the accused and another party that are reciprocally indictable.

It is in his breakdown of stasis headings, however, that Hermogenes is usually held to have achieved unprecedented elegance, for there Hermogenes links the headings in an orderly progression of contrary predicates—clear/unclear, complete/incomplete, and others—in a way no earlier writer had done before. The actual headings, it should be stressed, are not much different from the ones in earlier treatises, but Hermogenes arranges them in a more logically coherent, and therefore more easily remembered, fashion. It must also be stressed that we should not make too much of the apparent diaeretic divisions of Hermogenes. While interesting and helpful to the student struggling to master his system, they are far from pervasive and do not control the structure or contents of the work as a whole. The treatment of the conjectural stasis, for instance, lists no fewer than 10 headings, including "the demand for proofs" (*elenchōn apaitesis*), "will and ability" (*boulesis kai dynamis*), "persuasive defense" (*pithanē apologia*), and one heading titled "from beginning to end" (*ap' archēs achri telous*), a sort of narrative in which the course of events is seen as a series of natural consequences. Hermogenes calls his treatment here a *diairesis*, but his divisions obviously have nothing to do with diaeretic division by contraries. Nor does division by contraries in any way structure his discussion of the 10 headings for the stasis of definition, the 15 headings of the stasis of quality, or those of the stasis called *metalepsis*, which comprise the bulk of the treatise. Hermogenes' use of such divisions seems to have been motivated by pedagogical concerns—not, as one commentator on his works (the neoplatonic Syrianus) suggested, by some philosophical agenda.

Hermogenes' *On Invention* consists of four books. The first two are brief, treating of prologues and narratives. Books Three and Four discuss the proof and its amplification at length. In this treatment of proof, we find a reconceptualization of argumentation that is quite different from that of Aristotle, for instance, one closer perhaps to the conception of argument in Cicero's *De inventione*, in which "arguments" are invented by determining the stasis and developing the appropriate "places." Hermogenes' treatment is, however, more complex and subtle than his predecessors'.

Hermogenes' notion of argument is, to begin with, far broader than that of Aristotle, and takes us well beyond the Aristotelian enthymeme. In Book Three of *On Invention*, Hermogenes discusses headings, their kinds and sources; *lyseis*, or solutions to logical difficulties; epicheiremes and the topics from which they are derived; and the method of *ergasia*, the working up of arguments. *Epicheireme* in Hermogenes does not refer to the five-part syllogism familiar to us from Cicero's *De inventione*. It means, rather, the contention or claim being advanced about the question at issue, drawing support from the standard topics about persons—what they have said, what they have done—and things. These epicheiremes are backed up in *ergasiai* worked up by developing *topoi*: comparisons, examples, arguments from the greater and the lesser, from equal or equivalent cases, from opposites, and other lines of argument. They may also be supported by enthymemes, which, in Hermogenes, does not mean "a syllogism with a suppressed premiss," and/or "epenthymemes," or other supporting statements. This notion of argument is closely related, on the one hand, to the procedures in *On Staseis* and, on the other, to the pattern guiding the *ergasia* of the *chreia* that Hermogenes lays out in the *Progymnasmata*.

Some idea of the shape of a Hermogenean argument may be gathered from an example he provides, which I here abbreviate severely:[2]

CLAIM PUT FORTH (LYSIS): Contrary to what my opponent has said, it will not be difficult to dig through the Chersonese,

(ARGUMENT): for we shall dig earth and digging is child's play [epicheireme, from kinds of persons and deeds]; after all, the king of Persia dug through Athos when he had to, and if he could do that, certainly we can [*ergasia*, from comparison, perhaps from an *a fortiori* argument]; and in any event, he had to dig through a mountain, while we only have to dig earth [enthymeme, pointing up a crucial contrast], and he had to use recalcitrant slaves, while we shall employ free men [epenthymeme, from contraries].

In schematic form, then, a Hermogenean argument consists of the following elements:

1. The principal "point" (stasis issue)
2. Development by *topoi* concerning persons and things (the so-called *peristaseis*)
3. Development by "logical" *topoi* (e.g., contraries)
4. Enthymemes and epenthymemes drawn from *peristaseis*

Any "principal point," moreover, can be developed along six separate lines of argument; and each line of argument can, in turn, be developed along a half-dozen subsidiary lines. Fully analyzed, in fact, any position may be supported by a total of two hundred or so arguments, Hermogenes claims (145.18f., 149.4ff., Rabe). And a competent orator will have command of the entire abundant repertoire of arguments available from the various combinations of *topoi* and *peristaseis*.

This is clearly a long way from the sort of syllogism-based notion of argument familiar from, say, Aristotle's *Rhetoric*. But it is coherent, and it is closer to what orators actually do in advancing a claim than the syllogism model. Moreover, much of the plausibility of this sort of argument will stem not from the formal relationship of claim and premisses but from the vividness and plausibility of the comparisons and contrasts, the examples and assertions of *a fortiori* probability that are the concern of the *ergasia*. The argument's plausibility will also benefit from the way it is arranged, and the chief mode of arrangement, Hermogenes tells us, is "from beginning to end," one of the conjectural headings we saw in *On Staseis*.

More important perhaps than an argument's form is its expression—that is, the actual, discursive arguing. Hence it is necessary in invention to be concerned also with the devices of style and expression. This is the concern of Book Four, where Hermogenes discusses at length two general categories of style: (1) the political, which is compact, with an air of subtlety (*drimytēs*), and employs tight periodic composition; and (2) the panegyrical, which is expansive, using longer clauses and permitting even periods that cannot be enunciated in one breath. Related devices for presentation include the mode of dilemma, involving opposing rhetorical questions—this possesses *drimytēs* and has about it an air of truth; paronomasia, or "word play"; and deviations from normal usage (*tropē*).

Hermogenes' *On Invention* was very important in rhetorical curricula for centuries, and it is clearly the book one must consult if one hopes to understand what Byzantine orators were up to in the many speeches we have from them. The authenticity of *On Invention* has been questioned, as has that of the *Progymnasmata*; but in view of the close connections evident in it to *On Staseis*, it is hard to imagine that *On Invention* could have been composed by anyone who was not thoroughly imbued with Hermogenes' teachings. Another work ascribed to Hermogenes but almost certainly not written by him is *On the Method of Forcefulness*, which was, along with *On Invention*, universally attributed to him by rhetoricians of the Greek Middle Ages.

Hermogenes' most influential work is *On Qualities of Style*, or *On Ideas*. In this extended treatise, Hermogenes describes seven basic qualities that characterize ideal types of style: Clarity, Grandeur, Beauty, Vigor, Character, Sincerity, and Decorum.[3] These he breaks down in turn into subtypes, yielding, in all, 20 forms. Hermogenes considers each *idea* (a word used to mean a type of style as far back as Isocrates) as a combination of three basic elements: the thought (*ennoia*); the stance, or approach (*methodos*); and diction and composition (*lexis*), which covers the use of figures, the formation of clauses, word order, and prose rhythms. By combining these in different ways, rhetoricians can produce many different stylistic effects.

As is the case with Hermogenes' works on stasis and invention, it is unlikely that the theory of style laid out in *On Qualities of Style* was an entirely original one. The basic list of the kinds of styles can be traced back to Aristotle's student Theophrastus. Still, Hermogenes' system is considerably more refined than those of such predecessors as "Demetrius" or Dionysius of

Halicarnassus and came to exercise considerable influence on rhetoricians up to the fall of Constantinople in 1453, and beyond.

Some idea of the precision Hermogenes achieved in describing styles can be gathered from his discussion of stylistic Grandeur (*megethos*). Grandeur can be divided into six subtypes, which can in turn be grouped in three sets: Solemnity (*semnotēs*) and Brilliance (*lamprotēs*); Abundance (*peribolē*); and Asperity (*trachytēs*), Vehemence (*sphodrotēs*), and Florescence (*akmē*). The thoughts characteristic of *semnotēs* are about elevated topics such as divine things, glorious deeds, justice, and virtue. These thoughts must be expressed directly, without qualification (this refers to the stance, or *methodos*), using short clauses and more nouns than verbs. A sentence may also be given more dignity by the use of long vowels (long *o* sounds, in particular) and diphthongs. It is difficult to convey in English the stylistic features of Greek composition, but some idea of what Hermogenes saw as the "solemn" style may be gathered from this rendering of a passage from Demosthenes:[4]

> But it is impossible, it is impossible, men of Athens, that you acted wrongly when you decided to fight for the freedom and safety of all of Greece; no, I swear by your ancestors who fought at Marathon, by those who formed the ranks at Plataia, by those who fought at sea at Salamis and Artemesium, and by the many other brave souls who lie in the public cemetery, all of whom the city buried at public expense, thinking them worthy of that honor, all of them, Aeschines, and not only those who were victorious and successful.[5]

Brilliance is close to Solemnity, except that the thoughts are not as lofty and its clauses tend to be longer and more expansive. Abundance is like Solemnity and Brilliance in that it can make a thought vivid and impressive, but it seeks maximum emphasis by the use of long clauses and such figures of amplification as synonymity, enumeration, and polysyndeton.

Asperity, Vehemence, and Florescence are all used in accusations and reproach, and give a speaker's style an air of spontaneity and indignation— that is, they all share similar thoughts and "methods." The style of *trachytēs*, however, is short and choppy, using figures such as interrogation and hyperbole, looking for sounds that clash and grate:

> When, therefore, Athenians, will you do at last what must be done? What are you waiting for? Until, by Zeus, it is necessary. But now how should one consider what has happened? I think that for free men shame because of their position is the greatest compulsion. Or, tell me, do you want to run around asking one another "Is there any news?"..."Has Philip died?" "No, by Zeus, but he is ill." And what does it matter to you?[6]

Vehemence is like Asperity, but even more strongly expressed. By contrast, Florescence is used when an orator wants to attentuate his accusations. It shares the *ennoiai* of Vehemence, but adopts a different "method." Florescent style uses long clauses, not short ones, and such figures as anaphora and polysyndeton.

As can be seen, Hermogenes' typology is quite sophisticated. In fact, it can be used to describe any and all passages one might find in a given composition, as is clear from the many examples he gives from Demosthenes (the most frequently cited author), Lysias, and others. Its utility to subsequent generations is shown not only from the frequency with which it was recopied and from the persistence of Hermogenean critical vocabulary among Byzantine commentators and schoolmasters but also from the actual literary production of Byzantine writers and adaptations by Renaissance authors throughout Europe.

THE SECOND SOPHISTIC

With this brief look at the works of Hermogenes completed, we can turn now to the milieu in which they were produced, the so-called "Second Sophistic." This phrase was coined by Philostratus, author of *The Lives of the Sophists*, to characterize a literary-rhetorical movement, but it will serve just as well to mark off a period in the history of rhetoric that might be considered to begin with the fall of the Roman republic and to end some time in the sixth century. It is an age in which professional sophists—rhetoricians—practiced their art as teachers of rhetoric (sometimes occupying imperially endowed chairs of rhetoric), as itinerant performers invited by municipal governments to deliver orations on the occasion of public celebrations. Some of them served as diplomats and negotiators and as social attractions in the salons of various members of the Roman nobility, including the emperor himself. During this age, also, were composed all of the texts (including those of Hermogenes) that would be authoritative in rhetorical theory and practice for over a thousand years; attempts were made to reconcile the competing claims of philosophy and rhetoric; and the stage was set for the assimilation of "pagan" rhetorics into the culture and activities of early Christianity.

The importance of the Second Sophistic, whether as a literary movement or as a historical period, has been widely underestimated and misrepresented in standard treatments of the history of rhetoric. In the entry "Sophistic" in *The Oxford Classical Dictionary*, a standard reference, we read that rhetoric in this period "was tending to become a purely literary exercise practiced for its own sake. It was, however, a very popular pursuit, and successful practitioners in it enjoyed a high reputation." For many Classical scholars, the term *Second Sophistic* is synonymous with a decline in literary standards, of wild extravagances of style accompanied by a corresponding decline in the social and political spheres. Such characterizations persist, despite the fact that in recent years other students of the period have begun to question them.

Rhetoric, it is true, seems to retreat from courtrooms and assemblies into a scholastic setting, as it had in Hellenistic times. This should not, however, be taken to suggest that rhetoric was no longer considered relevant in the "real" world. If that were the case, one might ask with good reason why Vespasian, for instance, was motivated to fund an imperial chair—the term is not an anachronism, since the *thronos* or *cathedra* was the symbol of the professor's office—which Quintilian occupied. Why should Hadrian and Marcus Aurelius endow imperial chairs in provincial cities, at Antioch, Gaza, Alexandria, Ephesus, and elsewhere? Why would the empire establish salaried imperial chairs at Athens and Constantinople? Large sums of money were allocated from the imperial budget over four centuries not because rhetoric was irrelevant but rather because it was important training for the administrators of imperial policies in an empire of vast proportions.

A good part of the necessity for supporting an educational system can, in fact, be explained by the need for literate and articulate bureaucrats. For them, the rhetorical studies prescribed by the traditional *enkyklios paideia*, or "rounded education," would be sufficient. But rhetorical education was not limited to the elementary curriculum. "Sophistry" was a profession, not just a literary indulgence, that enabled a successful student to enter public life in one of the many municipal assemblies that were active in the provinces—at Antioch, for instance—or to take on the duties of the office of *defensor*, whose job it was to act as a civil advocate. Unfortunately, the activities of such practitioners in the art of rhetoric were not thought worthy of preservation (although some records do exist in papyrological collections). Hence the illusion that the practice of rhetoric in this age all but disappeared, with the exception of imperial panegyrics and showcase orations by commissioned professionals like Dio of Prusa (c. 40–115) or Aelius Aristides (c. 117–181). The notion that rhetoric declined in the Second Sophistic is largely based on an argument from silence, which does not prove anything, much less establish a social reality.

What manuscript evidence we have is limited to school texts and a large number of (mostly epideictic) speeches, many of which are polished versions of actual public orations. In addition to the treatises of Hermogenes, there are three school texts from this period that were particularly influential. *On Epideictic and Its Divisions*, by Menander of Laodicea (Menander Rhetor) was composed in the third century.[7] This work (actually two separate treatises) contains detailed instructions as to the proper subjects, forms, and commonplaces for a variety of epideictic speeches: speeches in honor of a city, imperial praise (*basilikoi logoi*), birthday speeches (*genathlaikoi logoi*), and wedding speeches (*epithalamia*), among others—about 20 types in all. Menander's work is better understood as a handbook detailing conventions that had already been established by his time and with which any aspiring rhetor would need to become familiar. The second text, the *Progymnasmata* of Aphthonius (fl. c. 400), a student of Libanius, defines, in all, 14 exercises, more than Hermogenes' work.[8] This book became a standard one in Byzantine schools, mainly (as later commentators tell us) because of its clear exposition and inclusion of sample versions for each exercise. The third text is called *Types of Letters* (*Epistolimaioi characteres*), dating to the late fourth or early fifth century and attributed by some to Libanius.[9] Forty-one types of letters are defined in it, along with advice on the standards of decorum for each. Here again, what should be stressed is that the prescriptions contained in this treatise define social as well as literary conventions, much in the way the arts of letter writing (*artes dictaminis*) composed centuries later in the West did.

These school texts must be viewed in an educational setting designed to prepare students for public life, not simply to refine received traditions. As dry as they are, they frequently offer intriguing insights into the standards and mores of their times. In the case of Menander's *On Epideictic*, in particular, we see reflections of the ways in which orators actually handled their themes. We know this because of the existence of the second body of evidence referred to earlier, the corpus of speeches from the Second Sophistic.

Perhaps the most conspicuous activity linked with the Second Sophistic was the display oration. Those speeches were delivered by professional sophists at public celebrations—triumphs, birthdays, funerals of emperors, rhetorical competitions sponsored by various municipalities—and were delivered in theaters, council chambers, even in specially constructed lecture halls (*akroateria*). Dio of Prusa, for instance, delivered his famous Speech to the Alexandrians (*Or.* 32) in the great theater of Alexandria. Polemon's speech at Hadrian's dedication of the temple of Olympian Zeus in Athens (Philostratus, *Lives* 1.533) was delivered before an enormous outdoor audience. Aristides' encomium of Rome was probably delivered (in AD 143) in the Atheneum, which sat upward of a thousand, that Hadrian had ordered built.

The number of extant orations composed by the great orators of this time is quite large, even larger if one includes compositions that are called *orations* but were never meant to be delivered. To give a detailed account of them is beyond the scope of the present chapter. But since this body of literature constitutes a large part of the evidence we have about the Second Sophistic, we shall have to say something about the functions of such oratory.

Generally speaking, the prime function of imperial oratory—that is, speeches given at imperial functions—is held to have been mainly one of conveying to the public the ideas and values of the rulers, thus performing many of the functions of a state-controlled press in a society without newspapers. By the same token, the prime function of much of the oratory of public celebration has been seen as mere entertainment, a sort of humane substitution for gladiatorial matches and bear baiting. While there is truth in both characterizations, one must be wary of their biases and limitations. The mention of a "state-controlled press," for instance, conjures images of contemporary totalitarian states; but one must not forget that societies have a radical need for regular reassertions of public values and ideals. Seen in that light, such a function of rhetoric seems not only legitimate but necessary. At the same time, another, perhaps more subtle side of such celebrations may be appreciated when one considers that what seems on the surface to be abject flattery may in fact be a reassertion of continuing standards of kingly or other virtue against which an emperor—or whoever is being praised—might be compared and measured. This is an aspect of epideictic that is often missed, but it seems to explain some of the speeches we have (such as Dio's panegyric to Trajan or, three hundred years later, Julian's encomium to the emperor Constantius) better than a reading that recognizes only the conventional praise. Another consideration in mitigation of the specter of totalitarianism is the fact that imperial orations are hardly equivalent to a state-controlled press inasmuch as they did not constitute any sort of medium for mass communication. The audiences of these speeches were confined to the elite insiders. Thus, while such speeches may certainly be seen to embody an ideology, they cannot be equated with propaganda.[10]

The public display speeches, on the other hand, might well be so considered, which makes them more than mere entertainment. Aristides, for instance, traveled widely to give speeches at great festivals throughout the Hellenic world. In so doing, he brought to widely disparate populations the image of a sort of cultural homogeneity, not exactly the Panhellenism of Isocrates, but certainly a common set of cultural themes and standards of taste and behavior cast in terms that are thoroughly Greek. "Propaganda" thus becomes an educational thing, an instrument of acculturation and cultural cohesion. That those cultural ideals may not have squared with social realities should not necessarily be seen as resulting in, or caused by, delusion and deception. If either were the case, one could not expect the ideologies to withstand for very long the pressures of material conditions—yet they did, and for a very long time. The "Hellenes" of late Antiquity saw the preservation of a common heritage as a matter of literal survival in the face of real and pressing threats from various *barbaroi*. And in large part, they saw accurately.

The socially integrative powers of rhetoric were perceived eventually by Christians as well. Very early Christianity was profoundly mistrustful of "pagan" rhetoric, partly because it was not Christian and partly because it was seen as unnecessary. Christ, after all, did not find it necessary to study rhetoric or to indulge in inflated bombast to bring his message to the world. But major leaders of the Church in the fourth and fifth centuries adopted features of that rhetoric on an unprecedented scale. The extant works of Gregory Nazianzus (330–390), for instance, include 45 orations, well over 200 letters, and a large corpus of poetry. The influence of "pagan" rhetoric is pervasive. His five "Theological Orations" comprise a set of highly developed forms of composition whose origins are clearly to be found in progymnasmata, particularly in the first of the orations, which is directed at the followers of the heretic Arius. His speeches are all for the most part homiletic, but can be classified roughly into three types—moral (deliberative), dogmatic (mainly apologetic, i.e., forensic), and panegyrical—as indeed Gregory himself had classified the orations of the Latin Father Cyprian in an encomium addressed to him (*PG* 35.1185f.). The picture drawn in the *Apologeticus* of the ideal Christian preacher is, as well, quite close to that of the ideal orator of Isocrates. So, too, with the dozens of speeches of John Chrysostom (349–407), even those on biblical subjects. In spite of his often-professed disdain for the "superfluous embellishments" of pagan writers (*Or.* 4.1), Chrysostom's preaching makes abundant use of tropes and figures, indeed of all the devices of the Hermogenean "ideas" of Grandeur and Beauty. Clear evidence of progymnasmatic training appears in the *ekphrasis* (extended description) on Antioch, for instance (*Or.* 2.5–6), that on the works of creation (9.6), and in Chrysostom's use of *synkrisis* (comparison) in many of his most famous encomia. More important than his stylistic qualities, however, is the sense we get from the orations of his concept of what a preacher's rhetoric ought to accomplish. Above all, it should result in salvation—naturally. But Chrysostom's rhetoric was effective not only in the Church but also in the city of Antioch, as its evident from his 21 sermons *On the Statutes* (AD 387) in which he sought to console and encourage unity among the citizens of that city in the face of oppression by local magistrates.

The real strength of the Greek rhetorical tradition becomes evident in its success in obtaining as firm a footing in the preaching of the Church as it did. This is often seen as a paradox, but the reasons for the Fathers' attraction to and assimilation of that tradition are really not hard to find. Virtually all the early Fathers were converts who had studied and, in many cases, taught rhetoric. Chrysostom, for instance, along with Theodore of Mopsuestia, was a student of the great pagan rhetorician Libanius. In fact, Chrysostom was so highly thought of by his master (it is reported by the historian "Sozomen") that Libanius thought he should succeed him in his chair of rhetoric, "if only the Christians had not stolen him." Many of the Fathers had been at first disdainful of Christian Scripture as boorish and barbaric on stylistic grounds alone. Later, these same Fathers faced the task of transmitting the message of Scripture not only to the common people but to the educated ruling classes as well. Their training in rhetoric gave them, it is true, the tools to praise their friends, attack their enemies, and enhance their written correspondence; but it also provided a way of rehabilitating the eloquence of Scripture and of achieving an authoritative platform from which to spread the Word, even in elite circles. Hence, although they display a consistent aversion to the "pagan" mythologies and the spiritual dangers of the non-Christian milieu, the most famous of the Fathers cultivated rhetoric to a degree that extends far beyond the mere appropriation of stylistic devices.

BYZANTINE RHETORIC

The end of the Second Sophistic coincides roughly with the rise in importance of the now Christian Roman Empire in the East and the decline of the Western Roman Empire in the fifth and sixth centuries, and hence with the beginnings of the Byzantine Empire, which was to last through many cycles of growth and decline until the fall of Constantinople. The term *Byzantine* is a fairly recent one, first used by Europeans in the sixteenth century. What we call the Byzantine Empire was called by its inhabitants the *basileia tōn Rhomaiōn*, literally, "the Roman Empire." And, to be sure, their political heritage was Roman, whereas their cultural heritage was unequivocally Greek. *Byzantine* is, however, the conventional term, so we shall use it here.

Historians of rhetorical theory consider Byzantine rhetoric to be of little interest since no new theories were developed in that setting—which is true, but unimportant. If we can name no major Byzantine theorist, we can point to a rhetorical production of staggering proportions, which is not surprising since we are dealing with so long a period. Byzantine rhetoric is, however, frequently dismissed as at once dry and inflated, imitative and mummified, and in general a great bore.[11] Fortunately, there is an increasingly strong current of scholarly opinion to the contrary, mainly the result of the reediting, or in some cases the publication of first (modern) editions, of the texts that comprise the rhetorical legacy of Byzantium.

So complex is the field of Byzantine rhetoric that we can hope here only to render a crude sketch of its main outlines. In what follows, the history of rhetoric in Byzantium will be divided into four periods: (1) the so-called Dark Ages, from the sixth to the ninth centuries; (2) the period after the controversy over Iconoclasm, the ninth and tenth centuries; (3) the period from the end of the tenth century to the sack of Constantinople, in 1204, which includes the Comnenan Age; and (4) the Paleologan Age, from the mid-thirteenth century to the capture of Constantinople by the Turks in 1453.[12]

The Dark Ages

The earliest period saw the codification of the Hermogenean corpus and of the works of Aphthonius and Menander in a commentary tradition that continued more or less unbroken for close to eight hundred years. These commentaries (of Sopater, Syrianus, and others) are important to us because they are the means by which the tradition was preserved and because they provide a glimpse of the intellectual currents of a period otherwise documented chiefly in various *Lives* of saints. They were important to those who used them because there was little in the way of an educational system wherein the tradition could be passed on *viva voce* from teacher to pupil, as most instruction was conducted privately—and very sporadically. The commentaries frequently reveal attempts to reconcile the art of rhetoric with philosophical concerns, mainly by scholars influenced by neo-Platonism, such as Syrianus. It is difficult to tell whether such traces of neo-Platonism as there are in the earlier commentaries are indicative of a systematic concern with the reconciliation of wisdom and eloquence, of an attempt to regain intellectual esteem for the commentators (which was certainly the case later with Michael Psellus, in the eleventh century), or merely a convenient vehicle for introducing into an otherwise tangled array of teachings the kind of coherence demanded by pedagogical concerns.

Rhetoric was taught as part of the traditional *enkyklios paideia*, which had persisted largely because the empire had a continuing need to train literate persons who could run its bureaucracies. In order to keep records, collect taxes, and draft and disseminate reports and decrees, Byzantine governments, both in the capital and in the provinces, required widespread literacy. And there is evidence that literacy in Byzantium, even in the so-called Dark Ages, was not restricted to an "elite mandarin caste" (a phrase one writer has characterized as suggestive of a meal of mixed French, Chinese, and Indian cuisines). Of course, what might be termed "high literacy"—which meant, basically, mastery of Attic Greek—was pretty much restricted to those who held high office.

The needs of the bureaucracy explain why Aphthonius' *Progymnasmata* and the works of Hermogenes were so important, for they were at the core of the rhetorical part of the *enkyklios paideia*. The needs of the bureaucracy also explain why the *Epistolimaioi characteres*, with its 41 distinct types of letters, enjoyed the popularity it did. The clear influence of Menander Rhetor and Hermogenes is evident in the few speeches we have from this period, that of Theodore Synkellos, for instance, which celebrated the retreat of the "Persians" (Turks) from the countryside around Constantinople in 627. Similarly, the speeches of Theodore Studites, from early in the ninth century, are composed according to the rules of Menander, traces of whose teaching are obvious as well in the many *Lives* of saints composed during the Dark Ages.

Considering the difficulties experienced by Byzantium as a result of constant invasions, and the loss of manuscripts that resulted from the invaders' depredations and hostility within the Church to "pagan" influences during the Age of Iconoclasm, it is surprising that the Greek rhetorical tradition was not lost altogether. But it survived, partly because of administrative necessities, to be sure, but also because of the continuing admiration for and emulation of such Fathers as Nazianzus and Chrysostom. The hostility to profane writings, in some ways, was only an aggravated instance of the ambivalence toward them that Christians had always exhibited.

After Iconoclasm

The failure of the Iconoclasts to maintain control over the Eastern Church and the defeat of the Arabs in 868 provided the occasion for the reestablishment at the heart of imperial institutions of the Greek cultural heritage. A systematic program for searching out and recopying manuscripts of Classical authors and of rhetorical classics was carried out during the reigns of Basil I and his successor, Leo VI (Leo the Wise), in the late ninth century. Its success can be measured by the large number of manuscripts that have survived from the tenth century, including, for instance, the very important *Parisinus graecus* 1741, which contains works by Dionysius of Halicarnassus, Menander's treatise on epideictic, Alexander Numenius on figures, and others; and *Parisinus graecus* 1983, which contains the complete works of Hermogenes, Syrianus' commentary, the *Progymnasmata* of Aphthonius, and other treatises used in the schools.

This period is one of considerable literary output, much of it in an encyclopedic vein: new commentaries (both on Scripture and on the standard rhetoric texts); chronicles; compendia of medical, astronomical, geographical, and ethnological lore; and, perhaps most notable, the *Bibliotheca* of the enormously erudite Photius. There are dozens of polemical works of a theological nature extant from this period; poetry, both sacred and secular— that of John Kyriotes Geometres (fl. 975), for instance; and of course speeches. Most of these exhibit the strong influence of classical models and a sensitivity to stylistic decorum; all of them reveal a thorough familiarity with the lessons taught by the rhetoric masters.

Perhaps the most famous figure from this period was Photius, Patriarch at Constantinople twice late in the ninth century, a strong opponent of Iconoclasm, and the greatest scholar of his time. The works of Photius that have a bearing on rhetoric for this period are his *Lexicon*, the encyclopaedic *Bibliotheca* (sometimes found with the title *Myriobiblos*, "Of Ten Thousand Books"), and a corpus of 18 sermons. The *Lexicon* is, essentially, a dictionary of Attic Greek, the dialect of high literacy and of the grand style in rhetoric. His *Bibliotheca* is a collection of almost 300 entries of varying length containing descriptions and criticism of the books he had read. The terminology of his criticism is borrowed in the main from Hermogenes' *On Qualities of Style*, as is also the general principle that he applies in judging a work of literature: that the ideal is attained through the proper mixture of the seven "ideas" of style. Photius' sermons also exhibit strong Hermogenean influence.

Another important figure from this period is John Kyriotes Geometres, who taught in Constantinople in the second half of the tenth century and composed commentaries on Aphthonius and Hermogenes. Geometres' commentaries are not extant as such, but are known from several extracts incorporated into later commentaries (that of John Doxapatres in the eleventh century, for instance). If his work is not exactly original, it is certainly not slavishly conformist either. In his commentary on Aphthonius, Geometres has some harsh things to say about John of Sardis (fl. 800 or so) for his failure to understand a phrase in Thucydides; and Doxapatres quotes him in his *Lessons on Aphthonius* as having observed that "not every instance of stylistic obscurity (*asapheia*) is a vice (*kakia*); rather, it may even be a virtue"—a notion that seems quite contrary to the tradition (including Hermogenes)[13] that held clarity of style in the highest regard, but that also seems to have been an unacknowledged conviction of Byzantine writers all the same.

Eleventh and Twelfth Centuries

This period is the high point in the history of Byzantine rhetoric—or, if it is not, it is the period for which we have the richest and most varied body of material to examine. We know more about the settings in which rhetoric was taught during this time than we do for any other, and the evidence suggests that during this period the imperial government—indeed, the various emperors themselves—put a high premium on rhetorical education. This period also produced some creative commentary activity, as is evident in the extensive commentaries of Doxapatres, in various *opuscula* of Michael Psellus, in the commissions granted by Anna Comnena (daughter of Alexios I Comnenus, 1081–1118) for commentaries—the first—on Aristotle's *Rhetoric*, and in efforts to bring traditional materials into contemporary perspective, as in the *Progymnasmata* of Nikephoros Basilakes (fl. 1145) and in the commentary of Gregory Pardos (Gregory of Corinth) on the pseudo-Hermogenean *On the Method of Deinotēs*.

This last, composed in the first quarter of the twelfth century, is interesting as an example of Byzantine attempts to consolidate various strands of received rhetorical lore, as represented by Hermogenes, Demetrius, Dionysius of Halicarnassus, and Apsines—all of whom were widely read during this time. Gregory spends considerable time explicating, for instance, the notion of *Perittotēs* ("superfluity") that is so important in the *Method*. Part of his explication consists of borrowings from Demetrius' *On Style* and Apsines designed to make it clear that "Hermogenes" often uses unfamiliar terms for figures and tropes discussed in other sources. Gregory also tries to indicate more fully than "Hermogenes" which figures and tropes will take precedence in a rhetor's attempt to achieve certain effects. In the case of *semnotēs* ("Solemnity"), for instance, hyperbaton is not only appropriately charming (*kalon*), it is absolutely necessary (7:2, 1244 Walz). So, too, a rhetor who seeks stylistic *megethos* ("Grandeur") will use figures involving *perittotēs*: repetition, *anaphora*, amplification by parts, etc. Gregory's examples are generally taken from Demosthenes and Homer, which is usual, but we also find citations of Genesis, the Gospel of John, and the Epistles of Paul.

Another area in which rhetoric seems to have attracted renewed interest is in commentaries on Scripture, particularly that of Euthymios Zigabenos on Psalms, a commentary that soon became the standard reference. Zigabenos' commentary is remarkable for the keen interest he shows in grammatical and rhetorical matters, most of them revolving around the question of how David's use of various stylistic devices (most frequently, as it happens, those involving *perittotēs*) to achieve rhetorical effects such as vividness, clarity, and emphasis.

But the richest source of all lies in the many dozens of speeches that survive, most of them epideictic in one way or another. These speeches not only show incontestably how thoroughly pervasive the lessons of Menander and Hermogenes had become, but may explain why, and to what end, the rulers of the period valued education in rhetoric as highly as they did.

Perhaps the most remarkable feature of these speeches—particularly the *basilikoi logoi*, or imperial praise—is their erudition, the striking extent to which all of their authors were able to construct long units of discourse filled with quotations from and allusions to the "Ancients" (*palaioi*), both Classical and biblical authors. The most frequently cited text is *Psalms*, as it happens, which is cited over and over in comparisons of the emperor with David the prophet and king; in virtual *centos* of psalmic passages that elevate the style of the description of a victory (for instance) to prophetic heights; and in explicit appropriations of thematic materal by the orators in order to express themselves in a way suitable to the ceremonies for which their orations were composed. There emerges from these speeches a "Davidic" eloquence that is unparalleled in the history of rhetoric.

As with the panegyrics of the Second Sophistic, it is clear that these speeches performed political and social functions by aiding in the construction of ideal models and defining values in such a way as to constitute a cultural identity for Byzantine society. So pervasive is the Davidic style in the speeches from the Comnenan era (c. 1080–1203) that it is tempting to conclude that the Comnenan emperors, in collaboration with the orators of the court—specifically, those who held the office of *maistōr tōn rhētorōn*, "master of the orators"—deliberately shaped their role as rulers on the model of David, who was of course both a forerunner and image of Christ himself. If that was the case, then rhetoric was as important for achieving domestic solidarity as the arts of war were for achieving supremacy over the hostile peoples against whom the emperor campaigned year after year.

As a final observation on rhetoric in this period, it should be noted that the low opinion of the rhetorical quality of these speeches held by the more conservative philologists is probably due to a combination of the genuine difficulty of construing the speeches and a failure to place them in their proper rhetorical context. The speeches must, above all, be read from the perspective of the Second Sophistic panegyric. They must, consequently, be read with a view toward Hermogenes, for it is Hermogenean rhetoric, not Aristotle's or Plato's or Demosthenes', that clarifies both their stylistic motivations and their method of argumentation. *Ergasia* is the proverbial name of the game.

The Paleologan Era

For over 50 years after the sack of Constantinople by Crusaders from the West in 1204, the Byzantine world was dominated by an unsympathetic Latin administration. In the nearby provinces to the south of the capital city, Byzantine scholars attempted to preserve the Greek heritage that they counted as their own. The eventual expulsion of the Latins and restoration of the capital to Byzantine authority witnessed yet another effort to recover and reinstate the Greek cultural heritage during the Paleologan era.

This is a period of far less brilliance than the one that preceded it. It is as if, while keeping the external trappings of Hellenism and Orthodoxy—and it is during this period that we find the most strident claims for both—Byzantine rulers and scholars alike let something slip away. Part of the reason for this may be that prolonged contact at close quarters with Western thinking produced an unplanned openness to it, which would explain, for instance, why it is that during this period various Latin works (including some by Thomas Aquinas) were translated into Greek. This had never happened before. Again, the ecclesiastical conflicts between Constantinople and Rome became more intense. One result was the Council of Florence, at which attempts were made to avoid, in vain, a final schism between the Catholic and Orthodox churches. In their diplomatic efforts, Byzantine intellectuals rediscovered the rhetorical importance of adapting one's arguments to one's audience. Hermogenean *ergasia* was forced to give way to Scholastic syllogistic; scholars felt required to look again at Aristotle, with the unhappy discovery that they could not understand him (Theodore Metochites complained that the *Metaphysics* was too obscure to be intelligible), try as they might.

The problems experienced by Byzantine intellectuals hardly put an end to the Greek tradition, however. The commentaries of Maximus Planudes on Hermogenes may seem insufferably dry, but Planudes was able to assimilate much new material, including some attributed (wrongly) to Aristotle, into the commentary tradition. The literary disputes between Nikephoras Choumnos and Theodore Metochites over the issue of stylistic obscurity resulted at least in the frank articulation by Metochites of rhetorical ideas that had in fact dominated rhetorical performance for a long time already. And the synopsis of rhetoric by George Gemistius Plethon achieved a synthesis of Hermogenean and Platonic notions to a degree no one since Syrianus had suspected was possible. Finally, at the end of this period, George of Trebizond composed a rhetoric mingling elements of Hermogenes, Aristotle, and Plato that was not only a synthesis of major importance from an intellectual point of view but also had a considerable impact on the West, as it was for Westerners a surprising, perhaps shocking, exposure to a rhetoric that was Greek and therefore new to them. The results of that encounter with Trebizond's work will become clear when we turn to the early Renaissance in the West.

SUMMARY

The Greek rhetorical tradition in the East spans almost fifteen hundred years. The dominant influence was exercised by the works, both genuine and spurious, of Hermogenes. In this tradition the notion of argument differs significantly from that of Aristotle, as the central element is not the syllogism but the procedure of topical *ergasia*, a sort of argument close to that in Cicero. Epideictic and Christian homiletic make up the greater part of what rhetoric survives from the Second Sophistic. That rhetoric should not be read as abject flattery or as a Platonic transmission of the Truth, but as an instrument of social cohesion in the tradition of Isocrates. Byzantine rhetoric follows the traditions established in the Second Sophistic. Its history can be divided into four periods: the so-called Dark Ages, which were not nearly as dark as some have imagined; the period immediately after the Iconoclastic controversy, of which Photius is probably the most outstanding figure; the very rich period covering the eleventh and twelfth centuries; and the Paleologan era, which takes us up to the fall of Constantinople in 1453.

FURTHER READING

The best survey of the material discussed in this chapter is G. Kennedy's *Greek Rhetoric under Christian Emperors* (Princeton, 1983), which contains much useful bibliography. There is to date no comprehensive study—in any language—on Hermogenes. His *On Staseis* was translated by R. Nadeau (*Speech Monographs* 31 [1964], pp. 361–424 (including an informative, although not completely accurate, introduction to Hermogenes' work). C. W. Wooten has done a valuable service with his translation, *Hermogenes' On Types of Style* (Chapel Hill, 1987) A new text of Menander Rhetor, with translation and commentary, was published recently by N. Wilson and D. A. Russell (Oxford, 1981). Nadeau published a translation of Aphthonius' *Progymnasmata* in *Speech Monographs* 19 (1952), pp. 264–285. A text and translation of the *Epistolimaioi characteres* can be found in A. J. Malherbe's "Ancient Epistolary Theorists," *Ohio Journal of Religious Studies* 5 (1977), pp. 3–77 (text on pp. 62–77).

Philostratus' *Lives of the Sophists* is available in a Loeb Classical Library edition, ed. W. C. Wright (Cambridge MA, 1952). Scholars have recently begun to look anew at the Second Sophistic. See Bowersock's *Greek Sophists in the Roman Empire* (cited in note 25 for Chapter 2) and E. L. Bowie, "The Importance of Sophists," *Yale Classical Studies* 27 (1983), pp. 29–59. Some orations of Libanius have been published in the Loeb series, ed. A. F. Norman, 1977. A good survey of the relations between Christianity and Classical culture can be found in I. Ševčenko's "A Shadow Outline of Virtue: The Classical Heritage of Greek Christianity," in *Age of Spirituality: A Symposium*, ed. K. Weitzman (New York, 1980), pp. 53–73. The introduction to R. Ruether's *Gregory of Nazianzus: Rhetor and Philosopher* (Oxford, 1969) is also good on this. Various homilies of Nazianzus and Chrysostom can be found in *A Select Library of Nicene and Post-Nicene Fathers of the Christian Church*, ed. P. Schaff and H. Wace (New York, 1890–1900; rpt. Grand Rapids, 1955). See also N. Wilson's *Basil the Great on the Value of Greek Literature* (London, 1975).

Detailed bibliography for the study of Byzantine rhetoric can be found in H. Hunger's monumental *Die hochsprachliche profane Literatur der Byzantiner* (Munich, 1978), vol. 1, pp. 65–196. G. Kustas' *Studies in Byzantine Rhetoric* (Thessalonike, 1973) and his "The Function and Evolution of Byzantine Rhetoric," *Viator* 1 (1970), pp. 53–73, are useful but far from comprehensive. See W. Treadgold, *The Byzantine Revival: 780–842* (Palo Alto, 1988) and P. Lemerle, *Le première humanisme byzantin* (Paris, 1971; trans. H. Lindsay and A. Moffatt, Canberra, 1986, as *Byzantine Humanism*). Both of these are important for background. Also important, but in need of updating, is J. M. Hussey's *Church and Learning in Byzantium* (London, 1937). The Greek texts of the Byzantine commentaries on Hermogenes and Aphthonius (among many others) can be found in C. Walz, *Rhetores graeci* (London/Tübingen, 1835–37; rpt. Osnabrück, 1968). A. number of imperial orations from the twelfth century were published by V. Regel and N.

Novosadskij in *Fontes rerum byzantinarum* (St. Petersburg, 1892–1917; rpt. Leipzig, 1982). There are no English translations of these works. Photius' sermons have been translated; see *The Homilies of Photius: Patriarch of Constantinople* (Cambridge, MA, 1958), which contains translations and commentary by C. Mango. On Byzantine masters of the orators, see R. Browning, "The Patriarchal Schools of Constantinople," *Byzantion* 32 (1962), pp. 167–202; 33 (1963), pp. 11–40. See also the more recent *Studies on Byzantine Literature of the Eleventh and Twelfth Centuries* (Cambridge, 1984) by the distinguished Byzantinist A. Kazhdan. On George of Trebizond, see J. Monfasani's *George of Trebizond: A Biography and a Study of His Rhetoric and Logic* (Leiden, 1976).

NOTES

1. Kennedy's *Greek Rhetoric under Christian Emperors* (in Further Reading) has made this less true today than it was before 1983.
2. See the explanation of the inventional process in L. Pernot in "Lieu et lieu commun dans la rhétorique antique," *Bulletin Association Guillaume Budé* 1986, pp. 267ff., which improves on Kennedy's in *Greek Rhetoric*, pp. 90f.
3. "Vigor," not "Rapidity," is the correct translation of the Greek *gorgotēs*; "Decorum" is more accurate than "Forcefulness" as a translation of the term *deinotēs* in Hermogenes. See Monfasani (in Further Reading) on this, pp. 286ff.
4. For much of the following discussion of style, I am indebted to C. Wooten, *Cicero's Philippics and Their Demosthenic Model* (Chapel Hill/London, 1983), pp. 23–42.
5. Demosthenes *On the Crown* 280.
6. Demosthenes *Philippics* 1.10.
7. See the introduction in Wilson and Russell (cited in Further Reading).
8. Text in Walz 1.55–120. See Nadeau's translation of Hermogenes cited in Further Reading.
9. See Malherbe's translation cited in Further Reading.
10. A. Kazhdan has some important observations on this in his "Certain Traits of Imperial Propaganda in the Byzantine Empire," in *Prédication et propagande au moyen âge* (Paris, 1983).
11. Maximilian Treu, an important nineteenth-century scholar, once characterized a Byzantine rhetorician as *adnumeratus . . . in sordido illo grege rhetorum byzantinorum quorum si noveris unum noveris omnes* ("one of that sordid herd of Byzantine orators of whom it may be said, 'If you know one, you know them all' "). This is still a common opinion of Byzantine orators in general. For an interesting account of how such a bias took hold among scholars, see B. Croke's "Mommsen and Byzantium," *Philologus* 129 (1985), pp. 274–285.
12. This division was proposed by G. Kustas in "The Function and Evolution of Byzantine Rhetoric" (listed in Further Reading).
13. Hermogenes ranked Clarity as the prime "idea" of style. He notes in passing (see p. 241 of Rabe's edition), however, that lack of Clarity may sometimes have a place in the style characterized by Grandeur.

CHAPTER 4

Rhetoric in the Latin Middle Ages

The history of rhetoric in the Latin West is, if anything, rather more complex than that in the Greek East. While Constantinople imposed a measure of cultural and political homogeneity on her subjects and fostered a fairly consistent tradition in rhetoric, the history of rhetoric in the West is marked by a succession of intellectual upheavals and conflicts no less striking than the cultural and political ones. The collapse of the Western Roman Empire in the fifth century AD, the inauguration and spread of the Holy Roman Empire after 800, the fragmentation and isolation that persisted despite the efforts of such rulers as Charlemagne to unify Europe—all of these in a sense had their counterparts in the intellectual production of the Latin Middle Ages. Consequently, it is far more difficult to capsulize or even to isolate distinct periods in the history of rhetoric from Augustine to the beginnings of the Renaissance.

In a superficial sort of way, it is of course possible to speak of three major periods. The first might be held to extend from the end of the fourth century to the beginning of the eleventh century and to have been dominated by the teaching of Augustine's *De doctrina christiana** and marked by a determination to preserve the matter, if not the functions, of Ciceronian rhetoric as represented by the *De Inventione* and the *Rhetorica ad Herennium*. The second period would cover the eleventh century and the first half of the twelfth. During this time, interests of a more speculative sort in the theoretical relations between rhetoric and dialectic become evident, owing in part to questions raised about the value of rhetoric in theological enterprises—the interpretation of Scripture, for instance—and in part to questions about the place of rhetoric in the education of the young. The long tradition of commentary on the works of Cicero begins to falter, and interest in the revision of Cicero's doctrine of topics by Boethius quickens at this time.

The last period runs from the second half of the twelfth century to the middle of the fourteenth. This period is marked by the widespread production, from Oxford in the West to Prague in the East, of treatises with a distinctly practical orientation, applied rhetorics designed to help students acquire specific skills in performing tasks defined by institutional needs and programs. Thus the proliferation of the arts of preaching, of prose and verse composition, and of letter writing.

Although it is clearly possible to proceed in this manner, the more one examines the available material, the less advisable it seems to do so. An alternative method for organizing the history of rhetoric might be to trace the conflicts and tensions among various traditions that were preserved by medieval scholars. Thus, for instance, both Ciceronian and Boethian strands persist and interact throughout the Middle Ages. On the one hand, Cassiodorus (sixth century), Alcuin and Hrabanus Maurus (ninth century), and Honorius of Autun (twelfth century) all agree in defining rhetoric as an *ars* that is part of "civil science," as Cicero had in his *De inventione*. On the other, Martianus Capella (fifth century) and his ninth-century commentators, including John the Scot, agree with Boethius in assimilating rhetoric to dialectic, as do Hugh of St. Victor and John of Salisbury in the twelfth century and Bonaventure in the thirteenth. Vigorous scholarly debates flare up in the eleventh century over the nature, scope, and status of rhetoric and become acrimonious in the twelfth, in part because of the development of distinctly theological methods of inquiry, which reach maturity in the scholasticism of the thirteenth century, and to the growing conviction that logical demonstration is to be preferred over both dialectical disputation or rhetorical argument. As with the attempt to construct an account around chronological periods, however, tracing strands of tradition becomes more and more difficult the closer one examines the arguments; the strands intertwine in unexpected ways; and the result is often too complicated to be intelligible.

Nevertheless, two inescapable points emerge from even the sketchiest of accounts. First, there is far more going on in the history of medieval rhetoric than was once thought. Indeed, since the 1960s, it has become a scholarly commonplace that it is no more possible to speak as though there were a "medieval rhetoric" than it is to speak of "Classical rhetoric" as though it were a unitary concept. Second, medieval rhetoric was far more than a mere transmission of mummified traditions that were poorly understood by those who transmitted them. The Middle Ages are often represented as stagnant and backward, well deserving of the contempt Renaissance scholars were to heap upon them. It is clear, however, that such a representation fails dismally to do justice to the intellectual complexity and sophistication of medieval rhetorics.[1]

Accordingly, in our account of rhetoric in the Latin Middle Ages we shall proceed in a roughly chronological order, but without attempting to delineate any strictly defined periods. Such a division into periods seems to work for the history of rhetoric in the East but is unsuited for the West. And rather than trying to trace the convoluted trajectories of various traditions across centuries of continually shifting and changing circumstances, we shall concentrate on particular authors and their works. Concerns and achievements peculiar to different circumstances, of course, will emerge from our discussions of those works, and so will the particularities of various positions taken by their authors. But it seems appropriate to let the material speak more or less for itself rather than to try to impose perfabricated designs, whether temporal or categorical, upon it.

RHETORIC IN AUGUSTINE

In 395, when he was yet a priest, Augustine wrote a letter to Alypius, bishop of Tagaste, in which he reported his recent pastoral activities. It seems that some members of Augustine's congregation reverted to their old pagan ways in the course of observing a Christian holy day, celebrating it by getting drunk. On being told of this, and noting that his sermon text for the day was providentially appropriate, he set about chastizing them. The text was from Matthew (7:6): "Give not what is holy to the dogs, nor cast your pearls before swine." Inspired by the appropriateness of the day's reading, he spoke on the subject of dogs and swine "in such a way as to make them blush for shame who were pigheadedly snarling and brawling against God's commandments and were abandoning themselves to foul pleasures." News of this sermon attracted a larger congregation the next day, when the reading was the episode from Matthew in which Jesus drives the moneylenders from the Temple (*Mt* 21:12f.). Augustine was able to adapt this text, too, to the subject of the drunkenness of the members of his flock. So vividly did Augustine set before them the gravity of their bad behavior that he moved this larger audience to tears. On the third day, news of his second sermon drew an even larger crowd to his church. When it came time for that day's sermon, Augustine put aside the one he had prepared and launched into another. This one so captivated his congregation that they stayed until nightfall, singing hymns. After this report, Augustine adds another piece of news to finish off his letter. The Circumcellions who had broken into the church some time before and smashed the altar, he tells the bishop, were currently being tried before a magistrate.[2]

In addition to giving an indication of how powerful a preacher Augustine was, and how able he was to speak *ex tempore*—he had, after all, spent some years teaching rhetoric—this letter provides a glimpse of the sort of society he had to deal with as a priest and, later, as a bishop. It was, to begin with, relatively new to Christianity and still very much given to beliefs and practices more typical of the pagans that surrounded it than of the official Christian way of life. Astrology and magic still played an important part in the lives of many Christians, and the exposure of infants to the elements as a method of population control, for instance, was not uncommon even among them. Above all, it was a society that had almost daily to endure bloody violence, at the hands both of marauding tribesmen who roamed the countryside and of some of their fellow Christians. The Circumcellions Augustine mentions were not pagans but members of the Donatist sect of Christianity in the region, a gang of thugs who had become notorious for their acts of vandalism and, indeed, mayhem. The Christian congregation typical of North Africa at the end of the fourth century was, in short, not an easy flock to care for.[3]

Knowing this, we can see that Augustine's rhetorical successes were perhaps even more impressive than they might have seemed at first. To be sure, he was a past master of the art, as we have noted. He was also himself a rather recent convert to Christianity; and in the process of his conversion, he had not only resigned from his position as a teacher of rhetoric, but he had rejected rhetoric itself. As he wrote in a letter he composed on another occasion, "these subjects are not in harmony with my current profession [of faith]" (*Ep.* 118.34). In this light, the successes he reports to Alypius are not just impressive but seem almost contradictory.

The contradiction here is, of course, the same one we saw in the case of the Greek Fathers who expressed mistrust and contempt for rhetoric while practicing it. On the one side, the sort of eloquence rhetoricians promoted was vain and misleading, virtually a near occasion of sin. On the other side, as all of them recognized as clearly as did Augustine, it was not only useful but sometimes necessary for assuring cohesion within Christian society. The tensions inherent in the notion of "Christian rhetoric," although they were alleviated somewhat by the example of the eloquence of Scripture, were never eliminated completely in Augustine's own mind. Not long after his letter to Alypius in which he boasted of his rhetorical success, he abandoned a treatise he had been writing that would provide the Christian preacher with instruction in rhetoric. That treatise he would eventually complete, about 30 years later, and call *De doctrina christiana.* In the meantime, in 397, he composed a set of instructions on how to instruct new converts, *De catechizandis rudibus,* which might be rendered *On Indoctrinating the Uncultivated.* *De catechizandis rudibus*[4] is worth a brief look since it exhibits Augustine's ambivalence toward rhetoric. The treatise, written in the form of a letter to the Carthaginian deacon Deogratias, is in two parts, the first (cc. 1–15) laying out some principles of catechetical indoctrination and the second (cc. 16–27) giving some examples of model instruction. Chapters 1–7 give general guidelines for the *narratio*, the story of Christianity, and the sort of exhortation a teacher should address to the aspiring convert. Chapters 8–15 are more specific. Augustine goes over the types of candidates for conversion, the dispositions one can expect of them and the causes of those dispositions, and the sort of character the instructor should convey. Chapters 16–25, the longest single section of *Rudibus*, is a model speech, a fervent declamation aimed at inspiring the would-be Christian to submit to baptism and the ways of the Church. What is interesting about these matters is that, although Augustine's attitude toward rhetoric is just short of contemptuous (see ch. 9), most of what he says about audience adaptation and the problems of "instructing" the "uncultivated" reads as though he had the *De oratore* of Cicero, if not at his elbow, at least in the back of his mind, although he scrupulously avoids any mention of Cicero or any other rhetorician. Moreover, the declamation, which is presumably a model of genuine eloquence, contains many of the devices one might expect Augustine to relegate to the realm of the false eloquence of the sophistic rhetoricians of his time.

This should perhaps not be very surprising. Augustine, born in 354 to a fairly wealthy family, underwent until he was 20 years old a rigorous training in rhetoric. Before his conversion, in 386, after a prolonged intellectual crisis that had him wavering between rival schools of thought, he was a teacher of rhetoric. His initial impression of Christianity, in fact, was that it was hardly worth pursuing, since the Christians he heard and read were so ill-spoken and lacking in the graces of eloquence. Eventually, of course, he was to become the bishop of Hippo and one of the foremost theologians and apologists the Church has ever known. In most of his writings, questions about the legitimacy of rhetoric are far less important than questions about free will or original sin. But in his early years as a Christian, he seems to have been deeply interested in reconciling his new profession of faith and his old profession of eloquence.

The first three books of *De doctrina christiana* were originally composed before 397. In 426, Augustine wrote the fourth book, completing the work. It is not unlikely that he also revised what he had written 30 years before. The fact that he dropped this project in favor of completing his catechetical treatise shows that, at the time, he was still uncertain as to how to present instruction in rhetoric to his fellow preachers, who had not had the benefit of his education. By 426, four years before his death, the resolution of this problem had evidently been achieved.

The treatise falls into two major parts. In the first, Augustine addresses the question of how to discover (the *modus inveniendi*) what is to be understood in Scripture; and in the second, the question of how to teach (the *modus proferendi*) what has been understood. Part One, Books 1–3, therefore, is about *inventio*, and Part Two, Book 4, about *elocutio*. Augustine's theory of invention is not concerned with the discovery of arguments or justifications, but with the discovery of meaning in Scripture. Only when these meanings have been grasped can one achieve the goals of teaching through adequate expression of them. Thus, *elocutio* is understood by Augustine in its broadest sense—roughly as what we might call *communication*.

Augustine's treatment of the ways in which Scripture can be understood begins with a discussion of words as the signs of things, a discussion that centers on the nature of things. Here he introduces the distinction between things as final ends that are to be loved or enjoyed (*frui*) and those that as intermediate ends are to be used (*uti*) for further ends. This classification produces a virtual hierarchy of being, with the triune God at the top. Book 2 deals with words as conventional signs, dividing them into known and unknown signs, on the one hand, and literal or figurative signs, on the other. This set of distinctions is elaborated by philological treatment of the nature of words in relation to Scripture and the arts and institutions of the pagans.

Book 3 deals with the problem of ambiguity and the means of removing it by identifying the manner of statement and the circumstances of fact.

Book 4 has been called the first manual of Christian eloquence. After a brief defense of rhetoric, which he defines as the art by which we acquire "through exercise and habit a most skillful use of words and an abundance of verbal devices (*ornamenta*)," Augustine demonstrates that eloquence is not alien to Christian discourse. This he shows from Scripture itself, exhorting his readers to attend to and imitate the eloquence of David and Paul. The next major section (4.27–33) lays out the duties (*officia*) of the orator—as in Cicero, to teach, delight, and move—as they apply to preaching the Word. Sections 33–58, the longest in the book, illustrate the Ciceronian *genera dicendi*—the high, middle, and low styles—with passages from Paul, Ambrose, and other Christian writers. The character of the preacher is the subject of sections 59–63. Here Augustine shows how character supplements the *officia* and is in turn the product of style and attention to decorum.

Since the three books devoted to *inventio* seem to argue that good rhetoric must be based on knowledge of the Truth in Scripture, Augustine's notion of the art has frequently been compared, if not equated, with the notion of rhetoric Plato set out in the *Phaedrus*. That comparison becomes more plausible when one reads in *De doctrina* (2.35) that dialectic supplies the means of stating truths once they have been discovered. Book 4, on the other hand, contains little if anything that cannot be found in the *De oratore* of Cicero, except the examples Augustine uses. As a whole, then, *De doctrina christiana* seems rather inconsistent, unless it is merely the superficial devices of Cicero that have been co-opted by Augustine and put to the service of a Platonic ideology. Certainly, Augustine cannot have intended to import a basically controversialist theory of rhetoric into the City of God, one might argue.

The Platonism of *De doctrina christiana* is probably as overstated, however, as the influence of Cicero on Augustine has been understated. It is true Book 4 is more obviously Ciceronian than the others. But Augustine's defense of rhetoric (at 2.54f. and 3.3) is not much different from Cicero's. What is more, the "platonizers" of Augustine fail to see that Augustine's dialectic is not Plato's, but Cicero's: a mode of rhetoric (see 2.48ff.). The methods for resolving ambiguities at 3.34ff., moreover, are precisely those laid out by Cicero at *De inventione* 2.116ff. And while it is clear that Augustine believes that the truth can be found in Scripture, his discussion of the principle of charity at 1.35ff. makes it equally clear that his "Truth" is a long way from Plato's.

The detection of gross inconsistency in *De doctrina christiana*, it can consequently be argued, is based on a partial, perhaps partisan, reading. Augustine's rhetoric is not simply the means by which the Truth can be conveyed to a congregation most effectively, but a rhetoric whose fundamental spirit is that of *caritas* ("charity") and whose ends, beyond teaching, delighting, and moving, are summed up in *communitas*. Augustine's view of rhetoric is, in the final analysis, the same as that of Chrysostom and

Nazianzus.) Such a view is not without its problems, for it always involves the sort of tensions we spoke about before. But it is noteworthy that late in his life, after decades of trading polemics with Pelagians and Donatists, and in the midst of barbarian invasions of North Africa, Augustine should take the trouble to complete a work he had begun 30 years before. If we remember the social conditions under which Augustine began to compose *De doctrina christiana*, however, and understand that those conditions hardly improved during Augustine's lifetime—indeed, they got far worse—then his motives for returning to that work and completing it are fairly clear.

De doctrina christiana was very important to later generations of Christian rhetoricians. The value they placed on it, obviously, had a great deal to do with Augustine's reputation as a philosopher and theologian. In those realms, his influence continued to be enormous. But in a sense, his treatise on Christian eloquence continued to be read and copied for as long as it did, even during the darkest of the Dark Ages, because it made any other such treatise unnecessary, if not impossible to supersede. Its existence, moreover, may in fact explain why Cicero continued to hold the position of importance he did in the Middle Ages. From the perspective of *De doctrina christiana*, the study of Cicero was at once justified by and a supplement to the ideal of Christian eloquence.

We shall look again at the influence of Augustine, when we discuss the rhetorics of the Carolingian renaissance in the ninth century and the rise of scholasticism in the thirteenth. We must turn now to another important figure in the history of medieval rhetoric, Boethius.

BOETHIUS

Anicius Manlius Severinus Boethius was born of an old Roman family (the Anicii) about 475 and was groomed for public life from infancy. He pursued encyclical and advanced studies under the great scholar Symmachus, from whom he acquired an unusually thorough knowledge of Greek for his time. Later in life, he determined to translate the works of Aristotle into Latin and compose commentaries on them. Boethius did complete a translation of Aristotle's *Organon* and of some of the commentary on it available to him. Instead of translating Aristotle's *Topics*, Boethius compiled a commentary on the *Topics* of Cicero, which he supplemented with a relatively brief, but very important, treatise titled *De differentiis topicis, On Topical Differences*. We will look at this work shortly.

Boethius accomplished all this, it should be noted, while pursuing an active public life. He became consul in 510 under the emperor Theodoric, and in 520 he became *magister officiorum*, the empire's chief administrator. While holding that office, Boethius fell out of favor, for obscure reasons, and was accused by political rivals of treason and dabbling in magic. He was subsequently tried, convicted, and sent to prison, awaiting execution. While in prison, he composed the work he is probably most famous for, *On the*

Consolation of Philosophy. After a long term in prison, he was finally executed in 524.[5]

De differentiis topicis, known in the Middle Ages as the *Topica Boetii*, is an important text in the history of rhetoric since it influenced for so long the perception of the resources and limitations of rhetoric as a method of inquiry and so profoundly affected the way Cicero was understood by medieval readers. We know of more than 170 manuscripts that were in circulation between the sixth and the thirteenth centuries—an enormous number, considering the small number of people at the time who could read. It was still mandated for study at the University of Paris in the thirteenth century, as we learn from the University statutes handed down in 1215. Indeed, it was still taught at Oxford as late as the fifteenth century.

The treatise is divided into four books. Boethius begins Book One by dividing logic, understood broadly as the *ratio disserendi*, or method of discourse, into two parts: analysis (or judgment) and discovery (invention). It is in invention that "topics" play their role as "seats of argument" (*sedes argumentorum*). He then distinguishes between arguments that are probable and arguments that are necessary, setting up a critical new distinction between two types of "topic": the "topical principle" (or "maxim," in some translations) and the "topical difference" (*maximae propositionis differentia*: see 1174D, 1185A). Boethius cites Aristotle, Cicero, and Themistius as his authorities; but as we shall see, he was up to something very different from what Cicero tried to achieve. In Books Two and Three, he outlines and attempts to explicate and synthesize the theories of Aristotle—in the *Topics*, not the *Rhetoric*—and Cicero (see 1200Bff.). Book Four treats of rhetorical topics and how they relate to dialectical topics. It is with this last book that we are chiefly concerned, but we need to see how he prepares the ground for his interpretation of rhetoric in Books Two and Three.

"Topical principles" are propositions that can be used to prove other propositions but do not themselves require proof, as they are self-evident and universal. They are, as it were, the kernel units of argumentation that give support to argumentative inferences (see 1185D). Boethius gives as examples of kernel units such "maxims" as "If the definitions of two things differ, then the things themselves differ" or "What inheres in the part also inheres in the whole" (1185D, 1188D).

Because the number of such principles is great, Boethius introduces the notion of topical differences, which provides him with a method of grouping and arranging principles in a manageable way. These differences define different relationships that can obtain between the terms of a proposition in question and the particular inference to be made. The analysis of these differences produces a three-way division of topics as intrinsic (definition, whole, part, causes), extrinsic (similarities, comparisons, proportionate relations, opposites), and intermediate (inflections, divisions) (see 1189Aff.). These dialectical topics, then, are abstract premises that express basic modes of syllogistic inference and the fundamental ways in which one can organize the kernel units, or principles.

Book Four begins with the observation that rhetoric and dialectic are both alike and different, the major difference being that rhetoric deals with *hypotheses* (Cicero's *causae*), questions "attended by many circumstances," such as person, place, time; and dialectic deals with *theses*, questions "without circumstances." They differ also in method, means, and end. Rhetoric's method is "continuous discourse"; dialectic's, question and answer. Rhetoric's means are enthymemes; dialectic's, syllogisms. While rhetoric seeks to persuade, dialectic seeks victory in disputation. At this point, Boethius tries to summarize the whole art of rhetoric—a hard thing to do, he says (1207D)—and presents a brief review of the *status* system familiar from Cicero (1209Bff.). Having established the kernel theory of inference in Book Two, the distinction between intrinsic and extrinsic topics in Book Three, and this basic positioning of rhetoric in relation to dialectic, he is ready to begin his analysis of rhetorical topics.

Boethius seems to follow Cicero's analysis of *loci* in the *De inventione* quite closely, but in fact he does something new and different as he discovers in Cicero's *loci* a pattern identical to that which describes the basic differences among dialectical *loci*. Rhetorical topics, too, are either intrinsic, extrinsic, or intermediate. The distinction between rhetorical and dialectical topics turns on their involvements with circumstances: rhetorical topics are circumscribed by particular circumstances; dialectical topics are not. Since dialectical topics are thus universal, they are prior in nature to rhetorical topics and encompass the forms of inference that are at the basis of arguments used in rhetoric. Any rhetorical arguments that cannot be resolved into a dialectical form of inference, for Boethius, would be little more than idle rambling. In other words, rhetorical topics derive their force from the abstract propositional rules provided by dialectic. Dialectic therefore governs the genus of argumentation, and rhetoric becomes a subordinate part of dialectic because it is a species of that genus.

As we noted, Boethius cites Aristotle and Cicero as his authorities. But if we recall that, for Aristotle, dialectic and rhetoric are parallel and coequal arts for dealing with different aspects of the same process and that, for Cicero, dialectic is subordinate to rhetoric, we begin to see that Boethius has effected a sort of revolution in *De differentiis topicis*. By making rhetoric into a species of dialectic, he makes rhetoric an appendage of dialectic and removes particular circumstances from the consideration of whether a given rhetorical argument is a good one or not. This repositioning of rhetoric in relation to dialectic in fact turns Cicero on his head in ways that were to have far-reaching consequences for rhetoric, extending down to the fifteenth century.

Augustinian and Boethian "Tensions"

Augustine and Boethius were dominant authorities throughout the Middle Ages, particularly in theology and philosophy, but also in rhetorical pursuits. Their influence, however, was by no means a unified one. Although Boethius was much affected by Augustine's spirituality and agreed with him on many doctrinal points, the two diverged somewhat when it came to the subject of rhetoric. These divergences between the Boethian and Augustinian programs were, in turn, the source of tensions that later emerged and multiplied over the nature and precedence of the arts of the trivium. A brief overview is in order here.[6]

In the system of Boethius, dialectic held precedence over rhetoric, as we saw. This was to justify later determinations that rhetoric should be taught before dialectic, since rhetoric was the natural bridge between grammatical— that is, literary—studies and dialectic, the art that teaches how to state true propositions; or, by the same token, the determination that dialectic ought to be taught before rhetoric to insure that the eloquence of a speaker be properly governed by wisdom. On the Augustinian side, it would be determined in some cases that rhetoric should be taught after dialectic because only in rhetoric—the art of Christian eloquence—could the word of God be adequately treated. Among those drawn more closely to Cicero, dialectic was seen as a form of rhetoric that, because it was more intellectually demanding, was better taught after rhetoric than before. More radical Ciceronians, such as the late-tenth-century reformer Gerbert of Reims, went so far as to equate rhetoric with the art of living the virtuous life. Theological commitments sometimes, as in the case of the first rule of the monastic community at Cluny in the early tenth century, rejected the "pagan" arts altogether. On the other hand, political commitments, whether bound up with the propaganda of the faith or the maintenance of social order, tended to value those "pagan" arts more highly. All of these kinds of tensions are implicit in the differences between Augustine's view of rhetoric and Boethius' view, and all of the positions we have indicated manifested themselves in the centuries after those two giants.

Cicero, of course, remained a powerful influence. But in various ways, medieval readings of Cicero were conditioned by Augustinian or Boethian programs. Boethians might be contrasted to Ciceronians—including, in this context, Augustine—by way of an opposition between a centripetal concept of *argumentatio* and a centrifugal concept of *argumentatio*. The centripetal concept emphasizes the kernel unit that is explicated by the *argumentatio* and the validity of the argument. It is in this respect that Boethius can be characterized as an Aristotelian. For him, as for Aristotle, the "argument" of a speech is its underlying enthymeme, "a sort of syllogism." Cicero's emphasis (and Augustine's) is on eloquence, "wisdom speaking copiously"— hence the centrifugal quality of Ciceronian argumentation. The "argument" of a speech is to be found not in any underlying scheme but precisely in the development of *loci*, their amplification, and the graceful connections made in it among the particulars of the case. These different emphases reappear, one's dominance repeatedly replaced by the other's, in commentaries and citations of Cicero throughout the Middle Ages.

The availability of texts of Cicero during this period can also be explained, at least in part, by the conflicting emphases of the Boethians and

Augustinians. Thus, the *De inventione* was the most frequently copied and most widely circulated text not because it was so useful to practicing rhetoricians but because it was the repository of Ciceronian doctrine concerning rhetorical places. Cicero's *Orator* and *Brutus*, and Quintilian's *Institutes*, were by contrast almost impossible to obtain; and the *De oratore* was available only in a severely mutilated form. These works were, in the final analysis, redundant, since all that needed to be known about eloquence could be found in the fourth book of the *De doctrina christiana*; hence the fact that it was copied far more frequently than those books of Cicero and Quintilian. In general, it must not be imagined that medieval scribes copied those works simply because they were there to be copied, as long as they were old.

Differences in theoretical emphasis, however, do not really explain much. Few rhetorical works, whether commentaries or arts of rhetoric, were composed by authors who were simply interested in promoting a doctrinal position until rhetoric became "scholasticized" in the twelfth century, when the university masters attempted, with only partial success, to take it over. As is usually true, the motives behind the composition of commentaries or treatises on rhetoric were rather concrete; and unless we begin to see that, we can hope only for the most superficial understanding of rhetoric in the Middle Ages. Let us revert, then, to the method we adopted at the beginning of this chapter.

THE FIRST RENAISSANCE OF RHETORIC IN THE MIDDLE AGES: ALCUIN

During the centuries after the death of Boethius, Europe in the north was the scene of constant migration and invasion by barbarian tribes, and in the east and south the battlefield where wars between Christians and Moslems were conducted. Rome ceased to be a center of learning, and even the Gallo-Roman schools in what is now France were reduced. The proponents of Latin learning came more and more to occupy the fringes of the old Roman Empire, particularly Ireland and Britain. There, the educational aims of Cassiodorus' program of liberal arts, a Latin version of the Hellenistic *enkyklios paideia*, were maintained with some success, as is clear from the writings of, for instance, the Venerable Bede (fl. c. 730). There is some evidence of residual awareness of technical rhetorical lore, but it is very sketchy. Although the schools at Bobbio, in the north of Italy, and St. Gall, in Switzerland, were in operation at this time, it is important to remember that both were founded by Irish monks—St. Columban and his entourage—between 600 and 613. In the ninth century, this situation was to change. We see then a remarkable increase in scholarly activity on the Continent and some interesting and innovative developments in rhetoric, largely owing to the influence of Alcuin and his students. It is to these that we now turn.[7]

Alcuin's *Disputatio de Rhetorica*

Alcuin was born in England around 735 and educated at the cathedral school at York, at the time one of the leading centers of learning in Europe. In 782, his reputation as a scholar widely known, he was invited to the Frankish court at Tours by Charlemagne as part of that king's efforts to consolidate his kingdom and develop its cultural and legal institutions, which were at the time relatively undeveloped. To that end, Alcuin was asked to assume leadership of the Palace School and work out the means of assuring the kingdom of a Latin-speaking priesthood capable of performing their required tasks. Alcuin succeeded in doing more than that, however. He not only reorganized the course of studies at the Palace School but established a school at the cathedral of St. Martin in Tours to educate teachers who were in turn to imbue the Germanic population of Charlemagne's realm with Latin culture. For 20 years, he served both the king, as an educator, writer, administrator, and statesman, and the Frankish Church, as its leading theologian and liturgical reformer. Far from being a humble schoolmaster, Alcuin was a shrewd and energetic functionary in Charlemagne's court, who was until his death in 804 at the center of virtually all that transpired there before and after the coronation of Charlemagne as Holy Roman Emperor in 800.[8]

On the face of it, the *Disputatio de Rhetorica et de Virtutibus sapientissimi Regis Karli et Albini Magistri,** the formal title of the work, is a fairly elementary treatise made slightly more interesting by the fact that it was composed in the form of a dialogue between Charlemagne, as student, and Alcuin, as master. In addition, it is noteworthy that about 90 percent of the *Disputatio* can hardly be described as original, since it is in some ways merely a pastiche of material from Cicero's *De inventione*, with bits and pieces of other authors thrown in. As we shall soon see, it is all of those things, but it is a much more complex document than its surface features would suggest.

The *Disputatio* might be seen to consist of three main parts: the introduction (lines 1–30), the discussion concerning rhetoric (31–1175), and the final disquisition on the virtues of a good orator (1176–1368). The treatment of rhetoric, in turn, consists of six parts, the first of which (31–465) lays out the standard lore on the parts of the art and the system of *status*, and the next five of which cover each of those parts and the parts of a speech. As the outline of the work appended to this chapter shows, the discussion of rhetoric is a brief but thorough compendium of Ciceronian doctrine drawn from the *De inventione*, the *rhetorica prima* of the age, the *Ad Herennium*, the *rhetorica secunda* wrongly attributed to Cicero, and the *Ars rhetorica* of the fourth-century writer Julius Victor. A few aspects of this compendious account are especially worth noting here.

To begin with, Alcuin is quite successful in summarizing what, in Cicero, occupies rather long discussions: for instance, the "circumstances" of a *causa* are summed up in a few lines as a set of questions: who? what? where? when? This becomes a formula in theology as well as rhetoric in the course of the Middle Ages. A second section of the discussion of rhetoric that catches our attention is Alcuin's description of legal proceedings and even the layout and trappings of a courtroom (see 399–465). This is all new to the character "Charlemagne," and it is an indication of the novelty of Roman legal procedures in the context of the prevailing Frankish system of justice.[9] Third, in the discussion of argumentation itself (*ipsa argumentatio*), "Charlemagne" asks "Alcuin" whether probable proofs can ever be considered geniune (see 733); and "Alcuin" answers "Yes," an indication of how thoroughly Ciceronian the notion of rhetoric in this treatise is. While Alcuin greatly admired the *Consolatio philosophiae* of Boethius, he apparently did not have as high a regard for the *De differentiis topicis*.[10] And fourth, we should notice that "Alcuin" spends a relatively long time (see 1077–1175) talking about memory and delivery—more, in fact, than he spends on style (see 986–1076)—noting that "this surpasses [the other parts of the art] by such a degree that, in the opinion of the superlative Tully [Cicero], a speech devoid of learning may be praised if it is well delivered, while a speech of consummate composition will meet with mockery and contempt if poorly pronounced." All of these features contribute to the basically practical orientation of the *Disputatio*.

The section on virtues at the end of the *Disputatio* does not seem to have much to do with rhetoric and is consequently often ignored. Its structural connection to what precedes it is, to be sure, a little loose. What motivates it dramatically is the observation that, just as, in speaking, the general axiom "Nothing in excess" must be observed, so must it be in life itself. But that does not seem enough to justify the discussions of prudence, justice, courage, and temperance that take up the next three hundred or so lines of the treatise. On the other hand, the verse introduction at the very beginning of the work tells us it should be read by one who wishes to learn about civic morals (*civiles mores*). Moreover, the treatment of virtues in the final section of the *Disputatio* corresponds almost exactly to the delineation of the *mores* that made Charlemagne a great king in Alcuin's letters. The virtues discussed, in fact, are the stock virtues of the ideal king. Implicitly, therefore, the *Disputatio* is not merely a compendium of rhetorical lore, but a political work that, in effect, commends to Charlemagne's subjects the exemplary character of their ruler. The *Disputatio de Rhetorica*, then, was meant as a handbook to be used by students in the schools Alcuin established, but it was also meant to hold up to those students an exemplary image of kingship in the person of Charlemagne himself.

The political aspect explains in large part why the *Disputatio* was so often copied in the ninth century and so seldom—or so it seems—after the collapse of the Carolingian royal line in 987. The other explanation is that there were many manuscripts of Cicero's works already available, which in effect made the *Disputatio* redundant. But the fact that all 16 manuscripts extant from the ninth century are in such a good state of preservation suggests that, as potentially useful as Alcuin's compendium of Ciceronian rhetoric would be for students, it was not widely used, particularly in the centuries that followed. So Cicero's popularity cannot explain everything. It seems, rather, that the *Disputatio*, politically charged as it was, lost its relevance for later generations of students.

Hrabanus Maurus

Alcuin was responsible for the founding and staffing of numerous schools throughout Charlemagne's realm. These attracted a second wave of Irish scholars, including among others the philologically sophisticated John Scotus Eriugena. These, together with Alcuin's own students, produced in turn a generation of scholars who expanded his influence even beyond the borders of France to cover the entire Holy Roman Empire. Monasteries flourished under Charlemagne and his successors, Louis the Pious and Charles the Bald, particularly at St. Gall, Fulda, and Corbie. Before long, the libraries at Tours, St. Gall, and Fulda were unparalleled in Europe. The *scriptoria* produced manuscripts at an unprecedented rate, written in the new, easier to read minuscule script; and from what we can gather from library catalogues compiled at the time, a relatively large number of those manuscripts were devoted to rhetoric.[11]

One of Alcuin's most distinguished students was Hrabanus Maurus (784?–856), who had come from Germany to Tours and was to return to his homeland to become abbot of the monastery at Fulda, about 50 miles northeast of Frankfurt, and eventually archbishop of Mainz, the city of his birth. Hrabanus was a prolific writer, the author of a treatise on grammar distinctive because of the attention it pays to the difficulty of teaching Latin to German-speaking students; of extensive commentaries on Scripture; of an encyclopedic dictionary (the so-called *De universo*) based on the *Etymologies* of Isidore of Seville; and of a pedagogical work in three books, *De institutione clericorum* (On the Training of the Clergy).[12]

De institutione was probably written some time between Hrabanus' ordination in 814 and his elevation to the abbacy at Fulda in 822. The first two books contain a compendium, or handbook, of theological and liturgical information that every priest would need to know. Book Three is a brief treatise on preaching and eloquence, consisting for the most part of a telescoped version of Augustine's *De doctrina christiana* and relevant passages from the *Pastoral Rules* of Gregory the Great. In fact, by far the greatest part of Book Three consists of direct quotation of Augustine's *De doctrina*, with not much of consequence added by Hrabanus himself. It is, however, not just a slavish imitation of the Bishop of Hippo, but an effective adaptation of Augustine to Hrabanus' times and indeed a document that clearly reflects the spirit of his age.

At the time of the composition of *De institutione*, the Church in Germany had been organized barely one hundred years, although Christianity flourished there from the third century. The work done by St. Boniface between 716 and 747 to order the internal administration of the Church was taken up by Charlemagne himself on his accession to the Frankish throne and continued with Alcuin's assistance after his arrival. We know the details of the attempts made to unify the liturgy and the rules governing monasteries because the decrees (*capitulae*) determining those matters, many of them actually written by Alcuin, are extant.[13] They extend to almost every detail: the shape of the Mass and its required parts, the official days of religious observance (all Sundays and various holy days, such as the Feast of All Saints), the requirement that the Creed be chanted in the Gregorian mode, rules for monastic discipline—all are laid out in the ecclesiastical *capitulae* that emanated from Charlemagne's court.

The fact that these ordinances comprise the content of most of the first two books of *De institutione* (see, for instance, 2.42 on Sunday Mass, 2.47ff. on chanting) should alert us to the pragmatic nature of Hrabanus' work. It also explains why the work was so widely circulated even after his lifetime. *De institutione*, in short, is not just a liturgical treatise but a sort of official manual whose rules were to be followed by the Saxon Church. What is more, the third book is practical in its orientation, too. Hrabanus there takes the essential materials from Augustine and presents them anew to his German students. These students, apparently, were relatively uncultivated; thus Hrabanus' assurances that there is nothing really wrong with rhetoric (3.19) and that drawing even on pagan sources is permissible—perhaps called for—in the interests of spreading God's word (3.18). These assurances are to be found in Augustine, of course, but they take on a good deal of relevance for Hrabanus' program. Indeed, the Church's situation in ninth-century Saxony was very like that of the North African Church of Augustine's time.

In both Alcuin and Hrabanus, therefore, we see efforts to adapt the old to fit the new—more specifically, to fit the vision of Charlemagne and his successor, Louis, of a unified, and unifying, Church and of the restoration of the cultural glories of the Roman Empire. To the Carolingians, the empire was not just a political structure; it was a rebirth of the past and of the Roman spirit. The chief promoters of Charlemagne's vision were Alcuin's students, and their students: Grimald, friend of Hrabanus and in the mid-ninth century abbot of the monastery at St. Gall, one of the most important centers of learning; Hrabanus' student Servatus Lupus (805–62), who spent a good part of his life collecting and editing Cicero's rhetorical works; and Remi of Auxerre (c. 840–908), who composed a massive commentary on Martianus Capella's allegorical treatise on the *artes liberales*, *The Marriage of Mercury and Philology*, that so fascinated Carolingian scholars; and many others.[14]

"THE AGE OF IRON AND LEAD": GERBERT AND NOTKER

During the tenth century, Europe was gravely threatened by dissent among its rulers and the depredations of successive invasions by Norse, Slavic, and Muslim armies. The royal line of Charlemagne ceded its preeminence to the Saxon House of Otto and eventually died out with the accession to the throne in France of Hugh Capet in 987. In addition to the apprehensions brought on by earthly conflicts, the impending arrival of the year of our Lord 1000—the Millennium—made for anxieties of a less mundane sort. Many feared that the arrival of the Antichrist predicted in John's *Apocalypse* and the end of the world were at hand. All of this, in turn, may explain the reaction against Classical learning that apparently developed at the time, epitomized, perhaps, by the dream of the abbot of Cluny, St. Odilo, in which a beautiful vessel is seen to be full of writhing serpents. The vessel is Classical poetry, Odilo writes. Hence the characterization of this century as an "age of iron and lead" by one historian of the Church.[15]

Of course, even if Classical studies were banned by the so-called Clunaic reforms enforced in many monasteries, the view of the tenth century as a primitive age of iron and lead is only a partial one. In many ways, this century can also be seen as an extension of the Carolingian "renaissance." Hostility to the classics was hardly peculiar to the decades after 900, for one thing. It was a prominent attitude during the reign of Louis the Pious. Study of the classics continued, in any event, to occupy the scholars at St. Gall and Tours, as the large number of manuscripts from the time attests. Among these is a remarkable collection of Ciceronian texts, the so-called *Collectaneum* produced in Tours by Hadoard, which contains a large selection from the *De oratore*. This century saw many literary innovations: the remarkable plays of Hroswitha of Gandersheim, for instance, and the meditative lyrics of Ratherius of Verona, a native of Liège. It is also the century that saw the emergence of a revitalized interest in rhetoric in the works of Gerbert of Reims and Notker Labeo, both active in the last decades before the Millennium. It is with these that we shall be concerned next.

Gerbert of Reims

Gerbert (c. 940–1003) wrote no treatise on rhetoric, but we learn much from his letters and from the biography by his disciple Richerius about his attitude toward rhetoric and his notion of its place in education. Gerbert's first (though by no means primary) claim to our attention is as an educational reformer. Gerbert's own education was not typical. His early studies at the monastery of St. Géraud in the south of France grounded him thoroughly in Classical literary studies. Somewhat later, he studied at Barcelona, where he acquired an unusually rigorous training in the mathematical arts. Barcelona was particularly strong in those fields, probably because of the influences of the most advanced mathematicians of the age, the Muslim scholars in southern Spain. Such an education could not fail to inspire him to reorganize the educational priorities of the school at Reims, where he became the master.

His most important reforms were instituted on what he saw as a Greek model, the idea that theology must be studied only after a thorough and systematic grounding in the liberal arts. Impressed by the efforts of Boethius to make the contributions of the Greeks in geometry and astronomy available to Latin readers, Gerbert sought to give more prominence to those disciplines in the arts curriculum, and toward that end composed a number of important treatises on those subjects. One of his pedagogical innovations was the use of charts and outlines that summarized the essential materials in an easily comprehended and remembered form, both in the mathematical and the literary arts. The rhetoric course underwent changes, as well. Instead of limiting instruction to methods of organizing and composing, Gerbert revived the practice of actual forensic declamation by students before their masters. The important thing for students to learn was not the rules of eloquence but how to stand up and argue a case. Gerbert wanted rhetoric to be more than a mere literary study.[16]

The chief influence in Gerbert's conception of rhetoric is, clearly, Cicero, for whom he had the greatest respect. And it is not just the *De inventione* that he had in mind, but the *De oratore* and the *Topics*, and most of all, the actual orations "which the father of Roman eloquence wrote for the defense of the many" (*Ep.* 86). Gerbert went to great pains to acquire a text of the *De oratore* because it was there that the truly important lessons from Cicero could be found—namely, the connections between eloquence and action. In 985, he wrote to Ebrard of Tours a letter that shows this: "I am not a man," he says,

> to separate the useful from the honorable, but constantly try, as Cicero did, always to join the one to the other. . . . Since philosophy does not separate the science of morals (*ratio morum*) from the science of speaking (*ratio dicendi*), I have always considered as equal the study of the good life and the study of good speaking (*bene dicere*). To a man exempt from the cares of government the one suffices perfectly well without the other. But when one is—as I am—entangled in public affairs, both are necessary. For it is of the highest importance to be able to speak persuasively and to restrain the fury of wayward spirits by the sweetness of eloquence (*suavi oratione*). It is for this activity, which must be prepared for beforehand, that I am diligently forming a library. (*Ep.* 57)

Gerbert's rationale for teaching rhetoric, and for teaching it the way he did, is of course the same as Cicero's. And while Alcuin, for instance, seems to have considered rhetoric a civil science, Gerbert is here far more specific than his predecessor about the practical implication of such a conception of the art. That rhetoric should be useful in the active life is more than a scholastic commonplace for Gerbert. What he believed, and what he taught his students, he also put into practice. He was recognized in his time as a consummate stylist and as a powerful advocate in political causes—the "public affairs" to which he refers in his letter—with no little justification. Gerbert's primary distinction in history is not that he reformed the curriculum at Reims, but that he eventually became the Bishop of Rome, as Pope Sylvester II, in the year that marked the Millennium.

Notker Labeo

Notker Labeo (950–1022), so called because of his pendulous lower lip, never rose as high in the Church as Gerbert and seems to have avoided public affairs altogether. He spent most of his life, as a student and, later, as a teacher, within the confines of the monastery of St. Gall. Nevertheless, we can see in his *Nova rhetorica** the same innovative spirit and pragmatic orientation as we saw in the teachings of Gerbert. This orientation is due in part to the practical problems he and his fellow teachers faced in providing the students at St. Gall with a means of access to Classical learning. Since the students had difficulty working on Latin texts, Notker plunged himself into a long-term translation project, "something totally unaccustomed," as he says in one of his letters, of works not only by Boethius and Aristotle but by Terence and Virgil as well. In his *Rhetorica*, too, Notker supplies German terminology where the Latin might have been obscure to his students. No doubt it was for such efforts that he was dubbed "Notker teutonicus" ("Notker the German") and eulogized as a "most benevolent teacher" (*benignissimus magister*) after his death.[17]

Notker's conscious efforts to be innovative in his *Rhetorica*, however, go far beyond the inclusion of German terminology. True, there was a need for a textbook appropriate to current circumstances at St. Gall. But in addition, he notes that the cycles observable in the history of rhetoric show that the time was ripe for a "new" rhetoric. The novelty of Notker's rhetoric is clear both from his formulation of the basic process by which *eloquentia* is attained and from the consequent organization of the *Rhetorica*.

Eloquence is attained by way of a two-step process of comprehension and artistic transformation. Thus one needs first to comprehend the "substance of the controversy," or the "nub of the issue"—what Notker calls the *materia* of the case—and its rhetorical limits and resources; and then, in view of those, to bring about the artistic shaping of controversial discourse. These two steps determine the format of the *Rhetorica*, as the first part (pp. 645–662) treats of rhetoric from the perspective of *materia*, which comprises all things and deeds that may give rise to controversy (*machunga dis strites*); and the second (pp. 663–683) from the perspective of rhetoric as the *ars* or *scientia* that shapes one's treatment of the controversy. These two perspectives are complementary, as is evident from Notker's parallel treatments of them (see the appended outline), two sides of a single process of rhetorical invention, which is, he says, "mightier than all the other parts of rhetoric" (p. 670).

Notker's rhetoric is innovative at virtually every level, from the introduction of vernacular terminology to the format of the entire work. Notker's parallel treatment of *materia* and *ars* is unique and unprecedented. While the format differs greatly from the standard one based on the *De inventione*, however, it is both faithful to the spirit of Cicero's work and an improvement on the versions of Ciceronian rhetoric in circulation in Notker's time. In his view, the tendency of the "old" rhetorics was to allow expression (*elocutio*) to take precedence over invention (p. 681) and consequently to value embellishment over substance. Given the relative amount of attention paid to elocution at the expense of invention we have seen even in Alcuin and Hrabanus, it might be argued that Notker's point is not far off the mark. The concentration on invention in Notker is, in any event, another novel aspect of his work.

That concentration, in turn, is a consequence of a new breadth that Notker grants to rhetoric. Standard treatments in his day tend either to restrict rhetoric to Cicero's three genres or to Augustine's "sacred eloquence." Notker, however, broadens the notion of rhetorical *materia* to embrace any issue in question whatsoever, and the scope of rhetoric to include the whole process by which dissent can be put to an end "according to a rational method" (p. 650). Thus the end of rhetoric is not just "speaking well," but the vital purpose of eliminating conflict and establishing concord. That this is Notker's conception of the art is clear from the *Nova rhetorica*, but it comes out with greater clarity in a passage from his commentary on the *Consolation of Philosophy* in which, in elucidating Book II, section 10, he answers the question "What is rhetoric?" He writes:

> The second [art] is rhetoric, which takes us further [than grammar] because it gives us that eloquence which one requires in court and in deliberations and wherever any sort of agreement (*dehéin éinúnga*) is a common need. . . . Whoever he may be, a man who can eliminate (*uerzéren*) conflict with speech—and if he has learned to do it by studying rhetoric—that man is an orator, in whose mouth is to be found rhetorical sweetness (*rhetoricam dulcedinem*).[18]

It is perhaps in this vision of what rhetoric is and what it is for that Notker was most innovative. He was not, of course, alone. From what we can tell, Gerbert would have shared Notker's view. Perhaps it is the fact that both lived in "an age of iron and lead" that explains this new emphasis on eliminating discord through discourse marked by "rhetorical sweetness." In any event, we do not find it in the other rhetorics of the age, and we will not see it so emphasized again until it is articulated by the humanists of the Renaissance.

MEDIEVAL "CICERONIANISM"

The decades after Notker's death were appreciably less turbulent, politically, than those before. In addition, technological innovation such as the introduction of the horseshoe and horse collar brought about improvements in agricultural efficiency, although it could not eliminate famine. Expansion of trade and improved conditions for travel and communication brought about a new prosperity in the towns and a general increase of urbanization. This, in turn, created educational needs that schools attached to cathedrals could and did satisfy: St. Martin's in Tours, Notre Dame in Paris, and perhaps most notably, the school at the cathedral at Chartres.

Alongside these developments, we see an intense interest in rhetoric, both as a school discipline and as an art that could usefully be exploited. In the eleventh and twelfth centuries there was an outburst of manuscript production that put new copies of Cicero and of Victorinus' commentaries on his works in circulation. Otloh of St. Emmeram and Anselm of Besate both wrote in the mid-eleventh century. By the end of the eleventh century, new commentaries on the *De inventione* and the *Ad Herennium* appeared—that of Lanfranc of Bec, for instance, and that of Manegold of Lauterbach; and in the first half of the twelfth, the masters at Chartres, Thierry of Chartres, for instance, produced even more commentaries. The jurists of Pavia and Bologna began to introduce rhetorical methods of interpretation borrowed from Cicero into their teaching, techniques that were later to take a Boethian dialectical turn and influence theologians in the twelfth and thirteenth centuries. And toward the end of the eleventh century the first examples of new systematic treatises on letter writing, poetic composition, and preaching begin to appear, the *artes dictaminis* and *artes praedicandi* that reached their full development in the thirteenth century. In this section and in the next, we shall examine some of these developments in some detail, looking first at the "Ciceronianism" of the eleventh and twelfth centuries and then at the characteristics of the new *artes* that appeared during that period and after.

"Ciceronianism"

Recent scholarship has greatly increased our knowledge of the commentaries on Cicero produced in the eleventh and twelfth centuries, although an enormous amount of work has yet to be done. Most of these remain unpublished; many do not survive. Similarly, studies on such writers as Otloh and Anselm of Besate are few and far between, and much that was previously accepted as fact has come in for serious reconsideration in recent times. But enough has been done in these areas to make it fairly clear that medieval Ciceronianism evolved along two lines: one traces a shift from practical to theoretical concerns, which eventually led to the sterile "rhetoric" that Renaissance humanists were to revile. The other reincarnated the Ciceronian notion of rhetoric as a "civil science" in the handbooks devoted to letter writing and preaching. In some ways, this double development may be attributed to regional differences. The schools in France seem typically to have been inclined to theoretical rigor; teachers in Italy, Germany, and England, to the practical side of rhetoric. What emerges from a closer study of the materials from this period is suggestive of something more than national predilections, however: a persistent tension between what we have called Boethian and Ciceronian orientations toward rhetoric.

To begin with, the Ciceronianism of Otloh of St. Emmeram and Anselm of Besate, both of whom wrote in the mid-eleventh century, is glaringly un-Boethian. Otloh (1013–66) was heir to the learning of St. Gall and Fulda. He was deeply familiar with Cicero's rhetorics, and seems particularly alert to the importance of style (*PL* 146.57Bff.) and was convinced that argument involves much more than syllogisms, as the dialecticians had it. In fact, his own eloquence is conspicuously centrifugal, drawing on the whole range of devices in Cicero to the extent that the cogency of an argument seems to be a function of sheer quantity (see, for instance, 146.64ff.). A man of wide acquaintance with Classical literature, Otloh was openly opposed to the tendency to reduce argument to syllogisms and feared that the authority of Boethius was overcoming that of the Church. Anselm of Besate's *Rhetorimachia* openly professes his allegience to the art of rhetoric and to the (obscure) Drogonic movement in philosophy, a movement so committed to the belief that the proper province of rhetoric was not truth but verisimilitude that it could dispense with the logical principle of the excluded middle. In any event, *Rhetorimachia* is an interesting attempt to make the lessons of the ancients intelligible to and adaptable by his contemporaries.

Somewhat later in the eleventh century and in the first half of the twelfth too, we see expressions of the conviction that rhetoric should be useful in life. In a commentary by Manegold of Lauterbach (1030–1103) on the *Ad Herennium*, we see rhetoric placed in the context of the sort of knowledge that pertains to the management of the affairs of citizens: architecture, military science, carpentry, "and also the science of pleading, that is, handling legal cases, that is, rhetoric, eloquence learned from rules" (see *Durham* MS. C.IV.29, f.197r).[19] In the preface to Thierry of Chartres' *Heptateuchon*, composed in the first quarter of the twelfth century, we read that learning and knowledge, as gained from the study of the liberal arts, must "minister to the cult of humanity"; and in John of Salisbury's introduction to the *Metalogicon* (c. 1160), we see his insistence that the arts should be put to the use of society.

In Thierry's commentary on the *De inventione*,[20] however, we see a different slant. Thierry tries hard to show that rhetoric is autonomous, not just a part of logic (see p. 218); but he was deeply influenced by Boethius, too, sometimes substituting not only the terminology but also the conceptions of Boethius for those of Cicero. It is thus likely (but not certain, since we have only part of his commentary) that Thierry's view, while giving lip-service to the notion of rhetoric as a "civil science," is in the end Boethian. Evidence of a tendency to read Cicero through Boethius' eyes is more apparent in the commentary by one of Thierry's predecessors. William of Champeaux (b. 1070), whose conception of invention was thoroughly Boethian, although he too defines rhetoric as part of civil *scientia*. Thierry's contemporary, William of Conches seems also to have taken a Boethian stance toward rhetoric. Peter Abelard (1079–1142), who was a student of William of Champeaux and became the most influential theologian of the time, shows total dedication to the methods of dialectic, as do John of Salisbury (d. 1180), student of Thierry and of William of Conches, and Hugh of St. Victor.

In short, at Chartres and Notre Dame, at least, the concerns seem to have been largely theoretical and the tendency to place rhetoric in the same position regarding dialectic as Boethius does in Book 4 of the *Differentiis topicis* seems to have prevailed. Indeed, what characterizes observations on rhetoric after 1150 is painstaking analysis, determining the exact meaning of terms or the exact nature of "issues," and the attempt to restore a coherence to rhetorical theory that scholars thought lacking in it. One exception to this general tendency may be seen in the commentary on the *Ad Herennium* by one "Alanus"—possibly Alain of Lille—from late in the century. This is for the most part much like other commentaries emanating from the cathedral schools in France, but the attention Alanus pays to, say, the matter of what figures of speech are appropriate to what sorts of issues or types of style reminds us more of Otloh than of William of Champeaux. Nevertheless, dialectic prevailed. In a way, the coda had long before been set in France by the likes of Berenger of Tours (d. 1088), who wrote in the midst of his dispute with Lanfranc that "it is by reason that man resembles God." Dialectic is the exercise of reason, and reason is "incomparably superior to authority when there is a question of ascertaining the truth." By the same token, the stimulus given to dialectical research by the translation of Aristotle's *Sophistic Refutations* in the mid-twelfth century by James of Venice cannot have failed to promote an attitude toward rhetoric that eventually separated rhetoric altogether from the realm of inquiry and consigned it to ethical studies as a source of psychological and sociological commonplaces.

Elsewhere—in Italy and Germany, for instance—rhetoric was otherwise conceived and transformed. The eleventh-century *Expositio* of the Lombard code of law begins with an exordium situating the study of law within the tradition of the *artes liberales*; and the principles of legal interpretation formulated by Berthold of Konstanz (d. 1100) are taken mainly from Cicero's *De inventione*. Later generations produced the so-called brocards (a corruption of "pro and contra") that became for jurists what *loci* had been to rhetoricians. Rhetoric and law went hand in hand in the schools of Pavia (where, incidentally, Lanfranc had practiced law before becoming a priest) and Bologna until, eventually, jurisprudence achieved independent status as a discipline in the twelfth century and rhetoric was consigned to the status of handmaiden not to logic but to the law.

In these areas, then, the study of the influence of Cicero and the decline of that influence present a rather complex picture, the detailed history of which has yet to be written. As we have observed, however, that influence was not totally negated by the ascendance of dialectic but simply took different forms in the practical *artes* that began to appear from the eleventh century on. It is to these that we now turn.

CICERO IN THE *ARTES*

Ciceronian rhetoric was adapted and transformed in three different kinds of *artes*: the arts of letter writing (*artes dictaminis*), of preaching (*artes praedicandi*), and of prose and/or verse composition (*artes prosandi/poetriae*). Such arts constitute by far the greatest part of available material on rhetoric in the Middle Ages from about 1100 to the first decades of the Renaissance. In the following, we merely sketch the broad outlines of their contents and of what can be concluded from them.[21]

Artes dictaminis

The connection between rhetoric and letter writing had been recognized as early as the fourth century. Julius Victor adds to his *Ars rhetorica* a brief section on the subject (see Halm 447ff.) in which he distinguishes among the different rhetorical requirements of official and informal letters on the basis of subject, occasion, and recipient. Instruction on the subject of letter writing in the early Middle Ages seems limited, however, to the *formulae*—stock formats for different types of official correspondence—from the pre-Carolingian era. Study of letters seems to have been part of the arts curriculum after Alcuin, and was certainly part of monastic experience, as the large number of extant collections of letters by the Church Fathers attests. But the first more or less formal treatise we possess on letter writing is the *Breviarium de dictamine* of Alberic of Monte Cassino, composed about 1087.[22]

More systematic treatises begin to appear in the first decades of the twelfth century, including the *Praecepta dictaminum* of Adalbertus Samaritanus (c. 1115), in which Alberic is attacked; and Hugh of Bologna's *Rationes dictandi prosaice* (c. 1123), in which Alberic is stoutly defended. Common to all of these is an acute sense of the principles of decorum of style; and all of them are, implicitly or explicitly, indebted to the rhetorics of Cicero. An anonymous *Rationes dictandi* composed somewhat later, in about 1135, shows, on the one hand, that Cicero's influence was pervasive and, on the other, that the basic outlines of the *ars dictaminis* had become pretty well settled. A list of the sections will give us an idea of its Ciceronian qualities and of the shape of the standard *ars*:

1. Prologue (p. 9 Rockinger)
2. Definition of terms (10)
3. Definition of *epistle* (10)
4. The five parts of a letter: *salutatio, benevolentiae captatio, narratio, petitio, conclusio* (10)
5. *Salutatio* (salutation) (10–18)
6. *Benevolentiae captatio* (making the reader attentive and well-disposed to the writer) (18–19)
7. *Narratio* (laying out the facts) (19)
8. *Petitio* (the request) (20–21)
9. *Conclusio* (the closing) (21–22)
10. How to shorten letters (22–23)
11. Rearranging parts (23–25)
12. The constitution of letters (25–26)
13. Principles of variation (26–28)

This general pattern reappears in most treatises written afterward, both in Italy and, after 1135 or so, north of the Alps. It must be borne in mind that letter composition here, as elsewhere in the period, is oriented toward oral presentation in a formal setting. Indeed, the anonymous author of this treatise defines a letter as "an *oratio* consisting of parts, harmoniously and clearly written."

The fact that the earliest treatises were all composed in Italy is hardly an accident. On the one hand, many of Alberic's students were probably trained for positions in the papal court. One of them, John of Gaeta, later became Pope Gelasius II. On the other hand, Adalbert and Hugh taught in Bologna, as did the author of the anonymous *Rationes*. Bologna and Pavia, the source of still other *artes dictaminis* from this period, were centers of legal study, as we have seen, where the preparation of notaries and secretaries was an important activity. All of these Italian *artes*, in short, were responding to the needs of growing bureaucracies, papal and secular, for literate, if not eloquent, functionaries.

By the middle of the twelfth century, *artes dictaminis* begin to appear in France (for instance, the *Ars dictandi aureliensis*, out of Orléans); and in the early thirteenth century, they appear in Germany. The *formulae* tradition going back to the pre-Carolingian era was very strong in the north, so there was some resistance to the new model. In 1239, however, one Ludolf of Hildesheim composed his *Summa dictaminum*. Eventually, too, the new model was adapted in Spain—Juan Gil de Zamora wrote *Dictaminis epithalamium* (c. 1275)—and, rather later, in England. By the mid-fourteenth century, the format that had been developed by the twelfth-century Bolognese writers had, in short, become the basic convention throughout Europe. In many of these treatises, it might be added, the name of Cicero (or "Tully") is never mentioned; but he is always lurking not very far in the background.

Artes praedicandi

In 1149 the abbot Wibald of Corbai wrote a long letter to his friend, one Manegold of Paderborn, in the course of which he makes some observations on the utility of Classical learning, noting among other things the fact that much of it, chiefly instruction in forensic rhetoric, had lost its point. At the end of the letter, Wibald writes:

> However, within the Church, there do exist some opportunities for rhetoric which incur no one's reproach, namely, within the office of preaching. The acknowledged king of this is, in my judgment, Bernard, the abbot of Clairvaux, a most famous man in our time. Him I can justly call a true orator according to the definition of a rhetorician, "a good man skilled in speaking." . . . Him you would call truly eloquent who does not destroy with his hand what he preaches with his lips. . . . So, if you too want to be renowned for your preaching, choose someone whose sweetness of speech charms your heart. For the greatest of rhetoricians agree that highly polished and copious eloquence is better achieved by imitation of good speakers than by slavishly following the textbook's precepts.[23]

This last thought Wibald takes directly from Augustine's *De doctrina*. But in his day it is difficult to see what "textbooks" he can have been referring to.

Aside from the third book of Hrabanus' *De institutione clericorum*, possibly the actual source of Wibald's knowledge of Augustine, there were no such textbooks, as far as we know, unless we count as a textbook the brief remarks of Guibert of Nogent at the beginning of his *Commentary on Genesis* (c. 1087), sometimes referred to as the *Liber quo ordine sermo fieri debeat*, roughly, A Book on How a Sermon Should Be Organized. Similarly, the instructions given by Honorius of Autun (d. circa 1150) on how a preacher should adapt to his audience, how to speak, and what gestures to use (see *PL* 172.815ff.) hardly constitute a work expressly treating the technique of sermon composition.

Within 50 years, this would all change; for in the thirteenth century we begin to see a number of manuals for preaching, *artes praedicandi*. Up to that time, it seems that imitation was the preferred mode of learning how to preach a sermon, if we can infer that from the large body of homiletic collections that are extant from as early as the ninth century. In a way, it is strange that so few manuals of preaching predate 1200. Preaching had always been a crucially important Church activity. The sheer number of sermons that were given, both in Latin and, after the third Council of Tours, in 813, in the vernacular, must have been staggering. Why there should, all of a sudden, be such an outburst of *artes* for preaching after 1200 is mysterious, although it undoubtedly had something to do with the arrival of the mendicant Dominican (Order of Preachers) and Franciscan orders at the gates of the universities in Paris and Oxford about that time.

Artes praedicandi come in various sizes. Earlier treatments tend to be rather short and are often attached to sample "sermonettes," suggesting that it was still thought essential to give the reader some exemplars to imitate. We must bear in mind that these *artes* were primarily practical, not in any significant way theoretical. Alexander of Ashby's *De modo praedicandi* (On the Method of Preaching, c. 1200), for instance, consists of only 7 folio pages; and William of Auvergne's *De arte praedicandi** (c. 1228) is similarly brief. By contrast, the *Forma praedicandi* of Robert de Basevorn* (c. 1320) is quite long, about 25 folio pages in most versions; and Raymond Llull's *Liber de praedicatione*, probably composed a decade or two before Robert's, fills over 200 folio pages, not including the 100 sample sermons attached to the *ars* proper.[24]

All of the *artes* presuppose a sermon format that had become rather standard by 1200 and was further refined during the thirteenth century, the so-called university sermon. This format, which is discussed in detail in Thomas of Salisbury's *Summa de arte praedicandi* (c. 1210), prescribes the following six parts:

1. Opening prayer for divine assistance
2. Protheme, or introduction of the theme
3. Theme, or statement of the scriptural text
4. Division of the text, statement of parts of theme
5. Development (*prosecutio*) of the parts
6. Conclusion

The "division" is almost always into three parts, each one suggested by a word in the scriptural citation; and the development of the theme consequently occurs in three stages, each of which may be further divided and developed.[25] Most of the treatises in question (for example, William of Auvergne's *De arte* and Richard of Thetford's *Ars dilandi sermones* [c. 1235]) say little about the format itself and concentrate on the modes of amplification.

As a final general observation, we should note that the influence of Cicero, or at least of a strongly Ciceronian notion of eloquence, is pervasive in these treatises. This can be seen most clearly in the similarity between the standard format and the standard arrangement of a Ciceronian oration, making allowances for the change of scenario from courtroom to church service. It can even be seen in the structure of some of the *artes*. Robert de Basevorn's *Forma*, for instance, is laid out in accordance with the arrangement of the Classical speech: ch. 1–23 (pp. 233–260 in Charland), introductory material; ch. 24–32 (pp. 260–273), exordium material; ch. 33–34, the partition or division; ch. 35–46 (pp. 273–307), the argumentation and its amplification; ch. 47f. (pp. 307–323), conclusions. But the most Ciceronian feature of all is the constant emphasis in early as well as late *artes* on *copia*, abundance of eloquence. This is obvious in a treatise such as Richard of Thetford's *Ars dilandi*, which is, after all, a treatise on amplification; and it is clear in William of Auvergne's *De arte*, the stated goal of which is to provide preachers with an *ars praedicandi et copia dicendi*. As for the later *artes*, it should be noted that the greater part of Robert de Basevorn's *Forma praedicandi* is devoted to what he calls the *ornamenta* to be employed; and Llull's *ars*, perhaps tyically for him, contains an elaborate system—almost a calculus—of invention and amplification.[26]

What we see in all of the *Arts of Preaching*, then, is an emphasis on the sort of eloquence we earlier characterized as centrifugal. In the fourteenth century, we see treatises such as John de Chalons' *Ars brevis et clara faciendi sermones secundum formam syllogisticam* (A Brief and Clear Handbook on Composing Sermons Following the Syllogistic Form) (c. 1370). But on the whole, the arts of preaching are steadfastly anti-Boethian. The job of the preacher, after all, was not simply to instruct but to move and edify as well. In short, while the commentators on Cicero and those arguing over the coherence of rhetorical theory moved steadily over to the Boethian side, the teachers in the Dominican and Franciscan houses of study (*studia*) close by, but not part of, the universities promoted a notion of eloquence based on the Ciceronian ideal.

Artes poetriae

The twelfth and thirteenth centuries saw the emergence of another kind of handbook, what might loosely be called the *Ars poetriae*. This type of handbook was meant primarily for students of grammar in the cathedral schools, those at Orléans and Chartres, for instance. As we shall see, however, poetry is later conceived in rhetorical terms as well, and the operative rhetorical perspective was Ciceronian.

Before we turn to a few representative treatises, we must recall that grammar, as it was taught in the trivium, is regularly held to include both the *ars recte loquendi* ("the art of speaking correctly") and the *ennarratio poetarum* ("the explanation of poetry"). The development of grammar in the twelfth century took two directions. The first emphasized the *recte loquendi* aspect of the art and was quickly appropriated by the dialecticians—Abelard, for example, who had no use for "poetic figments and inane fables" (see *PL* 178.1040f.)—who went on to create the so-called speculative grammar that became important in the thirteenth and fourteenth centuries. The other held on to both parts of the art but came to see that the materials learned in grammar were essential not only to the proper understanding of literary texts but also to the production of discourse, particularly poetry. As for poetry, we must bear in mind that the term covers a whole range of discursive types, from the mere versification of a theme provided to the student by the teacher to the impressive cosmological allegories that began to appear about the same time as the *artes*, and that the word *poetry* in the Middle Ages always refers to oral discourse.

The earliest *ars poetriae* we have is the *Ars versificatoria*[27] (*The Art of Versifying*) by Matthew of Vendôme. Matthew taught grammar at Orléans and, later, Paris and was conspicuous in the literary debates of his day. The *Ars versificatoria*, composed some time before 1175, consists of four parts:

I. General definitions and modes of generating ideas (118 sections)
II. The forms of words (46 sections)
III. The qualities of expression (schemes and tropes, 52 sections)
IV. The execution of the subject assigned (51 sections)

Matthew's *Ars* was intended for use by beginners in the part of grammatical study dealing with versification, the composition of a version in verse of some approved theme assigned by the teacher. The general aim of the work is clear from his exhortation to his reader to study these matters "lest you be misled into mistaking the intentions of the authors you read" (1.60, Faral p. 32). Hence it should not surprise us to find the many examples he gives, some of them quite long, and to see that he says nothing about such matters as invention and disposition except as they may refer to the selection of the apt figure or the composition of a single line of verse. Nevertheless, there is a strong rhetorical undercurrent in the *Ars versificatoria*. This comes out particularly in the attention paid to style, both in Matthew's admonitions to avoid a "dry and anemic" (*aridum et exsangue*) style and in his analysis of the faults of style in Parts II and III. The rhetorical lore on *loci* and the modes of amplification, moreover, is behind the treatment of "ideas" in part I. It must be stressed, however, that this is an elementary grammar treatise, not a work geared to the advanced student.

By contrast, the *Poetria nova* of Geoffrey of Vinsauf—frequently subtitled in manuscripts as "Galfredi rhetorica"—is addressed to rather more advanced students who studied poetry either in upper-level grammar class or in conjunction with their rhetorical studies. It is something of a tour de force, as it is written in verses that, while laying out the doctrine, exemplify the very things Geoffrey is discussing. It can be summarized thus:

I. Preface (vv. 1–42)
II. General observations on the subject (*materia*) to be treated "poetically" (vv. 43–86)
III. Disposition (vv. 87–202)
IV. Amplification and abbreviation (vv. 219–736)
V. Ornamentation (figures and tropes, vv. 737–1968)
VI. Memory and delivery (vv. 1969–2065)
VII. Epilogue (vv. 2066–2116)

About the same time that he wrote his *Poetria nova* (c. 1210), Geoffrey composed the *Documentum de modo et arte dictandi et versificandi*, a prose treatise covering the methods of both prose and verse composition. The approach taken in it is essentially the same as that of the *Poetria*.[28]

John of Garland, in another extant *ars*, the so-called Parisian Poetic, goes even further. John, who was born in England but taught for most of his life in Paris, complains that his predecessors were far too narrow. Hence his *De arte prosaica, metrica, et rithmica* (c. 1230) attempts to bring all three recognized categories of composition under one rubric—like Geoffrey's essentially rhetorical, but placing even more emphasis on methods for inventing *materia* and amplifying it than his predecessors.

These three *artes* are generally recognized as the most important examples of their genre. While they are all included under the category of *Ars poetriae*, it is necessary to recognize that they had different audiences: Matthew's was the elementary student, Geoffrey's the advanced, and John's—from all appearances—teachers of composition, not students. Yet all three reveal, as should be clear even from the sketchy account we have given here, the pervasive influence of Cicero and a tendency to move grammar further and further away from the concentration on *recte loquendi* and bring it into line with arts of producing discourse.

The various new *artes* that begin to appear in the twelfth century, in short, are all deeply Ciceronian, both in content and in spirit, running contrary to the other dominant trend in rhetoric represented by the increasing degree to which rhetoric was being assimilated to dialectic that we see at that time. These arts continue to be taught in the *studia* run by the various orders and in notarial schools well into the Renaissance. Some of the more important works not only continue to circulate in manuscript form but appear among the earliest printed books in the West, the so-called *incunabula*. In the universities, the dialectical methods of scholasticism become increasingly dominant, particularly after the arrival in the West of Aristotle's works in Latin translations by William of Moerbeke and Hermannus Germanus. Interestingly, Aristotle's *Rhetoric*, one of those newly translated works, exercised no visible influence.[29] It was used not in rhetorical instruction but in the ethics course. As a formal discipline of study, however, rhetoric ceased to be important in university curricula. After two successive, and very different, rebirths, in short, rhetoric lost its intellectual vitality in most European centers of learning after about 1300. But from the dormant state into which it fell it would eventually be, once again, reawakened, reborn once again, so to speak, in the Renaissance. It is to that reawakening that we turn in the next chapter.

SUMMARY

In 721 Luitprand, king of the Lombards, moved the remains of Boethius from the ancient basilica at Pavia to the Church of San Pietro in Cieldoro, where the remains of Augustine were also interred. In a sense, the presence of both in the same place is symbolic of their continuing double presence in the minds of medieval rhetoricians, a presence that, as it developed, became a virtual preoccupation. We can now see that the shifting oppositions between the rhetorics Augustine and Boethius stood for and the tensions inherent in that opposition between eloquence and certitude do, indeed, succinctly summarize the history of rhetoric in the Middle Ages.

Aside from a few shadowy traces, the history of rhetoric in the two centuries after the beheading of Boethius is invisible. With the reforms of Charlemagne, that changes. Alcuin's program eventuated in a succession of scholars and teachers that ranged from his student Hrabanus, to Lupus of Ferrières and Remi of Auxerre, and on into the early eleventh century, with Gerbert and Notker. All of these were motivated in their attempts to edit and collect and comment on the works of Cicero by practical considerations, centering on both ecclesiastical and secular needs that their educational plans were meant to fill.

While the monks at St. Gall and Fulda continued to copy and study and teach Cicero, there occurred in the eleventh and twelfth centuries a shift both in the dominant centers of learning and in the perspectives brought to bear on Cicero's works. This second renaissance of Ciceronian studies produced the commentaries of William of Champeaux and Thierry of Chartres, which so clearly reveal a reading of Cicero through the eyes of Boethius and a consequent turn to abstract issues of definition and scope. This theoretical impulse eventually resulted in rhetoric's disenfranchisement in the business of inquiry evident in the distinctions of the Parisian scholastics.

As rhetoric declined in the universities, it continued to thrive in the centers of legal and notarial instruction, first in Pavia and Bologna and then north of the Alps, and in the Dominican and Franciscan *studia*. New genres of rhetorical literature begin to appear in the *artes praedicandi* and *dictaminis*, treatises with a strong pragmatic thrust designed to produce effective preachers and articulate administrators and advocates. In this pragmatic literature we see a tendency to range all modes of discourse under one rhetorical rubric. In these new genres, which persist up to the Renaissance, Cicero's presence is always felt even when it is not explicitly recognized.

FURTHER READING

J. Murphy's *Rhetoric in the Middle Ages* (Berkeley, 1974) is still the standard comprehensive treatment of the Latin medieval rhetorical tradition. Useful brief surveys can be found in R. McKeon's seminal "Rhetoric in the Middle Ages," *Speculum* 17 (1942), pp. 1–32; R. Bolgar's "The Teaching of Rhetoric in the Middle Ages," in *Rhetoric Revalued*, ed. B. Vickers (Binghamton, NY, 1982), pp. 79–86; and M. Camargo's chapter in *The Seven Liberal Arts in the Middle Ages*, ed. D. Wagner (Bloomington IN, 1983), pp. 96–124. Many of the texts discussed are to be found in Migne's *Patrologia Latina*, here cited by volume, page, and section (e.g., *PL* 164.800D). There are informative entries on virtually every writer mentioned in this chapter in *The Catholic Encyclopedia*.

On Augustine's life and career, see the thorough study by F. van der Meer, *Augustine the Bishop* (London, 1978); and on the social background, R. MacMullen, *Christianizing the Roman Empire* (New Haven, 1984). On the subject and structure of *De doctrina christiana*, see G. Press in *Augustinian Studies* 11 (1980), pp. 99–124. On Augustine's rhetoric, see W. R. Johnson, "Isocrates Flowering: The Rhetoric of Augustine," *Philosophy and Rhetoric* 9 (1976), pp. 217–231. On Boethius, see H. Patch, *The Tradition of Boethius* (New York, 1970). E. Stump has given us an excellent translation of and commentary on the *De differentiis topicis* (Ithaca, NY/London, 1978); and, more recently, of Boethius' commentary on the *Topica* of Cicero (Ithaca, NY/London, 1988). See also M. Leff, "Boethius' *De differentiis topicis, Book IV*" in *Medieval Eloquence*, ed. J. Murphy (Berkeley, 1978), pp. 3–24.

For traces of rhetorical training in the early Middle Ages, see G. Kennedy, "Forms and Functions of Latin Speech, 400–800" in *Medieval and Renaissance Studies* (North Carolina), n. 10 (1984), pp. 45–73. I have used W. S. Howell's text and translation of Alcuin's *Disputatio*, but have found L. Wallach's quite different reading of that work in *Alcuin and Charlemagne* (*Cornell Studies in Classical Philology* 32 [1959]) more persuasive.

The letters of Servatus Lupus (Lupus of Ferrières) are available in a translation by G. Regenos (The Hague, 1966). On Lupus' scholarship, see C. Beeson, *Lupus of Ferrières as Scribe and Text Critic* (Cambridge, MA, 1930). For Remi's commentary on Martianus Capella, see. C. Lutz, "The Commentary of Remigius of Auxerre on Martianus Capella," *Medieval Studies* 19 (1957), pp. 137–156.

On the tenth-century background, see H. Focillon, *The Year 1000* (New York, 1969). Gerbert's letters can be had in English in the version by H.

Lattin (*The Letters of Gerbert* [New York, 1961]). S. Jaffe's "Antiquity and Innovation in Notker's *Nova rhetorica*: The Doctrine of Invention," *Rhetorica* 3 (1985), pp. 165–181, is most informative. On Anselm of Besate, see B. Bennett, "The Significance of the *Rhetorimachia* of Anselm de Besate to the History of Rhetoric," *Rhetorica* 5 (1987), pp. 231–250.

The intellectual upheavals of the eleventh and twelfth centuries are lucidly discussed by T. Stiefel in her *Intellectual Revolution in Twelfth Century Europe* (London, 1985). On the teaching of rhetoric, see K. Fredborg, "The Scholastic Teaching of Rhetoric in the Middle Ages," *Cahiers de l'Institut du Moyen-âge Grec et Latin* (Copenhagen; hereafter *CIMAGL*) 55 (1987), pp. 85–105. On the cathedral schools, see P. Dronke, "New Approaches to the School of Chartres," *Anuario de Estudios Medievales* 6 (1969), pp. 117–140. On Otloh of St. Emmeram, see I. Resnick, "'Scientia liberalis,' Dialectics, and Otloh of St. Emmeram," *Révue Bénédictine* 97 (1987), pp. 241–252; and G. Evans, "Studium discendi: Otloh von St. Emmeram and the Seven Liberal Arts," *Recherches de théologie ancienne et médiévale* 44 (1977), pp. 29–54.

On Ciceronianism, see. J. Ward, "From Antiquity to the Renaissance: Glosses and Commentaries on Cicero's Rhetorica," in *Medieval Eloquence* (ed. Murphy, cited above), pp. 25–67. F. Quadlbauer's *Die antike Theorie der genera dicendi im lateinischen Mittelalter, Sitzungsberichte d. Österreichische Akademie der Wissenschaften* 241:2 (Vienna, 1962) is still the most thorough study of that subject to date. On Thierry of Chartres, see K. Fredborg, "The Commentary of Thierry of Chartres on Cicero's 'De inventione,'" *CIMAGL* 7 (1971), pp. 1–36; and, especially, her *Latin Rhetorical Commentaries by Thierry of Chartres, Pontifical Institute of Mediaeval Studies: Studies and Texts* 84 (Toronto, 1988). See also "The Uncompleted *Heptateuch* of Thierry of Chartres," by G. Evans in *History of Universities* 3 (1983), pp. 1–14. Developments in medieval jurisprudence and their connections with (Ciceronian) rhetoric are sketched by P. Stein in *Regulae Iuris: From Juristic Rules to Legal Maxims* (Edinburgh, 1966), pp. 134–179.

The literature on the various *artes* is extensive (see the citations in Murphy, *Rhetoric*, cited above). Among the more interesting on the *artes dictaminis*, see, e.g., G. Constable, "The Structure of Medieval Society according to the *Dictatores* of the Twelfth Century," in *Law, Church, and Society: Essays in Honor of Stephan Kuttner* (Philadelphia, 1977), pp. 235–267; R. Spence, "A Twelfth Century Treatise on the Writing of Privileges," *Bulletin of Medieval Canon Law* 12 (1982), pp. 51–63; and R. Witt, "Medieval 'Ars Dictaminis' and the Beginnings of Humanism: A New Construction of the Problem," *Renaissance Quarterly* 35 (1982), pp. 1–35. H. Caplan's "Classical Rhetoric and the Medieval Theory of Preaching," *Classical Philology* 28 (1933), pp. 73–96, is still important. On all aspects of preaching and the *artes praedicandi*, see J. Longère, *La prédication médiévale* (Paris, 1983), which provides an overview and an enormous bibliography. L.-J. Bataillon's "Approaches to the Study of Medieval Sermons," *Leeds Studies in English*, n.s. 11 (1980), pp. 19–35, and, most recently, D.

D'Avray's *The Preaching of the Friars* are also necessary reading. For further study of the *artes poetriae*, see the extensive bibliography in P. Klopsch, *Einführung in die Dichtungslehren des lateinischen Mittelalters* (Darmstadt, 1980), pp. 167ff. D. Kelly's "The Scope of the Treatment of Composition in Twelfth- and Thirteenth-Century Arts of Poetry," *Speculum* 41 (1966), pp. 261–78, is commendable reading.

NOTES

1. For various ways of organizing the history of rhetoric in the Latin Middle Ages, see Murphy, *Rhetoric in the Middle Ages*, and R. McKeon (both cited in Further Reading).
2. The letter described is *Ep.* 10 in the Loeb edition of Augustine's letters, ed. J. Baxter (London, 1930), pp. 69–91.
3. On the social background, see MacMullen (cited in Further Reading).
4. I have used the translation of *De catechizandis rudibus* by J. Christopher (*Catholic University of America Patristic Studies* 8 [Washington, 1926]). For *De doctrina christiana*, see the translation by D. Robertson (Library of Liberal Arts edition [Indianapolis, 1958]). The best available text is that of J. Martin in the *Corpus christianorum* edition, vol. 32 (Turnhout, 1962).
5. On the career of Boethius, see Patch (in Further Reading). I have used the Migne text of *De differentiis topicis* IV (*PL* 64, col. 1174Cff.). See also the work of E. Stump (cited in Further Reading).
6. On this tension, see McKeon and Camargo (both as cited in Further Reading).
7. On Cassiodorus and his influence, see Murphy, *Rhetoric* 64ff., with notes; on Bede, ibid. 74ff. For traces of the persistence of rhetorical training, see Kennedy, "Forms and Functions" (cited in Further Reading).
8. On Alcuin, see Wallach (cited in Further Reading). I have used the text of the *Disputatio* in K. Halm, *Rhetores latini minores* (Leipzig, 1963), pp. 532–550 (hereafter, Halm), and cite by line as in the edition and translation by W. S. Howell.
9. For an account of Frankish law and procedure, see S. Dill, *Roman Society in Gaul in the Merovingian Period* (London, 1926), pp. 40ff. As in the Lombard system, Frankish procedure substituted trial by oath or ordeal for trial by debate. On the rationality of this procedure, see C. Radding, *A World Made by Men: Cognition and Society 400–1200* (Chapel Hill, 1985), chapter 1.
10. Alcuin's *"Dialectica"* (see *PL* 101.949A–74C)—also a dialogue between "Alcuin" and "Charlemagne" and evidently meant to be read along with the *Disputatio*—shows few traces of anything that might be described as Boethian influence.
11. On activities at St. Gall, see L. de Rijk, "On the Curriculum of the Arts of the Trivium at St. Gall from c. 850–c. 1000," *Vivarium* 1 (1963), pp. 35–86. For Cicero's *De inventione* alone, the numbers are impressive. See R. Mattmann's inventory in *Studie zur handschriftlichen Überlieferung von Ciceros "De inventione"* (Freiburg, 1975), pp. 174ff.
12. On Hrabanus, see Murphy, *Rhetoric*, pp. 82ff. I have used the Knoepfler edition of *De institutione clericorum* (Munich, 1900).
13. These *capitulae* can be found in *Monumenta germania historia. Leges* 2:1, ed.

Boretus (Hanover, 1883), pp. 56ff. See also *Neuf capitulaires de Charlemagne concernant son oeuvre réformatrice par les "missi,"* ed. C. LeClercq (Milan, 1968).

14. On Martianus' influence, see Murphy, *Rhetoric* 43ff. and Lutz (both cited in Further Reading).

15. Namely, Caesar Baronius in the sixteenth century, cited by L. Wallach in "Education and Culture in the Tenth Century," *Medievalia et humanistica* 9 (1955), p. 18. In Hesiod, the ages of iron and lead mark a decline from those of gold and silver.

16. On Gerbert, see Focillon (cited in Further Reading), pp. 127ff. I have used the edition of Gerbert's letters by J. Havet in *Collection de textes pour servir à l'étude et à l'enseignement de l'histoire* 6 (Paris, 1889). These are also available in English, thanks to Prof. Lattin (see Further Reading).

17. For Notker, I have used the text in *Die Schriften Notkers und seiner Schule*, ed. P. Piper (Freiburg/Tübingen, 1882), pp. 645ff. On the text of the *Nova rhetorica* and Notker's career, see Jaffe (cited in Further Reading).

18. Passage quoted by Jaffe, p. 178.

19. The text of Anselm's *Rhetorimachia* can be found in *Gunzo epistola ad Augienses und Anselm von Besate Rhetorimachia, MGH Scriptores* 2, ed. K. Manitius (Weimar, 1958), pp. 95–183. On Manegold, see Ward (cited in Further Reading) and M. Dickey, "Some Commentaries on the *De inventione* and *Ad Herennium* of the Eleventh and Early Twelfth Centuries," *Mediaeval and Renaissance Studies* (London) 6 (1968), pp. 1–41.

20. The text of Thierry's commentary was first published by W. Suringar in *Historia critica scholastarum latinorum* (Leyden, 1834), pp. 213–253. On this commentary, see Fredborg, "Thierry" (cited in Further Reading) and J. Ward, "The Date of the Commentary on Cicero's *De inventione* by Thierry of Chartres and the Cornifician Attack on the Liberal Arts," *Viator* 3 (1972), pp. 219–274.

21. On the *artes*, see Murphy, *Rhetoric*, chapters 4–6; and the works cited in Further Reading.

22. I have used the texts in L. Rockinger's *Briefsteller und Formelbücher des eilften bis vierzehnten Jahrhunderts*. Quellen und Erörterungen zur bayerischen und deutschen Geschichte 9 (Munich, 1863; rpt. New York, 1961). The *Rationes dictandi* can be had in English (tr. J. Murphy) in *Three Medieval Rhetorical Arts*, ed. J. Murphy (Berkeley, 1971), pp. 1–25.

23. Text in Fredborg, "Scholastic Teaching" (cited in Further Reading), pp. 89f. (Latin text in *PL* 189.1254B–1255C).

24. Texts of the *artes praedicandi* can be found in T. Charland, *Artes praedicandi: Contribution à l'histoire de la Rhétorique au moyen âge*. Publications de l'Institute d'Etudes Médiévales d'Ottawa 7 (Paris/Ottawa, 1936). The text of William of Auvergne's *De arte predicandi* can be found in A. DePoorter, "Un manuel de prédication médiévale," *Revue néo-scolastique de philosophie* 25 (1923). pp. 196ff. The *Ars* of Raymond Llull can be found in *Raimundi Lulli opera latina* 118. *Liber de predicatione*, ed. F. Stegmüller (Majorca, 1961), pp. 139–407. Robert de Basevorn's *Forma praedicandi* (tr. L. Krul) can be read in English in Murphy, *Three Medieval Rhetorical Arts*, pp. 109–215.

25. On the theory of sermon composition, see Charland, pp. 109ff. Organization in threes, contrary to Charland, predates the thirteenth century. See J. Leclercq, "Sur la charactère littéraire des sermons de saint Bernard [of Clairvaux]," *Recueil d'études sur saint Bernard et ses ecrits* 3 (Rome, 1969), pp. 185ff.

26. See William of Auvergne's *De arte*, see De Poorter, p. 196. For Llull's "calculus,"

see Stegmüller, pp. 143ff.
27. Most of the texts of these *artes poetriae* can be found in E. Faral, *Les arts poétiques du XIIe et du XIIIe siècles*, Bibliothèque de l'école des hautes études, fasc. 238 (Paris, 1924; rpt. Paris, 1958). The work of John of Garland is available in English, trans. T. Lawler in *The Parisiana poetria of John of Garland* (New Haven, 1974). Matthew of Vendôme's *Ars* has been translated by R. Parr in *Mediaeval Philosophical Texts in Translation* n. 28 (Milwaukee, 1981). Parr's introduction is a good brief survey.
28. Geoffrey's *Documentum* has also been translated by R. Parr in n. 17 (Milwaukee, 1968) of the series cited above.
29. On the survival of the *Rhetoric*, see Murphy, *Rhetoric*, pp. 94ff.

AUGUSTINE, *DE DOCTRINA CHRISTIANA*, BOOK 4

(References to paragraph numbers in Robertson translation.)

Book 4. Setting forth what has been understood, that is, in Part II.
  A. Introduction (1–5) Truth ought to be armed with eloquence, which can, but needn't, be learned from precepts.
  B. [General characteristics of a Christian speaker] (6–26) The teacher must both teach what is right and correct what is wrong; must instruct, move, and conciliate at the appropriate times in his exordium, narration, proof, and peroration.
    1. Wisdom and eloquence (7–21) Wisdom consists in understanding Scripture (8); several examples (11–21).
    2. Clarity (22–25) It is of paramount importance to make ourselves understood, even at the expense of elegance.
    3. Pleasantness (26) The preacher must make the subject appealing.
  C. [Offices of the speaker] (27–33)
    1. (27–28) Organic relationship among three offices
    2. (28–33) We must not only convey truths but persuade audiences to act accordingly.
  D. [Style] (34–58) The three offices are related to three styles: subdued, moderate, and grand.
    1. The three styles are appropriate to different subjects (35–37).
    2. Examples from Scripture and the Fathers (38–51).
    3. Styles should be blended for maximum effect (52–58).
  E. [Moral requisites of the Christian speaker] (59–63) If you cannot be both virtuous and eloquent, you should prefer speaking wisely to speaking eloquently.
  F. Conclusion (64)

ALCUIN, *DISPUTATIO DE RHETORICA*

(Text is based on Halm, 532–550; line numbers are according to Howell.)

  I. Prologue
    A. Verse *propositio* (lines 1–8)
    B. Dramatic introduction (9–34)

II. Preliminary material
   A. The origin of rhetoric (31–51)
   B. The ends and concerns of rhetoric (52–65)
   C. Divisions and definitions (66–84)
   D. The three kinds of *causae* (85–104)
III. *Loci* and *status causarum*
   A. The seven *circumstantiae*: person, deed, time, etc. (105–117)
   B. Doctrine of *status*: conjectural, definitive, etc. (118–214)
   C. The question, reason, point to be judged, etc. (215–232)
   D. The qualitative *status* (233–398)
      1. Practical (*status negotialis*) (240–255)
      2. Juridical (*status iuridicalis*) (256–398)
[IV.] The nature of legal proceedings, arrangement of courtroom (399–465)
   V. The six parts of a speech (466–935)
   A. Exordium (473–535)
   B. Narration (536–562)
   C. Partition (563–581)
   D. Proof (582–830)
      1. Definitions (592–644)
      2. Strategies (645–684)
      3. Arguments about events (685–704)
      4. Argumentation itself (705–830)
   E. Refutation (835–869)
   F. Conclusion (870–935)
[VI.] The difference between rhetoric and sophistic (936–970)
VII. Arrangement (971–985)
VIII. Style (986–1076)
   IX. Memory (1077–1087)
   X. Delivery (1088–1175)
[XI.] The treatise on virtues (1176–1368)

NOTKER LABEO, *NOVA RHETORICA*

(Outline is based on text in Piper, pp. 645–684.)

Part One (pp. 645–662)
   A. As regards the *materia*
      1. On the *materia* of rhetoric in general (645–646)
      2. The three kinds of *causae* (646)
      3. All three divided into
         a. *Status legales* (dealing with written documents) (647)
         b. *Status rationales* (dealing with facts) (647–648)
            i. The subdivisions of the *status qualitatis* (648)
            ii. The sources of *status* (648–649)
      4. The nature of rhetoric itself and the parts of a speech (650–651)

WILLIAM OF AUVERGNE, *DE ARTE PRAEDICANDI*

(Line numbers are according to text published by De Poorter.)

---

* All of the following are modes of amplification.

8. Vehement detestation of vice (27)
9. Commendation and praise of virtues (19)
10. Exemplification (19)
11. Promise of joys and threat of punishment (88)
12. Distinctions (35)
13. Divisions (7)
14. Derivations and combinations (24)
15. Interpretation (28)
16. Definition (20)
17. Relations (26)
18. Praise of the words used (with examples, 62)

ROBERT DE BASEVORN, *FORMA PRAEDICANDI*

(Section numbers are from Charland's *Artes praedicandi.*)

[Introductory material]
1–12. Of preaching and preachers
13–14. Wisdom and eloquence; preview of work
15–23. Invention of The Theme; various modes
24–25. Winning over the audience; necessity of prayer
    26–30. Digression on invention
31–32. Introduction
33–35. Division; statement of parts of sermon
    36–38. Digression on Parisians vs. Oxonians
39. Amplification
    40. Digression on Oxonian preaching
[Modes of amplification]
41. Transition
42. Correspondence
43. Congruence of correspondence
44. Circuitous development
45. Convolution
46. Recapitulation
47. Concluding the sermon
    48. Digression on modes of invention
49–50. Types of variation; concluding remarks

CHAPTER 5

Rhetoric and Renaissance Humanism

The apparent decline of rhetoric during the Middle Ages was reversed during the Renaissance, when rhetoric, mainly because of the rise of humanism, achieved an importance that is difficult to overestimate. *Humanism* is not easy to define, for there are various claims as to what it means. For some, it is a lofty ideal, according to which human intellect reigns supreme in the universe. For others, it is merely an episode in the history of education, in which newly available materials for study replaced the older ones. Moreover, figures as diverse as Lorenzo Valla, Erasmus, and John Calvin have all been identified as humanists, despite crucial differences in outlook and purpose that set them widely apart from one another. We shall examine those differences, insofar as they relate to the history of rhetoric, in this chapter, but we need first to get a sense of some common denominators that underlie the apparent diversity, some basic attitudes that characterize humanism as a whole.

One common denominator that serves to make humanism intelligible is the keen interest in Classical texts that emerged during the Renaissance, particularly in the newly available texts of works by Cicero and Quintilian and, a little later, of works by Greek writers unknown in the West until that time. While Renaissance scholars were fascinated by anything Classical and had particular esteem for historians such as Livy and Tacitus and for the *Lives* of Plutarch, they seem to have valued rhetorical works most of all. This interest in rhetoric, in true eloquence, may be seen as a second common denominator. The eloquence these scholars sought to master was not an empty pomposity of language or the extravagant artifice sometimes associated with rhetoric, but the harmonious union of wisdom and style whose aim was to guide men toward civic virtue, not to mislead them for the sake of winning the day. This ideal of eloquence was counterposed by Renaissance humanists to the scholasticism of the Middle Ages, which they criticized on aesthetic grounds and, more important, for its concentration on the abstract and merely intellectual and its consequent failure to touch on essential matters of relevance to human life. That this perception of scholasticism may have been distorted is immaterial. That is the way in which scholars of the Renaissance saw it. In connection with this, we can point to another common denominator, the conviction that knowledge ought to serve practical ends. Human learning ought to have some utility for life; education should instruct not only the intellect but also the will; and the only effective means of conveying truth is by persuasion and eloquent discussion, not by logical demonstration. In sum, what holds the notions of humanism together is, in large part, its preoccupation with rhetoric—more particularly, with rhetoric conceived, as it was by Cicero, as political wisdom. The next question is, Why was rhetoric seen to be so important?

The familiar picture of the Renaissance as an age of erudition and eloquence, an age in which there emerged a sort of enlightened and committed stance toward the life of the mind, is factual enough, but unbalanced. Perhaps the Renaissance was all of those things, but it was also an age with a darker side, and this darker side must be taken into account if we expect to understand why rhetoric was accorded such a high status among humanists. The Renaissance was, to begin with, a violent and turbulent age. The primary occupation of the common and uneducated man in a time when the rich and literate comprised just a tiny fraction of the population was not farming or commerce, but fighting. The list of wars, skirmishes, invasions, and campaigns that occurred during the Renaissance would be very long indeed. In some ways, the opening scene from *Romeo and Juliet* is a good representative anecdote for the period. Even the Pope commanded a large army. Second, the Renaissance was an age of disturbing uncertainty, and not just among intellectuals who perceived the bankruptcy of much traditional thinking. The whole picture of the world was changed by the discoveries of the great explorers and conquerors of the age. The effects of those discoveries, like the effects of the new theories of Copernicus and Kepler about the shape of the solar system, were far more pervasive than the shock of discovery intellectuals experienced with the influx of new texts. Violence and uncertainty, finally, came to a head late in the Renaissance in the religious conflicts that the Reformation brought about, conflicts that, paradoxically, sought to put an end to uncertainty, both intellectual and political, by force.

If it is nothing else, rhetoric is an alternative to the use of force, as it is the art *par excellence* of persuasion in place of coercion, of deliberation by examination of alternatives in place of autocracy. As Cicero had observed in his *De inventione*, rhetoric is the *moderatrix* of force, which is "a very untrustworthy servant." Rhetoric, too, provides not so much an alternative to uncertainty as a way of managing it, of employing the fact of uncertainty for constructive ends by providing a mode of analysis and judgment suited to the resolution of problems of fact and of action. This aspect of rhetoric emerges not only from the idealistic pronouncements of the scholar-statesmen of the time (Salutati, for instance) but from the fact that even scientists (Galileo, among others) turned to its methods and from the applications of rhetoric in commerce, as the roots of double-entry bookkeeping can be traced to rhetoric. Finally, rhetoric pervades the disputations aroused by the actions of the great reformers (Luther, Calvin) and counterreformers (Erasmus, the Jesuits) alike. In the absence of consensus on established meanings in Scripture, and in the interests of minimizing or avoiding violence, both parties availed themselves of the resources provided by rhetoric.

With this backdrop in view, then, we turn to a brief account of the history of rhetoric in the Renaissance, an account that is of necessity brief and incomplete but that may nevertheless provide a starting point for more detailed study. In this chapter, accordingly, we will examine first the impact of the transmission of new texts with a bearing on the Renaissance understanding of rhetoric and then move on to an account of the critical roles rhetoric played in Renaissance intellectual history up to the end of the sixteenth century.

NEW TEXTS, OLD RHETORICS

There are two parts to the story of new influences on Renaissance humanism. The first concerns the discoveries in the fourteenth and fifteenth centuries of texts of works previously known only in part and of works previously unread, although their existence had been reported. The second concerns the transmission of Greek rhetorical works previously unknown in the Latin West, first in pieces, and in translation, by George Trebizond, and later in the form of manuscripts of Greek works collected in Italian libraries, published by the great Venetian printer Aldo Manuzio and subsequently disseminated all over Europe.

As we saw in Chapter 4, rhetorical works by Cicero and Quintilian had been in circulation throughout the Middle Ages. The *De inventione* of Cicero and the *Rhetorica ad Herennium* attributed to Cicero continued to exercise important influence, both directly and indirectly, over a thousand-year period. Quintilian's *Institutes* was also known but was not as influential, since Quintilian was considered nothing more than an imitator of Cicero. His work, additionally, was known only in part, as the majority of medieval copies of the *Institutes* were full of *lacunae* so large as to render the work almost incoherent. Of Cicero's *Brutus* and *Orator*, two major treatises on style, nothing was known. The *De oratore*, like the *Institutes*, was known only in parts. None of Cicero's speeches were known except indirectly; his philosophical works were familiar to medieval readers only in the form of extracts in *florilegia*; and no one had even suspected that a large body of Cicero's correspondence to his friends was still extant.

Hence the discoveries by Petrarch (1303–74) of manuscripts containing two speeches by Cicero and of the corpus of his correspondence with Atticus;

by Coluccio Salutati (1331–1406) of copies of Cicero's correspondence with various friends and associates; and by Poggio Bracciolini (1380–1459) of two new speeches (the *Pro Roscio* and the *Pro Murena*)—all of these caused a great deal of excitement among Italian humanists. For the first time, they were able to see a fleshed-out picture of the great Roman orator and for the first time they were exposed directly to his political and philosophical ideas, at the core of which was the notion of the orator who was both a philosopher and a statesman. For the first time, they were able to read Cicero's precepts for true eloquence and obtain a glimpse of the importance in rhetoric of *actio*, not simply of the schemas transmitted by Cicero's scholastic commentators.

Two other discoveries during this period were of major importance. The first was the discovery claimed by Poggio of the complete text of Quintilian's *Institutes* in 1416 at the monastery of St. Gall. Poggio, a papal secretary, had stopped there en route to the Council of Constance, where the papal court had moved in 1414. Poggio copied the entire work (in great haste) and brought it back with him to Italy, where his version was copied and distributed among a large group of scholars. Some 40 manuscripts of the St. Gall version of the *Institutes*, all copied between 1418 and 1489, including the personal annotated copy of Lorenzo Valla, are extant. This number probably represents only a portion of the total number of manuscripts that were then in circulation. Later, with the introduction of movable type, 43 editions of the *Institutes* were produced between 1470 and 1539. The demand, in other words, was enormous.

The new version contained the parts of the work that had been missing in the manuscripts previously available—important parts, including the preface and opening chapter of Book One, the entire section on figures of thought in Book Nine, and the last half of Book Twelve. Scholars were now able to appreciate and contemplate the most comprehensive treatment of rhetoric ever composed. Quintilian's reputation was considerably enhanced, and such key notions as that of the core relation between *virtus* and eloquence and that of the universal range of rhetoric took on a new significance. Together with the new picture of rhetoric as actually practiced, which the Renaissance humanists were able to get from the newly discovered speeches of Cicero, the *Institutes* provided them with new inspiration and increased motivation for total devotion to the study of Roman rhetoric.

The discovery of the complete text of Cicero's *De oratore* was no less influential. The manuscript of this work was found along with copies of *Orator* and *Brutus* by Gerardo Landriani, bishop of Lodi (just outside of Milan) in the cathedral cellar. Landriani was unable to decipher it, so he passed it on to a Milanese humanist, Giovanni Omodi. Omodi was also unable to make it out, so he gave it over to skilled paleographer, Cosmas Cremonensis, who painstakingly transcribed two copies of the manuscripts (copying even the errors), one for the bishop and one for himself. As was the case with Quintilian's *Institutes*, scholars eagerly ordered copies of the *De oratore* for their own libraries, and the manuscripts in Cosmas' possession were transcribed over and over. *De oratore* was important to its Renaissance readers because now, for the first time, they were able to encounter a coherent and comprehensive treatment of rhetoric by Cicero himself, a treatment unlike any they had known before. Unlike the *Ad Herennium*, moreover, the *De oratore* was a beautifully composed dialogue in which the interlocutors not only set out the standard parts of the art but discuss and debate their nature and significance, always taking care to root the importance of rhetoric in practical affairs and not just in theoretical consistency. Scholars found inspiration in a treatise on rhetoric that was not dry and plodding (as both *De inventione* and the *Ad Herennium* tend to be) but that exhibited wit and *suavitas* ("charm") and portrayed "real" orators comparing and defending their respective positions, engaging in *controversia*, and not simply dogmatizing.

The humanist's enthusiasm for Quintilian and Cicero was due, in large part, to the political conditions that obtained in Florence and elsewhere on the Italian peninsula. Since the late thirteenth century, Florence has been a republic governed by a senate and presided over by a chancellor. The Florentine republic was, at least in theory, a new version of the old Roman republic. At the beginning, Florentine politicians and scholars had only the sketchiest idea of what such a system entailed, except that they knew that rhetoric was always a conspicuous part of it. Cicero taught two important lessons: that the primary duty of man is action and that the *vita activa* does not distract one from one's intellectual powers but stimulates them. Petrarch's "face to face" encounter with Cicero's career, as it could be glimpsed in Cicero's letters, and Salutati's later on (in 1392), gave new depth to their perception of the old republic and new inspiration, a fervid desire to realize the old republican ideal and a concrete exemplum of the statesman-orator.

Most of those Florentines who could by virtue of their education and standing call themselves "humanists" (although, we might note, they would not have used that term) were not just scholars but politically active men. Many of them were professional orators who were esteemed because they advocated a code of civic duty, gave education a genuine relevance to political life, and were themselves accomplished speakers, as close as could be imagined to Quintilian's *vir bonus dicendi peritus*. Some of the more famous among them—Salutati, Bruni, and Lorenzo Valla, for instance—served long terms as chancellor of the republic. All were buried at state expense and given lavish funerals at which their eloquence and consequent contribution to the reputation of the city were praised publicly. Because of their political commitments, in short, Florentines took their rhetoric very seriously.

The impact of the new texts on Renaissance scholars can also be seen working on a more properly philosophical level. The new picture of Cicero allowed Renaissance humanists finally to discard the medieval version that held up for admiration not Cicero's politics and eloquence but his flight from active life, a view that prevailed well into the thirteenth century. It was now possible to understand more clearly what *philosophia* implied to Cicero: a liberal education, the possession of technical skills that made the active life feasible, and good character. The fundamental bias of such a view is ethical, not speculative. Hence, as Salutati observed in his *De nobilitate* (ch. 23), the good is to be more highly valued than the merely true, virtue preferred over knowledge, the will over the intellect, and thus rhetoric over philosophy and eloquence over wisdom.

Cicero had provided some clues as to the relationship between rhetorical training and political virtue in the newly discovered sections of Book 3 of the *De oratore*. But that relationship continued to be problematic—could such training *guarantee* wisdom?—as did that between rhetoric and philosophy. The acquisition of the new text of Quintilian, however, made it possible to clarify those relationships as it both provided a comprehensive, coherent curriculum and subsumed all knowledge to rhetoric, which, Quintilian taught, embraces everything that concerns the human being. These issues are at the heart of Lorenzo Valla's work, and Valla's intimate understanding of Quintilian explains both his preoccupation with eloquence and his critique of the old philosophy in two of his most famous works, the *Elegantiae linguae latinae* and his *Disputationes dialecticae*.

In short, these new discoveries provided a firm philosophical basis for the celebration of eloquence, and gave new meaning to the slogan long familiar to humanists from Cicero's *De partitione oratoria*: *nihil...est aliud eloquentia nisi copiose loquens sapientia*, "Eloquence is nothing other than wisdom speaking copiously." The doctrines of Quintilian prepared the ground for Valla's repudiation of abstract theory and made it possible to integrate the resources of eloquence with the political preoccupations and exigencies of the day.

TREBIZOND AND THE ALDINE *RHETORES GRAECI*

The second part of the story of new influences on Renaissance rhetoric is that of the infiltration of Greek rhetorics into the universities and studies of Western scholars. This, in turn, occurred in two stages, the first George of Trebizond's *Rhetoricorum libri quinque* and the second the acquisition and eventual publication by Aldo Manuzio of manuscripts of the Greek authors themselves—in particular, of Aristotle's *Rhetoric* and of the works of Hermogenes, both for the first time.

George Trebizond (Trapezuntius) was born in Crete in 1395. Of his early years not much is known, but it is obvious that he received an excellent education in grammar and rhetoric, probably at Candia from the renowned master John Simeonachis. In 1416, he traveled to Venice at the invitation of the eminent humanist Francesco Barbaro, a friend of Simeonachis, and greatly impressed scholars there. He never returned to Crete, but spent the rest of his life in Italy. By 1421, Trebizond had mastered Latin and become thoroughly familiar with the works of Cicero. During his rather turbulent lifetime, he held various academic positions (at Padua, Florence, and elsewhere) and served under a number of popes, including Eugenius IV, who appointed him a member of the papal delegation to the Council of Florence in 1439. Trebizond was an ambitious man, a fierce competitor (as one had to be) among the scholars of his day, somtimes choleric (he was once jailed for punching Poggio Bracciolini on a street corner in Rome), and, like his Italian counterparts, a prolific writer and translator. He died in Rome in 1472 or 1473.

Trebizond's most important contribution to the history of rhetoric is his *Rhetoricorum libri quinque* (hereafter, *RLV*), certainly the most comprehensive treatment of rhetoric in the Renaissance, possibly of all time.[1] In fact, Trebizond intended that *RLV* should displace Quintilian's *Institutes* as the most comprehensive text on the subject. Although he follows Quintilian on some matters, his conception of rhetoric was, as he makes clear in the preface to the book, devoid of the requirement that the orator be a good man, in the moral sense. Rhetoric was, rather, a pragmatic political art indifferent to morality. The chief contribution Trebizond made in *RLV*, however, was the assimilation of Hermogenes into the Latin rhetorical tradition.

Aside from the sixth-century Latin translation by Priscian of his *Progymnasmata*, the works of Hermogenes were completely unknown in the West. His name and reputation were known to some Western scholars (although they often confused him with others of the same name), but his works were inaccessible until Greek scholars like Trebizond found their ways to the centers of European learning in Italy and, eventually, north of the Alps.

We shall have more to say about Trebizond's role in introducing Hermogenes to the West later. Here we will sketch the contents of *RLV* in order to convey some idea of the book's comprehensiveness and of the contributions made in assimilating Hermogenean doctrine into what Trebizond conceived of as a basically Ciceronian framework.

Book One begins with an echo of Cicero: *Rhetorica est civilis scientia*, "Rhetoric is a civil science," and goes on to celebrate it as the most illustrious and necessary of the arts. There follows a fairly standard treatment of the three kinds of speeches—juridical, deliberative, and demonstrative—and of the duties of the orator. His discussions draw heavily on Cicero and Quintilian (as would have been obvious to his Western readers), but Trebizond makes no reference to Quintilian. These in turn are followed by some detailed remarks on each of the five standard parts of a speech, also based on Cicero but augmented by some material from Hermogenes' *On Invention* on the subdivisions of the exordium. Trebizond finishes this book with a sketch of the different staseis, using the dichotomous division technique of Hermogenes (see, for instance, p. 78).

Book Two is, essentially, a paraphrase of Hermogenes' *On Staseis* grafted on to standard treatment of the subject in Latin sources. *On Staseis* was unknown to Trebizond's readers. As we have seen, the treatment of stasis by Hermogenes employs dichotomous division, making for clear organization and a certain theoretical elegance. Trebizond was evidently proud of his exposition of stasis theory in *RLV*, as he later boasted in his defense of it addressed to Guarino that he had introduced order where his predecessors had left chaos.

Book Three is devoted to the subject of argumentation, and the fullness of his discussion is almost staggering. It is also interesting in that it minimizes the role of syllogistic reasoning (which he treats in another treatise, on dialectic) almost to the vanishing point, something we might expect from the definition he gives of argumentation (p. 246): *est enim argumentatio argumenti per orationem explicatio, quae sine ornamento fieri non potest*, "Argumentation is the explication of an argument through discourse, which [explication] without embellishment cannot exist." The first part of this definition is rather common; the second is not, but is fully in keeping with a Hermogenean perspective (and justified finally in the last book of *RLV*, as we shall see). The bulk of Book Three consists of an exhaustive listing, with examples, of rhetorical places (*loci*). There are, he explains, ten principal modes of argumentation. These he draws from Cicero's *De inventione*, the *Ad Herennium*, and Hermogenes' *On Invention*. There are also, he continues, those secondary *loci* that are limited to special fields—and almost unlimited therefore in quantity. Next, Trebizond runs through some 35 dialectical places (genus, species, property, and the others), some of which are subdivided further (as, for instance, "cause" is divided into "formal," "material," "efficient," and "final"). Trebizond continues by listing the 7 standard "circumstances" (*peristaseis*) of person and deed, each of which can be treated using all 10 principal modes, along with the secondary modes and all of the dialectical *loci*! He then goes on to enumerate and discuss 15 methods of confutation; lists over 30 commonplaces for the peroration, some, again, subdivided further (9 are given for *indignatio*); and records 15 "solutions," or ways of weaseling out of tight spots. For all of these, Trebizond draws on Hermogenes, as well as on Cicero and Quintilian (who is, again, not cited). The result of all this is a virtual engine for generating discourse, discourse that, in the absence of situational constraints, could very well become endless as, for instance, any and all of the *peristaseis* could be amplified by any and all of the 35 dialectical places and treated in any of the "modes," both primary and secondary. As a resource for invention, therefore, Trebizond's system is almost infinitely productive.

Book Four contains Trebizond's discussions of deliberative and demonstrative oratory. These discussions make it clear that he is not yet finished with his topical treasures, for he details 31 places proper to deliberative rhetoric, for instance. He then goes on to the subject of arrangement (following Hermogenes' *On Invention*), memory, and delivery (drawing on Quintilian, but once again neglecting to cite him).

Book five, finally, concerns *elocutio*, the most artistic and the most noble part of the art of rhetoric. Memory and delivery, Tebizond points out, are gifts of nature, matters of talent more than of learning. Skill in invention and arrangement can be acquired through experience alone, as, indeed, must have been the case with the ancient orators. But only from instruction by one who knows the art of rhetoric can one learn eloquence, the most eminent gift given to humankind, since it is not rhetoric in general but style in particular that is peculiar to humankind, and thus the perfection of humankind. It is, therefore, eloquence that makes rhetoric the true *ars humanitatis* (p. 457). What follows is a list of figures (drawn mainly from the *Ad Herennium*) with examples from both Greek and Latin authors; a discussion of composition; and, at the end, an introduction to the Hermogenean system of "ideas" of style, to which no one in the West had up to that time been exposed.

Trebizond's achievement in *RLV* is impressive, but there is so much in his book that his discussions can be at times bewildering. If, for instance, the ancients could compare the store of *loci* to a large mansion with many rooms or to a grove of trees where one might acquire the "timber" needed in forensic or political debate, Trebizond's topical system at times more resembles a maze or a jungle. The confusions that can arise from such comprehensive treatment as we see in *RLV* set the stage for later reforms by Agricola and Ramus, who set about the task of simplifying matters, as we shall see later in this chapter.

Another aspect of *RLV* deserves comment because it bears on the nature of the transmission of Hermogenean doctrine to the West. Much of what was new to Trebizond's audience can be attributed to his command of the Greek tradition of which his readers were ignorant, particularly Hermogenes and the commentaries on his works. Trebizond is careful to demonstrate his command of that tradition by identifying himself clearly as a Greek and by introducing his readers to Greek technical terminology, which would have been new to them. "These things *we* call in Greek...," he says repeatedly, and then gives the Greek term. But Trebizond actually mentions Hermogenes only twice: once in Book One at the beginning of his discussion of the qualitative stasis; and again in Book Five, where he cites Hermogenes' *On Ideas* explicitly. In other words, Trebizond did pass on to his Western colleagues a good bit of Hermogenes, as our sketch of the contents of *RLV* shows; but they did not know it was Hermogenes. They cannot have avoided the impression that Trebizond himself was the source of all that new material. Granted, Renaissance scholarly conventions were not very strict about acknowledging one's sources. But the impression left by Trebizond was perhaps more self-serving than one might have tolerated even then. Trebizond, as we have noted, was an ambitious man. The extent of his ambition might be gauged, it would seem, by his apparent unwillingness to share the credit with his most important source, Hermogenes of Tarsus.

The appearance of editions and translations of Hermogenes under his name eventually rendered *RLV* virtually superfluous, although in spite of that the book continued to be found useful as a compendium well after 1600. Erasmus was familiar with it (and appears to have caught Trebizond out, one might add),[2] Nizolius (1488–1567) admired it greatly, and it was the source for a good deal of sixteenth-century literary criticism. Soon after Trebizond's death, however, the actual texts of Hermogenes, along with the works of other Greek rhetoricians from late antiquity and Byzantium, became widely available. The one who made them widely available was the great Venetian printer and patron of the arts Aldo Manuzio.

Mention of Manuzio brings us to the second stage of the transmission of Greek rhetorics to Western Europe. The fall of Constantinople to the Turks in 1453 was the occasion for many Greek scholars to flee to the South of Greece, to Corfu, and above all to Crete, where, as we saw, there was an established center of learning at Candia. Many of these scholars eventually made their way to Italy, where, like Trebizond before them, they had been invited by various patrons of learning—Cardinal Bessarion and Lorenzo de Medici among others, as well as Manuzio himself. There was at this time a large demand in Italy for Greek manuscripts, due partly to the desires of people like the Medici to assemble impressive libraries and partly also, no doubt, to the Council of Florence, where prolonged contact and disputation with the Greek delegation had convinced Westerners that there was much to be learned from the East. Little did they know how much.

Refugee Greek scholars played a crucial role in promoting Greek studies in Europe, if only because they were the only ones qualified to teach Greek and produce the grammars necessary for systematic study of the language. Some, such as Janos Laskaris, Musurus, and Jerome Aleander, were commissioned to travel to the East to collect manuscripts. Among the manuscripts brought back by Laskaris were various collections of rhetorical texts that contained not only the works attributed to Hermogenes but Aphthonius' *Progymnasmata*, Menander Rhetor's *On the Divisions of Epideictic*, and various treatises on figures and tropes as well. Manuscripts such as these fell into the hands of Manuzio, and he used them as the basis of his 1508 edition of *Rhetores graeci*, a landmark in the dissemination of the Greek rhetorical tradition throughout Europe. Within a few years after its publication, Manuzio also produced an edition of the canonical Attic orators: Demosthenes, Isocrates, and the rest. Western scholars could now read for themselves what the Greek rhetorical treatises had to say, and also to experience the eloquence those treatises were concerned with.

The development of the printing trade in the late fifteenth and early sixteenth centuries made possible a dissemination of information much faster and more extensive (both geographically and quantitatively) than anyone could have imagined before then. Manuzio was not only the first to publish the Greek rhetoricians, among many other Greek authors; he was by far the most prolific and influential publisher of the time. In a 35-year period, the Aldine press produced first editions of more than ninety Classical and post-Classical Greek writers. Recent investigations have determined that the average Aldine press run was about one thousand copies, and that the total output of the Aldine press of Greek and Latin works may have exceeded 120,000 volumes, a very large number, considering the relatively low literacy rate at the time. These handsomely produced volumes in octavo were easy to carry about, unlike the folio manuscripts and codices that scholars had to work with before printed texts were easily available (although very expensive). In addition, Manuzio cultivated a circle of scholars from all of

Europe—Thomas Linacre from Oxford, Reuchlin from Heidelberg, the young Erasmus from the Netherlands, and various Poles and Hungarians— who returned to their homelands with Aldine editions. Within a few decades, other printers in Paris, Basel, Vienna, and elsewhere used Manuzio's editions to produce their own. Hence, in the 50 years after the publication of *Rhetores graeci*, we find at least 10 editions of works by Hermogenes and far more of the *Progymnasmata* of Aphthonius, for instance.

The first half of the sixteenth century, then, saw a virtual explosion of Greek studies, an important part of which was the assimilation of Greek rhetorics into the Western tradition. By 1550, Hermogenes and Aphthonius were being taught in Paris, Florence, Heidelberg, Vienna, Budapest, and Krakow. In 1535, the teaching of Hermogenes at King's College, Cambridge, was mandated by Henry VIII. Of course, the impact of these texts was not nearly as profound as that exerted by the earlier discoveries of texts of Quintilian and Cicero, chiefly because political transformations had pretty much resulted in the exclusion of humanists from active careers in the civil sphere. But at the same time, the impact was felt by more scholars over a shorter period of time and was in general more intense. We might see the effect of the newly available texts as comparable to the effect on modern teachers of physics if they were to be suddenly confronted with works by Newton and Einstein that challenged the established view of those authors, not to mention of physics itself. It is true that the influence of those new texts was sometimes oddly misplaced. Johannes Sturm, who taught Hermogenes in Paris (Ramus was one of his students), transformed Hermogenes' *methodos* into a refinement of the old Scholastic "method"; and Fabio Paolini, in his *Hebdomades* (1589), saw a mystical significance in Hermogenes' seven *ideai*, identifying them with the seven (*sic*) planets and finding in them clues to the Orphic nature of the power of oratory. Nevertheless, the impact was profound. The study of rhetoric could never be quite the same.

In general, we must bear in mind that the Greek tradition never displaced the Latin, but was grafted onto the key conceptions of Cicero and Quintilian. The result was a hybrid that increased the yield of the traditional inventional systems, provided new sources of *copia* of eloquence—"Nothing else," we will recall, "than wisdom speaking copiously"—and multiplied perspectives within the established Ciceronian view of rhetoric as rooted in *controversia*. The basic current of Ciceronian rhetoric was, then, not diverted but augmented and carried to more scholars to nourish and satisfy more resources and needs.

The augmentation of the established view brought about by the influx of new perspectives, however, was also to have a destabilizing effect, particularly in the schools, where the nature and content of the rhetorical curriculum became the subject of considerable controversy, as is clear from the repeated calls for reform, which continue well into the sixteenth century. The question of how habits of rhetorical analysis could best be inculcated brought about demands for the simplification and clear organization of the curriculum. The very abundance of lore then available led to the perception of a need for a "short, certain *way*," as Johannes Sturm (1505–89) put it, "which is simple, clear, and straightforward." Sturm's call for such a "method," as he characterized it, set the stage for the subsequent reformation of rhetoric that was crystalized in the work of Peter Ramus. But that reform must be seen in the context of another and more profound reformation, the Protestant Reformation. It is in the context of that movement for reform, the significance of which can be seen in the conflict between Erasmus and Luther, that the educational reform of the mid-sixteenth century must be viewed. And it is in the context of the Reformation that we can best understand subsequent reconceptualizations of the nature and end of rhetoric that eventually led to the virtual extinction of the old humanism based on *controversia*.

ERASMUS AND LUTHER

Erasmus was not a professional rhetorician, nor did he ever write a treatise on rhetoric. Born illegitimate in humble circumstances about 1466, he became the foremost Classical scholar as well as one of the most conspicuous and controversial theologians of his time. In spite of his continual struggles against poverty and illness, he was a prolific writer and scholar who, in addition to his many educational tracts, satires, translations, and theological diatribes, produced an enormous corpus of commentary on Classical authors and Scripture. What holds this astonishingly large body of work together is the humanist rhetorical perspective, the controversialist cast of mind, which pervades it all.

The end of education, in Erasmus' view, was the development of eloquent persons of character, an ideal he shared with Quintilian, for whom he had great respect and from whom he borrowed much. Toward that end, Erasmus composed early in his career his famous *De copia*, On Fullness of Expression, a treatise designed to inculcate linguistic sensitivity and fluency, which would enable speakers or writers not only to achieve an impressive ability to say the same things in different ways but to have at their disposal a fund of expressions that could be tapped according to the situational demands they might encounter. A crude example of the kind of thing Erasmus had in mind may be seen in the variety of salutations students might learn in the course of normal grammar school instruction devoted to letter writing. In the 1520s, when Erasmus was deeply involved in composing commentaries on the Latin version of the New Testament, he somehow found time to write, as well, three major educational treatises: *On Letter-Writing, On the Correct Pronunciation of Greek and Latin*, and *On the Education of the Young*, the first and last deeply influenced by Quintilian's *Institutes*, the other a detailed treatment based on Quintilian but far more comprehensive. All of these may be seen as laying a foundation for eloquence in exposition, social activity, and of course disputation—in short, the ability to function truly as a *vir bonus dicendi peritus*.

Sensitivity to language and a clear view of the social dimensions of eloquence are the main themes of another of Erasmus' works, the *Ciceronianus*, a satiric dialogue lampooning the so-called Ciceronians of his day.[3] All of them, save Valla and Rudolf Agricola (at whose work we shall look later), for whom Erasmus saves special commendation, are guilty of idle, aimless, and pedantic posturing, posing as Ciceronians by using only words and expressions found in Cicero. Such erudition, Erasmus points out through his spokesman Bulephorus, misses the point of studying Cicero, for it ignores decorum—appropriateness to the given situation—thus sacrificing true eloquence for the sake of sounding good without really being so.

Nowhere do the themes of humanist rhetoric come out more clearly, however, than in two quite different works, the mock encomium in *Praise of Folly** and the treatise (Erasmus called it a declamation, as he had *Folly*) *On Free Will*, in which he challenged Luther's dogmatic denial of free will to humankind. The argument of *Praise of Folly*,[4] in which Folly (*Stultitia*) praises herself, is that Folly is the source of all good things, that all men (whether they know it or not) pay homage to Folly, and that Folly is the genius of true Christianity. This elegantly composed *declamatio*, rich in allusion to Classical writers and in hilarious satire of virtually every group imaginable, is profoundly ironic, a point missed by many of its original readers. What Erasmus intended to show in *Folly* is that much of what is held conventionally to be serious (business, the law, even literature itself) is actually foolish and misses the true wisdom to be found in appreciation of the sort of "folly" or "foolishness" represented in the penetrating observations of Folly herself, as well as in the words of Christ. The last point is the one that attracted the most virulent attacks by Erasmus' contemporaries, as Erasmus undoubtedly knew it would—"Those who feel injured," he says in the dedication of the work to Thomas More, "will reveal their consciences, if not also their cowardice."

The form of *Folly* is that of the encomium, as prescribed in the *Progymnasmata* of Aphthonius or in the *Divisions of Epideictic* of Menander Rhetor, both of which Erasmus knew (in their Aldine version, as it happens). But it is not its formal success in following Classical models that makes *Folly* a paradigm of the old humanist cast of mind. It is, rather, the argument embedded in that form, not a direct argument proceeding from certainties and establishing facts, but an indirect one. Nor is the irony of *Folly* a "stable" irony, the sort that invites the reader to penetrate to the author's message by means of simple reversal of what is said to perceive a contrary thesis, as is the case with Swift's *A Modest Proposal*, for instance. While it may be true at one level that Folly, in praising Folly, is actually praising its opposite, Wisdom, *Folly* is more complex than that. Erasmus, in taking the stance of the Academic Skeptic who can argue all sides of a question, avoids any hint of dogmatism, indeed of any consistent point of view. As one critic has put it, if Luther could say "*Hier stehe ich!*" Erasmus could say of himself, "Here *I* stand...and here...and here..."[5] Thus, on the one hand, Folly may be seen as "true" wisdom; but surely Erasmus does not actually counsel stupidity and foolishness (though Folly seems to), but condemns it. The greater part of his satire is, moreover, quite on target, exposing the vanity and (ironically, perhaps) foolishness of merchants, scholars, princes, and popes. Are we then to take seriously Folly's "reading" of Christ's words when he counsels his disciples to be as little children? Evidently, very seriously indeed. And surely, Erasmus is not really attacking those whose life is dedicated to letters (he would be attacking himself, as well as his old friend Manuzio); but is he saying that the virtue of grammatical studies is to be measured precisely by the degree of foolishness attained in them? In whose eyes? That is a decision to be made by the reader, not one demonstrated by Erasmus, nor even by Folly.

Like the dialogue form so loved by earlier Renaissance humanists, *Folly* is in a sense open-ended. Erasmus does not tell us what to believe (although Folly does); we have to come to that on our own after sorting out those points that seem probable and those that do not. Nor does Erasmus intend us to feel secure in any higher knowledge. On the contrary, his *declamatio* makes us feel uneasy, uncertain, yet knowing, in the end, that there is something wrong with the traditional wisdom. And that is precisely the effect Erasmus intended—but not overtly. Consequently, if *Folly* was meant to sting the conscience of the guilty, it was also meant to provide the innocent (so to speak) an occasion for reasserting the primacy of virtue and for clarifying worthwhile goals. The end of *Folly*, therefore, is not praise, nor even mock praise, but deliberation by the reader, a sorting out of competing views and the determination of which course in life proves to be both *honestum* and *utile*, the stock topics of deliberative rhetoric. In this respect, *Praise of Folly* belongs to that tradition of eloquence allied with wisdom that was embraced by Erasmus' predecessors and models in Italy.

The Debate over Free Will

Erasmus' controversialist perspective, with its concomitant irony and diffidence, comes out even more clearly in his *Diatriba de libero arbitrio*, which was aimed at Luther's contention (Luther proclaimed it, typically, as an *assertio*) that "free will" is really "an empty name...a fiction and a label without reality" (*Assertio*, article 36).[6] The method of the *Diatriba* is evident both in Erasmus' own words and in the construction of his argument. Erasmus' method is that of Ciceronian *controversia*, arguing both sides of the question *in utramque partem*, advancing his opinion as being "sufficiently probable" (*satis probabile*), and in effect suspending final judgment. Thus, after a preface and introduction in which he expresses his intention to "analyze and not to judge" and appeals to the valid presumption that the tradition possesses ("Who can believe that Christ has allowed his Church to overlook error for 1300 years?" he asks), Erasmus sets out the arguments from Scripture supporting free will and the apparent arguments against it, throwing the two sets into the balance. He concludes that "as many passages as there are in Holy Scripture mentioning [the necessity] of God's grace, there are as many establishing the freedom of the will." What must be avoided is exaggeration; since the exaggeration in Luther's position seems to result in the impossibility of sin, a middle ground is the only reasonable one to occupy.

Erasmus' examination of the arguments for and against proceeds as follows. On the one hand, texts in both the Old and New Testaments abound supporting belief in free will. Looking for support for that belief, he says, "is like looking for water in the ocean." On the other hand, the citations Luther appeals to (mainly from *Romans* 9 and cognate texts from the Old Testament) are all found to be open to contrary interpretations. In general, Luther's readings are, though not always unreasonable, far from certain, as are other citations Luther seems to have overlooked. Luther and his followers fail to see this, Erasmus explains, because "their case is like that of the young man who loves a girl so much that he sees her image everywhere." The result is (in keeping with the stock arguments of the Classical *diatriba*) both "useless" and "pernicious" (the opposites of *utile* and *honestum*) and, even more, immoderate and divisive. Erasmsus himself, it is to be noticed, does not use the diatribe form to promote a thesis of his own as to the existence or nonexistence of free will: he merely points up (by detailed analysis) the reasonability of believing that there is such a thing and the uncertainty of the evidence appealed to by Luther.

The argumentative tactics of Erasmus are appropriate to his method. Like Socrates, Erasmus does not claim knowledge but has only questions and some tentatively held opinions. Also like Socrates, Erasmus does not attempt to construct watertight proofs but argues with mundane parables and comprisons. At the same time, of course, his "ignorance" is belied by the enormous erudition he displays, and his humility and diffidence seem to be undone by the pointed wit and sarcasm of his characterizations of the opposition. His repeated apologies for "verboseness" have an air of the *praeteritio* about them: "I should not have gone on as I did (but I've already done it, so you'll have to deal with it anyway)," Erasmus seems to be saying. And the comparisons seem to make his position so obviously reasonable as to be irrefutable, yet he dismisses them as incidental to what he "really" means to say. As in *Folly*, we see a slippery debater here, one not above arguing *ad hominem*, at one level, but an intensely serious intellect at another. One conviction persists steadily in spite of such tactics, however. It is not that man's will really is free (he describes himself later as "vacillating in the middle" on that question), but that the only way to arrive at a tenable position is by subjecting it to the skeptical methods of *controversia*. In this, Erasmus is an exemplary Renaissance Ciceronian, for whom philosophizing is at heart a matter of invention and eloquence—that is, rhetoric.

The distinctiveness of Erasmus' position can be seen clearly if we compare it briefly with Luther's manner of arguing in his response to the *Diatriba, De servo arbitrio* (*The Bondage of the Will*). Luther does not address the issue of whether man's will is free. He concentrates entirely on a series of refutations of the conclusions drawn by Erasmus and on denunciations of his method. For Luther, no amount of traditional authority will be enough to put in doubt the "plain fact" that good works cannot lead to salvation. Not for Luther is Erasmus' method of comparing arguments and weighing probabilities. At the end of *De servo*, he says, "I have not compared, but have asserted, and do still assert." Not for Luther is Erasmus' reading of Scripture as open to a variety of equally plausible interpretations: "Let this be our sentiment," he says, "that no implication or figure be allowed to exist in Scripture. . . . We should adhere everywhere to the simple, pure, and natural meaning of the words, according to the rules of grammar and the habits of speech which God has given unto men." And for Luther there is no middle ground, no excuse for diffidence or vacillation. The universe is dichotomous: "If God is with us, Satan is absent; if Satan is present, God is absent."

The conflict between Erasmus and Luther is far more than a conflict between two learned and eloquent theologians. It is, rather, a conflict between two quite different mentalities, one of which proceeds cautiously and uncertainly, the other of which asserts with confidence what an irrefutable authority has revealed by inner illumination. The one insists on establishing and comparing probabilities, the other on playing out the consequences, grim as they may be, of utter certainties. Both men, of course, are steeped in erudition, skillful in the arts of debate and refutation, and eloquent, each in his own way; and therefore both may be seen as in some way basically "humanist." But we see two very different faces of humanism in Erasmus and Luther. These two faces of humanism continue to compete throughout the sixteenth century and explain why it is that Renaissance rhetorics take the shapes that they do during the rest of the century, both on the Continent and in England. We turn in the following section to a consideration of those complex developments, beginning with an examination of the emergence of Ramus' reforms.

REVOLUTIONS IN RHETORIC: AGRICOLA AND PETER RAMUS

The reforms in rhetorical education and the transformation of rhetoric itself effected by Peter Ramus in the mid-sixteenth century are seen by most historians of rhetoric as a watershed. Important as Ramus is in that history, the significance of his work has perhaps been overestimated.[7] It has certainly not been properly contextualized. On the one hand, Ramus' importance must be measured against that of one of his most influential predecessors, Rudolf Agricola; on the other, Ramist reforms must be situated within the larger context of the Protestant Reformation in order properly to account for the influence Ramus exercised on subsequent rhetorical theory. Hence we shall examine in the section that follows both Agricola and Ramus, and in the case of Ramus we shall look not only at his *Dialectic* but also—and perhaps more to the point of the present study—the *Rhetoric*, on which he collaborated with his colleague and confidant, Omer Talon.

Agricola

To Erasmus, who had apparently encountered him as a young student, Rudolf Agricola (1444–85) was a kind of culture hero. It was he, Erasmus says in his *Ciceronianus*, "who first brought with him from Italy some spark of better literature." Like Erasmus, Agricola was born in the Netherlands and educated by the Brethren of the Common Life. Agricola studied at Erfurt and then at Louvain, where he held the chair of rhetoric and developed an interest in Greek and studied theology. In 1469, he traveled to Italy, where the humanist Renaissance was in full bloom. There he remained for 10 years, gaining a reputation for both his learning and his elegant style, until he returned to Germany in 1479. Agricola died in Heidelberg at the age of 41. His works were all published posthumously.

Agricola's works have always been recognized as influential by students of the Reformation (as they influenced the German scholar Melanchthon, whom we will discuss later, and, through him, Luther), but his importance in the history of rhetoric has only recently begun to be fully appreciated.[8] Agricola, it is now clear, was not just a reformer of the curriculum and a precursor of Ramus, although he was both of those. He was at the center of a semantic revolution that reinaugurated the Classical view of invention as fundamentally rhetorical, breaking with the Boethian tradition, which restricted *common*places (as distinguished from particular places) to dialectic, and returning to the Ciceronian view that had established invention and commonplaces primarily in rhetoric and later extended them to dialectic. Agricola's critique of the tradition that separated rhetoric and dialectic parallels that of Valla's in the *Disputationes dialecticae*, but Agricola goes further by redefining "dialectic" not as an art designed, as it was in the scholastic tradition, to secure the validity of an argument, but rather as the art of inquiry itself—that is, a dialectic which is at its core rhetorical.

In this respect, Agricola's "revolution" seems paradoxical. After all, his chief work is *De inventione dialectica*, not *rhetorica*; and at one point he explicitly removes invention from the realm of rhetoric.[9] But in doing such things, he is actually extending the domain of the methods of rhetoric in all branches of knowledge, thus reestablishing, among other things, Quintilian's claim that rhetoric embraces all.

Boethian dialectic, it will be remembered, was conceived as a universal verbal art whose application was connected to specifically verbal acts—statements (propositions) and arguments. Invention in dialectic discovered and provided the maxims (*maximae propositiones*) that would guarantee the validity of assertions made in disputation. This sense of "dialectic" ties invention to logical necessity, supplying the criteria by which an argument may be taken as valid and true. But in the process it removes dialectic from the realm of invention aimed at *generating* statements and arguments when they are needed and from the widest field of application, probabilities. It is probabilities and problems, after all, that occasion efforts to generate discourse. Moreover, only probabilities are by and large accessible to anyone (*De inv. dial.* 2.6, p. 207).

Agricola's understanding of "dialectic," like Cicero's, is by contrast oriented toward invention rather than judgment. For Agricola, every disputed matter can be reduced to a question that asks whether a given predicate may be said to inhere in its subject. Agricola's dialectic, then, involves the comparison of subject and predicate to see whether there are points of agreement (*consentanea*) or disagreement (*dissentanea*). The sort of comparison Agricola has in mind can be made clear by observing the dialectical application of places (in Agricola, there are 24) to a proposition or question using a procedure Agricola called *ekphrasis* (2.28f., pp. 362ff.). For example, let us say (using Agricola's own example)[10] that the question is "Should a philosopher take a wife?" (The subject-predicate structure of this is clearer in the Latin: *Philosopho habenda est uxor?*). In a schematic presentation, Agricola's analysis (which we shall reproduce only in part) would look like this:

Place	*Subject: "Philosopher"*	*Predicate: "Wife"*
1. Definition	A man virtuously seeking knowledge...	A woman leading a married life for the sake of children
2. Genus	Man (*homo*)	Woman (*mulier*)
3. Species	Peripatetic, Stoic, etc.	"This one, that one..."
4. Property	Care for knowledge with virtue	To bear children virtuously
5. Whole/ part	Human attributes	Human attributes
6. Conjuncts	"Philosophy," "philosophizing,"...	"Wifely," "wifehood,"...
7. Adjuncts	Pallor, severe expression, care for work,...	Wifely love, modesty,...
8. Act	Studying, laboring...	Smiling, correcting, educating...
...		
12. End	Living virtuously...	Procreating in marriage...

By analyzing the question in this way, we can on the one hand generate discourse about both philosophers and wives. Dialectic shows what sorts of things we can say but—and this is crucial—only particular, concrete knowledge about philosophers and wives can tell us *what* to say (see 2.7), which is diametrically opposed to Boethian doctrine. On the other hand, we can use our lists to generate arguments. Where we see *consentanea*, we can develop an argument to the effect that it is quite appropriate for a philosopher to take a wife (see, for instance, no. 4, emphasizing "virtue," no. 5, and possibly no. 12, emphasizing "life") or, to the contrary, that it is not appropriate on the basis of the evident *dissentanea*. The "place logic" of Agricola, in other words, by this process of *ekphrasis*, can generate probable arguments aimed at creating conviction on both sides of the question. Unlike Boethius, Agricola is not interested in judging validity but in devices that will facilitate invention. What drops out, accordingly, is the syllogism as a central concern. To the extent that it can be said that *consentanea* are equivalent to middle terms in syllogisms (and indeed Agricola calls them *media*, or "middles"), we seem to be back with Boethius; but by virtue of Agricola's "semantic revolution" the emphasis here is, again, not judgment, not the discovery of maxims, but vehicles for invention.

Dialectic, therefore, is a universal art because any proposition can be handled in this way, not because it possesses universal premises or inferential axioms. Dialectic provides a generalized organization for the acquisition of data in support of inquiry into particular questions, for the discovery of appropriate particular arguments using the known particulars of special fields for application in the resolution of particular questions. In this respect, Agricola recovers the rhetorical topical tradition as Cicero had sketched it out in his *Topica*, for instance.

This observation, however, brings up the paradox referred to before—that Agricola gives us a treatise on *dialectical* invention, not rhetorical invention, and in fact removes invention from rhetoric altogether, assigning to rhetoric the task of teaching only the embellishments of speech (2.25, pp. 314, 318). But Agricola's distinction between dialectic and rhetoric is fundamentally different from the Boethian distinction. By drawing his new dialectic into the realm of probabilites, Agricola puts all inquiry on the same footing. Moreover, the arguments and proofs of Agricola's dialectic cannot be based on purely formal validity but depend rather—and Agricola is explicit about this in Book 3—on the force or power (psychological power?) of the accumulated weight of particular knowledge and evidence. It is in this light that Agricola's discussion of amplification and his characterization of it as *vehemens argumentatio* (see 2.4, p. 201) can be understood. Rhetoric, therefore, cannot be distinguished from dialectic in respect to the source of the certainty of the knowledge it displays. When Agricola says that all invention belongs to dialectic, then, he means that rhetoric requires no *separate* system of invention, as it did in Boethius. While Agricola seems to affirm the divorce between rhetoric and dialectic, he does so in a way quite different from the scholastic way. Only as it is taught is rhetoric distinct from dialectic. The "divorce," therefore, is more apparent than real, as dialectic is at its heart rhetorical, able to invent arguments that move audiences as well as instruct them—that is, which persuade them.

The Agricolan "reform," therefore, was quite fundamental. From the moment of its publication in 1515, *De inventione dialectica*, with its resituating of rhetoric in relation to dialectic, appears to have struck a responsive chord. It took Paris by storm in the 1520s and went into 40 editions, issuing mainly from Paris and Cologne, before the end of the century. Eventually, it was displaced by one who claimed to be following Agricola's lead, Peter Ramus.

Whether Ramus' debt to Agricola can be taken as seriously as he suggests it should is a matter we will have to look into. There is no doubt that Ramus' familiarity with Agricola made his task easier. But, obviously, before we can address the question of influences, we need to look at what Ramus succeeded in doing. We turn, therefore, to consideration of Ramus' reform of rhetoric.

Ramus

Born of a poor farming couple in Picardy in 1515, Ramus was more or less adopted by an uncle who succeeded in getting a good education for him. Having attained the degree of master of arts in 1536, Ramus was able to secure a position at the Collège du Mans and, later, at the Collège de Presles, where he taught until his death. From the beginning of his career, Ramus was evidently bent on establishing his status within the Parisian university community, and to that end composed a number of polemic treatises aimed at undermining the authority of Aristotle, Cicero, and Quintilian. These treatises served only to arouse the anger of his colleagues, however, and he was briefly forced to withdraw from his teaching post. He was soon restored to it, partly as a result of the intervention of an old friend Charles of Lorraine, a cardinal in the Church, and eventually (in 1551) was appointed Regius Professor.

The problem with the traditional authorities, in Ramus' view, was that they failed to delineate clearly among the various arts of discourse, with the result that there was often confusing overlap—figures and tropes, for instance, were taught in both grammar and rhetoric—and an unwieldy body of traditional lore that it was a professor's task to clarify and interpret to his students. Such criticism would of course apply not only to the ancients but also to Agricola. Both he and Quintilian, to whom he owed so much, compounded the problems inherent in the subject by implying that rhetoric was the ultimate art of discourse, to be taught after the student had mastered grammar and logic. Aside from being wrong "in principle," Ramus argued, such a progression, with rhetoric at the apex, ill accorded with normal pedagogical practice, which offered rhetoric (at the time, in many ways, little more than the teaching of good Latin style) before dialectic. Thus in both theory and practice, the traditional view was problematic.

Ramus developed his critiques in various treatises (for instance, the *Aristotelicae animadversiones*—Remarks on Aristotle—in 1543), showing that since the traditional definitions of the verbal arts were so fatally flawed, it was no wonder that both rhetoric and dialectic taught invention; that both rhetoric and grammar taught figures and tropes; and that rhetoric, although it had no claim to either invention or arrangement (as Agricola seemed to Ramus to have demonstrated), continued to count them both among its five parts. Ramus' solution was to redefine those arts, in a strictly logical fashion, so that grammar was restricted to matters of syntax and etymology and rhetoric to style and delivery, thus resolving some of the ambiguities of the old classifications. Most important, however, he restricted the study of invention and arrangement to dialectic, and insisted that they not be considered in any way part of rhetoric.

Having demolished the old and having newly defined those arts, it remained for Ramus to work out each one in its new form. His *Dialectique* (1555, revised a year later as *Dialecticae libri duo*)[11] accomplishes that task for dialectic, or logic, in both of its parts, invention and judgment. On the face of it, Ramus' treatment of invention is not radically different from Agricola's. Ramus further streamlines Agricola's system of places, cutting their number from 24 to 14 (later, to 10) and continues to use those places to discover "points of agreement " (*consentanea*) and "points of disagreement" (*dissentanea*). But in fact there is something very different going on in Ramus.

Dialectic, Ramus says, is the art of speaking decisively on matters in doubt. Faced with a question, Ramus' dialectician must search for a means of joining or dissociating a proposition's subject (which he calls "the minor part") and its predicate ("the major part") when that proposition is stated on one side or the other of a given question. For instance, for the question "Is man dialectical?" the assertion might be "Man is dialectical." In order to argue decisively for this assertion, one must find a middle term that links itself both with "man" and with "dialectical."[12] There is, Ramus teaches, a regular method for discovering such a middle. Like Agricola, Ramus sets up a list of places, in which all possible middles are stored. These places are, in fact, themselves generic *arguments*, he says. When one runs through these "arguments" (in a manner reminiscent of Agricola's *ekphrasis*) with the terms "man" and "dialectical," one comes to "species" (or "form") and recalls that the specific difference of "man" is "rational," which is evident from the definition "Man is a rational animal." One sees, too, that man's rationality is the cause of dialectic, and since what is true of the cause is true of the effect, "dialectic" is also linked with "rational." It now becomes possible to construct a valid syllogism:

· Major: Whatever is rational is dialectical.
· Minor: But every man is rational.
· Conclusion: Therefore, every man is dialectical.

Note that the subject in the conclusion is a term in the minor premiss, the predicate in the major—hence the labels "minor part" and "major part." Note also that in view of the fact that this method cannot fail to turn up "rational" in its review of the places, it is not possible to argue the contrary of the assertion that man is dialectical; this can be seen in the impossibility of constructing a valid syllogism that negates either the premises or the conclusion.

For Ramus, the syllogism is the proper mode of "decisive speaking" in disputes, if not in rational discourse in general. Its power as a tool is evident in Ramus' use of it in his Remarks on Quintilian, for instance, where he proceeds point by point to demonstrate syllogistically how Quintilian went wrong. Syllogisms yield certain conclusions; thus the promise of Ramus' dialectic is not probability but certainty. One now begins to see why Ramus' own statements about what he owed to Agricola have to be qualified. Ramus in fact ignores the "semantic revolution" accomplished by Agricola's *De inventione* and in the end reduces Agricola's importance to the use of examples from Classical poets and orators. The differences between the two as regards theory are, moreover, insurmountable. For Agricola, the aim of dialectic is persuasion by probable discourse—that is, communication, *oratio*. For Ramus, the aim of dialectic is the truth, *ratio*. Agricola's commitment was to Classical rhetorical education, a curriculum like Quintilian's, which nurtures patterns and habits of thinking and speaking together. Thus his topical logic and Erasmian *copia* are completely compatible. Ramus' commitment is to certain truth arrived at (as in Plato and Boethius) by dialectical invention and set out according to the "natural method," arranging ideas in descending order of generality. Rhetoric is simply the vehicle for the transmission of that truth to an audience unprepared to accept it. As Ramus observes:

> All the tropes and figures of style, all the graces of delivery, which constitute rhetoric as a whole, truly and distinct from dialectic, serve no other purpose but to lead the vexatious (*fascheux*) and mulish (*rétif*) auditor.... These have always been studied on no other account than that of the failings and perversities of the audience, as Aristotle himself taught.... (*Dialectique*, p. 153)

We shall take a closer look at Ramist rhetoric shortly, but for now we need to complete our examination of dialectic.

The second part of dialectic is judgment, "the art of collocating (or assembling) what invention has discovered and judging that collocation."[13] Since such "comparisons" require that one be able to keep in mind or recall apt comparisons, memory is assimilated to dialectic along with arrangement. There are three steps in judgment. First, one must render all discourse into syllogistic (or enthymematic) form. Here, of course, we are in the familiar territory of Boethian dialectic. Second, we must examine the links in lengthier concatenations of arguments to be found in extended discourse to discover "that which provides the collocation and arrangement of many arguments cohering with one another and linked as by an unbroken chain so as to lead one to a determined end." From this perspective, the traditional Exordium, Narration, Confirmation, and Peroration are nothing but a syllogism or series of syllogisms amplified by ornaments (*Dial. inst.*, p. 30). Third, we must see whether the substance of the discourse agrees with religion, by which all men are freed "from the shadows of the cave," Ramus says, echoing Plato. Indeed, properly conducted, dialectical inquiry, to which one arrives after moving up through grammar and rhetoric, puts us in contact with "all the multitude of things as they are in God's own mind" (*Dial. inst.* 38f.).

With invention, arrangement, and memory all made parts of dialectic, only style—the use of figures and tropes—and delivery are left to rhetoric. Grammar is the study of syntax and etymology only. Style and delivery are the subjects of the Ramist *Rhetorica*, which was written by Ramus' colleague and confidant Omer Talon but almost certainly revised by Ramus himself after Talon's premature death in 1562. Talon's *Rhetorica* is, aside from its Ramism, a very perceptive book composed by someone thoroughly grounded in Classical oratory and poetry (Homer, Virgil, and Horace are cited frequently) and obviously devoted to their study.[14] He is also clearly disappointed with the way eloquence was treated by the ancients—the author of the *Ad Herennium*, Quintilian, and (if Talon's reference[15] to *Turci mansuetiores...in Grecia* means what it appears to) Byzantine writers, with whom Talon may have become familiar by way of the Aldine *Rhetores graeci*.

With the exception perhaps of an early Byzantine work, Phoibammon's *Peri schematōn*,[16] the old treatments of tropes and figures are characterized chiefly by their apparent lack of any organizing principle. The Ramist method of dichotomous division (which Ramus must have got from Sturm's 1529 lectures in Paris on Hermogenes) provides a rigorous organization and a highly economical way of comprehending the whole of traditional lore on tropes and figures in the space of relatively few pages. Thus the *Rhetorica* fills barely one hundred pages, where by contrast Quintilian's treatment covers two entire books of the *Institutes*. This rigor, it ought to be emphasized, is not merely a means for clearly distinguishing among the various devices of eloquence and rendering them easy to remember. The method is quite thoroughly logical, as it proceeds from genus, as it were, through species to the point where no further divisions are possible. Such a procedure is not only rigorous; it is also complete.

There are, then, two parts to rhetoric, style and delivery. Style, in turn, has two parts, tropes (semantic mutations) and figures (changes in the manner of expression); and so, too, does delivery, which consists of voice and gesture. Tropes can be divided into two broad classes: those involving part-to-whole relations (metonymy and synecdoche) and those involving part-to-part relations (metaphor and irony)—thus yielding four master tropes. Figures, too, can be so divided into figures of diction and figures of thought, and these, in turn, can be subdivided dichotomously until we have accounted for 12 figures of diction and 14 figures of thought. Talon makes some brief remarks on the specific effect of each trope and figure, citing examples from poets and orators for illustration. The discussions of voice and gesture are not so carefully structured, but there are few enough things to say about these that dichotomous division may not be required: it is enough, for instance, to discuss gestures of the head and eyes, the arms and fingers, and the torso, hips, and feet, in that order, to introduce a sufficient measure of coherence.

Compared to the *Dialectica* the *Rhetorica* is highly original; and compared to the treatments in Cicero's *Orator* or Quintilian's *Institutes*, the *Rhetorica* is immensely more clear and easy to comprehend. Hence the popularity of the book in Paris, particularly, and in England, where it was in effect translated by Abraham Fraunce and presented in *précis* form by Dudley Fenner (these will be discussed in the final section of this chapter).

The vast differences between Agricola and Ramus should now be clear. Agricola was still firmly in the controversialist tradition, which cultivated arguments *in utramque partem*, "on both sides," and the principles of amplification, of *copia*. Ramus' intellectual tendency is quite different, reflecting a kind of Platonist stance toward rhetoric as a subordinate adjunct to dialectic, the third moment (after invention and arrangement) in communication, as it were. Thus Ramus' work can hardly be viewed in the way he himself characterized it, as a fulfillment of or advance upon Agricola's. Rather, Ramus reflects a major change in attitudes toward communication in the mid-sixteenth century, not just in Paris, but all over Europe.

This change was clearly not one engineered by Ramus himself, but was the occasion for his rethinking of the rhetorical tradition and explains why his work became so popular. The publication demographics of the *Dialectic* and the *Rhetoric* help us to understand the nature of the shift in attitudes toward rhetoric. To begin with, Ramus' impact on his immediate intellectual milieu was mixed. During his lifetime, eight editions of the *Dialectic* were printed in Paris by his friend Wechel. At least two of these editions were revisions in which Ramus responded to criticisms leveled at the *Dialectic* by Pierre Galland (over its implications for the curriculum) and Jakob Schegk, who had embarrassed Ramus by pointing out numerous inconsistencies. After Ramus' death—more specifically, after the St. Bartholomew Day Massacre—the numbers fall off sharply, perhaps because Wechel, a Protestant, had fled to Frankfurt. By contrast, Talon's Ramist rhetoric does much better (26 editions up to 1610, as opposed to 13 of the Dialectic during the same period). Only two editions of each were printed in Spain, and no editions were published in Italy. In Germany, however, the picture is quite different. Between 1573 and 1610, over one hundred editions of the *Dialectic* came out there, many produced by the prolific house of Wechel. Among the other German editions, there are many with commentary by various Protestant theologians, both Lutheran and Calvinist, such as Johannes Piscator, Friederich Beurhaus (a 1583 edition), Rudolf Snell (1597), and Konrad Dietrich (1609). Likewise, Swiss printers produced a proportionately large number of editions of Ramus and Talon. In short, Ramist dialectic and rhetoric made their greatest impact on Protestant readers, and almost none at all on Catholic populations. This pattern is evident also in England and Scotland, where, as we shall see, Ramus was most influential in Calvinist Puritan circles.

Why this should be the case is not altogether clear, but it certainly had a great deal to do with the renewed commitment to certainty and the belief that such certainty could be attained by the understanding of Scripture, held by Luther and Calvin alike to be not only inerrant but also unequivocal. The most immediate rhetorical consequence of this sort of commitment was an enormous outpouring of Protestant propaganda between 1530 and 1555, propaganda aimed at vilifying the Church of Rome. At the same time, the Reformation brought about in its intelligentsia an extremely ambivalent attitude toward humanism, in respect both to the authority of the ancient and patristic writers and to the question of how best to educate Protestant youth, an ambivalence that comes out clearly in the writings of Luther and Calvin. On epistemological, doctrinal, and pedagogical grounds alike, the early Reformation was at variance with the tradition from which it sought to liberate itself. The problem was that Reformation intellectuals had no systematic alternative to that tradition and no rationale for grounding their protest save for "inner light" and Scripture itself. Hence, perhaps, the reliance on propaganda and, all too often on violent force to achieve their ends.

Ramus met his death at the hands of Catholics during the bloody St. Bartholomew Day Massacre. His "conversion" to the Protestant cause came late in his life, we are told by his biographer Nancel, but he had long been suspected of harboring "heretical" (Lutheran) sentiments. In his last years, evidently before he had proclaimed his defection from Rome, Ramus traveled widely and was welcomed enthusiastically by his hosts in Protestant strongholds such as Strasbourg, Basel, Frankfurt, and Augsburg. His death was mourned deeply in those cities and, within a very short time, Ramus was called a martyr to the Protestant cause.

The reason for this high esteem is clear. Ramus' *Dialectic* provided an apparently rock-solid foundation for the definitive critique of the ancients, a sure method for attaining certainty, and a set of criteria for judgment that enabled one to test the validity of that certainty. Johannes Piscator, for instance, was able to apply Ramist canons to Scripture itself and in the process demonstrate that, in effect, Christ's message took the form of a syllogism and that the accounts of his message were concatenations of syllogisms—once he was able, that is, to strip away all of the "ornament" added to them to entertain the untrained reader. The *Rhetoric* provided a way of recognizing what was ornament and what was not, as well as a way of adjusting the manifest sense to the latent "real" meaning. And for Protestant poets and playwrights such as Agrippa D'Aubigné (1550–1630), Ramist rhetoric supplied a powerful vehicle for attacks against Rome *par un chemin tout neuf*, or "by an entirely new route."[17] And of course, the divorce between rhetoric and dialectic was compatible with the Puritan ideal of preaching from axioms, "plaine delivery of the Word without painted eloquence," as one seventeenth-century divine put it. In sum, the Protestant Reformation, and not some purely theoretical issue, is what explains the nature of Ramus' achievement and why Ramus was so important for so long to so many.

ENGLISH RHETORICS: 1530–1600

The development of rhetorical studies in sixteenth-century England took two forms, one shaped by the contacts with Continental humanism; the other, later in the century, by the introduction of the works of Ramus and Talon to English audiences. Rhetoric, it is true, had been taught at Oxford and Cambridge since the Middle Ages in a curriculum dominated by Cicero (including the pseudo-Ciceronian *Ad Herennium*), and only slightly modified in such works as 'Traversagni's *Rhetorica nova*, which he composed while teaching the subject at Cambridge. Rhetorical instruction underwent significant transformations, however, under the influence of the Agricolan revolution, particularly as it was articulated in the influential works of Philip Melanchthon (1497–1560), which reached England in the 1520s. In similar ways, the production of editions of Ramus and Talon and of Ramist rhetorics by Englishmen had, after 1550, a rather short-lived impact.

On the whole, the English rhetorics of this period were derivative, not much more than translations or patchworks of close paraphrase of Continental authorities who wrote their treatises in the traditional Latin. In the end, these Continental authorities were to prevail over the vernacular rhetorics in the schools as well as in the universities. At the same time, the majority of those who actually practiced rhetoric—the lawyers of the Inns of Court— paid scant attention to the controversies of the schools and continued to train candidates for the bar as usual. The language of English law then was neither English nor Latin, but Norman French. Aspiring lawyers learned to argue cases not by reading books but by observing actual pleadings conducted in the courtroom. The transformations brought about by Ramism never succeeded in displacing the humanistic orientation of English rhetorics, except in Puritan circles. This undoubtedly had as much to do with Tudor English resistance to Evangelical Protestantism (which did gain the upper hand in the next century) as with the peculiarity, by Continental standards, of English academic and political institutions. The English, after all, had their own Protestant Church, an established one; and the contempt expressed later by Francis Bacon for Ramus' "axioms" was perhaps predictable, given the professional traditions of Elizabethan lawyers and diplomats.

The Influence of Continental Humanism

The first rhetoric in English was composed by Leonard Cox.[18] Not much is known about Cox's life, but we know that he took a degree at Cambridge some time before 1518 and left England about that time for the Continent. In 1518, he was invited to Krakow to give an oration, a dated copy of which is preserved in the Muzeum Czartoryskich in that city. It is unlikely that such an invitation would have been extended to Cox before he received a degree. By 1524, records show, he was a master at the Krakow Academy, and in 1527 we find Erasmus writing to him about affairs in Hungary. Cox was acquainted with Melanchthon as well, and was renowned for his erudition both on the Continent and in England. In 1527 or 1528, Cox moved back to England, where he became master of the school at Reading. It was then that he composed *The Arte or Crafte of Rethoryke*, which was published in London in 1530 and again in 1532.

The Arte or Crafte is a brief book covering only invention. Cox's conception of rhetoric is quite Ciceronian, as is clear, for instance, from his restriction of the applicable *loci* to Definition, Cause, Parts, Likes, and Contraries, a configuration found in Cicero's *De oratore*. But his chief inspiration came from another source, *Institutiones rhetoricae* of Melanchthon, the "werke of Rethoryke wrytten in the lattyn tongue" he refers to in his introduction, as well as a contemporary outline, or study guide, of that book by Melanchthon's student Georgius Maior. From Melanchthon Cox borrows the basic organization of his book; his four-part model of the art (Judgment, Invention, Disposition, and Elocution); and the corresponding subdivisions of the kinds of invention into dialectical ("logical"), demonstrative (sometimes "methodic" or "didactic"), deliberative, and juridical. The inclusion of "judgment" and "logical invention" as parts of rhetoric in both Cox and Melanchthon must of course be viewed in a distinctly Agricolan context: the most general principles of invention emerge in dialectical and demonstrative invention, and more particular topical invention, in deliberative and juridical rhetoric. While Cox's examples are obviously designed to appeal to an English reader, in short, his work as a whole is little more than a filling out of the section on invention in Maior's outline, often with material borrowed directly from Melanchthon's *Institutiones* itself.

Melanchthon, it should be noted at least in passing, was very well known and highly respected. This is true not only of his *Institutiones* (1521, and revised later as *Elementa rhetorices* in 1531*), but of his theological works as well. The reason seems to be that, on the one hand, his devotion to the liberal arts was shared by influential English intellectuals. He was the only one of the Lutheran "heretics," for instance, who was not attacked in the *Dialogue Concernynge heresyes* (c. 1526) of Thomas More, the old friend and colleague of Erasmus. It was in fact that very devotion to humanism that led to Melanchthon's break with Luther. On the other hand, as the author of the text of the Augsburg Confession in 1530 and of the doctrinal *Loci communes theologici*, Melanchthon and his views were seen as compatible with Archbishop Cranmer's program for Reformation in England under Tudor rule. In the area of rhetoric, however, Melanchthon's importance was particularly conspicuous. Virtually every rhetoric produced in England from 1530 up to the end of the century shows marks of his influence.

Richard Sherry (1506–56?) was a contemporary of Cox, although there is no evidence that the two ever came into contact. After taking a degree at Magdalen College, Oxford, Sherry was appointed master of the Magdalen College School, a position he held until 1540. Sherry then retired to London to devote himself to his writing. His best-known work is *A Treatise on Schemes and Tropes* (1550, revised in 1555),[19] which he conceived as an introduction for grammar school students to "elocution"—that is, expression. This, in keeping with the Melanchthonian (and Agricolan) scheme of things, Sherry calls the third part of rhetoric.

The book is divided into two major parts, the first treating schemes and tropes considered from a "grammatical" perspective and the second treating them from an "oratorical" perspective. The grammatical section consists of three parts: (1) a survey of the "schemes" (figures) of diction and composition; (2) the faults and virtues of diction and composition; and (3) tropes. These topics are "grammatical" because they have to do with clear, proper, and refined usage and expression. The "oratorical" section takes up rhetorical figures, presenting them according to the Melanchthonian three orders of figures: (1) figures of expression, such as repetition, exclamation, and interrogation; (2) figures of thought: partition, enumeration, and the like; and (3) modes of amplification, the "heeping of probacions," as he puts it. In all, Sherry lists over two hundred terms, giving for each the Greek and Latin name, a definition, and, for most, examples.

A Treatise on Schemes and Tropes is far from a slavish imitation of Continental sources, but it nevertheless reveals significant influence from that quarter. Sherry's notion of how the study of figures and tropes fits into a rhetorical curriculum owes much to Agricola and to Melanchthon's treatment of that subject in his Institutiones. This should not be surprising, since Sherry heard lectures on those writers while he was at Oxford by William Paget, to whom he dedicated the second edition. Second, the order of discussion of the first part of the treatise owes much to a little work that circulated widely along with Maior's outline of the Institutiones, the Tabulae schematorum ac troporum, by Petrus Mosellanus, a colleague of Melanchthon.[20] This is clear from a comparison of Sherry's work with the Tabulae. Ultimately, of course, all the lore on figures and tropes goes back to Quintilian and the Ad Herennium, but the organization is Melanchthon's. Finally, while it is true that Sherry devotes the last quarter of his work to material not found in the treatments of elocution by either Melanchthon or Mosellanus, he follows Maior's outline of the section on modes of amplification, which in Melanchthon are treated in the section on invention. Sherry, of course, has no section on invention, but saw the necessity of including the modes of amplification in his treatise.

In so following his Continental sources, Sherry introduced his readers to the most up-to-date literature on the subject. His Treatise did not much impress his fellow schoolmasters, however, as they rejected his compromise with the vernacular in favor of retaining the Latin core of their instruction. Thus it happened that Susenbrotus's Epitome schematorum et troporum (1540, published in London in 1562)[21] won the field in the mid-sixteenth century, as it was both in Latin and even more up to date than even Melanchthon and Mosellanus.

Henry Peacham's Garden of Eloquence[22] came out first in 1577, its aim being, in his words, "to profyte this my country, and especially the studious youth of the Realme, and such as have not the understanding of the Latyne tongue." Where Peacham (1546–1634) was educated is not known, but he clearly was a good Classical scholar—at least in Latin—who kept abreast of developments in rhetorical education in the generation after Sherry even though he spent most of his adult life serving as a curate to a Hertfordshire church, well away from the centers of learning.

His familiarity with recent developments in rhetorical teaching is especially clear from his use of the more current Susenbrotus as his main

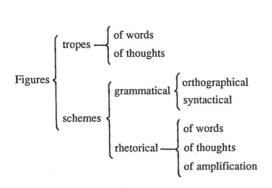

Figure 5.1

source—a use so extensive that one scholar has characterized the *Garden* as "a vernacular Susenbrotus for a Bible-reading public." But many parts of it are very like sections of Melanchthon's *Institutiones* and not like anything in Susenbrotus. Peacham also had Sherry's *Treatise* at his elbow, and he obviously knew Erasmus' *De copia* and his Cicero and Quintilian well. The basic outline of the work is, in one way, clearer than Sherry's (see Figure 5.1).

Within most of these larger divisions, however, Peacham introduces more refined subdivisions ("orders") that serve to complicate things. For instance, he adds six orders of syntactical schemes to the (by now) traditional three orders of rhetorical schemes "of words," "of thoughts," and "of amplification." The result, then, is more refined than Sherry's. In the single later edition, printed in 1593, Peacham simplifed his original layout somewhat, diminishing the number of orders within orders. He also adds for each scheme and trope a note on the use and a caution against misuse. It may be significant, too, that he drops out of the later version the whole section on orthographical schemes, since cutting it may be a sign of Ramist influence. Such influence would not be surprising, because Peacham was a rural cleric who was never as thoroughly imbued with the humanist spirit as his predecessors, such as Cox or even Sherry, both of whom had traveled widely and met or corresponded with the great Continental humanists.

In their attempts to schematize eloquence for their readers, Cox, Sherry, and Peacham were not unique and did not advance far beyond their Continental counterparts. But they may all be seen as running against a strong pedagogical current in their attempts to present the principles of eloquence in the vernacular instead of in the established language of the schools and universities, Latin. Their attempts were not very successful, at least not until the end of the century; but they represent, nevertheless, the emergence of a conviction as to the propriety of vernacular education, a conviction that had already emerged in the Established Church and was therefore part of a larger national trend. Peacham's work, and perhaps Sherry's, too, may represent, as well, another side of the growth of national consciousness—namely, the economic. Peacham, who never held an academic appointment, evidently aimed his book at an audience of young scholars who wished to obtain a rhetorical education without first troubling to learn Latin, an audience that grew during the sixteenth century. Although it is probably an overstatement to characterize Peacham's (or Sherry's) project as "a get-rich-quick scheme,"[23] it is clear that there was money to be made by publishing such books as theirs.

Another whose project may be seen in the double light of nationalism and economic gain is Thomas Wilson, England's foremost humanist next to Thomas More.[24] Wilson wrote what is perhaps the most important work on rhetoric to issue from Tudor England. *The Arte of Rhetorique** was first published in 1553 and soon became quite popular, going into more than half a dozen editions before its author's death. Wilson himself was an extraordinary man with an extraordinary career: a Cambridge graduate who found himself in the middle of the conflicts between Protestants and Catholics after the death of Henry VIII (he himself was a Protestant); mastered "civilian" (Roman) law as well as English common law; was appointed ambassador to the pope, then named privy councilor to Elizabeth I and a secretary of state; and retired as the lay dean of Durham cathedral.

Two features of this book may explain its popularity. First, Wilson succeeds in it, as no other writer before ever had, in anglicizing Continental humanist rhetoric. Second, Wilson's *Arte* treats not only invention (as Cox's had) nor elocution alone (as in Sherry), but all five traditional parts of the art of rhetoric.

Although Wilson draws heavily on Quintilian and on the *Ad Herennium*, he adapts these writers (and others, as we shall see) to an English audience, writing in English and recasting the lessons from the old Latin standard authorities to fit into an English institutional milieu. It has been suggested that Wilson's intended audience consisted not only of schoolboys and perhaps preachers, but students of the law as well, young noblemen at the Inns of Court who did not have the time or patience to master rhetoric from the Latin textbooks and who would ordinarily not be subjected to systematic training in rhetoric as such in the course of their legal studies. A famous passage from the *Arte* brings out some of these aspects of Wilson and his readers:

> When is the lawe profitable? Assuredly, both now and evermore, but especially in this age, when all men goe together by the eares, for this matter, and that matter. Soche altercation hath been heretofore, that hereafter nedes must ensue much altercation. And where is all this ado? Even in little England, or in Westminster hall, where never yet wanted businesse, nor yet ever shall. Wherefore is the lawe profitable? Undoubtedly, because no manne could beide his owne, if there were not an order to staie us, and a Lawe to restrain us. And I praie you, who getteth the money? The Lawyers no doubt. (f. 19^v)

Wilson is always careful elsewhere to give familiar examples for the particular part of rhetoric he happens to be discussing, calculated to appeal to his English readers and strike them as apt:

> for example, if I shall have occasion to speake in open audience of the obedience due to our sovereigne king I ought first to learne what is obedience, and after knowledge attained, to direct my reasone to the only profe of this purpose, and wholly to seke confirmacions of the same, and not turn my tale to talke of Robyn Hoode and to shewe what a goodly archer was he, or to speake wounders of the man in the Mone. (44^v)

Both of these passages are fairly typical of Wilson's lively and direct style and tone, features that make the *Arte* rather more readable than most comparable treatises—from any age. The first brings out another quality of Wilson's mind, however, one that shows him to be a man who thinks in an argumentative fashion, who considers possible objections, and who is quite at home in a sort of give-and-take with his reader. It is this side of Wilson that many have recognized as a sign of his deeply humanistic stance toward his subject and as putting him in the company of another great humanist, Erasmus.

Wilson's humanism comes out, as well, in his conception of rhetoric and in the structure of the *Arte*. Book One, on invention, discusses the nature and ends of rhetoric, the three kinds of "causes," and the division of *status*. Book Two, on arrangement, covers the six parts (Wilson counts partition as a separate part) of "every Oracion"; and the "figure Amplification," which includes sections on moving emotions and humor. Book Three, on elocution, lays out the virtues of a good style, the modes of "Exornation," and the principles of memory and delivery.

Wilson's division of rhetoric into three parts—invention, arrangement, and elocution (to which are attached the discussions of memory and delivery)—is borrowed from Melanchthon, as is the organization of tropes and schemes into three orders and the procedure by which he discusses each genre, beginning with "demonstrative" and treating each according to the argumentative parts appropriate to it. It should be noted also that Wilson places amplification in the section on invention, not elocution. This, too, is in keeping with Melanchthon's *Institutiones*, which Wilson evidently knew. The emphasis on "plainness" in the section on the virtues of style is consistent with the primacy given to the demonstrative, which includes the "didactic"— again, as in Melanchthon. These Melanchthonian structures are, it is true, filled out with material taken from Quintilian, Erasmus, and the *Ad Herennium*, as well as of his own invention; but it is clear that Wilson's conception of rhetoric owes more to Melanchthon than to the others. In short, Wilson's *Arte* is very much in a Continental vein—that is, in the humanist tradition, as anglicized as it is.

Some students of Wilson have detected tensions between his humanism and his Protestant declarations. If there are any such tensions, they certainly do not show up in his treatment of invention, which is thoroughly rhetorical and, like Melanchthon's, wary of claims to certainty. Wilson subordinates style to invention, it is true, but not in any way that remotely resembles the Ramist approach. In the preface to the second edition of the *Arte*, after his unfortunate experience in Europe, where he suffered imprisonment at the hands of Pope Paul IV, Wilson makes it clear that experience has taught him that one had better know what one wants to say before opening one's mouth. But Wilson hardly slights style. On the contrary, he makes a special effort to provide the fullest treatment he can, given the proportions of his work, often turning to Sherry for material. It is perhaps significant, too, that the only big change he made in the second edition in 1563—and there were no more changes in subsequent editions—was the addition of several anti-Catholic jokes to the section on humor. While that may indicate a more fervent commitment to the Protestant cause, it is surely no evidence of his having in any way accepted the new Protestant rhetorics that had been produced on the Continent.

As an intellectual movement, then, Ramism made no impression on Wilson, although it must have been known to him. He seems to have found it no more difficult to ignore it than did his counterparts at Oxford, notably John Rainold, who continued to lecture on Aristotle, Cicero, and Hermogenes up to the end of the century—Protestants all, but not by any stretch of the imagination Ramists.

Ramism, in fact, made rather less difference in English rhetorics than has commonly been supposed. This is not to say that it made no impression, for there was indeed a flurry of Ramist activity in Scotland, particularly at St. Andrews, a center of Calvinism after Knox established the Reformed Church, at St. John's College, Cambridge and, to a lesser extent, within Puritan circles at Magdalen College, Oxford.

The first, and perhaps most influential English Ramist we know of is Gabriel Harvey (c. 1550–1631).[25] Harvey's *Rhetor* (1575) and *Ciceronianus* (1576), delivered as inaugural lectures at Cambridge, are the earliest interpretations of Ramist rhetoric in England. Harvey published these in London in 1577. Along with Foquelin's translation of Talon's *Rhetorica* into French and MacIlmain's English rendering of Ramus' *Dialectique*, which had been published in London three years earlier, Harvey's lectures supplied would-be Ramists in England with a manifesto whose program was to be fulfilled, insofar as it was, by two of his students at Cambridge, Dudley Fenner and Abraham Fraunce.

It is clear from their very nature that both *Rhetor* and *Ciceronianus* were intended to be programmatic. Inaugural lectures, which were seldom given, much less published, in England, are designed to introduce a series of lectures—in this case, lectures concerned with the analysis of rhetorical models that students were expected to master and imitate. So at the end of *Ciceronianus*, Harvey announces that he will begin next time with an analysis of Cicero's *Post reditum*.

The *Ciceronianus* is an interesting document. On the one hand, it is quite ordinary in its construction. It breaks down into a conventional five-part structure and is written in an energetic and sometimes elegant Latin style. On the other hand, Harvey's argument is quite unconventional, at least from the perspective of mid-sixteenth-century Cambridge. His general line of thought is not much different from Ramus' *Ciceronianus* or Erasmus' work (unacknowledged by Harvey) with the same title: that most of those claiming to be "Ciceronians" are mere poseurs and that a true Ciceronian will not "refrain from reading on occasion other writers who are outstanding in their genres, but should always return to Cicero as the eldest son and true heir of Eloquence" (p. 56). In Harvey's view, this means that future Ciceronians— his students—should not limit themselves to Ascham and Aphthonius (whose *Progymnasmata* had been revived in Richard Rainolde's *Foundacions of the Arte of Rhetorick* in 1563), but look rather to Ramus and Talon. They, at least, were wise enough to distinguish clearly among the several arts, and their example must be followed lest his students "be like worthless pharmacists who select a different medicine instead of the right one" (p. 96). Rhetoric, says Harvey, must be restricted to style and delivery, so as not to copy the scholastic redundancies of treating invention and arrangement in both rhetoric and dialectic. All of this, clearly, amounts to a presentation of the Ramist program as implicitly endorsed by Cicero and as the one to be followed by any "true" Ciceronian.

For holding and disseminating such views, Harvey was soon attacked by this enemies for his "straunge opinions." But the two students mentioned before, Fenner and Fraunce, were evidently undaunted by their master's failure to sway his peers. Like their master, both were committed Ramists. But each took his Ramism in his own direction.

Dudley Fenner (1558?–1587)[26] is remembered in the history of rhetoric as the author of *The Artes of Logicke and Rethorike* (1584). This slim volume consists of abstracts of Ramus' *Dialectique* and of Talon's *Rhétorique*, both of which had been published in London at the press of the Huguenot refugee from France Thomas Vautrollier. Ostensibly, Fenner's *Artes* is intended to be useful to "Ambassadors, Captains, and Ministers" (p. 80). But it is clear from his preface "To the Christian Reader" that Fenner's versions are intended explicitly to contribute to the spiritual growth of their readers; in keeping with that end, Fenner's examples are all drawn from Scripture. It may be significant, too, that Fenner's version leaves out the opening pages of Talon's treatise, where Talon had invoked the tradition of Plato, Aristotle, the Romans, and the "*Turci.*" The religious side of the *Artes* is consistent with the larger program Fenner sought to develop in his work—namely, the promotion of the newly articulated presbyterian "discipline," a Scriptural discipline that could enforce "godly conversation" on all church members and that would result in "a major increase," as Fenner put it in one of his tracts, "in the kingdom and glory of Christ." Fenner was most famous, and most notorious, in his day as a Puritan divine whose writings promoting the presbyterian cause got him into trouble with Establishment ecclesiastical authorities. As a consequence, Fenner spent the better part of his adult life in virtual exile, first in Antwerp and later in Middleburg, a haven for English Puritans in the Netherlands. It was at Middleburg, in fact, that the *Artes* was published, anonymously, in the same year that saw the publication of his "Defence of the Reasons of the Counter-Poyson," an apology for the presbyterian position. In Fenner we see the application of Ramism to the advancement, therefore, of Calvinism.

Abraham Fraunce (1561?–1633)[27] heard Harvey's lectures while a student at St. John's, where he was a scholarship student and a protegé of Sir Philip Sidney. While at Cambridge, Fraunce began an English version of Ramus' *Dialectique*—which would have been the third English version—but never published it. In 1583, he left St. John's and enrolled at Gray's Inn, where he studied common law and was admitted to the bar. Fraunce was known chiefly as a poet and translator and as a champion of a school that sought to "naturalize" Classical meters in English.

While he was at Gray's Inn, evidently, Fraunce composed *A Lawier's Logike*, a paraphrase of Ramus' *Dialectique*, and *The Arcadian Rhetoricke*, a virtual translation of the 1567 version of Talon's *Rhétorique*. Both were published in 1588. If Fenner used Ramus to aid the cause of the presbyterians, Fraunce's use of Ramus went in a very different direction. The primary purpose of his *Lawier's Logicke* seems to have been to introduce his fellow aspirants to the bar to Ramist dialectic in English. Likewise, his *Arcadian Rhetoricke* sought to accomplish for England what Talon's rhetoric had for France—a vernacular poetic. Hence, where Talon's examples were drawn from Homer and Virgil, and those in the *Rhetorique* from French poets, Fraunce's examples are mainly from his patron, Sidney, and his friend Edmund Spenser. Fraunce preserves intact the structure of Talon's work, as Fenner had; but unlike Fenner, he turns Talon to another purpose, one consistent with a growing interest in an English poetic but without any theological agenda.

Significantly, Fraunce's *Arcadian Rhetoricke* was never reprinted, nor for that matter was his *Lawier's Logicke*. Fraunce's work may have failed to rival the popularity of Talon's because English poets saw no need for a systematic poetic, or because Sidney died before the book was completed, leaving Fraunce without a sponsor. Talon himself, however, remained popular, as is evident from the fact that an adaptation by Charles Butler, first published in 1598 and many times afterward, was quite a commercial success. Not even Fraunce's Ramist promotion of the vernacular could secure an important place in English letters. The humanists, after all, had already contributed greatly to that cause. Fenner, too, failed to make a measurable impression on his countrymen with his *Artes*. True, the *Artes* was once reprinted, in 1588; but it was reprinted in Middleburg, not in England. Fenner, in fact, was to have far more influence in the Puritan colonies in the century that followed than he ever had in England.

Ramism, then, never quite succeeded in England. By contrast, as we have seen, Wilson and Peacham were quite successful. The competition was stiff, and the Ramists could not prevail except in narrow Calvinist circles. Ramus' *Dialectique* attracted serious attention only in the next century, when Puritantism had gained the upper hand in English literary and political affairs. Why this should have been the case is a question with many answers. It may be simply that English Protestantism was not receptive to the movement that had become so pervasive in Germany, for instance. The certainty promised by Ramist dialectic was evidently not trusted, not even, it seems, by the presbyterians. What seems clear, in any event, is that in England the controversialist tradition in Renaissance rhetoric was not supplanted—at least not in the sixteenth century—by the "platonizing' dialectic of the Ramists, as it had been in many places on the Continent. When it finally was supplanted, it was not by Ramists but by fiercely anti-Ramus empiricists. But that part of the story needs to be told in the next chapter as part of a much larger picture of new developments in the history of rhetoric.

SUMMARY

The notion of "humanism" in the Renaissance is held together chiefly by the preoccupation with rhetoric, particularly with rhetoric as it was conceived by Cicero, as political wisdom. The discovery of new texts of important works by Cicero and Quintilian and of Greek rhetorics was important not only because of their novelty, but also—and mainly—because they were perceived as relevant to contemporary conflicts in education, politics, and philosophy. Rhetoric provided an ideal alternative to the violence that was so characteristic of the age and a means for managing uncertainty in a time when traditional beliefs and values were being questioned. Even when rhetoric ceased to have direct political relevance, the habits of mind, the concern with eloquence and the methods of analysis rhetoric provided, continued to saturate the literary production of the age. In short, far from being "a monstrous aberration," as the historian Burckhardt once characterized it, rhetoric is in many ways the key to a proper understanding of the culture of the Renaissance.

Among the most important works of the period, three stand out. Trebizond's *Rhetoricorum libri quinque* (*RLV*) is perhaps the most comprehensive treatise ever composed, but it is of interest chiefly because it served as a vehicle for the transmission of Greek rhetorics to the West. Agricola's *De inventione dialectica* is important because in it Agricola attempted a "semantic revolution," which reasserted the primacy of rhetoric over logic, or dialectic. Peter Ramus' *Dialectica*, often seen as revolutionary in its separation of invention, arrangement, and memory from rhetoric, was extremely important, but more as filling a void in intellectual discipline brought about by the Reformation than as contributing anything genuinely new to rhetorical theory.

The Renaissance up to the end of the sixteenth century is characterized by an emerging conflict between the humanism of Ciceronian *controversia* and the newer expressions of a platonizing tendency to restore dialectic as the fundamental intellectual discipline. This conflict comes out clearly in the debates between Erasmus and Luther, which pit a view of rhetoric that is basically bilateral and symmetrical and that aims at the *satis probabile*, against a view like Plato's, where the Truth is to be communicated effectively in a unilateral, asymmetrical setting. The latter view came close to achieving dominance on the Continent but had trouble gaining a strong foothold in Tudor England. Eventually, the humanistic controversialist rhetoric gave way, first, to the platonizing Ramists and, afterward—as we shall see in the next chapter—to the empiricists' and Cartesians' "motivistic" rhetorics. But in general, it is important to observe that both rhetorics coexisted in the sixteenth century and that Ramism, while an important movement, fell far short of its goal to revolutionize the study of rhetoric in Europe.

FURTHER READING

Some idea of the enormous literature on Renaissance rhetoric can be gained from a perusal of J. J. Murphy's *Renaissance Rhetoric: A Short-Title Catalogue* (New York, 1981). On the meaning of *"humanism"* and the history of the discovery of new Classical texts, see R. Pfeiffer, *History of Classical Scholarship from 1300 to 1850* (Oxford, 1976), pp. 3–123. Also very informative on Classical influences is R. Bolgar, *The Classical Heritage and Its Beneficiaries* (New York, 1954). The story of the transmission of Greek texts to the West is recounted in D. Geanakoplos' *Greek Scholars in Venice* (Cambridge, MA, 1962). H. Gray's "Renaissance Humanism: The Pursuit of Eloquence," *Journal of the History of Ideas* 24 (1963), pp. 497–514, is still important. See also J. Seigel, *Rhetoric and Philosophy in Renaissance Humanism* (Princeton, 1968); and V. Kahn, *Rhetoric, Prudence and Skepticism in the Renaissance* (Ithaca, NY, 1985). On the social background to early humanism, see L. Martines, *The Social World of the Florentine Humanists* (Princeton, 1963). M. Lowry's *The World of Aldus Manutius* (Ithaca, NY, 1979) is most informative about Manuzio's career and production.

For Valla, Salutati, et al., see Seigel, cited above. A short introduction to Valla's career can be found in M. Anderson's "Laurentius Valla (1407–1457): Renaissance Critic and Biblical Theology," in *Concordia Theological Monthly* 39 (1968), pp. 10–27. Valla's works have recently been reedited and published by scholars in Padova and Paris. His *De vero falsoque bono* can be had in a translation by M. Lorch (Bari, 1970), as can his *De voluptate*, trans. and ed. A. Hieatt and M. Lorch (New York, 1977).

Erasmus' *Ciceronianus* is available in English in a translation by I. Scott (*Columbia University Contributions to Education* no. 21, New York 1908; reprinted 1972). The huge University of Toronto project to bring all of Erasmus' works to English readers has already produced a translation of *De copia* and *De conscribendis epistolis*. English translations of *Praise of Folly* abound. On the dispute over free will between Erasmus and Luther, M.

Boyle's *Rhetoric and Reform* (Cambridge, MA, 1983) is the best treatment to date.

On Agricola's life and career, see the chapter devoted to him by L. Spitz in *The Religious Renaissance of the German Humanists* (Cambridge, MA, 1963). M. Cogan's "Rodolphus Agricola and the Semantic Revolutions in the History of Invention," *Rhetorica* 2 (1984), pp. 163–194, is an essay to which the discussion in this chapter owes a great deal. See also J. R. McNally, "Prima pars dialecticae: The Influence of Agricolan Dialectic upon English Accounts of Invention," *Renaissance Quarterly* 21 (1968), pp. 166–177.

Most of the works of Peter Ramus remain untranslated into English. The exception is the recent edition of his *Rhetoricae distinctiones in Quintilianum*, in *Peter Ramus, Arguments in Rhetoric Against Quintilian*, trans. Carole Newlands, with an introduction by J. Murphy (DeKalb, IL, 1986). The Scolar Press put out a facsimile edition of Ramus' *Logike* (the 1574 London edition) in 1966. W. Ong's treatment of Ramus in *Ramus, Rhetoric, and the Decay of Dialogue* (Cambridge, MA, 1983) is still important, but many of Ong's claims have recently been disputed. See, for instance, P. Sharratt, "Recent Work on Peter Ramus: (1970–86)," *Rhetorica* 5 (1987), pp. 163–194; and N. Bruyère, *Méthode et dialectique dans l'oeuvre de La Ramée* (Paris, 1984). Kees Meerhoff's *Rhétorique et poétique au XVIe siècle en France*, Studies in Mediaeval and Reformation Thought 36 (Leiden, 1986), is very important. For Nancel's *Life* of Ramus, see Sharratt, "Nicolaus Nancelius *Petri Rami Vita*, Edited with an English Translation," *Humanistica Lovaniensia* 24 (1975), pp. 161–277. Most of the information on figures associated with the dissemination of Ramism can be found in the entries on each in *ADB, BU*, and *DNB*.

Very little work has been done on Melanchthon's rhetorical treatises. On Melanchthon's career in general, see L. C. Green, "Melanchthon in His Relation to Luther," *The Mature Luther*, Martin Luther Lectures 3 (Decorah, MI, 1959). On Susenbrotus, the best treatment to date is still J. Brennan's 1953 University of Illinois dissertation, The Epitome troporum ac schematum: Text, Translation, and Commentary. On J. Sturm, see P. Mesnard's "The Pedagogy of Johann Sturm (1507–1589) in Its Evangelical Inspiration," *Studies in the Renaissance* 13 (1966), pp. 200–219. On the influence of Ramist rhetoric on drama, particularly Protestant martyr plays, see J. Enders, "The Rhetoric of Protestantism: Book I of Agrippa D'Aubigné's *Les tragiques*," *Rhetorica* 3 (1985), pp. 285–294.

The standard account of rhetoric in England for this period is still W. S. Howell, *Logic and Rhetoric in England: 1500–1700* (Princeton, 1956), although the book needs to be superseded by a more careful and balanced account. A good short account of rhetoric in Tudor England (with bibliography) can be found in L. D. Green's edition and translation of John Rainold's Oxford lectures on Aristotle's *Rhetoric* (Newark, DE, 1986), pp. 9–90. On the teaching of dialectic in sixteenth-century England, see. L. Jardine, "The Place of Dialectic-Teaching in Sixteenth-Century Cambridge," *Studies in the*

Renaissance 21 (1974), pp. 31–64. On the training received by aspirants to the bar in the Inns of Court, see W. Prest, *The Inns of Court under Elizabeth I and the Early Stuarts: 1590–1640* (Totowa, NJ, 1972). There is now a study of the life and works of Thomas Wilson in the Twayne Author Series, by P. Medine (Boston, 1986).

NOTES

1. I have consulted the 1532 Paris edition of *RLV* printed by the firm of C. Wechel.
2. In a letter to Budé in 1516 (*Ep.* 480. 99f.), Erasmus refers to Trebizond as one "who has pillaged Hermogenes." See *The Correspondence of Erasmus*, vol. 4, ed. J. McConica (Toronto, 1977), p. 105.
3. The full title is *Dialogus Ciceronianus, sive de optimo genere dicendi* (1528). English translations are available in the editions of Scott and by the members of the Toronto group currently active (see. Further Reading).
4. A convenient translation is found in *The Essential Erasmus*, trans. and ed. J. Dolan (New York, 1964), pp. 98–173. The best treatment of the structure of the work, on which I have relied for the appended outline below, is that of J. Chomarat in *Grammaire et rhétorique chez Erasme*, vol. 2, pp. 970ff.
5. For this characterization, see W. Kaiser, *Praisers of Folly: Erasmus, Rabelais, Shakespeare* (Cambridge, MA, 1963), p. 39.
6. For Erasmus' *Diatriba libero arbitrio* I have used the text in *Erasmus von Rotterdam Ausgewählte Schriften*, vol. 5, ed. W. Lesowsky (Darmstadt, 1969), pp. 1–196 (facing Latin and German texts). For Luther's *De servo arbitrio*, I have consulted the text in *Luthers Werke in Auswahl*, ed. O. Clemen (Berlin, 1966), vol. 3, pp. 94–253. For English versions of Erasmus and the relevant parts of Luther, see *Erasmus-Luther: Discourse on Free Will*, trans. and ed. E. Winter (New York, 1961). On the debate generally, see Boyle, *Rhetoric and Reform* (in Further Reading).
7. This realization has taken a long time to develop. In addition to Sharratt "Recent Work" (see Further Reading), see B. Vickers, "Rhetorical and Antirhetorical Tropes: On Writing the History of *Elocutio*" in *Comparative Criticism* 3 (Cambridge, 1981), pp. 105–132.
8. A good example is Cogan's "Rodolphus Agricola" (see Further Reading).
9. I have used the 1539 Cologne edition (reprinted in facsimile as *Monumenta Humanistica Belgica* 2 [Niewkoop, 1967]).
10. *De inv. dial.* 2.28, pp. 368ff. The example is a traditional one.
11. In the discussion that follows, I have used the 1543 Bogard edition of the *Dialecticae institutiones*, and the Dassonville edition of the *Dialectique* (1555) in *Travaux d'humanisme et Renaissance* 67 (1964).
12. On what follows, see Ong, *Ramus*, 182f. The importance of the syllogism as a critical tool is obvious from Ramus' attacks on Quintilian in *Arguments in Rhetoric* (see Further Reading), *passim*.
13. Ong, *Ramus*, pp. 184ff., 210f.
14. For Talon's *Rhetorica*, I have used the augmented 1572 Paris edition published by Wechel.
15. In Talon's preface, p. 6., I take the reference to be not to Turks but to Byzantine writers, including perhaps Phoibammon, with whom Talon might have been familiar from the Aldine *Rhetores graeci*.

16. Phoibammon's sixth (?) century treatise, available in the Aldine *Rhetors graeci*, is one of the few systematic treatments. The others are merely lists of names and definitions. Talon, of course, was not the first to try to reorganize the lists of tropes and figures in the traditional Latin and Greek treatises, as is obvious from the earlier works of Melanchthon and Susenbrotus, for instance.

17. See J. Enders, "The Rhetoric of Protestantism" (see Further Reading), p. 93. "Martyr drama" was an important genre in late Renaissance literature.

18. For Cox's text and an informative introduction, see the edition of F. Carpenter, *University of Chicago English Studies* 5 (1899). Carpenter shows, among other things, that the 1528 date commonly given for the publication of *The Arte* is too early. The information on Cox in *DNB* is unreliable.

19. Sherry's text has been published in a Scholars' Facsimiles edition, (ed. H. Hildebrandt (Gainesville, FL, 1961). For biographical data on Sherry, see the entry in *DNB*.

20. Mosellanus and Maior were repeatedly published along with a study guide to Erasmus' *Copia* during the first half of the sixteenth century.

21. Susenbrotus' work went into several editions on the Continent, at least four in England (the latest in 1635). See Brennan (cited in Further Reading).

22. *The Garden of Eloquence* is available in facsimile (Scolar Press, 1971).

23. This characterization is T. Baldwin's, *William Shakespere's 'Small Latine & lesse Greek'* (Urbana, 1944), vol. 2, p. 34.

24. Wilson's *Arte* has recently been reedited, by T. Garrick (New York, 1982), with emendations and a full (although not always trustworthy) introduction.

25. Harvey's *Ciceronianus* is available in the edition (with English translation) by H. Wilson and C. Forbes, *University of Nebraska Studies*, 1945. It is this edition that is referred to in the text. On Harvey's career, see the entry in *DNB*.

26. I have used the 1584 Middleburg edition. Fenner's work is available also in R. Pepper, *Four Tudor Books on Education* (Scholars' Facsimiles, Gainesville, FL, 1966).

27. I have used E. Seaton's edition (Oxford, 1950), based on the 1588 edition of *The Arcadian Rhetorike*.

ERASMUS, *PRAISE OF FOLLY*

(Page references are to *The Essential Erasmus*, ed. J. Dolan.)

Exordium (pp. 101–103) *Insinuatio*; credentials, apology and attack
Argument (pp. 103–172)
  I. Lineage, birthplace, education, consorts (103f.)
  II. Proposition: Folly (*Stultitia*) as the source of all good for men and gods alike (104–136)
    A. Benefits
      1. Life itself is the result of foolishness (105).
      2. Pleasures of a carefree (foolish) life
        a. Happy times of life (106f.)
        b. Comparison with gods (108f.)
      3. Passions (follies) create good relations among men (110ff.).
      4. Self-love (*philautia*) (113f.)

5. Folly responsible for great feats, virtues (114–120)
6. Foolishness a cure for the miseries of life (120ff.)
B. Refutation of the philosophers
  1. Ignorace is bliss (122–124).
  2. Idiots are happy (125f.).
  3. Madness is sweet (126–131).
  4. High self-regard is good (131f.).
  5. Flattery is a virtuous thing (132f.).
  6. Illusions are good (133f.).
  "Epilogue" to first part of the argument (135f.).
III. Proposition: All men (whether they know it or not) worship folly. That this is true can be demonstrated by surveying the many classes of men (136–161).
  1. Ordinary men (especially merchants) are devotees of foolishness (136f.).
  2. So are "learned" persons.
    a. Grammarians (138f.)
    b. Poets and rhetoricians (140f.)
    c. Lawyers (142)
    d. Scientists (142f.)
    e. Theologians (143ff.)
    [f. Contrast with apostles and Church Fathers (145f.)]
  3. Monks, as their sermons clearly show (148ff.)
  4. Princes and courtiers (153ff.)
  5. Popes, cardinals, and bishops (157–159)
  6. The Church as a whole (159f.)
IV. Proposition: Authorities agree that *Stultitia* lies at the heart of life itself (161–173).
  1. Pagan writers (161f.)
  2. Scripture
    a. Old Testament (162f.)
    b. New Testament (164ff.)
  3. Christ himself (167f.)
  4. The whole concept of Christianity (169ff.)
Peroration (abrupt) (173)

PHILIP MELANCHTHON, *ELEMENTA RHETORICES*

(Page references are to the text in *Corpus Reformatorum* 13, ed. C. Bretschneider [Halle, 1846].)

Book One. The elements of Rhetoric (417–458)
  I. The nature and ends of eloquence; distinction between rhetoric and dialectic (417–421)
  II. The three genera of *causae* (421–455)
    A. Preliminaries: dialectical foundations, *loci communes*

THOMAS WILSON, *THE ARTE OF RHETORIQUE*

(References are to page and folio numbers in the facsimile edition of the first [1553] edition, ed. R. Bowers [Gainesville, FL, 1962].)

CHAPTER 6

Rhetoric in the Seventeenth Century

If the Renaissance can be said to have been an age of conflict, so can the seventeenth century, only perhaps with more confidence. As historians have pointed out, only five years of the sixteenth century were free from political conflict; for the seventeenth, the total is four. This century saw radical political upheavals and protracted wars in every European country: the assassination of Henry IV of France and the beheading of Charles I of England; the emergence of political Absolutism under Louis XIV and the Glorious Revolution in England; the Thirty Years' War, Louis XIV's War of Devolution against the Netherlands, the Holy League's war against the Ottoman Turks carried on by the Hapsburgs and their Polish allies—the list is a long one. The century also saw scientific innovation of enormous consequence—Copernicus, Galileo, and Newton; the refinement of the microscope by Descartes' colleague Huygens; Harvey's treatise on circulation—as well as Bacon's "New Instauration," Hobbes' *Leviathan*, Descartes' *Discourse on Method*, all of them works that altered philosophy in radical ways. We see all at once, as it were, Bernini's *David*, the invention of the calculus, the emergence of Gustavus Adolphus as "the Copernicus of warfare" with his tactical use of heavy artillery, and Pascal's *Pensées*.

The history of rhetoric in the seventeenth century is no less complex, and no less difficult to summarize in a brief compass. The seventeenth century brought to a complete and, at least in retrospect, predictable end to the humanism of the two or three centuries that preceded it, although not as decisively or as rapidly as is often thought. It also set in motion reformations in literature and philosophy that were to achieve their ends only in the century that followed; and with these came significant shifts in the way rhetoric was conceived, shifts whose nature and importance have recently undergone serious reconsideration.

In this chapter, we shall try to get an idea, first, of the institutional and intellectual forces that conspired to bring those shifts about. Without understanding what happened in this century in those areas, it is not possible to understand what occurred in rhetoric afterward, even into the twentieth century. That seems an obvious observation, but it is not as trite as it might seem. The seventeenth century is usually studied, it seems, not for what happened during it as much as for what happened after. It is more often viewed as the beginning of our age than as the end of another. Consequently, the most accessible accounts of the history of rhetoric in the seventeenth century have consistently neglected important individual works and philosophical themes that had crucially important impacts on how rhetoric came to be viewed in that period and that have deeply affected views of rhetoric held to this day by an alarmingly large number of those whose interests and academic professions center on the subject of rhetoric. Accordingly, a second purpose of this chapter will be to restore a perspective lost in most standard treatments by exhuming, so to speak, a number of works and movements whose importance has been left too long to lie in an uneasy peace. Among these are the increasing focus on affect, or emotion, in rhetoric; the complementary division created between reason and persuasion; and the consequent replacement of the controversial and dialectical models current in the Renaiassance by what we called at the beginning of this book an *operational*, or *motivistic*, model.

JESUIT RHETORICS

If only in sheerly demographic terms, but certainly not only in those terms, the most significant influence on the history of rhetoric in the seventeenth century was that exercised by the Society of Jesus, the Jesuits. This religious order, whose members are to this day referred to as "the Pope's commandos," was chartered by the Vatican in 1540, its mission "to teach the young and convert the heathens." It quickly became the vanguard of the Counterreformation as well as the leading educational force in Europe. Within two years of its foundation, the order had established colleges for young men in Coimbra, Portugal, and in the far-away city of Goa in India. By 1556, there were 12 Jesuit "provinces" and 79 Jesuit communities serving over a thousand students. Sixty years later, the number of college had grown to 372 and the number of students to over 13,000, in Portugal, Spain, Italy, France, Germany, Hungary, and Poland. In 1627, it is recorded, the province of Paris alone supported 14 colleges with a student population of more than 12,000. In all, Jesuit colleges, by the middle of the seventeenth century, taught more students than almost all other such institutions in the rest of Europe. Even Protestant families sent their sons to Jesuit schools, as those schools were supported by the order and hence for the most part tuition-free.

Rhetoric, at least after the institution of the Jesuit *Ratio studiorum*

(Program of Studies) in 1599, was a central element in the curriculum of those schools. The *Ratio studiorum* directed that all students were to be trained in eloquence, "both in oratory and in poetry," and that the instruction be based on Cicero, Aristotle, and Quintilian. The rapid growth in the number of students created a heavy demand for both elementary texts and handbooks for teachers that would supply, as required by the *Ratio*, a uniform perspective and the rigorous pedagogy for which the Jesuits became so famous—or, in some quarters, notorious. Hence, we find Soares' *De arte rhetorica*, a school text designed for easy comprehension, going into a 100 editions in over 40 different cities by the middle of the century. Textbooks more voluminous and more comprehensive appeared and were used in Cologne (Strada's *Eloquentia bipartita* [1638], for instance), Vilna (Radau's 1640 *Orator extemporaneus*), Lyon (Pomey's *Candidatus rhetoricae* [1659]), and Prague (Czernoch's *Quaesita oratoria* [1677]), as well as in Paris, the origin of the greatest number of Jesuit rhetorics. So large is the number of textbooks written by Jesuits, and so large the population reached by them, that it is difficult to arrive at any precise estimate of the total number of such books and of the extent of Jesuit influence. But even a cursory glance at the available bibliographies shows the numbers to have been gigantic and the influence correspondingly great.[1]

A detailed study of Jesuit influence in rhetoric has yet to be written, and this is clearly not the place to attempt such a task. Some idea of the nature of that influence, of the role played by Jesuit rhetorics in the seventeenth century, may be had, however, from a brief look at two of the more widely used: Soares' *De arte rhetorica* and Caussin's *De eloquentia sacra et humana*.

Cypriano Soares' *De arte rhetorica*,[2] published just 20 years after the foundation of the Society of Jesus, is a modest book (about 200 pages) written in a lucid and straightforward Latin style, as befits the audience Soares had in mind. It was, as noted before, one of the most widely used school texts of the century, particularly in France, where between 1620 and 1635, for instance, it went into at least 22 editions printed in 10 different cities. The preface makes it clear that Soares' conception of rhetoric, while designed for Christian youth (see p. 12f.), was solidly in the tradition of Cicero, Aristotle, and Quintilian, and thus "antimodernist" in its agenda. Thus, he begins Book One with Quintilian's definition of the art, stressing that the end of rhetoric is persuasion, "the moving of men's minds." Soares continues in a classicizing vein by dividing rhetoric into three kinds: the rhetoric of demonstration (which he calls *exornatio*), that of deliberation, and that of judgment. Rhetoric deals with particular, not general questions; but as in Quintilian (3.6.80ff) can derive particular lines of argument from consideration of general questions.

Book One consists of two parts: first, a treatment of invention proper, by which one finds arguments by drawings on the "artistic" *loci* (16 in number) and on the "inartistic," such as the ones Aristotle lists at the end of *Rhetoric* 1. He enumerates the artistic places here, and exemplifies them from Cicero's orations. In the second part, Soares discusses the central role played in persuasion by emotion, exploring the connections between amplification and emotional reaction and listing the modes of achieving it, particularly as it plays a role in demonstration and deliberation.

Book Two (pp. 75–113) is devoted to the second part of the art, arrangement (*dispositio*). Soares distributes his discussion over the five traditional parts of a speech, beginning with the exordium and the *loci* to be used in exordia to speeches in each of the three main genres, drawing heavily on Cicero. He then goes on to discuss narration, the confirmation (where he presents the traditional lore on *status* and its role in argument), the confutation, and the peroration (pp. 109–113).

Book Three, on *elocutio*, comprises close to half of the entire book (pp. 114–214). In it, Soares covers the four virtues of style—*latinitas*, clarity, ornament, and decorum—and their corresponding vices; discusses quite thoroughly the various tropes and figures and principles of composition; and, at the end, makes a few observations on memory and delivery (ch. 52–57).

Soares presents in the three books of *De arte rhetorica* very little that could not have been learned from reading his chief authorities. Indeed, he states clearly that his intention is simply to make the lessons of those authors easier to comprehend: Quintilian is too long and diffuse for the average student, the *De oratore* too subtle, and the two books of *De inventione* jejune—"*inchoatos et rudes*," he says. At the same time, Soares' agenda is not that of Cicero and Quintilian. One conspicuously absent item in his book is any treatment of the *genus iudiciale*; and the sections covering argument are quite short by comparison to the treatments in Aristotle, Cicero, and Quintilian. Soares' rhetoric is less interested in argument as such, in fact, than it is in providing the means of generating persuasive discourse in a broader sense. In that connection, we find an increased importance attached to affect, or emotion. This, he says, is "the greatest force (*vis*) of the orator" (1.32, p. 44) and is accomplished by amplification, "the weightier sort of argumentation which, by the moving of souls (*motu animorum*), brings about believability (*fidem*) by speech" (1.56, p. 73).

Emotion had of course always been recognized as an important element of persuasion, and hence of concern to rhetoricians. It was the emotional aspect of rhetoric that horrified Plato and that gave Aristotle the most trouble in justifying. Cicero's interlocutors in *De oratore* spend a long time discussing it, and Quintilian devoted a significant part of the *Institutes* to it, especially in connection with amplification. In all, however, the use of emotion is rather suspect and certainly needs to be placed in a correct relationship to the process of argumentation. Agricola and Melanchthon, in the same way, betray a distincly dialectical bias in their treatments of invention, and have much to say about reason, but little about affect.

Soares, by contrast, seems to place an unusually high premium on emotion as a component of persuasion, for it is evidently emotion that mainly *moves* the souls of men—that is, persuades them, in addition to teaching them. In some ways, the featuring of emotion by Soares may be seen as a reflection of actual rhetorical practice, particularly in the realm of preaching, where emotion was sanctioned if manipulated for the right reasons. It is also arguable that what we see here is the influence of Ignatius, whose *Spiritual Exercises* consist in large part in the arousal and orientation of emotion achieved through vivid amplification—on the Passion of Christ, for instance. What best explains this new role of emotion, however, is more generally the rhetorical activity spawned by the Reformation and Counterreformation. And as the rhetoric of emotion became more prominent in the churches, it began to affect also the rhetoric of the royal court and, indeed, of the courts.[3]

NICOLAS CAUSSIN

Nicolas Caussin, S.J. (1580–1651), taught rhetoric at the Jesuit college in Rouen and later at the College of La Flèche. He was a man of remarkable erudition and a powerful preacher. His success in the pulpit eventually brought him to the attention of Cardinal Richelieu, who also served as prime minister in the court of Louis XIII. Richelieu had Caussin appointed confessor to the king, a position of great sensitivity, if not vulnerability. In time, Richelieu sought to involve Caussin in palace intrigues, the details of which are recorded in Caussin's extant correspondence. When that plan failed, Richelieu ordered him to be sent away from Paris, preferably as far away as Canada. Caussin, however, got only as far as Brittany, where he lived in exile until the death of Louis XIII. He was then able to regain his position in the Court, mainly by virtue of the perceived brilliance of his attacks on the academics in Paris.

Caussin was a prolific writer and was widely read, even in England, where his *Cour sainte*, or *Holy Court*, was published in 1634 and became popular among recusant Catholics there. It is, however, his *De eloquentia sacra et humana** that is of interest to us here. Caussin wrote it while at La Flèche, and was able to get it published in Paris in 1619. By 1643, the book had gone into four separate editions printed 10 times in cities in both France and Germany.

De eloquentia is a huge volume filling over a thousand pages, treating sacred and human eloquence in 16 books—far too long and complex to be discussed in detail here.[4] The book is notable for its exhaustive treatment of standard, and until that time not-so-standard, topics; for his inclusion of examples and models from Classical and post-Classical authors at virtually every stage of the book's development; and for the enormous erudition Caussin displays.

Caussin's treatment of the emotions in Book 8, of epideictic in Book 10, and of civil eloquence in Book 12 are particularly noteworthy for the thoroughness of his discussions. While Soares, by comparison, says almost nothing specific about the emotions despite the importance he attaches to them, Caussin devotes almost a hundred pages to the subject in Book 8. Much of this draws upon Aristotle's *Rhetoric*, but not slavishly. The discussion of epideictic in Book 10, which owes a great deal to Menander's *On the Divisions of Epideictic*, is the most complete one of its time, to be surpassed only by Radau's 20 years later in his *Orator extemporaneus*. Likewise, the discussion of civil eloquence, which Caussin traces all the way back to Exodus, is astonishingly detailed—to the point, sometimes, of excess.

Caussin evidently felt that it was necessary to include in his book, since imitation is so important (see Book 3, ch. 17ff.), numerous models, not only of exemplary passages but also of the sorts of "eloquence" one ought to avoid (as at, see instance, 2.17–27). Perhaps most interesting about the models Caussin holds up for his students' admiration is the fact that most of them are not, as is usual in rhetorics of his time, from Cicero and Virgil, but such authors as Aelian, Libanius, even Philo of Alexandria, as well as Basil, Gregory Nazianzus, and, above all, Chrysostom. Caussin is clearly promoting a quite different canon for determining the nature of true eloquence— namely, the Second Sophistic, a rhetoric of extravagance and vividness, rather exotic and grandiose. This is not to say that Cicero and Virgil are ignored, for they are not. But it is obvious from his selections that Caussin, whose elevated style caught the attention of the king, was no orthodox Ciceronian.

Caussin's exemplars give us an idea—only the merest idea—of his wide learning and sophisticated tastes. He appears to have read everything and retained it well enough to be able to cite apt passages without much effort in illustration of points he wished to make. He knew his Hermogenes well (see 2.27ff.; 5.1; 12.24f., etc.). But he also could call on Aelian, Libanius, and the *Suda* in his treatment of narration (6.14ff.); on Demetrius and Alexander Numenius, as well as Bede and Rutilius Lupus, on figures (7.17); on Philo, Hermes Trismegistus, and Michael Psellus on affect (8.1ff.); and on the *Procheira* of Leo the Wise, the ninth-century Byzantine emperor, and the handbook of Byzanto-Roman law by Harmenopoulos in his discussion of civil questions (12.21ff.). In short, Caussin was at home in material that few others had read, much less mastered, at that time.

As remarkable as it is for its erudition, *De eloquentia sacra et humana* was still thought useful in schools—perhaps more useful to rhetoric masters than to rhetoric students. It is also remarkable for its systematic emphasis on emotion—both the orator's and the audience's—as a crucial component of eloquence aimed at persuasion. This emphasis explains, at least partly, the book's success, for it accords neatly with larger programs underway in literature, art, and politics at the time. To explore the relevance of Caussin's work to his age would take us far afield. But it is clear that Caussin's conception of rhetoric reflects the so-called Baroque spirit—that dramatic anti-"Classical," post-Reformation mentality so given to striking conceits and the juxtaposition of clashing imagery. This Baroque mentality, to the formation of which the Jesuits contributed significantly in music, drama, art, and architecture, stressed the communicative potential of the arts, their ability to have an effect on audiences, to move it and involve it. Hence a keen interest in the mysteries of hieroglyphics and emblems begins to emerge in Caussin's time, and artists begin to experiment with the raw emotional content of subjects both great and trivial and with the tensions between unity and variety, light and darkness, the sacred and the profane, in an effort to achieve maximum impact on the senses and feelings. This same emphasis on affect is apparent in Soares, and even more in Caussin, and is characteristic of most rhetorics of this period, both Jesuit and non-Jesuit. Affect will continue to play an important part in rhetoric until the end of the century.

KECKERMANN AND VOSSIUS

We shall have more to say about the Jesuits later, but here it is necessary to note that the Jesuit tradition did not wholly dominate the first half of the seventeenth century, although it came close. Jesuit rhetorics, as such, did not have much influence in England, for instance, even if it is true that Thomas Farnaby's *Index rhetoricus* (1625) cites Soares as an authority. Nor did Jesuit rhetorics, to give another example, much affect the rhetoric of legal advocacy in England or on the Continent—a significant exception considering the large number of legal rhetorics published in France during this period for the edification of a population of lawyers so great as to prompt one contemporary observer to exclaim, "*Advocats! Les rues de Paris en sont pavées!*" ("Advocates! The streets of Paris are paved with them!").[5] And in any event, there were many writers on rhetoric besides Jesuits, some of them Ramists, others drawing on Aristotle for inspiration, most of them quite consciously anti-Jesuit by study or temperament.

In terms of their popularity and importance, two such figures stand out, Bartholomeus Keckermann (1571–1609) and Gerhard Johann Vossius (1577–1649). Keckermann was very influential in northern Europe and in England. Bacon was familiar with his *De rhetorica ecclesiastica* and probably also with his *Systema rhetoricae*.* The latter, which we shall look at shortly, was used in Dissenting English schools until the end of the century. Daniel Defoe studied it as a boy at Dr. Morton's Academy, for instance. Vossius' work in rhetoric, too, was important, not only in the Low Countries but also in Scotland, Germany, and Sweden long after his death. Vossius considered himself an Aristotelian and found Ramus repugnant. Yet his books were used even in schools where Ramus' influence was quite pronounced—at St. Paul's School, for instance, when Milton studied there. Since both Keckermann and Vossius are always mentioned in histories of rhetoric but never accorded the exposition they deserve, we turn now to a brief look at their rhetorics.

Keckermann

After studying at Wittenberg and Heidelberg, both centers of Protestant learning, Keckermann became master and professor at the Reformed (Calvinist) Gymnasium at Danzig (Gdansk), at the time the leading city in Prussia. His *Systema rhetoricae* is only one of many works he composed: he wrote widely on scientific and theological matters, and was the author of a systematic grammar of Hebrew, for instance.[6]

Keckermann's rhetoric is frequently characterized as vaguely Ramist because of his interest in "system" and his use of dichotomous division as an organizing principle. But his contribution to rhetoric and its connection with Ramism is rather more complex than is usually recognized. Dichotomous division does play an important part in his painstakingly detailed exposition of rhetoric (the *Systema* is over 700 pages long); but his use of it is more in keeping with pedagogical aims that go back to Agricola and Melanchthon—indeed, to Quintilian—than with any Ramist ideology. While he distinguishes rhetoric clearly from logic (see, for instance, Part One, Book 1, c. 9, pp. 98ff.), he insists on preserving all of the traditional parts of the art. His *Systema*, in fact, is concerned as a whole with the traditional part of rhetoric studiously avoided by the Ramists—invention. Keckermann's separation of "general" rhetoric from "special" rhetoric and his procedure of working from the general to the particular may also be called Ramistic, but he is up to something quite different. Rather than scrapping the traditional doctrines, he is interested in reorganizing them in a way that is not simply theoretically elegant but that makes sense of them in terms of what he sees as the primary goal of rhetoric, "to move the emotions and the wills of men" (Part One, 1.1, p. 11f.), which he stresses throughout his treatment. Finally, one might note with interest Keckermann's observation that the orator considers circumstances and audiences "prudently" (*prudenter*), and thereby be reminded of Ramus' assignment of "prudence" to rhetoric—a matter not explored by him or by Talon.[7] But as will become clearer as we look more closely at *Systema rhetorica*, Keckermann's "prudence" is more concerned with affect than with style and more with what to say than with how to say it. In view of the fact that *Systema* is really about invention, it is more accurate to place Keckermann solidly in the humanistic tradition than in even the most loosely defined Ramist tradition.

As firmly grounded in humanism as his conception of rhetoric is, however, Keckermann's notion of the art is significantly different from those laid out by his sixteenth-century predecessors. Those rhetorics, whether Agricolan or other, put a premium on "dialectical" invention, on the primacy of "straight thinking" in constructing cogent and effective discourse. Unlike Agricola or Melanchthon, Keckermann sees the primary function of rhetoric not as teaching (*docere*) but as "the moving of the heart" (*motum cordis*). Just how central affect is in Keckermann's conception of rhetoric is not very evident from an outline of the book such as will be found at the end of this chapter; so a closer look is in order.

For Keckermann, affect is central as the primary goal of the art as a whole and of its constituent parts and, additionally, as the principle that allows us to understand how different traditional kinds of rhetoric are related to one another. Part One of *Systema* (pp. 9–401) demonstrates how central emotion is to rhetoric broadly conceived; Part Two (pp. 402–720) how every conceivable form of rhetoric can be differentiated in terms of the qualities and intensity of affect aimed at in each. Thus "the principal object of eloquence is the will or feeling of man; for the orator looks especially (*praecipue*) to the heart, that he might move it and excite it to different emotions" (see *vario affectu* Part One, 1.1, p. 11). Echoing Quintilian, Keckermann adds that the orator aims at exciting *good* emotions (p. 13f.). Some kinds of rhetoric aim more at informing (*ad notitiam*), others more at feelings (p. 49); but all rhetoric aims "primarily at the exciting, indeed compelling, of the heart to bring about action" (p. 14). So amplification is the most important part (the *caput*, or "head") of the art, as it relates directly to the moving of emotion in the auditor (1.7, pp. 67ff., and indeed all of Part 1, Book 2). Disposition ought to accommodate itself wholly to that aim (see pp. 99ff.). Euphony, too, is important for the moving of souls (*animorum motionem*) (2.20, p. 257ff.). Even delivery is directed toward that end (pp. 394ff.).

In Part Two of *Systema*, Keckermann turns to "special" rhetorics. The principal distinction he makes is between "dogmatic" rhetoric (*dogmatica oratio*) and "affective" rhetoric (*oratio affectuosa*). Both, it must be stressed, involve affect, even though the former, in principle, is the sort of rhetoric in which something is explicated "plainly" (*nude*) and "not expressly meant to move the emotions" (p. 419). At the heart of "dogmatic" oratory is vividness, not precision (see p. 439f.). *Oratio affectuosa* covers all of what traditionally fell under the three main kinds of rhetoric—epideictic, deliberative, and juridical. Most of Part Two is devoted to a detailed exposition of those kinds and their subtypes in which Keckermann regenerates the Classical canons on the basis of the kinds and intensities of emotions to be aroused in different circumstances.[8] It is in this context that he includes the chapters on emotions (ch. 10–13) as a prolegomenon to the more precise distinctions he draws later and to the detailed precepts regarding the amount of amplification and the appropriate stylistic devices for each of over three dozen "genres" of "primary" rhetoric and numerous "derivative" rhetorical forms, such as self-deliberation, letters, or the elaboration of *chreiai*.

Even without a highly detailed analysis of *Systema*, it is easy to see that the most important feature of Keckermann's notion of rhetoric is the role of affect and his determination to orient all the traditional lore on rhetoric toward the moving of souls. Indeed, we can see in his position an even more specific target than "souls," for Keckermann's rhetoric is aimed at the "*wills* of men" specifically (p. 11, cited above, and p. 465)—a concept we see introduced into rhetoric for the first time. In these respects, Keckermann shares more with his contemporaries, the Jesuits, than with the leading Renaissance theorists, Ramist or otherwise. He was, in short, a "new" rhetorician whose concerns and focus accord well with the effective perspective that defines rhetorics of the seventeenth century.

Vossius

Gerhard Johann Vossius was a learned man known and admired all over the Continent and in England. His rhetorical works, although by no means the full measure of his stature as a scholar and intellectual, are significant both because of their wide use and long publication histories and because of their representative qualities among seventeenth-century rhetorics.

Vossius came out of a Calvinist milieu, and to be sure never really left it. His career included successive posts as rector of the Latin school at Dordrecht, where he himself studied as a boy; at Leiden, where he took his degree; and, from 1631 to 1635, at the new Athenaeum Illustre in Amsterdam, where he taught until his death. He was far from being a Dutch provincial, however. While at Leiden, he came into contact with many scholars and students who had come there from Germany, Poland, and Bohemia to flee the horrors of the Thirty Years' War. He was a friend of Huygens and corresponded with Galileo. His reputation at Cambridge and Oxford was secure enough to prompt both universities to name him an honorary fellow. Despite his religious profession, he enjoyed the favor of Charles I; largely because of it, his name was proposed by Bishop Ussher for the post of dean of the Cathedral of Armagh.

Vossius published four works on rhetoric: the *Institutiones rhetoricae* (1606); *De rhetoricae natura et constitutione* (1621); *Rhetorices contractae, sive partitiorum oratoriarum* (also 1621);* and *Elementa rhetoricae* (1626). All went into numerous editions; but the latter two, both school texts, were particularly popular. The *Elementa* was reprinted in at least 22 Latin editions well into the next century, and was eventually even translated into Dutch, English, and Swedish. *Rhetorices contractae*, a compendium based on his early *Institutiones*, went into 33 editions (it was assigned as a state-endorsed text in the Netherlands after 1627) by the end of the century, including 7 Oxford editions and 14 German editions.

Although Vossius draws on a variety of sources in *Rhetorices contractae*[9]—including Hermogenes, Menander Rhetor, Keckermann, and Caussin—his leading influences are Cicero and, in particular, Aristotle. It is in fact the most "Aristotelian" of any treatise on rhetoric of the time. Vossius repeats Aristotle's definition of rhetoric at the outset, while drawing attention as well to the practical aims of the art (1.1); stresses, as had Aristotle, the interrelations of *ēthos*, *pathos*, and *logos* (1.2); relies heavily on Aristotle's discussion of emotions at *Rhetoric* 2.2–11 (see 2.1–14); and seems to agree with Aristotle that, in principle, only two parts of a speech are necessary, the proposition and the confirmation (see 3.1). At the same time, Vossius seeks throughout to reconcile Aristotle's doctrines with those of Cicero, as one might expect, given the continuing importance of Cicero's works in the curricula of the day. Moreover, what he does with Aristotle is guided by interests and emphases that have more to do with seventeenth-century Europe than with Aristotle's Athens.

In its earlier editions, *Rhetorices contractae* filled over four hundred pages; later editions pared it down to less than a hundred. The treatise in its longer form comprises five books, covering invention, arrangement, and elocution, very much in keeping with a Renaissance conception of the parts of the art. Vossius' discussion of invention in Book 1 is constructed around considerations of the status questions, including a fifth question unfamiliar from earlier treatments, the *status quantitatis*. Book 2, which is also on invention, treats of the emotions at length (ch. 1–14); contains a long chapter (15) on the ages and fortunes of man; and introduces principles of invention geared to specific forms of rhetoric. The treatment of the first two topics is heavily dependent—at least on the surface—on Aristotle; that of the last on Menander Rhetor and Dionysius of Halicarnassus. Book Three, on arrangement, is a relatively brief discussion arranged according to the six standard parts of a speech. Books Four and Five cover *elocutio*, including tropes (4.3–10) and figures (4.11–22), the levels of style (5.1ff.), and, very briefly, delivery (5.8f.).

From very early in his career, Vossius was violently opposed to Ramus, condemning him for his asinine (in Vossius' view) railing against Aristotle and Cicero. In that sense, Vossius could be characterized as an "ancient" holding out against the incursions of the "moderns." And much of what Vossius says is consistent with such a reading. But Vossius was a man of his time in his perception of the supremely important role of emotion in rhetoric. This side of Vossius, often unnoticed as the strong Aristotelian element in the book is emphasized, becomes evident when one notices, for instance, the subtle revision of Aristotle's definition of rhetoric: in Vossius' version, it is "the faculty of seeing in each instance what is *likely to lead to being persuaded*," which is not quite the same as "the available *pisteis*" in Aristotle. It also becomes clear when one looks again at his discussion of affect at 2.1–14. The principle of organization behind this section is more reminiscent of Keckermann than of Aristotle. Like Aristotle, Vossius arranges the emotions in contrary pairs; but like Keckermann, he orders the emotions according to their role and prominence in the kinds of rhetoric (see, for instance 3.1. pp. 91f.; 2.5, p. 105, 107); bases his discussion of the ages and fortunes of men on the emotions they feel; and goes on in chapters 16ff. to generate modes of invention for various subtypes of epideictic, deliberative, and juridical rhetoric according to the emotive principles laid down at the beginning of the book. Further, Vossius argues for the necessity—not just the fact, as in Aristotle—of emotion in exordia and perorations. Exordia, he says, aim at "moving the soul of the auditor as though by a sort of drug" (cf. *quibusdam medicamentis*, p. 215); perorations at *pathopoeia*, "the arousal of feeling" (p. 261f.). The aim of style is to reveal the emotions of the speaker and to arouse or allay the emotions of the hearer. There is little in these observations, to be sure, that cannot be seen as implied by Aristotle; but Vossius' reading of Aristotle is quite evidently guided and shaped by concerns more in keeping with his contemporaries' views on rhetoric than with Aristotle's compelling emphasis on argument. It would not be too much to say that Vossius gives us not Aristotle but *Aristoteles keckermannianus*.

The works we have just looked at, Jesuit and non-Jesuit alike—and all of them quite influential in their day—suggest a major shift in the conception of rhetoric from a dialectical/controversial model to another placing much emphasis on the speaker's ability to work the emotions of the audience. Such a view eventually replaces the earlier one completely in most of Europe and in all of the English-speaking world. But it was not the rhetoricians by themselves who brought this change about. New ideas among the philosophers contributed much also. It is to those ideas and their importance in the history to which, perhaps belatedly, we now turn.

PHILOSOPHERS AND RHETORIC

The seventeenth century trend away from Renaissance conceptions of rhetoric as an instrument of *controversia*—what we called in Chapter 5 the management of uncertainty—to the faculty of apprehending the means of persuasion through affect to action is clear from the rhetorics composed early in the century. That tendency is reflected as well in the observations made on the place and functions of rhetoric by philosophers of the time, chiefly Bacon, Descartes, and Hobbes. The influences on these men that rhetoric had and the influences they exercised in turn on rhetoric make for a very long and complicated story. But all three played an important part in the transformations rhetoric was undergoing and was to undergo later, some because of their new accounts of how human beings actually "work," others because of the revolutions they brought about in the theory of knowledge, revolutions that were no less shattering than the political revolutions that occurred in their time. So it is appropriate at this point to say something about those developments; but it is necessary that we limit ourselves, as far as is possible, to the precise ways in which philosophical issues raised by Bacon, Descartes, and Hobbes affected thinking about rhetoric.

It is important that we remind ourselves that philosophy does not arise of its own accord. The need to understand, or to understand better or differently, is the product of the failure to understand, or understand well, which in turn is prompted by disorder, conflict, and the collapse of confidence. One does not have to look very long at the first half of the seventeenth century to see why philosophy underwent significant changes. This was a period, above all, of the confusion of politics and religion, in England and on the Continent. In England, zealous Puritans competed with resentful Anglicans for control of Parliament, and Parliament in turn aspired to control over the monarchy, control that it eventually achieved as it brought the neck of Charles I to the block in 1649 by means of legal parliamentary procedure. Civil war gripped England for over a decade. In France, Mazarin and Richelieu, both cardinals of the Church, served as the king's prime minister. *Raisons d'état* were arbitrary and absolute justifications. A quarrel between two groups of German princes resulted in a war that ravaged all of Europe for three decades. Originally a petty conflict between parties whose religious affiliation was incidental, the Thirty Years' War became a fierce struggle between Catholics and Protestants. It then was transmuted into something puzzling, as Catholic France allied itself with Protestant Sweden and Holland against Spain. What Bacon saw and heard as a member of Parliament and as Lord Chancellor, what Descartes witnessed as a soldier serving both Catholic and Protestant commanders, the terror Hobbes endured as he was hounded by both ecclesiastics and politicians—such experiences could not have failed to convince these three that there must be a better way.

All three, it is evident, were aware that forces were remolding European society that were ill understood. All, it is clear, saw a need for thinkers and speakers who could find meaning and direction in the midst of confusion and be effective. It was not a free spirit of inquiry or a commitment to pure research that prompted Bacon to rethink human knowledge and outline the ways in which that knowledge could be attained, augmented, and communicated. Progress does not just happen; it has to be made to happen. Descartes may have concluded in the isolation of his "stove-heated room" that the sure way to knowledge was through doubt; but the need he saw for certainty and precision stemmed from his realization that certain conviction otherwise arrived at led to irresolvable dispute and consequent death and devastation. Hobbes' attempts to instruct those in power with his *Elements of Law* and *Leviathan* were based on his conviction that those in power were in serious need of instruction. A defense of political absolutism may strike us today as suspect, if not repugnant; but Hobbes saw in his time that nasty and brutish political chaos had somehow to be tamed by a sovereign power.

Although each was in some degree mistrustful of rhetoric, Bacon, Descartes, and Hobbes were all masters of it. Bacon's eloquence on the floor of Parliament, Ben Jonson reports, was so powerful that "his hearers could not cough or look aside from him without loss. He commanded where he spoke...[and] the fear of every man who heard him was lest he should make an end."[10] Readers of his *Essays* often feel the same. Descartes saw in rhetoric the potential for disastrous deception, yet he was a consummate stylist himself. Hobbes, too, feared the destabilizing rhetoric of the demagogues, but the passion of his own rhetoric was no less intense than theirs. The eloquence of these philosophers reminds us of the fact that all three were well trained in the art—Bacon at Cambridge and at Gray's Inn, Descartes at the feet of the Jesuits at La Flèche, Hobbes at Magdalen—all centers of rhetorical instruction that relied heavily on Cicero and Aristotle and to a lesser, but eventually more crucial, extent on the newest developments in the rhetorics of Talon, Soares, and Vossius.

In assessing the influences of these three philosophers on later theories of rhetoric, we must be careful to distinguish between what each of them thought rhetoric to be and what effects their ideas had on their successors. The two are by no means the same, nor indeed necessarily connected with each other. We shall therefore first sketch briefly the notions of rhetoric found in their works and then examine the impact their thinking had on subsequent rhetorics.

Bacon (1561–1626) wrote in his *De dignitate et augmentis scientiarum* (1623; English version, *On the Advancement of Learning*, 1605): "Rhetoric is subservient to the imagination, as Logic is to the Understanding; and the duty and office of Rhetoric, if it be deeply looked into, is no other than to apply and recommend the dictates of reason to imagination, in order to excite the appetite and will" (6.3, *Works* 4.455).[11] By "rhetoric" here, Bacon does not mean the art in all its conventional fullness as it was conceived by his humanist predecessors—Agricola, for instance, whom he studied at Cambridge, or Wilson, whose work he must have known. Memory is assigned elsewhere by Bacon, as one of the four major intellectual arts (6.2, 4.448); and delivery (*pronuntiatio*) is assigned to grammar, one of the arts of "tradition"—that is, the transmission of knowledge. Arrangement in Bacon belongs not to rhetoric as such but to "method," the second part of "tradition." Invention is radically devalued by Bacon as far as it pertains to rhetoric, for it is placed within the purview of the sole remaining conventional part, *elocutio*, or diction. Rhetoric is the means by which knowledge may be made "present" to the imagination; and the proper study of rhetoric is the systematic examination of the affective possibilities of language, which is used by reason to affect the imagination "to excite the appetite or will."

By comparison with Tudor rhetorics current in Bacon's time, and with Ramist or semi-Ramist works he may have known, Bacon's notion of rhetoric seems novel. But his idea of the importance of affect and of the relation between affect and will is in fact close to those views which we saw earlier in the works of other authors—Caussin, Keckermann, and Vossius—none of whom, obviously, could have influenced Bacon's view. The question here is not one of influences, however, but of just how unique or novel Bacon's view of rhetoric really was. In its general outlines, it seems not unlike those other views. Moreover, even in more refined aspects, Bacon's view is clearly in tune with the positions outlined by his contemporaries. For instance, rhetorical communication in Bacon can be described as occurring between the orator's reason, which formulates both the policy he wants to persuade others to accept and the means of presentation that will be persuasive, and the imaginations of the members of his audience. But it can also be said that, in a similar way, the solitary thinker uses rhetoric to excite his own appetite and will in a sort of intrapersonal negotiation—that is, one may be said, in Bacon's view, to "talk oneself into something." This idea is not uniquely Baconian. It appears also in Keckermann, in the section he devotes to "solitary deliberation" at *Systema* Part 2, 1.9 and in Vossius (2.20). Similarly, one might observe that Bacon's "appetite and will" is not an expression of alternatives: appetite and will are functionally the same. This identification was unknown before the seventeenth century; it is common to all the rhetorics we looked at earlier. In short, what Bacon has to say about rhetoric—which is not much, since he believed it to have been treated sufficiently elsewhere—is not as novel as it has sometimes been represented, however interesting it might be otherwise.

Descartes (1596–1650) says very little specifically about rhetoric aside from a fleeting reference to it in his *Discourse on Method* (1637), where he enumerates it among the subjects he had to learn at school but subsequently rejected in his search for pure philosophy. His rejection of rhetoric is interesting for what it tells us about his understanding of it—hence of his motives for rejecting it. That rejection put him in a quandary later. Descartes excluded rhetoric from philosophy indirectly in Rule 10 of his *Rules for the Direction of the Mind*, composed before the *Discourse*, where he rejects "dialectic": "The dialectic everyone learns (*vulgarem dialecticam*) is completely useless," he says, "to those who wish to discover the truth of things....It can only sometimes express to others reasons already known...and therefore should be removed from philosophy and transferred to rhetoric" (*Oeuvres* 10.406).[12] The precepts of dialectic, that is to say, are no more than the forms of discourse which comprise that part of rhetoric that is useful in laying out what one already knows from the analysis of problems by rigorous modes of deduction. If it seems odd to place dialectic in this relationship to rhetoric, one need only note that, in Soares and the rest, the rhetorical discussions of syllogisms and enthymemes appear in the section on arrangement.

As negative as Descartes' assessment of the intellectual legitimacy of rhetoric was, he perceived quite clearly in the course of his career that he could not do without it in communicating his discoveries to others. Descartes experimented with all of the available genres—autobiography, dialogue, "geometrical" demonstration, letters—and did not hesitate to bring vivid metaphor and analogy to the assistance of his "clear and distinct ideas." He did this, moreover, in spite of his conviction that, in principle, such ideas ought to persuade without the aid of *le fard et les couleurs de la rhétorique* (Alquié, 2.790).

The fact that he had to yield to the necessity of using rhetoric as he adapted his discourse to his various audiences in order to render his ideas "as clear as if [a reader] had himself discovered them" (*Oeuvres* 7.255f.) made Descartes extremely uncomfortable. The fact that he also found rhetoric necessary to sustain his own "will to overcome deception" (as one writer has put it)[13] cannot have made him any less uncomfortable. Descartes felt this need particularly when his ideas were under attack, when he needed to convince *himself* that he was right. In one polemical response to a detractor (see *Oeuvres* 7.439), he likens himself to the astronomer whose calculations have proved the sun to be many times larger than the earth but who, on walking out in the street, finds his senses arguing against his calculations—the sun looks much smaller. So, too, Descartes, having insisted that the mind must be freed from the senses if it is to reach the truth, and even after convincing himself of the indisputable truth of his deductions, needed to persuade himself—to "talk himself into," as it were—the truth of those deductions in order to continue to adhere to them.

The rhetoric Descartes rejected, but had to use on himself as well as on others, was the same rhetoric he learned from the Jesuits at La Flèche, where he had studied Soares and where his teacher was Denis Petau, whose edition of the Second Sophistic orator Themistius had come out not long before

Descartes entered his class. His use of that rhetoric shows that he had learned his lessons well. In short, what he understood by "rhetoric" was largely what it meant to Soares, Keckermann, and the rest.

Like both Bacon and Descartes, Hobbes (1588–1697) too understood by "rhetoric" what other writers of his time did. Hobbes is an interesting case. As tutor to the young Lord Cavendish in the 1630s, Hobbes dictated in Latin and then composed in English a "Briefe," or synopsis, of Aristotle's *Rhetoric*. Elsewhere in his writings, he shows that he knew his Aristotle well and found much of use in his works. As with Vossius, however, Hobbes' "Aristotelianism" is more interesting in its deviations from its source than in its restatements of the ancient philosopher's teachings. For instance, in the "Briefe" we find the same sort of slight alteration in Aristotle's definition of rhetoric that we saw in Vossius—namely, the emphasis on "winning," on changing minds (see *Works* 6.424).[14] Aristotle's discussion of emotion, as presented by Hobbes, is controlled completely by that perspective, and the discussion of style in *Rhetoric* 3 is likewise redirected.

In his more mature works, Hobbes has much to say about rhetoric, most of it in the context of politics. On the whole, he is suspicious of rhetoric. In *Leviathan*, for instance, we find the familiar denunciation of metaphor:

> Metaphor, and senseless and ambiguous words are like *ignes fatui*; and reasoning upon them, is wandering amongst innumerable absurdities; and their end, contention, and sedition. (Ch. 5, *Works* 3.37)

In *Elements of Law* (1640), his denunciation is more sweeping. Rhetoric is the art of an eloquence bent only on persuasion, "a commotion of the passions of the mind, such as hope, fear, anger, pity" (*Works* 2.161). Proper "instigation and appeasing," he says, "raises passion from opinion"; but persuasion raises opinion from passion. Will is at the mercy of the desire or fear that "conceptions" trigger. Raising passion (*appetitus*) sets the will in motion; in fact, appetite and will are the same (4.75f.). Democracies, he observes further, are "aristocracies of orators" who depend on such language; they are masters of the eloquence of persuasion. Even more, the authors of rebellion are "necessarily eloquent," although men of little wisdom (4.141ff.). Rhetoric, in short, is a kind of coercion that cannot but lead to strife and political instability.

Hobbes' observations are embedded in his attempt to explain how "commotions of the passions" affect both individuals and civil societies on the basis of his system of universal mechanism. We will be talking more about some of the effects of mechanism on rhetorical theories later; but for now we need to notice that many of Hobbes' political observations are similar to observations Aristotle made in his *Politics* and Cicero in *De inventione*. On rhetoric specifically, however, Hobbes sounds more like a man of his own age than like those ancient authorities. His characterization of persuasion as a "commotion" of feelings echoes the language of Caussin and Keckermann, whose works he may possibly have known. Like Caussin (8.7ff.) and Keckermann (Part 2, 1.10ff), again, Hobbes awards prime positions in his ordering of emotions to desire and fear. The difference, of course, is that Hobbes saw such rhetoric as threatening the security of any state. His alternative view demands that "a man must submit his opinions in a matter of controversy to the authority of the commonwealth" (*Works* 4.170f.).

What Bacon, Descartes, and Hobbes understood by "rhetoric," therefore, whether they accepted it or rejected it, is much like what the authors of the most widely used rhetorics of the period meant by the term. Their own visions had little to do with any reconceptualization of rhetoric. On the other hand, the philosophical systems they constructed provided others, who were interested in reforming, rethinking, and eventually replacing the "old" rhetorics, with strong philosophical grounds for doing so, or at least attempting to. Bacon and Descartes had an almost immediate impact on such reformers once their works became widely known—around 1650 or so. Hobbes' influence on rhetoric was not decisive or even easily distinguishable from Bacon's until long after Hobbes' death, in the next century. In order to measure Hobbes' importance, we shall eventually have to look at John Locke and David Hartley; but a discussion of those authors belongs in the next chapter. Accordingly, we shall concentrate in the final sections of this chapter on the legacies left to rhetoricians by Bacon and Descartes.

BACON AND THE NEW STYLE

Bacon's primary concerns with the acquisition of real knowledge and the accurate communication of it resulted, as we have seen, in another "semantic revolution" by virtue of which "invention" was removed from rhetoric altogether and transformed into the process by which new arts and new knowledge are brought into being (*Works* 3.389f.), not the discovery of arguments on given questions. Rhetoric was conceived by Bacon, as it had begun to be by Continental rhetoricians, in terms not of the occasions on which it was used but of its relation to and effects upon a given set of human faculties: imagination, affect, and will. For the Continental rhetoricians, this meant that the proper inquiry of a rhetorician concerns the "pathology" of eloquence, an interest clearly perceivable in various rhetorics that feature that term in their titles—Dannhauer's *Pathologia rhetorica sive disputatio de affectibus* (Strasbourg, 1632) or Valentin Thilo's *Pathologia oratoria* (Königsberg, 1647), for instance. To Bacon and his followers, it meant that rhetoric, along with its counterpart, dialectic, would have to be expelled from schools of serious thought about the real world.

Bacon's paramount contribution was seen to have been his demonstration that only experiment would yield real knowledge of nature. Dialectical questions, by contrast, Bacon characterizes as "vermiculate," on the analogy of the process by which "many substances in Nature which are sold do putrefy and corrupt into worms" (*Works* 3.285). Words should say something about things, not "ideas," or other words. Civil discourse, in Bacon's view, was particularly in need of purification from sophistry and muddle-headedness;

but civil life is unfortunately inaccessible to experimental method. Nevertheless, clear thinking and communication on the model of ideal scientific discourse might ameliorate the conflicts brought about by the insidious preference for words over "matter."

This idea took hold in the religious conflicts of the years after Bacon's death and emerges in, for instance, Henry More's (1614–87) attack against the "Dissenters" (any Protestant profession other than the Anglican, basically), who are characterized as "Enthusiasts." Fearful of "Enthusiasm's" contagion among the uneducated classes, More attacks it as an "affectation of Humor and rhetorick." "Enthusiasm," More writes in 1650, is a

> disease...viz., to desire to be filled with high-swoln words of vanity, rather than to feed on sober truth, and to heat and warm our selves rather by preposterous and fortuitous imaginations, than to move cautiously in the light of a purified mind and improved reason.[15]

Baconians became increasingly hostile to such "scientific" prose as that of Sir Thomas Browne in his *Pseudodoxia* (1646):

> For if Crystal be a stone (as in the number thereof it is confessedly receiv'd) it is not immediately concreted by the efficacy of cold, but rather by a Mineral spirit, and lapifidical principles of its own, and therefore while it lay *in solutis principiis*, and remained in a fluid Body, it was a subject very unapt for proper conglaciation. (p. 50)

This sort of expression is not only unclear and overblown—the first a genuine fault in scientific writing; the second a matter of taste—it is possibly politically subversive, as it depends so heavily on Latinate words at the expense of good English.

Organized reaction to Enthusiasm and to the alien pomposity of so much current writing issued from the Royal Society, founded in London in 1662. The Society's chief propagandist on this issue is Thomas Sprat, whose *History of the Royal Society* (1667)[16] articulates well the concerns and solutions attested to by its members. On the subject of those "other" writers, whose modes of expression the Society was to condemn, Sprat writes. "The ill effects of this superfluity of talking, have already overwhelm'd most other Arts and Professions," so much that Sprat is inclined to banish "eloquence...out of all civil Societies as a thing fatal to Peace and good Manners" (p. 111). He continues his invective:

> They make the Fancy disgust [*sic*: disguise?] the best things, if they are sound, and unadorn'd: they are in open defiance against Reason: professing, not to hold much correspondence with that, but with its Slaves, the Passions: they give the mind a motion too changeable, and bewitching, to consist with right practice. Who can behold, without indignation, how many mists and uncertainties, these specious Tropes and Figures have brought to our Knowledge? (p. 112)

The Royal Society, accordingly, took action against the excesses of style (particularly, Latinate diction and composition) in the natural sciences:

> They have...been most rigorous in putting in execution the only Remedy, that can be found for this extravagance: and that has been, a constant Resolution, to reject all the amplifications, digressions, and swellings of style: to return back to the primitive purity, and shortness, when men deliver'd so many things, almost in an equal number of Words. They have exacted from all their members, a close, naked, natural way of speaking; the positive expressions; clear senses; a native easiness; bringing all things as near Mathematical plainness, as they can: and preferring the language of Artizans, Countrymen, and Merchants, before that, of Wits, or Scholars. (p. 113)

And it is made quite clear by Abraham Cowley, one of the Society's original members and the author of the "Ode" prefaced to Sprat's *History*, that the inspiration behind these reforms was Francis Bacon:

> From words, which be but pictures of the thought
> (Though we our thoughts from them perversely drew)
> To things, the mind's right object, he it brought.[17]

We need to bear in mind that the Society did not set about to reform the English language as a whole, only the excesses of writing that were being represented as "scientific." Nor can we overlook the fact that even those who joined in the Society's resolution continued, in many cases, to write the same sort of prose they had condemned; or that there were social and ecclesiastical motives behind the resolution that are probably as important as the scientific, philosophical ones. Nevertheless, the effects of the Society's pronouncements on other kinds of writing became evident immediately. Just after the publication of Sprat's *History*, Robert South, University Orator at Oxford, speaks of the "absurd empire and usurpation of words over things" and the necessity of using plain terms that can easily be understood. In a matter of just a few years, the Society's resolution seems to have affected even the theater, in adaptations of plays by Shakespeare for Restoration audiences. Thus, early in *The Tempest* (I.ii.22–33), Shakespeare gives Prospero these lines:

> 'Tis time
> I should inform thee farther. Lend thy hand,
> And pluck my magic garment from Me—So.
> Lie there, my art. Wipe thou thine eyes, have comfort.
> The direful Spectacle of the wreck, which touched
> The very virtue of compassion in thee,
> I have with such provision in mine art
> So safely ordered that there is no soul,
> No, not so much perdition as a hair,
> Betid to any creature in the vessel

> Which thou heard'st cry, which thou saw'st sink. Sit down,
> For thou must know farther.

The 1670 adaptation of these lines by Dryden (a member of the Society, as it happens) reads:

> I should inform thee further: Wipe thine eyes, have comfort; the direful spectacle of the Wrack, which touched the very spirit of compassion in thee, I have with such a pity order'd that not one Creature on the Ship is lost.[18]

This literary phenomenon is repeated over and over again in Dryden's adaptations and in others, such as Nahum Tate's 1681 version of *King Lear*. Shakespeare's figures and tropes are discarded, and he is made to write a plain, direct, good English.

It is interesting, however, and probably significant, that Dryden and Tate saw nothing wrong with streamlining Shakespeare's language. Quite to the contrary, they saw themselves as improving upon Shakespeare and, if anything, making his plays more sentimentally powerful—one hesitates to say "tragic," in view of the fact that Tate wrote a new, happy ending for *Lear*—than the originals. Similarly, the famous preachers of the day, South and Isaac Barrow and the rest, surely did not have in mind a turn to plain style that would make their sermons less than effective in moving the souls of the members of their congregations.

The purpose of the Society's reforms was to clean up scientific writing in order to make it more efficiently communicative. The underlying reasons for believing that the plain style would in fact be more effective and accurate in scientific writing were the same reasons theatrical producers and preachers thought their respective vehicles could also be made more effective, as it happens. That is, the retreat from metaphor and from highly amplified prose was not a retreat, from a rhetorical standpoint, from affective prose, but an improved way of achieving emotional impact and moving wills. The plain style can be more effective because it is more concrete (therefore impressing the imagination more deeply), easier to follow (hence more directly affective), more precise in its diction (see "concrete"), and better fitted, as they thought, to the way the mind, appetites, and will of man work psychologically. All this was made abundantly clear by Robert Boyle, incidentally, in *Some Considerations Touching the Style of the Holy Scripture* (see pp. 147ff. of the 1663 London edition). The basic premises of the rhetorics of Caussin and Keckermann, that is to say, were never denied; the quarrel was rather with their ideas of the best linguistic, or discursive, means to achieve the desired persuasive effect.

In concentrating our attention as we have on the more or less immediate influence of Bacon, we have deferred a necessary discussion of the emerging psychological and philosophical consensus as to how the human mind works, which was consolidated just before the end of the century by Locke, in his *Essay of Human Understanding*. We have also left out part of the story of rhetoric in England in this century by ignoring a number of rhetorics produced after 1620. But there is not much to that story. Vicars' *Manduction to the Rhetorical Art* (1621) is little more than a school text, serving up a stew of Cicero and Ramus with a dash of Keckermann as seasoning. Farnaby's *Index rhetoricus* (1626) is likewise a mere study guide. While Farnaby invokes the names of Soares, Caussin, and Keckermann, there is no evidence that he learned anything from reading their treatises. The rhetorical works of Thomas Blount (*Academie of Eloquence*, 1654) and John Smith (The *Mysterie of Rhetoric Unveil'd*, 1657) amount, respectively, to a commonplace book for polite letter writing and a list straight out of Talon of the tropes and figures found in Scripture. Not many "mysteries" are "unveil'd" in the latter, in spite of its title. By contrast, Descartes' followers on the Continent were bringing about some important changes in the way rhetoric was conceived and valued. It is to the Continent, then, that we must return.

DESCARTES AND THE "NEW RHETORIC"

"Cartesianism" took hold in Europe within a few years of the publication of the *Principia philosophiae*, in 1647, and spread across the Continent with unprecedented speed. Its effects are with us even today. Some elements of Descartes' thought withered, chiefly the mind-body dualism it propounded; but others flourished and continued to exercise considerable influence. As far as the history of rhetoric is concerned, it is generally held that virually every important position on the nature of rhetoric enunciated since Descartes can be seen as extensions of, or reactions to, a few basic principles in his philosophy.

Descartes' position can be crudely summarized in terms of its foundations and broad implications. One of the most enduring innovations in Descartes is his notion of proper philosophical method, which has four "rules": (1) never accept anything as true that is not clearly and distinctly so: doubt until convinced otherwise by self-evident truths; (2) reduce all problems to their simplest components; (3) conduct all inference geometrically, by rigorous deduction, moving from the clear and simple to the complex; and (4) review and recapitulate.[19] Another major element in Descartes' position was neither entirely innovative nor wholly accepted for very long by many— namely, his notion that the thinking ego (the *Cogito*) is both distinct and separate from the body that incorporates it. This mind-body dualism goes back a long way, to Plato or before; and it was perceived by Descartes' critics, including Hobbes, as the major weakness in his system. But part of it, the part about the body, continued to be of major significance in psychology and in rhetorical theory for centuries to come.

The implications of Descartes' seemingly simple "method" are staggering. To begin with, Descartes' method proceeds from personal doubt by way of deduction from self-evident truths. Every person, that is to say, must begin afresh the work of building the structure of all knowledge. As a consequence, Descartes' theory turns out to be one that has no reference to history or prior belief by others. Descartes thus cut himself off from all the *eruditio* that his Jesuit teachers held to be the foundation of true learning and eloquence. Second, a proposition, for Descartes, is true only if it can be derived "geometrically" from that which is self-evident and uncontaminated by contingency. Proof, not argument, becomes the sole concern in rational inquiry. Moreover, a given proposition or thesis can only be true or false. Thus, if two people are in a room and disagree, at least one of them is wrong, says Descartes. By contrast, it is a central tenet among rhetoricians that the sort of proof called for by Descartes is generally not available and that two persons who disagree can both have justifiable positions, in fact usually do. Descartes' convictions about the necessity of proof eventually compelled him to admit that his method was simply not applicable to the activity of daily life, or to matters of faith. This, in turn, implied for him a radical divorce of value, as nothing more than sentimental preference, from fact, with the unavoidable consequence that human action was removed from the realm of truly rational inquiry.

Issues such as these have received far more critical attention in recent years than they did in the years after Descartes' death. We shall talk about them again in due course. His contemporaries and followers, however, saw in his "method" only further reinforcement of a growing conviction that persuasion was distinct from conviction and basically not a process appealing to reason. Claims to rationality must be reserved for geometry. More important were the implications of Cartesian dualism, particularly as it figured into his analysis of affect in his *Les passions de l'âme* (1649). This treatise, as deeply flawed as it is by Descartes' curious notion that the body communicates with the soul via the pineal gland, set in motion the mechanistic psychology that dominated Western thinking until the twentieth century, when it was replaced by another, more refined version of the same basic model—behaviorism. At the time, however, Descartes' study of the workings of the emotions was accepted as further support for an already widely discussed idea of how the mind works and as a philosophical explanation of the role of affect in persuasion.

The immediate extent of Descartes' influence is perhaps most evident in the fact that even the Jesuits, who were among his severest critics, seem to have taken on the cause of "geometric" rigor. Jesuit rhetorics after 1660 (for instance, Jouvency's *Ratio discendi* in 1692 and the 1711 revision of Pomey's *Candidatus rhetoricae*) began to reorder their expositions, treating now elocution first and only later invention and arrangement. Jesuit teaching of rhetoric dropped the traditional emphasis on *eruditio* and began to concentrate on abstract rules. Older rhetorics were revised so that the student would first be exposed to a multitude of preliminary definitions, subdivisions within subdivisions, and jargon. Interest in the emotions, although it had long been evident, also became keener (see, for instance, Du Cygne's *Rhétorique*

[1661]), and efforts were made not only to record the precepts for dealing with emotion but also to explain how emotion worked.

Such responses as these depended more on Cartesian format than on Cartesian principles. During the period after Descartes' death, however, another rhetoric was published that not only follows a Cartesian format but embodies Cartesian doctrine as well—Bernard Lamy's *L'Art de parler*. A comparison of this book with others we have seen in this chapter shows that, if only in organizational terms, a "Cartesian" rhetoric is quite a different sort of enterprise from the ones Caussin or Vossius undertook. And as we shall see, there are other differences aside from organizational revisions.

LAMY'S *RHÉTORIQUE, OU L'ART DE PARLER*

Bernard Lamy (1640–1715), a member of the Oratorian Order, which was the chief rival of the Jesuits in education and theological disputation, would not have called himself a "Cartesian." Nor would he have called himself a Jansenist, although his order is sometimes so characterized. He would have called himself an "Augustinian." Nevertheless, he might be called all three, since the teachings of Bishop Jansen articulated by so many Oratorians were, to be sure, within the Augustinian theological tradition, but also compatible with several aspects of Descartes' system. Chief among these was Cartesian dualism, but not far behind is the limited Cartesian acceptance of what counts as rational. Both dualism and rationalism are evident in the work of his fellow Oratorian at Port-Royal, Antoin Arnauld. Dualism dominates Arnauld's *Morale practique des Jésuites*, an extended attack filling 24 folio volumes. Cartesian rationalism is the foundation of the work Arnauld is more famous for, *De l'Art de penser* (On the Art of Thinking), the manifesto of the so-called Port-Royalist logic. Dualism is a major part of Lamy's conception of rhetoric; rationalism is hardly less important.

Lamy's *Art de parler** (1675, reprinted often in France and abroad)[20] begins with a discussion of the principles of the formation of speech and of signification. Lamy starts, in fact, by tracing differences in vocalization to the properties of the organs of the voice. Vocalizations represent the "designs" (*desseins*) in the mind; they are corporeal, the designs incorporeal—rather more visual than linguistic, it seems. Because the function of language is to transmit those designs to a hearer, clarity is the paramount virtue of expression. There are, however, distinct advantages to deviating from the "natural" order of expression. Hyperbaton, for instance, "quickens the interest of the hearer and makes him more attentive" (p. 50). Language is conventional, so linguistic signs must be distinguished from natural signs, which correspond directly to the *sentiments* (loosely, "sensations")[21] and to the external manifestation of emotion. The origins of language are to be traced to the agreements within primitive groups as to the references of various vocalizations, Lamy explains at length (chs. 13–14), and usage is the relevant guide in the determination of intended meaning.

Lamy's concern in Book 1 is clearly to ground what he has to say about speech in observable and recorded physiological fact and to explain in a scientific manner the "pathology" of discourse, why and how discourse affects its audience. He wants to be able to explain why the rules of speaking are binding, not just lay down precepts. His authority on most of these matters is Descartes.

Book 2 begins with the observation that no language is rich enough to provide words to stand for all the different dimensions of meaning conceived by humans. We need tropes and figures to supplement the "normal" semantic stock of our language. Chapters 2–6 (pp. 90–108) are, accordingly, devoted to the various tropes and their good usage. Figures, too, supplement the merely referential and comparative functions of words and metaphors as they contribute to the expression of the speaker's feeling, or *sentiment*, about the subject being communicated and to the successful communication of that feeling to the auditor. Tropes and figures, in short, are not just ornaments of speech.

The most interesting feature of Book 3, on composition, is its emphasis on the role clear and agreeable composition of sounds plays in bringing together sense and sentiment. Lamy reviews the subject thoroughly, working from individual sounds and their combinations (chs. 2–5, pp. 159–177) to the arrangement of words, the importance of proper length, pauses, and cadence in phrases and clauses. Ease of both expression and comprehension is stressed. But there is more. In the last section (chs. 22–24, pp. 230–244), Lamy sketches what might be called a "physics" of style in which the principles of "sympathy" between cadence and the motions of the soul are explained and exemplified. The process of communicating—of transmitting the sense of what one wants to say to another—is viewed as a physical process of sympathetic kinesthesia in which vibrations in the soul of the speaker are transmitted by sounds that produce like vibrations in the soul of the hearer. Significantly, this discussion of composition alone is almost as long as the entire last book, which covers the entire "art of persuasion."

The shortest part of *Art de parler* is Book 4, barely 60 pages long, on style. Style works along the same set of principles as composition more broadly conceived. Lamy is very clear here on the physiological basis of his theory about why it is that one individual's style differs from another's. These differences arise from differences in their faculties of imagination, memory, and judgment. Of imagination, Lamy writes:

> When the external object strikes our senses (*frappent nos sens*) the motion it makes is communicated by the nerves to the center of the brain, whose soft matter (*substance molle*) retains from this impression certain traces. The direct connection between the soul and the body causes the ideas of corporeal things to be associated (*liées*) with those traces.... The form, clarity (*netteté*), the good order of our ideas depends on the clarity and distinctness of the impressions of the objects on the brain.... The substance of the brain is not of the same quality in all heads; that is why one

ought not to be astonished if manners of speaking should be peculiar to each author. (4.2, p. 248)

Style, then, is grounded in the physical makeup of each individual. As for differences in style, some may be attributed to different immediate circumstances, even to differences in climate or racial characteristics or the differing conventions of different eras. Our choice of style ought to be governed primarily by the nature of the object we wish to communicate so as to achieve clear transmission to the imagination of the auditor; but conventional considerations of the forms of language in which we might communicate are important, too, as we must provide the auditor with discourse that will not run counter to expectations. Custom, after all, is the sovereign of all language.

Lamy completes his *Art de parler* in Book 5 by treating last of all those matters that were treated first in the old rhetorics: invention, arrangement, and the other traditional parts of the art. Invention is disposed of in three sections: chapters 2–9 (pp. 306–328), on "proofs" (*preuves*) and how to discover them; chapters 10–13 (pp. 328–342), on the character traits of the good orator; and chapters 14–16 (pp. 342–353), on how to excite the emotions of the auditor. Following these is a treatment of arrangement, running through the five traditional parts of a speech (chapters 17–20, pp. 354–363). Delivery and memory are dispatched in a few pages, as is *elocutio*, which of course was the real subject of Books One through Four. Lamy's last chapter, which is curiously left out of the 1676 English translation, contains a number of observations on preaching. His main point here, however, is that what he has said in the rest of the book should not be understood to pertain only to that special branch of rhetoric. The art of speaking, as he has dealt with it, is the art of speaking in general; and the principles he lays down pertain to all communication.

Lamy's treatment of invention may remind some readers of the way Aristotle organizes his discussion around *logos, ēthos*, and *pathos*. But Lamy has other things in mind. He makes that clear at the beginning of Book Five (see p. 303). The strongest proof, he says, is that afforded by logic or geometry, proof deduced from a self-evident truth (*une verité clair*, 5.2, p. 306). Orators will, consequently, find their strongest arguments where they can assimilate a contested proposition or thesis to an incontestable truth deductively. The old commonplaces, as useful as they might be for amplifying, are otherwise useless (5.5, p. 315) and tend rather to dilute what one has to say and to confuse the auditor. Reason, in any event, is not enough. Persuasion requires that we find the means of changing the auditor's *sentiments* to the ones we desire to impose: we need to make the audience come over to our side. To do this, cunning (*l'adresse*) is necessary; we must capture their hearts without revealing our artifice, as one must hide from a madman (*phrénetique*, p. 329) the fact that we are administering drugs to cure him. It is to this end that exhibiting certain qualities of character (probity and prudence especially, p. 330) are necessary as auxiliaries. Passion, in particular, is indispensable, for there is no other means by which we can lead those to whom we speak to act. "While we are without passion, we are without action" (p. 345). The key passions are admiration and contempt, the basic feelings we must arouse; and for that end, clarity, because it is vivid, is necessary. "Reasoning," or argument, is treated in a brief section on "confirmation" in the part of Book Five on arrangement, accordingly, in less than four pages. Persuasion, in short, is totally divorced from argumentation by Lamy.

As we saw earlier, this divorce had been long in the making. Lamy, however, hands down the final decree, citing Cartesian principles as grounds. He does more, of course, as he explicitly revises the whole notion of rhetoric, transforming a means for handling *controversia* into a unilateral process of influence. If the old rhetoric was a way of managing uncertainty, the new is, by contrast, a way of managing the uncertain by shaping the "movements of their souls" to conform to the proposition advanced by the orator.

SEVENTEENTH-CENTURY PERSPECTIVES

We have spent a relatively long time on Lamy partly in order to give some idea of how deeply Cartesianism affected ideas about rhetoric late in the seventeenth century. The "rationalism" and, so to speak, "applied dualism" in *L'Art de parler* are fairly representative of what happened to rhetorics all over Europe after 1660 or so. The implications of Cartesianism for rhetoric of course go far beyond mere alterations in the formats of those rhetorics and involve some fundamental revisions in the conception of human nature. At a less philosophical level, Cartesian rationalism and dualism fostered and eventually provided a rationale for a new critical perspective, what is commonly referred to as "classicism" or "neo-classicism." Lamy, in fact, was arguably the first to see the possibilities in Descartes' new system for a new theory of discourse that would supplant the old by encouraging the scientific study of literature. It is perhaps in this context that Lamy's larger significance can be seen.

The dominant critical aim of neo-classicism was to reduce to rational method the rules or precepts peculiar either to one of the various arts (poetry, architecture, music) considered as a whole or to some one of its genres or styles. Boileau's *L'Art poétique* (1674) and Rapin's *Réflexions sur l'éloquence* (1682) are representative of this approach to literature. Both works attempt to organize, with an unprecedented rigor, the various modes of expression and to lay down the rules for each. Both authors are extremely interested in applying the principles of those various modes of expression as they can be delineated in Classical authors to the production of eloquent discourse in the vernacular—in this case, French—as opposed to the traditional Latin. In both, the preference for the vernacular is to an important degree grounded in their concern for clear and effective communication. And in both, that concern leads to the promotion of the plain style. In terms of their interest in rigorous organization, the derivation of particular precepts from general definitions, and the preference for clear and distinct expression, both Boileau and Rapin can be viewed as typical proponents of the "geometric spirit" that dominated European intellectual activity after the death of Descartes.

Of course, in rhetoric, the groundwork for such developments had been laid by Keckermann and seems implicit in Radau's *Orator extemporaneus*, which was first published in Vilna in 1641 and was reprinted in Amsterdam in 1655 by Jan Maire, who also published Descartes' *Discourse on Method*, in addition to, among others, the works of Gerhard Vossius. Neither Rapin nor Boileau saw himself as a "modern" in the famous literary "Quarrel between the Ancients and the Moderns." Rapin, a Jesuit, never deviated from a fundamental commitment to Classical literary standards, as much as he recontextualized those standards; and Boileau's chief inspiration, by his account at any rate, was not Descartes, but Longinus. This choice, incidentally, makes perfect sense in view of Longinus' operational view of rhetoric as being chiefly concerned with the production of affect and his perception that the simplest unadorned style often elicits the most sublime response.[22] Boileau and Rapin, however, were among the first to attempt to bring all of discourse under the rubric of rigorous rationality, not just rhetoric.

True *neo*-classicism, strictly speaking, emerges with the attempts to ground those precepts for eloquence at a more fundamental level, on the psychophysiological realities of human nature, as Lamy had done. Matters of style, after Lamy, are discussed in terms of physical differences among individuals. Standards of decorum are based not on Horace or Cicero or Aristotle, but on human nature itself, a principle laid down by Lamy and later worked out in detail under his influence in Hutcheson's *Inquiry into the Origins of the Ideas of Beauty and Virtue* in 1725. In the wider context of contemporary and subsequent literary criticism, in short, the importance of Lamy is hard to dismiss.

What we see going on locally in Lamy and more regionally in the "neoclassical movement" in France and in England, with Dryden, for instance, reflects as well an even wider picture of change and transformation in the seventeenth century in other realms. If in comparing Donne, say, with Milton, it is possible to detect a shift from a humanist preoccupation with discourse as a mode of managing uncertainty to a Ramist preoccupation with the ways prefabricated forms of discourse can be placed at the service of transmitting inner convictions, it is also possible to detect in comparing Milton with Dryden a transformation by which social convention is made into moral imperative.[23] Galileo's hypotheses, which sought to explain phenomena observable by means of the new telescope, become in Newton unobservable laws of motion by which God governs the harmonies of the universe.[24] And in rhetoric and political philosophy alike, as we have seen in the instances of Lamy and Hobbes above all, the traditional understanding of reason as self-motivating and a faculty that can control the passions and direct the will is replaced by a new model. In the old model, reason proposes goods to the agent and provides that agent—a rational agent—with grounds for action. In the new model, reason is inert, incapable of moving to action.[25] Only affect can do that.

Finally, if we view these transformations in an even wider perspective, that of social and political developments, we can see that it is not a mere coincidence that such transformations occurred when and where they did: in France, during the reign of Louis XIV (1643–1715; and in England, after the brief reign of Charles II, in particular, about the time of the Glorious Revolution of 1688, which brought about the last of a series of restorations of monarchy—a monarchy whose absolute authority had been rationalized by Hobbes. The sort of rhetoric we see suggested by Hobbes and by Lamy, and even before them in the affective rhetorics articulated earlier in the century, seems particularly well suited to an atmosphere in which absolutism came to be seen as the only practical solution to social and political disorder. It can, in any event, be truly said that by the end of the seventeenth century, confusion had proven to be the mother of enlightenment, and enlightenment the mother of oppression.

This concludes our survey of rhetoric in the seventeenth century. As sketchy as present limitations have forced it to be, it may convey some idea of the extent to which, and some directions in which, further study might be recommended. In Chapter 7, we shall pick up some strands of the history of rhetoric that we have left dangling and try to see how the sorts of developments we have surveyed reached their fulfillment in the eighteenth century, sometimes called the "Age of Reason."

SUMMARY

An examination of rhetorics in use throughout Europe during the seventeenth century reveals an increased interest in affect and in the connection between passion and will in persuasive—eloquent—discourse. This observation holds not only for Jesuit rhetorics, with their important role in the Counterreformation, but in non-Jesuit rhetorics as well, as a glance at Keckermann and Vossius shows. The views of rhetoric held by Bacon, Descartes, and Hobbes are completely consistent with those of contemporary authors of rhetorics.

These philosophers did provide, however, philosophical bases for a partial reconceptualization of rhetoric toward the end of the century. It now became possible to ground a theory of rhetoric as essentially a matter of moving the will through the emotions on philosophical principles. Lamy's *Art de parler* is perhaps the most significant example of what such a rhetoric involves.

The "motivistic" view of rhetoric seems particularly well suited to an age where political absolutism came into its own. It is no accident that Cartesian rationalism, as it gave rise to the "geometric spirit," was realized politically in a social order that was deduced from the "self-evident" principle of absolute monarchy. Although there are many manifestations of the death of Renaissance humanism during this century, perhaps the manifestations in the political sphere provide the most intelligible context for the dominance of a unilateral and asymmetric rhetoric. Finally, it might be noted that this "managerial" rhetoric is structurally identical to the "dialectical" rhetoric of Plato and Ramus. The crucial difference, of course, lies in the concern of Plato and Ramus for the effective transmission of the Truth, whereas the new rhetorics of affect provide the means by which any unspecified motive may be accomplished in the persuasion of an audience by an eloquent speaker who is able to "move souls."

FURTHER READING

Most of the important literature on this very complex period is in French and German. There are very few modern editions of the important works, moreover, Jesuit and non-Jesuit alike. For general background, one might try reading I. Wade's *The Intellectual Origins of the French Enlightenment* (Princeton, 1971) alongside J. Polisensky's *War and Society* (Cambridge, MA, 1978) and H. Langer, *Thirty Years' War* (New York, 1980).

W. S. Howell's *Logic and Rhetoric in England: 1500–1700*, which we cited in the last chapter, is still the best source for English logics and rhetorics. For France, M. Fumaroli's *L'age de l'éloquence* (Paris, 1980), with an enormous bibliography, is indispensable. See also P. Bayley, *French Pulpit Oratory: 1598–1650* (Cambridge, 1980), which is good on the handbooks in the background of seventeenth-century preaching. For Germany, W. Barner's *Barockrhetorik* (Tübingen, 1970) is perhaps the best general treatment of Continental rhetorics of the time and has a good bibliography. J. Dyck's *Ticht-Kunst: Deutsche Barockpoetik und rhetorische Tradition* (Berlin/Zürich, 1966) is also important. Biographical information for individuals discussed in this chapter is from *BU* and *ADB*.

On the Jesuits, the masterful papers of F. de Dainville, S. J., recently collected in *L'éducation des Jesuites (XVIe–XVIIIe siècles* (Paris, 1978), are exceptionally informative. A fairly elementary, but still useful, brief account can be found in R. Lang, "The Teaching of Rhetoric in French Jesuit Colleges: 1556–1762," *SM* 19 (1952), pp. 286–298. The extent of Jesuit influence on the arts generally was examined in a set of papers collected in *Baroque Art: The Jesuit Contribution*, ed. R. Wittkower and I. Jaffe (New York, 1972).

The only full-scale study of Keckermann's career is one in Polish by B. Nadolski (Torún, 1961), but there is a brief entry in *ADB*. A vague idea of his place in seventeenth-century education can be had from J. Freedman's "Cicero in Sixteenth- and Seventeenth-Century Rhetorical Instruction," *Rhe-*

torica 4 (1986), pp. 227–254. For Vossius, by contrast, there is the excellent study by C. Rademaker, *Life and Work of Gerhardus Johannes Vossius* (Assen, 1981).

On Bacon, see K. Wallace, *Francis Bacon on Communication and Rhetoric* (Chapel Hill, 1943); and L. Jardine, *Francis Bacon: Discovery and the Art of Discourse* (Cambridge, 1974). M. Cogan's "Francis Bacon on Rhetoric and Action," *Philosophy and Rhetoric* 4 (1982), pp. 212–233, contains some valuable insights, as does Paolo Rossi's *Francis Bacon: From Magic to Science* (Chicago, 1968). For Hobbes, C. Hinnant's sketch in *Thomas Hobbes*, Twayne English Authors series, 215 (Boston, 1977) is a good place to begin. On rhetoric in Hobbes, see J. Zappen, "Aristotelian and Ramist Rhetoric in Thomas Hobbes' *Leviathan*: Pathos versus Ethos and Logos," *Rhetorica* 1 (1983), pp. 65–91, in some respects misleading but useful nevertheless. A convenient edition of Hobbes' "Briefe" can be found in J. Harwood, ed., *The Rhetorics of Thomas Hobbes and Bernard Lamy* (Carbondale, IL, 1986). The English version of Lamy's *Rhétorique* unfortunately omits the last chapter, "On Preaching," of the original French. Among the most interesting studies of Hobbes is L. Roux's *Thomas Hobbes: Penseur entre deux mondes* (St.-Etienne, 1981). P. France has an interesting chapter on Descartes in his *Rhetoric and Truth in France: Descartes to Diderot* (Oxford, 1972), but most of the valuable work on rhetoric in Descartes has been done, not unexpectedly, in French, particularly by H. Gouhier. See, especially, his essay, "La résistance au vrai et le problème cartesien d'une Philosophie sans rhétorique," in *Retorica e Barocco: Atti del III Congresso Internazionale di Studi Umanistici*, ed. E. Castelli (Rome, 1955), pp. 85–98. See also A. Benjamin, "Descartes' Fable: The *Discours de la méthode*," in *The Literal and the Figural*, ed. A. Benjamin, G. Cantor, and J. Christie (Manchester, 1987).

A mere beginning to the study of the rhetoric of the law courts in seventeenth-century France, an area not touched by Fumaroli or Bayley, can be found in C. Holmes, *L'éloquence judiciare de 1620 à 1660* (Paris, 1967). There is clearly a great deal of work to be done in this area. Adaptations of rhetoric to the demands of the royal court are explored in a set of papers published in *Travaux de linguistique et littérature* 22:2 (Strasbourg, 1984). B. Vickers' outstanding "The Royal Society and English Prose Style: A Reassessment" in *Rhetoric and the Pursuit of Truth: Language Change in the Seventeenth and Eighteenth Centuries* (Los Angeles, 1985), pp. 3–76, is required reading. W. Mitchell's *English Pulpit Oratory from Andrewes to Tillotson* (London, 1932; rpt. New York, 1962) is still extremely useful, as is the formidable study (with newly edited texts) in I. Simon's 1967 Liège dissertation, *Three Restoration Divines: Barrow, South, Tillotson* (Paris, 1967).

The literature on Lamy is sketchy and, by and large, unilluminating. A general study may be found in F. Girbal's *Bernard Lamy: Étude biographique et bibliographique* (Paris, 1964), and some useful information may be gleaned from Harwood's introduction to *L'Art de Parler* in the edition cited above.

Harwood publishes the 1676 English translation, which is quite incomplete, though it gives a reasonably fair idea of what Lamy succeeded in doing.

On Donne and Milton, see T. Sloane's *Donne, Milton, and the End of Renaissance Humanism* (Berkeley, 1985), a very interesting study of the transition from humanism to Ramism in English letters. On Galileo, see M. Finocchiaro, *Galileo and the Art of Reasoning: Rhetorical Foundations of Logic and Scientific Method* (Dordrecht, 1980). On French neo-classicism, see H. Davidson, *Audience, Words, and Art* (Columbus, 1965); and on the importance of Longinus in that movement, J. Brody, *Boileau and Longinus* (Geneva, 1958). On the emergence of the will in ethical theory, see A. Levi, *French Moralists: The Theory of the Passions, 1555–1649* (Oxford, 1964).

NOTES

1. C. Sommervogel's *Bibliothèque de la Compagnie de Jesus* (Brussels, 1891–97), 7 vols., contains the names of 13,000 Jesuit authors of works on almost every subject imaginable, most from the seventeenth century.
2. I have used the 1620 Rome edition of this work.
3. Preliminary work on this neglected area has been done by C. Holmes (cited in Further Reading).
4. References are to the 1626 Cologne edition.
5. Recorded in Holmes, p. 17f.
6. I have used the first edition of *Systema rhetorica* (Hanover, 1607). An edition of Keckermann's *Opera omnia* was published in Geneva in 1614.
7. Ramus clearly had problems with the "method of prudence." See Ong, *Ramus*, pp. 252ff, in Chapter 5.
8. Crudely put, "dogmatic" rhetoric is only slightly affective; judicial rhetoric, used to affect the judgment of a single judge, is strongly emotional, playing on fear and indignation; "social" rhetoric may be either strongly emotional, as in political deliberations, or weakly so, as in ceremonial noncontroversial situations; and so forth.
9. Citations are to the 1627 Leiden edition.
10. See *Timber: or Discoveries*, ed. F. Schelling (Boston, 1892), p. 30.
11. References to Bacon are to the 1900 Spedding edition, hereafter called *Works*.
12. References are to Adam and Tannery, eds., *Oeuvres de Descartes* (Paris, 1897–1901), hereafter *Oeuvres*; and to F. Alquié's edition of the works and letters (Paris, 1963–67).
13. The phrase is A. Benjamin's; see *The Literal and the Figural* (cited in Further Reading), p. 10.
14. References to Hobbes are to *The English Works of Thomas Hobbes*, ed. W. Molesworth, 12 vols. (London, 1840), hereafter called *Works*.
15. Quoted by Vickers (see Further Reading), p. 46. A later attack by More, in *Enthusiasmus triumphatus* (London, 1662), elaborates the connections between rhetoric and "Enthusiasm" (see pp. 6, 18, 38, etc.). This work is available in a facsimile edition published by the Augustan Reprint Society, no. 118 (Los Angeles, 1966).
16. I have used the facsimile edition, ed. J. Cope and H. Whitmore (St. Louis, 1958).
17. Ibid., p. iii.

18. See *Shakespeare Adaptations*, ed. M. Summers (New York, 1966), p. 14.
19. A convenient English text of the *Discourse* can be found in the Modern Library edition, ed. N. Smith (New York, 1958). For these "rules," see pp. 106f.
20. I have used the facsimile text of the 1699 Amsterdam edition put out by Sussex Reprints (Brighton, 1969).
21. This term becomes popular in the seventeenth century after Descartes. It has specific reference, in Descartes (as also in, for instance, Mme. de Sévigné, whose letters give an intimate view of life in the Court of Louis XIV), to movements of the soul, not to what we call today *sentimentality*.
22. Longinus became enormously influential in the seventeenth century due mainly to the publication of Boileau's translation of *On the Sublime* in 1674. That influence continued well into the next century, not only in France but in England and Germany as well.
23. On this, see Sloane (cited in Further Reading).
24. See Finocchiaro (Further Reading).
25. See Levi, (cited in Further Reading). The emerging importance of the will in rhetorical discussions has yet to be examined thoroughly.

NICOLAS CAUSSIN, S. J., *DE ELOQUENTIA SACRA ET HUMANA*

(Page references are to the 1681 Cologne edition.)

Book 1: On the eloquence of the ancients (pp. 6–77)
   The invention of rhetoric (ch. 1–10)
   Survey of Greek and Roman orators (ch. 11–61)
   Comparisons among orators (ch. 62–72)

Book 2: On the best qualities of eloquence (pp. 78–147)
   Vices of style (ch. 1–16)
   Examples of inferior style (ch. 17–27)
   Praiseworthy style: its kinds (ch. 28–40)

Book 3: On the foundations of eloquence (pp. 147–180)
   Talent: many varieties (ch. 1–6)
   Study and practice of eloquence (ch. 7–16)
   Imitation (ch. 17–21)

Book 4: On invention and *loci* (pp. 181–259)
   Broad erudition the source (*nutrix*) of invention (ch. 1–2)
   Survey of areas of learning (history, scripture, etc.) (ch. 3–12)
   "Rational *loci*": a "place logic" (ch. 13–57)

Book 5: On amplification (pp. 260–302)
   The necessity of amplification (ch. 1–8)
   The 12 basic modes of amplification (ch. 9–20)
   Examples of noteworthy amplification, index to Cicero passages
      for further study (ch. 21–43)

Book 6: On disposition and the parts of a speech (pp. 303–357)
   General remarks (ch. 1–5)
   The exordium (ch. 6–13)

BARTHOLOMEUS KECKERMANN,
SYSTEMA RHETORICAE

(Page references are to the 1608 Hanover edition.)

Part One: *Rhetorica generalis*
Book 1. On rhetoric, its nature, object, and parts (pp. 9–135)
    ch.   1. Definition, offices, etc. (9–16)
    ch. 2– 8. On invention (17–96)
              (2–6) Treatment and explication of simple and complex
                themes
              (7–8) Amplification and exaggeration
    ch. 9–11. On arrangement (97–134)
              (9, 10) General observations on parts (97–121)
              (11) The exordium (122–125)
Book 2. On "ornamentation" (pp. 135–350)
    ch.   1. General observations (135–143)
    ch. 2–10. Tropes (metonymy, synecdoche, etc.) (144–182)
    ch. 11–19. Figures (use in explication, amplification) (182–199)
              (13–17) Figures of thought (199–234)
              (18, 19) Figures of diction (235–256)
    ch. 20–22. On prose rhythm (257–329)
              (20, 21) On cadence (257–282)
              (22) Periodic composition (282–329)
    ch.   23. On ornament by means of *copia* (329–351)
Book 3. On delivery (pp. 351–402)
    ch.   1. Memory (351–377)
    ch. 2– 4. Delivery in general (377–403)
              (3) Voice (377–393)
              (4) Gesture (394–403)
Part Two: *Rhetorica specialis*
Book 1. On dogmatic and affective rhetoric (pp. 403–647)
    ch.   1. Principles of subject, audience, circumstance (403–416)
    ch. 2– 9. On dogmatic rhetoric (417–452)
              (2–7) Treatment of simple themes (417–443)
              (8–9) Treatment of complex themes (443–451)
    ch. 10–32. On affective rhetoric (452–572)
              (10, 11) Affect in general (452–463)
              (12–25) Affect and particular genres (463–525)
              (25–32) Levels of affective style (525–647)
Book 2. On teaching eloquence (pp. 648–703)
    ch. 1– 2. General principle (648–670)
    ch. 3– 4. Special exercises (by genre) (670–703)
Book 3. On judging eloquence (pp. 703–720)
    ch.   1. Judging delivered speeches (730–710)
    ch.   2. Derived principles of judgment (710–718)
    ch.   3. On "quasi-rhetoric" (letters, dialogues, etc.) (718–720)

GERHARD JOHANN VOSSIUS, *RHETORICES CONTRACTAE, SIVE PARTITIONUM ORATORIARUM LIBRI V*

(Page references are to the 1627 Leiden edition.)

BERNARD LAMY, *RHÉTORIQUE,*
OU L'ART DE PARLER

(Page references are to the 1699 Amsterdam edition; reprinted Brighton, 1969.)

Book 1. [Of language generally]
  A. General principles of expression (pp. 1–57)
   1. Words are corporeal signs of incorporeal "designs" (1–16)
   2. On the various parts of speech and their arrangements (17–57)
  B. On the origins of language (58–84)
   1. Distinction between natural and conventional signs; convention the norm (58–71)
   2. On good and bad usage (72–84)
Book 2. [Supplements to the referential capacities of language]
  A. Variety in expression provided by tropes
   1. Tropes, their species and use (85–99)
   2. Rules for using tropes (100–107)
  B. Figures and their connections with emotions (108–152)
   1. On the variety of figures and their functions (108–145)
   2. Reflections of their usage (146–152)
Book 3. [On composition]
  A. Combinations of sounds and words; bringing sense and *sentiment* together in different ways (153–198)
  B. On prose and verse rhythms; a physics of communication (199–244)
Book 4. [Of style generally]
  A. Different styles due to different physical makeup of individuals (245–262)
  B. On choosing different styles (263–302)
   1. Differentiations by type (263–276)
   2. Differentiations by genre (277–302)
Book 5. [Rhetoric, or the art of persuasion]
  A. Parts of the art of rhetoric (303–367)
   1. Invention of arguments (303–353)
   2. Disposition and the other parts of the art (354–367)
  B. On preaching, which works on the same general principles (368–374)

CHAPTER 7

Eighteenth-Century Rhetorics

The "New Philosophy," as it was articulated by Descartes, Hobbes, and Locke, drove Jonathan Swift almost to distraction. "It is the opinion of Choice *Virtuosi*," he wrote in 1704,

> that the Brain is only a crowd of little Animals, but with Teeth and Claws extremely sharp, and therefore, cling together in the Contexture we behold, like a picture of Hobbes' *Leviathan*, or like Bees in perpendicular swarm upon a Tree, or like a Carrion corrupted into Vermin, still preserving the Shape and Figure of the Mother Animal. That all invention is formed by the Morsure of two or more of these Animals, upon certain capillary Nerves, which proceed from thence, whereof three Branches spread into the Tongue, and two into the right Hand. They hold also, that these Animals are of a Constitution extremely cold; that their Food is the Air we attract, their Excrement Phlegm; and that what we vulgarly call Rheums, and Colds, and Distillations, is nothing else but an Epidemical Looseness, to which that little Commonwealth is very subject, from the Climate it lyes under. Farther, that nothing less than a violent heat, can disentangle these Creatures from their hamated Station of Life, or give them Vigor and Humour, to imprint the marks of their little Teeth. That if the Morsure be Hexagonal, it produces Poetry; the Circular gives Eloquence; If the Bite hath been Conical, the Person, whose Nerve is so affected, shall be disposed to write upon the Politicks; and so of the rest.[1]

Swift succeeds in this short passage in deriding the view held by Hobbes and Locke—their solution to Descartes' dualism—that the mind works in much the same way as matter and can therefore be treated in mechanical or physiological terms. He derides also their view that perception is a matter of putting together two or more "impressions," the "Morsures" of which he writes. He only hints at the connection between this theory of knowledge as impression and eloquence here, but a little later in the same work he gets more explicit:

> The Art of *Canting* consists in skilfully adapting the Voice to whatever the Spirit delivers, that each may strike the Ears of the Audience, with its most significant Cadence. The Force, or Energy of this Eloquence, is...taken up wholly in dwelling, and dilating upon Syllables and Letters. Thus it is frequent for a single Vowel to draw Sighs from a Multitude; and for a whole Assembly of Saints to sob to the Musick of one solitary Liquid. But these are Trifles; when even Sounds inarticulate are observed to produce as forcible Effects. A Master Work-Man *shall blow his Nose so powerfully*, as to pierce the Hearts of his People, who are disposed to receive the *Excrements* of the Brain with the same Reverence, as the *Issue* of it. Hawking, Spitting, and Belching, the Defects of other Mens Rhetorick, are the Flowers, and Figures, and Ornaments of his. For, the Spirit being the same in all, it is of no Import through what Vehicle it is conveyed.[2]

Just so. If words are reduced, as they are in the physiological account, to mere forceful sound capable of producing some affect in the hearer, all sound becomes operative.[3] To prevent this view from degenerating into such absurdity as Swift detects, one must find recourse in belief in the connection between words, thoughts, and things suggested by Sprat's slogan, "the deliverance of so many things almost in an equal number of words," or in Locke's careful explanation of the notion that words are "marks for the ideas" within a speaker's mind. But this "representation theory of meaning," a theory that had significant influence throughout the eighteenth century both on the Continent and in Britain, is also the butt of Swift's satire. Lemuel Gulliver describes the "most learned and wise" of the Academy of Lagado who

> adhere to the new scheme of expressing themselves by things, which hath only this inconvenience attending it, that if a man's business be very great, and of various kinds, he must be obliged in proportion to carry a greater bundle of things upon this back, unless he can afford one or two strong servants to attend him. I have often beheld two of these sages almost sinking under the weight of their packs, like pedlars among us; who, when they met in the streets, would lay down their loads, open their sacks, and hold conversation for an hour together; then put up their implements, help each other to resume their burdens, and take their leave.[4]

Descartes, Hobbes, and Locke had all, it is true, rejected the external object as relevant to the question of knowledge and expression: Descartes because the senses are not to be trusted, Hobbes because only subjective perception can explain why men speak the way they do, and Locke because it is impossible that words could be anything other than signs of the impressions of things rather than of the things themselves. On this account, Swift's attack seems to be a canard, but in fact Swift's insight is very penetrating, since the ideational version of the representation theory was caught up in the same conundrum as the strict objective version. If one wishes to assert that to each word there corresponds an impression (a "simple idea," in Locke) and to each impression a sensation, it is difficult to see how one can avoid adding an extra step supplying an object for each sensation; for without some such object it is impossible to explain how "ideas" are generated in the mind in the first place.

This is the sort of question the New Philosophy raised and debated in the eighteenth century. Swift's acerbic reaction to such speculation was by no means typical nor, to be sure, universally consented to. If there were many who had reservations about it—or who simply ignored it—there were as many who accepted at least some of its main tenets and even more who were comfortable with some version of the psychological model implicit in it. No history of philosophy in the eighteenth century can afford to ignore the variety of positions among those who took part in the controversies sparked by the New Philosophy. By the same token, the progress, or lack of it, of rhetoric during this period might be mapped in terms of the various responses to the New Philosophy that emerge in the important rhetorics of the period. That is what we will try to do in what follows in this chapter. And what we will find is that the picture is a great deal more complicated than it has been represented by some historians of rhetoric.

Before we begin, however, we must make sure once again to keep the role of philosophy in perspective. From the point of view of rhetoric, to put it in the bluntest terms, the New Philosophy was virtually peripheral, although it is obviously necessary to keep it in the picture. Whatever effects the philosophical positions of Descartes or Locke had on rhetoric, it is clear that rhetoricians did not decide that persuasion was a matter of impression and affect and "movements of the soul" because they had been converted to dualism and mechanistic naturalism. Rhetoricians appropriated the vocabulary of the New Philosophy because they had already become convinced, as we saw in the last chapter, that such things were precisely what persuasion consisted in; and they quote the philosophers accordingly—usually rather casually, it might be added, and for obvious tactical reasons. We will not therefore take the view that the New Philosophy itself brought about radical changes in rhetorical theory. In some cases it did result in changes: there are, after all, a few rather programmatic "philosophical" rhetorics that appear late in the century—*after* certain adjustments of some details of Lockean psychology had been made. Even in those cases, however, it is impossible either to deduce the shape of such rhetorics from, or to reduce them to, philosophical doctrine, although it is true that in some cases the idiom of the philosophers did infiltrate rhetoric. On the one hand, therefore, we must be careful not to overestimate the importance of philosophy for this period; but at the same time we must be prepared to recognize it, on a case-by-case basis, when it is necessary to do so.

In what follows, we shall first try to get a general idea of how philosophy and rhetoric interacted in the eighteenth century. We will then examine in some detail some of the more important rhetorics of the first half of the century, up to about 1760. After that we will turn to a consideration of some of the relevant social and educational conditions bearing on rhetoric. And finally, we shall turn to some rhetorics of the second half of the century—specifically, those associated with the so-called Scottish School.

PHILOSOPHY AND RHETORIC: AN OVERVIEW

The New Philosophers—Locke, in particular—were for the most part hostile to rhetoric, so it is little wonder that we see so few systematic applications of their teachings in the rhetorics of the time. Locke's psychology, in fact, presented rhetoricians with some serious problems. First, there was the mind-body dualism, which persists in his view. Descartes had solved the problem of how the "Spirit," to paraphrase Swift, could deliver words to the Voice by guessing that the transaction took place in the pineal gland. Locke simply ignored the problem. More importantly, perhaps, Locke's theory, as some of his early critics noticed,[5] dictates that communication is little more than a report on a speaker's inner state—that is, the content of a private world. The objects of mental perception—what we know—are not things but the "ideas" we have of them in our minds based on our sensory experiences and reflections. These "simple ideas" we compose and recompose into "complex ideas." Other "ideas" we simply construct with no prototype in sensible nature. Thus when I utter the word *dog*, I refer to my idea of "dog," not to any particular dog. Only if my vocalization of *dog* conforms to the sign that you have learned is associated with a similar idea in your head will you "understand" what I am saying. If I consciously assign that vocalization to some other idea, I have deceived you; if unconsciously, I am deranged, and you, the listener, have in either case been misled.

To avoid such problems, Locke says, the best way to explain to anyone the meaning of a word signifying a simple idea is "by presenting to his senses that subject which may produce [the idea] in his mind, and make him actually have the idea that word stands for" (*Essay* III.11.14). But there is always a disparity between the needs of communication and the accidents of personal experience, for my experiences are mine and yours are yours, sometimes similar but never exactly the same. Rhetoric only makes things worse, for rhetoric, in Locke, deliberately or spontaneously, indulges in private games with words. In metaphor, for instance, we use one word to stand for something other than what is conventionally referred to by it or, in some cases, we deliberately mix ideas that have no "natural" connection with one another. Hence, Locke observes at the end of *Essay* III, rhetoric is "a perfect cheat."

Responses by rhetoricians contemporary with Locke varied considerably. One response to the dualism problem was framed by J.-B. DuBos (1670–1742), who simply "aestheticized" the entire matter, using Quintilian as his authority, by defining persuasion in purely affective terms, as did some of his predecessors in the seventeenth century. As far as the problems arising from Locke's epistemology were concerned, a solution—a very influential one, as it developed—was proposed by Claude Buffier, a philosopher of considerable ability who was intent on saving the best parts of Descartes and making adjustments to take care of the worst. To escape the inevitable solipsism of Cartesian/Lockean psychology, Buffier proposed *un sentiment commun*, the common sentiment[6] of nature—that is, "common sense." We shall look more closely at Buffier's work later. For now it is pertinent to mention that this idea of "common sense," as it was transmitted by Thomas Reid to his colleagues in Aberdeen, became a key element in Campbell's *Philosophy of Rhetoric* (1776), as well as in Blair's *Lectures on Rhetoric and Belles Lettres* (1783). We shall look at these, too, in due course.

Another problem posed by Locke's psychology, at least as it relates to communication, is the problem of the stability of reference of words to ideas. Almost everyone agreed with Locke (*Essay* III.1.1) that meanings depended not on any "natural" connection but on convention. Hence the frequency, from Lamy to Campbell and Blair, of speculation as to the origins of language and the explanation of the multiplicity of languages. But that was only part of the problem. There is more.

In principle, every word stands for, or signifies, a single idea. But any set of sensory experiences will generate a multitude of ideas, not just one, and that multitude will in turn be increased by the composition of the simple ideas into complex ideas. Moreover, two successive experiences of the same sort of sensory object must in principle generate two separate ideas—that is, two different ideas. At this point, the power of "abstraction" comes into play, whereby what is common to those two ideas is drawn off, to become yet another idea. This idea, like the first two, will presumably have its own proper name or sign. As a consequence, one would have to have a vocabulary commensurate with the multiplicity of sensations, ideas, and abstractions if one should wish to communicate clearly and avoid acting the "perfect cheat." Unless experience were somehow suspended or terminated, however, one would have to generate an interminable list of names. But the semantic resources of a given language, indeed of all languages taken together, are finite.

As we saw before, Lamy resolved this problem by pointing out that tropes were designed specifically to overcome the disparity between the quantity of experience and the available vocabulary for communicating that experience. In the eighteenth century, DuMarsais made a related observation in his *Des Tropes* (1730) and proposed a systematic way, equivalent in its rigor to geometry, of organizing the basic modes of expressing thoughts "tropically": "by correspondence," "by opposition," and "by connection." DuMarsais' analysis provided, on the one hand, a psychological grounding for the traditional "master tropes" and, on the other, anticipated Hume's modes of association, which were in turn appropriated by some Scottish rhetoricians, such as Joseph Priestley. We shall examine DuMarsais later.

Buffier and DuMarsais, then, are representative of ways in which rhetoricians responded constructively to the New Philosophy and laid the groundwork for later, more programmatic "philosophical" rhetorics, such as Campbell's. But there is yet another side to this century that exhibits few traces of actual influence by the New Philosophy while seeming nevertheless to strike out in new directions. Such rhetorics as Vico's *Institutiones* (1711). Gottsched's *Ausführliche Redekunst* (1736), Mayans' *Retórica* (1757), and Ward's *System of Oratory* (1759), among others, betray no serious interest in the doctrines of Descartes or Locke. In order to present a balanced picture of the eighteenth century, therefore, we will have to look at those rhetorics as well as at the "philosophical" ones.

The reason there is such a strong strain of "nonphilosophical" rhetorics in this century of the Enlightenment is, basically, a nagging sense that nothing can be gained, in view of the roles rhetoric was meant to play in society, from trying to rethink rhetoric from a standpoint that was essentially antirhetorical. This perception was instinctive and immediate in many of the rhetorics of the age and, it will be argued, came eventually to dominate everyone's conception of the art. Philosophical speculation about the mechanisms of persuasion and communication may have provided explanations for how language works (or so some rhetoricians thought) and a rationale for the structure of the discipline—both for the connections among the constituent parts of rhetoric and for the pedagogical formats best suited for teaching it. But such speculations have a built-in tendency to "deinstitutionalize" rhetoric, as is evident both from the concentration on the workings of individual psyches and their mutual interactions and from the generalization of rhetoric, as it was transformed into the study of *belles lettres*, to cover a host of literary genres not ordinarily considered to be rhetorical. Such speculative approaches to rhetoric, that is so say, fail to address a paramount concern of rhetoricians in any age—namely, the practical demands of the social and political conditions governing where and how the art is exercised and by whom and for what ends. This failure creates tensions in even the most philosophically oriented rhetorics. In light of those tensions, it is not difficult to understand, for instance, why we see, side by side, the idolizing of stylistic clarity and the insistence on elegance. Hence, too, the disparity in the philosophical rhetorics between the "value-free" truths of psychology and the insistence by Fénelon, Rollin, and the rest that the rhetorician be "a good man." And hence the slow transformation of "common sense" as an epistemological warrant into "taste" as a mode of social redemption.

In the end, that is to say, because of the settings in which rhetoric was actually taught and in which eloquence was expected, even the philosophical rhetorics were compelled to recognized the social leverage afforded by the art. Even philosophy, as it was incorporated into rhetoric, became an instrument of social mobility; and its principles were appealed to not as much in the interests of truth as in the interests of success and of the exercise of power. It is arguable, in short, that it is not the "philosophical" rhetorics, but the "nonphilosophical" rhetorics that ultimately must control our understanding of rhetoric in the eighteenth century.

BUFFIER AND DUMARSAIS

We need now to discuss in some detail the contributions of two figures whom we characterized before as having made constructive adjustments to the New Philosophy, Claude Buffier, S. J., and César-Chesneau DuMarsais.

The work of Buffier (1661–1737) is not well known these days, but it was highly respected in the eighteenth century, not only in France but in England and Scotland as well—as we shall see later in this chapter. Claude Buffier was born of French parents in Poland in 1661, entered the Society of Jesus when he was 19, and distinguished himself, both within the order (as a founding editor of the influential *Mémoires des Trévoux*) and without, as a penetrating thinker. He was the author of two dozen scholarly works, including a treatise on memory systems (1705), a French grammar (1709), the *Traité des premières véritéz* (1724—his major work), and the *Traité de l'éloquence* (1728). The treatise on memory systems was enormously popular, going into 20 editions, including translations into Spanish and Polish. The *Grammar* was likewise widely read and was translated into English (1734), German (1738), Dutch, and twice into Italian.[7]

This is not the place to attempt a detailed examination of Buffier's philosophy, although it was as a philosopher that he was so highly thought of in his day. But in order to get his contribution to rhetoric into some sort of perspective, we should note here for the record that the two main influences on his *Traité des premières véritéz*, by his own account, were Descartes and Locke. In fact, Buffier carried on a long correspondence with Locke. After Buffier's death, the great *philosophe* Voltaire (*Oeuvres* 14 [Paris, 1848], p. 48) characterized him as the only Jesuit who was sensible enough to produce a rational philosophy by combining Descartes with parts of Locke. Bearing this in mind, let us turn to Buffier's *Traité de l'éloquence.**

The *Traité* is divided into two large parts, the first (pp. 295–365) dealing with general principles in 26 chapters, and the second (365–409) consisting of models drawn from various genres and some critical observations on the old rhetorics of Aristotle, Cicero, and Quintilian. The first part is not divided into the traditional sections, but it can be seen nevertheless to fall into four parts: I–XI discussing the nature and kinds of eloquence; XII–XIV laying out some brief guidelines for the various parts of a speech; XV–XXIII treating figures, especially that of "exposition," or vividness, and their effects; and XXIV–XXVI commenting on some general rules rhetoric provides. In such a bare outline, this part of the *Traité* does not look radically different from earlier treatments we have seen. Unlike those works, however, the progression of points both within and between its subparts is quite fluid, with one idea leading naturally, by extension or by exception, to the next. It is also worth nothing that Buffier is a virtual minimalist on the standard topics, paring the old lore down to absolute essentials and discarding what he sees as superfluous. His treatment of two subjects—the nature of eloquence and the figure *exposition*—is by contrast very full and, for the most part, quite original.

Buffier begins by drawing a distinction between true eloquence and apparent eloquence. The latter is frequently met with, he says, but is a mere matter of a certain facility with words, a pale copy of the true eloquence. True eloquence, much less frequently encountered but a natural capacity nonetheless, is "the ability (*talent*) to create in the souls of others by speaking (*parole*) the impression of immediate understanding (*sentiment*) and the emotion (*mouvement*) which we intend" (p. 297). Buffier's definition, then, is not much different from, and is expressed in a vocabulary similar to, those we saw in the affective rhetorics of the seventeenth century—at least, on the surface.

True eloquence depends little on rules (p. 313f.). It is closer to a natural *ingenium* of the sort Horace wrote about in his *Ars poetica*. This "talent" can be cultivated by adhering to rules and by practice, but it cannot be reduced to them (p. 323f.). And like the rules in Horace's *Ars poetica*, Buffier's rules are quite "natural," sensible, nonformulaic, and few. The "rules" in his section on the parts of a speech (XII–XIV) come down to: "state your case in the opening, divide it into two or three parts, and speak on each. At the end, sum up."

Buffier has something to say about "proof" in that section, too. He is concerned lest he be misunderstood when he uses that term, so he draws this distinction:

> If one desires not to abuse the term "proof," he will find, it seems to me, that it comprises a great deal of discourse where one has no business *proving* or *convincing* the mind of some *truth*, but is rather trying to communicate it, present it, and affect someone . . . so that he is *persuaded*. . . . "Proof" belongs properly to Logic; but the movement or *sentiment* of the soul is the proper end of eloquence. (p. 330f.)

Given the separation here of persuasion from conviction, it is clear that Buffier's notion of rhetorical proof has nothing to do with arguments and everything to do with powerful language.

Figures are the chief means for presenting thoughts and affecting audiences. There is far too much discussion about these, he says, for only six or seven are really important (p. 334f.). And in fact, common usage is full of them: they come quite naturally when we want to express ourselves to others and are thus not just the business of formal arts. By exploiting figures, we can express ourselves in different ways, moreover, which is a desirable thing, given the variety of audiences we might want to persuade.

The one universally useful figure is *exposition* (p. 338f.). In fact, eloquence as a whole is little more than the effective *exposition* of things, thoughts, and attitudes. Buffier then demonstrates the way of using this figure, distinguishing it from mere explication and showing how useful it is for achieving a kind of presence or vivacity in the mind (soul) of the auditor, particularly in its version as "repetition," which, far from causing *ennui* in the soul, is the secret of producing an impression or *sentiment* in it (p. 351f.).

Buffier's notion of rhetoric is, therefore, quite cogent and very much to the point. The gist of what he says in his *Traité* is: forget all the rules and taxonomies, and concentrate on the real end and basic means of eloquence— moving the soul by vivid expression. The sort of rhetoric we are dealing with here, then, is affective, a unilateral transaction between an active speaker and a passive listener, between mover and moved. Formal rules are all but completely discarded. Human nàture itself serves to explain how that sort of transaction can take place, as the slightest attention to what experience teaches allows us to see.

All of this seems quite clear. But it is strange, nonetheless, since it also seems to be at odds with the New Philosophy, to which he himself claimed to subscribe in his philosophical work, a sort of throwback to the affective rhetorics of his predecessors, both Jesuit and non-Jesuit. Is Buffier simply being inconsistent? How, in any event, could his rhetoric be reconciled with his apparent philosophical beliefs? In order to see that, we shall have to look again at his alleged Lockean Cartesianism.

Clearly, Buffier's philosophy would not have been what it was without Descartes, as devoted as it was to the question of the beginnings of knowledge. And, as clearly, Buffier owed a great deal to Locke, particularly on the issue of what sorts of things one could hope to have knowledge of. But in both Descartes and Locke there is a lurking solipsism. If all we know are the ideas in our own consciousness, we can be absolutely sure only of our own existence. If there is communication, what is communicated can only be the contents of our own consciousness. And this, as we have seen, poses serious problems, particularly for rhetoricians who speak so blithely about clarity of style and moving others' souls.

Buffier looked for some first principle that was not, as in Descartes, solely in consciousness nor, as in Locke, solely in sensation, in order to escape the trap of solipsism and avoid the problems solipsism creates for any theory of communication. The principle he hit upon is that of "common sense," "the disposition which nature has put in all men, or clearly in the greatest number of men, to form...a common and uniform judgment concerning objects different from the objects of one's own consciousness" (*Traité des premières véritéz*, p. 563). The first of these "primary truths," according to Buffier, is that "there are in the world other beings and other men than ourselves." In this, Buffier seems to follow Descartes in part. But Buffier goes further, taking it to be self-evident (see p. 565f.) that "there is something in man which is called truth, wisdom, and prudence, and it is not something wholly arbitrary"; that "all men are not in conspiracy to deceive me"; that "what is affirmed through the experiences and testimony of all men is incontestably true"; and that "a fact attested by a very large number of reasonable men who claim to have witnessed it cannot reasonably be revoked by doubt." This faculty of common sense, it must be stressed, is not physical but *quelque chose de spirituel*, something of a spiritual nature; but at the same time common sense is nothing like the innate ideas of Descartes. It is, rather, the principle that allows as valid starting points the experience of objects, the probable, and matters of sound opinion; and is thus something like the cognitive assumption behind Aristotelian dialectic, although not reducible to universality of consent.

Once Buffier had laid out this notion of common sense, he was able to rescue rhetoric from the oblivion to which both Descartes and Locke had sought to consign it. The essence of the art of rhetoric as it had been hinted at, but perhaps imperfectly grasped, by his predecessors could now be grounded firmly on "self-evident" truths, as could the faculty of taste, which had proved so difficult to account for after Locke.

The other author we have associated with the New Philosophy is César-Chesneau DuMarsais (1676–1756), most famous in his day for his work on grammar but important in the history of rhetoric as well. DuMarsais was far more taken with the New Philosophy than Buffier, probably because of his Oratorian education and his early exposure to the Port-Royal school. And unlike Buffier (with whom he occasionally takes issue), DuMarsais is no minimalist. His *Des Tropes, ou des differents sens dans lequel on peut prendre un mot dans une même langue* (1730)[8] fills some 360 pages of careful and copiously illustrated analysis.

Des Tropes went into numerous editions in France—in fact, it shaped rhetorical education in France well into the nineteenth century—and came out in German and English versions as well. One recent French critic has hailed it as "without a doubt the most important monument of all French rhetoric,"[9] although there are surely, even in France, many who would dispute that. For our purposes, *Des Tropes* is important because it is a good example of how rhetoric was recast under the influence of Descartes and Arnauld and because it promoted the process by which rhetoric was transformed from an art of persuasion into 'the study of unusal expressions.'"[10]

DuMarsais tells us in the preface to *Des Tropes* that he intends to treat his subject with "geometric rigor" (p. xiv). The treatise is in three parts. The first (pp. 1–51) presents definitions and general observations on figures and tropes. Both fall under the general heading of "tropes," since both "are ways of speaking remote from those which are natural and ordinary" (p. 2). One needs to understand such modes of expression both to be able to understand what one reads and to master the art of speaking and writing in general. Tropes are used to enliven an idea, to give more energy to expression, to ornament discourse and engage the imagination in an agreeable way, to dignify discourse, to disguise unpleasant (*dure*) ideas, and to enrich a language by multiplying the uses of single words.

Part Two consists of an exhaustive catalogue of particular tropes (pp. 52–247) and some observations on how they might be organized systematically (pp. 248ff.). Although DuMarsais distinguishes figures of speech from figures of thought in Part One, that distinction seems to play no role in the organization of the catalogue. In fact, it is difficult to see that there is any single controlling principle of organization, although DuMarsais implies that there is one in his rejection of the schemes of Vossius and of his contemporary Rollin (see pp. 36ff., 248f.).

Toward the end of Part Two (pp. 248ff.), DuMarsais begins reflecting on the 19 tropes he has analyzed and notes that all of them, at the same time as they represent deviations from "natural" usage, imply some *rapport* or *liaison* between the word or phrase as signifier and what is signified. Catachresis (see pp. 52ff.) and metaphor (pp. 155ff.), for instance, are founded on a *liaison* or correspondence or resemblance. Irony (pp. 199ff.) is based on a *liaison* of contrariety or opposition. Metonymy and synecdoche involve *rapports* that are neither those of resemblance nor those of opposition, but some connection —cause and effect, circumstance, and the like—is operative. One could, he says (p. 252), class all of the particular tropes along such lines.

The *rapports* DuMarsais discusses are not merely grammatical. Grammar and usage reveal mental processes in accordance with which thoughts are formed and expressed. In Part Three (pp. 263–360), DuMarsais inquires into the nature of these processes, looking now at modes of expression not traditionally counted as "tropic" but which are "tropic" nonetheless. For instance, by making an adjective out of a noun or a participle of a verb, or the reverse, one is implicitly articulating a judgment about what is the object signified and what the qualities attached to it. At a different level, words may express either more or less than their literal meaning; and if more, those words may express "objects" at multiple levels of abstraction (as in allegory, for instance). The entire discussion here is carried on the context of the psychological conditions by which words bear meanings, conditions that are on the whole consistent with Locke's psychology. But DuMarsais goes further than Locke had, freeing meaning from the limitations of the representational theory of meaning by demonstrating the rational principles of association that govern meaning even where the meaning is not literal. In introducing these principles of association, it might be added, DuMarsais anticipates Hume, as the resemblances between the modes of association in the two authors make clear.

DuMarsais, interestingly, betrays no interest whatever in communication as such. That is because he saw himself not as a rhetorician, at least not in the normal understanding of that term, but as a rational grammarian. Thus he restricts himself to the shapes of expression and what they can tell us about the mental states of those who apprehend meaning. His contribution to rhetoric is nevertheless worthy of note because his analysis of tropes provided a way for rhetoricians to escape the fate decreed for them by Locke's theory of meaning and to dodge the implications of that theory as they are laid out in *Essay* III. Figures and tropes—even ambiguities and covert meanings—could again, after DuMarsais, be seen as not only legitimate but central in language.

In Buffier and DuMarsais we see two thinkers who took the New Philosophy seriously but refused to surrender to the implications of that movement for rhetoric. The notion of "common sense" hit upon by Buffier and the analysis of the different modes of association by DuMarsais introduced into discussions about rhetoric were very influential later in the century in ways we shall examine in due course. But Buffier and DuMarsais give us only part of the picture. Not all rhetoricians took the New Philosophy as seriously as they did. Some ignored it, some actively opposed it. And it is to some of those that we turn now.

BOUHOURS AND ROLLIN

Numerous rhetorics published between 1700 and 1760 were self-consciously "classicizing" treatises. One might point, for example, to Giambattista Vico's *Institutiones oratoriae* (1711),* composed while Vico was professor of rhetoric at Naples; or, later in the century, to Ward's *System of Oratory*, based on his lectures at Gresham College, London, where he was professor of rhetoric from 1720 to 1758.[11] Both of these are strongly Ciceronian in conception and format. Both of them were also self-consciously opposed to the New Philosophy.

Bouhours and Rollin, on the other hand, deserve to be looked at rather closely. Unlike Vico and Ward, who exercised no visible influence in the eighteenth century (Vico's reputation has been considerably enhanced in the present century, however), Bouhours and Rollin were published frequently, widely read and quite influential.

Dominique Bouhours (1628–1702) was, like Buffier, a Jesuit. Unlike Buffier, he had little use for the problems generated by the New Philosophy. As professor of humanities at Paris and of rhetoric at Tours, Bouhours argued tenaciously that what needed to be known about true eloquence could be found in Cicero and, above all, Quintilian. His writings are far from unimaginative imitations of the old rhetorics, however. He was a creative and ingenious author of vast erudition whose *Pensées chrétiennes* was one of the most widely read books in the eighteenth century, in French and in translation (including Hungarian, Armenian, and Arabic versions!). His favored literary genre was the dialogue, and it is for his dialogues, *Les entretiens d'Ariste et d'Eugène* (1671) and *La manière de bien penser* (1687), that he is most famous in the history of rhetoric. *La manière* went into two dozen editions before 1800, most of them printed in Paris, but others in Lyon, Amsterdam, Augsburg (a German translation), Bologna (in Italian), and Rome. There were two versions in English, including John Oldmixon's 1728 paraphrase as *The Arts of Logick and Rhetorick*.[12]

La manière de bien penser is an extended dialogue (more than 460 pages) between Eudoxe, a devotee of the classics and of good taste, and Philanthe, who is quite taken with the new fashions in literature, particularly Italian and Spanish works. The dialogue is divided into four parts, as the discussion is imagined to take place over a four-day stay by Philanthe at Eudoxe's country estate. The topics treated in the four parts of the dialogue are as follows: (1) true and false thoughts, and the difference between them (pp. 1–83); (2) the fidelity of a thought to the truth is not sufficient to make for good thinking (pp. 85–274); (3) how the sublime can degenerate into bombast, the agreeable into affectation, and the delicate into oversubtlety (pp. 275–392); and

(4) a review of the doctrine that good thinking and expression should be unadorned, clear, and intelligible (pp. 393–463).

At first glance, the title might suggest that the work be placed in the mainstream of the New Philosophy. But Bouhours is careful to distinguish at the outset his aims from those of the Port-Royalist "arts of good thinking." *Penser* here refers rather to the ability to discriminate between true eloquence and false eloquence. "Good thinking" and "good expression" are, moreover, inseparable, indeed perhaps indistinguishable, from one another. One does not learn these things by deploying the rules of an arid system, but by wide acquaintance with all sorts of literary expression—with what Bouhours calls *belles lettres*. This acquaintance is, to be sure, informed by a few perennial truths about discourse, chiefly that perspicuity is the most important virtue of style and that affectation is the worst vice. But these principles do not function in Bouhours as they do in Lamy, for instance. Bouhours' "method" consists of a sort of "show-and-tell," exposing his reader to a staggering assortment of passages—sometimes as short as a single verse, sometimes quite extended—that are "discussed" by the interlocutors. These passages are drawn from all genres, from poetry to panegyric to history, and from authors in French, Latin, Italian, Spanish, and Portuguese. The order here, incidentally, is hierarchical, with French being by far superior to the other languages. Bouhours had such a low regard for German as a language suited for literary purposes that his characters all but ignore it.

Bouhours' method, then, is empirical. Moreover, it can work only if his readers already have some natural ability to discriminate between sense and nonsense, between expression that "rings true" and that which does not. In some ways, therefore, Bouhours makes assumptions similar to those of his "modern" counterparts; and indeed his emphasis on clarity and accuracy of expression resembles that of the New Philosophy. But one must be careful not to make of Bouhours a "crypto-modern." The method he uses is the same method as that in, for instance, Longinus or Hermogenes (both of whom Eudoxe appeals to), and the criteria he insists upon are the criteria articulated by Quintilian, not Descartes and Arnauld. There is evidently no need, in Bouhours' view, to take all that New Philosophy into account since, in the final analysis as it bears on eloquence, it supplies nothing new and only complicates matters by formalizing something that can be made obvious simply by looking at the ways various authors express themselves.

The popularity of *La manière* was due, then, not to its being *au courant*, so to speak, but to the fact that it provided a relatively painless and accessible way by which a reader could sharpen his (or her) sense of good literature— that is, acquire taste. It was a way that was easily adopted by other audiences, as well: hence, Oldmixon was able to claim that his version could do for English readers what Bouhours had done for the French. He had only to pick the appropriate English examples to replace Bouhours' French ones. Since there were large numbers of people in France and England—all over Europe, for that matter—who felt it necessary to acquire good taste, Bouhour's book could not have failed to attract a large audience as indeed it did.

Another work that proved very influential in the eighteenth century is Charles Rollin's *Traité des études: De la manière d'enseigner et d'étudier les Belles-Lettres.** Rollin (1661–1741) was perhaps France's most eminent man of letters in the first quarter of the century and dedicated himself to the cause of educational reform, particularly reform of the instructional regimen in the Paris rhetoric courses. This consisted in large part of memorization and recitation, amplification on assigned themes, and disputation exercises, a plan of instruction that undoubtedly owed much to the influence of the Jesuit *ratio studiorum*. In its place, Rollin called for the study of French along with Latin, the reading of "modern" authors, graduated exercises, and the eventual cultivation of good taste and of a simple yet elegant style that would enable the student to speak and write effectively. The *Traité*, originally published between 1726 and 1728, went into 27 later editions, well into the nineteenth century. It was translated into German (1750), four times into Italian, and into Russian (1789). There were no fewer than 10 English editions (the first in 1734), including 3 printed in Scotland and one in Ireland.[13]

The book is divided into two major sections. The first is a relatively brief discussion of the principles of rhetoric and of rhetorical criticism; the second consists of treatments of special forms of eloquence: the eloquence of the bar, that of the pulpit, and that of Sacred Scripture. Since it is a manual for teachers and not a textbook, Rollin's discussion concerns both the theory and its pedagogical applications. Relatively little time is spent dwelling on general principles, rather more on taking exemplary texts and explaining how they can be explicated. He observes, "It is easy to see that rhetoric without the study of good authors is lifeless and barren, and that examples in this, as in all other things, are infinitely more efficacious than precepts" (2.3). Rhetoric for Rollin, that is to say, is quite closely tied to what was traditionally grammatical studies, the subjects of which the new grammar had largely abandoned in the interests of inquiring into the nature of language itself after Descartes. The *Traité* thus fills a gap that had formed between rhetoric as a more or less academic exercise and grammar as an abstract science of language.

Rollin was a champion of the simple style, but recognized, first, that not all authors wrote in such a style and, second, that simplicity itself was no guarantee of eloquence:

> There are enemies of all ornament in discourse who find real eloquence only in the simple, naked style, like that of conversation, which regards as superfluous anything added to that which is absolutely necessary.... If one had to speak only to philosophers, or to people devoid of all emotion and all prejudice, perhaps that notion would appear reasonable. But that is not the way things are, and if the orator does not know how to win his audience over by pleasing them and turning them by a gentle force (*une douce violence*), jutice and truth will succumb beneath the onslaughts of the liars. (2.82)

Genuine eloquence, in turn, was not simply a matter of linguistic form; that is, one cannot ascertain the eloquence, or sublimity, of a composition by looking to stylistic principles alone. One must, rather, look to the effect on the audience. As a general rule, in fact, "A good orator is almost infallibly applauded by his audience" (1.158). What one discovers after examining exemplary passages is that, while the simple style is effective in transporting its auditors, the flowery style is not, since it impedes the understanding. The exemplary writers he commends to his readers, it should be noted, are Cicero and Demosthenes. Thus it is clear that Rollin, reformer that he was, did not intend to jettison the past nor the tradition it stood for, but to save its true genius.

To Rollin, what antiquity had to offer was the means by which the natural reason of children could be perfected by study in such a way as to produce an *honnête homme*, a phrase difficult to translate but that can easily be paraphrased by Quintilian's notion of "a good man skilled in speaking." This allusion to Quintilian is, in fact, quite relevant to Rollin's educational project, particularly as it includes training in rhetoric. Much of the *Traité* is drawn quite candidly from Quintilian's *Institutes*. In fact, some passages are virtual *centos* of lines from Quintilian (see, for instance, 2.85ff., drawing on *Inst.* 8.3 and 4.2; 135ff., from 8.5; 161ff., from 9.4 and Cicero's *Orator* 176ff.). Rollin himself had produced an abridged version of the *Institutes* in 1715 in response to the demand he saw for versions of that work, a demand evident in the keen interest in Quintilian shown in France at the time.[14]

The idea that a child's natural reason could be cultivated so as to produce an *honnête homme* was a relatively new one in Rollin's time. In the sixteenth century, *honnêtes hommes* would be found only among the aristocrats. In the wake of religious reform and the increasing attention paid to the idea of "natural reason" in the seventeenth century, the *honnête homme* became a sort of ideal into which, in theory, any rational child could be molded through education. In the wake of changes in society that made the elites of the literary salons and of the *parlements* accessible to the bourgeoisie, the production of *honnêtes hommes* regardless of bloodlines became possible in fact.

In Rollin's time, therefore, the *honnête homme* became more or less synonymous with a member of polite society, well versed in many areas, especially *belles lettres*. The study of those subjects, Rollin wrote, "enables us to pass correct judgment on other men's labors, to enter into society with men of understanding, to keep the best company, to have a share in the discourses of the most learned, to furnish subjects for conversation, without which we must be silent, to render it more agreeable by intermixing facts with reflections, and setting one off by the other" (1.7). The most necessary quality for such a person, "in a word...not only for the art of speaking but for the total conduct of life, is taste (*goût*), that prudence, that discernment which apprehends for each subject and for each occasion that which one must do and how one ought to do it" (1.171, citing, it should be noted, Quintilian 6.5!).

Such educational ideals were of course not peculiar to Rollin. In some ways, although Rollin's program is more austere than the programs of others, its goals and the notion that the way to reach those goals is through the cultivation of taste by exposure to *belles lettres* are ideas he shared with Buffier, DuBos, and Bouhours, however much he may have disagreed with them on other matters. And such educational ideals did not stop with Rollin. Within a few years of the publication of the *Traité*, we find these ideals articulated by authors all over Europe. Although the France of Louis XIV and XV spawned them, they were to spread to Italy and Spain, to England and Scotland, even to Poland and Russia, as we shall see in the next section.

RHETORIC AND FRENCH CULTURAL DOMINANCE

We have looked so far at rhetoric in terms of possible responses to the New Philosophy current at the turn of the eighteenth century. On the one hand, we have rhetorics like those of Buffier and DuMarsais, which might perhaps be understood as conscious adjustments to that philosophy; and on the other, we have the "classicizers," such as Bouhours and Rollin, who largely ignored the doctrines being promoted in the name of Reason. What ties all of these together, it now appears, is the common interest shared by those sympathetic and unsympathetic to the philosophers alike in the social leverage supplied by the study of rhetoric. This concern is evident in authors during the mid-century in various European countries. And we will examine some of that material later in this section. For now, we need to step back briefly and get a look at the broad picture of French cultural domination in the eighteenth century, particularly as it relates to social, political, and educational changes that occurred up to about 1760.

As we have seen, the works of Bouhours and Rollin circulated all over Europe and were translated into both German and English. We might add to these books such works as Fénelon's *Dialogues sur l'éloquence*, translated into English and German (Halle, 1734); Charles Batteaux's *Les Beaux Arts reduits à un même principe* (1747), of which German versions were published in Leipzig and Vienna; and Lamy's *Art de parler*, a German version of which came out in 1753. It significant that the majority of books on rhetoric published in both England and Germany up to 1750 were imports or translations from the French, while no English or German rhetorics were translated into French in that period.

While it might be argued that this is no more than a sign of French chauvinism, the fact is that French fashions, letters, and political ideas dominated Europe almost completely. French of course was the language of diplomacy and of polite company. It was also the official language of the court of Frederick the Great in Germany and of Catherine the Great in Russia. German princes, in particular, sought to reproduce French architecture, and perhaps the world of grace and finesse it stood for, in the châteux they commissioned: *Mon repos* in Württemburg, *Sans souci* in Potsdam, *la Gloriette* in Vienna. Most of all, perhaps, European rulers emulated the absolute monarchy of the "Sun King," Louis XIV. As we have noted, the so-called Age of Enlightenment might be better called the "Age of Enlightened Despotism."

In order to understand why Europe looked so intently at France, we need to recall that this was a period of consolidation, of the emergence of national consciousness in Germany, Russia, Spain, and Italy, among others. The paramount concern of the rulers of these countries, like that of Louis in France, was stability, the maintenance of social order. Traditionally, social hierarchies and the inequalities in the social rank were viewed as ordained by Providence. When theological justifications were eliminated by the *philosophes* as unwarranted by reason, rational justifications took their place. Voltaire, for instance, may have been radical in his anticlericalism, but he remained a believer in efficient monarchical government. The power accorded to the State by Rousseau was to have been derived from the General Will, a conception that borders on the totalitarian. Unfettered reason, in fact, would not produce the free play of ideas and opinions, but complete harmony by means of unanimity. Thus even the champions of Enlightenment adhered, in the final analysis, to some form of absolutism. And if absolutism was pervasive in France, it was equally so in the other nations of Europe, all of which looked to Louis XIV's example as their model.

Virtually every monarch in Europe faced two important problems. One was how stability and uniformity could be established and maintained. The ordinary way of doing this was by decree. The other was perhaps more serious. The expansion of trade due to colonization during the eighteenth century led to the growth of a wealthy urban class in every country in Western Europe, a class whose wealth came both from trade and from banking, from financing the expeditions to find more raw materials and financing the wars that resulted from the competition for markets. The emergence of this new class threatened the old order as it destabilized the order of privilege and shifted the centers of power. A partial solution to both of these problems came from an unexpected corner: institutions of higher learning. While increased support for existing universities and the foundation of new ones might be seen as mere window dressing for the continuation of the traditional powers of the monarchies, it was a way, first, to promote a sort of cultural homogeneity (and perhaps a measure of national pride) and, second, to provide an avenue by which nonaristocrats could be absorbed into the royal administrative apparatus. As in the case of Byzantium, then—ironically for an age that saw Byzantium as a huge cultural aberration—education was found to have its rewards for the ruling class. As we shall see, the part of that education devoted to rhetoric was thought to be particularly rewarding.

At the beginning of the eighteenth century, most universities in Europe, with the exception of a few healthy institutions run by the Oratorians and Jesuits, were in dire straits. Most universities in Germany in 1700 were barely able to function. The renowned old university at Heidelberg enrolled, on the average, only about 80 students per year between 1700 and 1715; 20 others had fewer than 700 students total. Vico's Naples University was poor and disorganized. Study of the liberal arts was on the decline all over Europe: the chair of Greek at Alcalá in Spain, for instance, was vacant for over 40 years (1693–1734). There was, moreover, a chronic shortage of qualified teachers at elementary levels in almost every country; and at the higher levels, the traditional classics-based curriculum was perceived to be inadequate for the times.

In response to this critical situation, the rulers of Europe increasingly intervened to bring about a revival of higher learning, looking, in almost every case, to France as a model. As Louis XIV had attempted to use education to reduce regional differences and to train bureaucrats, Catherine the Great decreed that an official "catechism" be published and mandated for use in schools. State commissions of education were created in Poland and in Austria. Older universities in Germany were granted large subsidies, and new universities were founded and richly endowed, as at Göttingen (1737) and Erlangen (1742). Curricular reforms designed to attract students were instituted at many universities, reforms that, in the main, diminished the importance of the theology faculties and built up the faculties of "philosophy," which included what would now be considered natural sciences as well as liberal arts. By the 1760s, history, mathematics, and rhetoric were lavishly promoted by faculties of philosophy not as mere propaedeutics to the professions but as important subjects of study in their own right. And as a result of reforms, greater numbers of students were enrolled from the middle class, educated, and placed in administrative positions. Between 1715 and 1750, the percentage of university-trained officeholders who were not of noble blood grew appreciably in every country in Western Europe, particularly in those states where bureaucratic administrations of a more or less despotic type had been set up.

It is against this background of educational reform instituted by royal decree and inspired by French cultural and political models that the history of rhetoric in the mid-eighteenth century must be viewed. Eventually, writers in Spain, Germany, and Italy rebelled against the cultural hegemony of France, but the rebellion was less a rebellion against the ideals of French culture than against the use of the French language as the official tongue of polite society. The ideals, particularly the ideal of the *honnête homme*, though in different national guises, remained intact.

In what follows, we shall look at two rhetorics from the mid-century, one from Germany and the other from Spain. It would be difficult to argue that these two treatises epitomize the period in any precise way, but they are nonetheless fairly representative. With that qualification, then, we turn to Gottsched's *Ausführliche Redekunst* and Mayans' *Retórica*.

Gottsched

Johann Christof Gottsched (1700–66) was one of Germany's most conspicuous literary figures. Professor of poetry at Leipzig from 1734 until his death, Gottsched was a champion of the German language and saw as his mission in life the creation of Germany literary standards that would enable German poets and dramatists to assimilate their work to the French models that had exercised so much influence. He was a leading figure, along with his wife, in the Deutsch Gesellschaft, a middle-class literary society that he hoped would do for German what the Académie Français had done for French. He was well known as a critic, most famous perhaps for his essay on poetic criticism *Versuch einer Critischen Dichtkunst vor die Deutschen* (1730), that led to his election to membership in the Prussian Academy, founded by Frederick I as the German equivalent to the Académie Française, and to his appointment to the chair of poetry. This work was consciously modeled on Boileau's *Art poétique.*

Ausführliche Redekunst (A Complete Rhetoric)* was first published in Leipzig in 1736 and republished in 1739, 1743, 1750, and 1759.[15] Its success can perhaps be more accurately gauged by the wide circulation of abridged versions of it up to the end of the century. These versions were published in facing German and Latin texts "for the benefit of the students in Poland and Hungary" in Wratislava, Vienna, Posnan, and Zagreb. It was also read and admired, as was his *Dichtkunst,* in Russia, where there was an active Gottsched Club.

Gottsched's work was of course not the first German rhetoric, but it succeeded in doing what the others had failed to do. It presented a curriculum of study firmly rooted in the classic tradition but up to date and thoroughly German. The rhetorics of Johannes Meyfart (*Teutsche Rhetorica,* 1634) and of Gottsched's colleague at Leipzig, G. P. Müller (*Idea eloquentiae novantiquae,* 1717), were but continuations of the old baroque rhetorics. Gottsched draws heavily on Cicero, who was, after all, still an important author in German schools, but at the same time he reinterprets traditional lore to bring it into line with the contributions of Lamy, Rollin, and, at times, his compatriot, the philosopher Christian Wolff. Most striking, however, is the fact that Gottsched not only appeals to the standards of good German prose but himself writes in good German prose free of the excesses of the francomania he saw in others' writing, of the aridity of the German chancery style, and of the bloated style of his baroque predecessors.

Ausführliche Redekunst consists of two parts that, together, fill over 700 pages. In the first, general part—the *allegmeiner Teil*—Gottsched presents the basic principles of good speaking; in the second, he provides over 300 pages of examples of good speaking, translations into German and imitations in German of Classical orations, samples of speeches from various genres, and letters. It is with the first part that we are concerned here.

Like Buffier's *Traité,* Gottsched's work is not divided into books but into chapters. The 18 chapters of Part One, however, cover the standard material in rather standard form: (1) chapters 1–2 deal with the definition of rhetoric and the character of the orator; (2) chapters 3–9 cover invention; (3) chapters 10 and 11 concern arrangement; (4) chapters 12–16 cover elocution and good writing; and (5) chapters 17–18 briefly treat delivery. The skeletal structure of the book, then, is familiar; but how does Gottsched flesh that structure out?

The most conspicuous feature of the first 11 chapters is their heavy dependence on Classical sources. Cicero, in particular, is very important in

Gottsched's exposition of the parts of a speech and the rules for invention for each of them (see pp. 123–192, chs. 3–7). Gottsched's ideal orator (see p. 107, ch. 2) is, basically, Quintilian's *vir bonus dicendi peritus* writ large. If his account of the qualities of the ideal orator is reminiscent of the catalogue of virtues of the *honnête homme* in Rollin, we should remember where Rollin found the inspiration for that catalogue. The treatment of amplification (pp. 193–220, ch. 8) includes a few German examples, but most of the citations are from Cicero and Demosthenes (they are, to be sure, cited in German). Chapter 11 (pp. 272–284) is little more than a paraphrase of Aphthonius' *Progymnasmata*.

Evidence of "modern" influences is, by contrast, less prominent, but the modern touches are not unimportant. His definition of rhetoric as an ability "to persuade a hearer of whatever one wills, and to move him in whatever way one desires" (see p. 89, ch. 1) and his reduction of emotions to the basic attraction/repulsion pair (see p. 226, ch. 9) are embedded in the context of rationalist thinking, despite the fact that he cites Aristotle and Quintilian (via Rollin, again) as support. Gottsched's seven-part structure for a speech (pp. 122ff., ch. 3) is not much different from traditional models, but the two basic steps of persuading the intellect and then moving the will are characteristically modern and not ancient. Add to this the fact that his whole conception of disposition seems governed by syllogistic form (see pp. 257ff., ch. 10) and that it is only the "substantive disciplines" that can give us knowledge—both post-Ramus notions—and we begin to see that Gottsched was far from immune to the developments in philosophy in his lifetime.

Yet we must be careful not to make of Gottsched's work a programmatic philosophical rhetoric. As with the French authors we saw earlier, the importance of philosophy is not as great as some would make it out to be— the influence of Locke is all but invisible, and that of Wolff not much more visible, although Gottsched cites them both. Gottsched's chief goal is the production of elegant and effective speakers. This should be obvious from the extensive treatment of style he pursues in chapters 13–16, approximately one-third of the treatise, and from the trouble he goes to in setting out the extensive array of examples in Part Two of the *Redekunst*. If we were to look among the many French rhetorics he cites for a treatise analogous to Gottsched's, it would probably be Rollin's, not Lamy's. In short, just as Gottsched's activities in the Deutsch Gesellschaft and his achievement in his *Dichtkunst* can be seen as attempts to Germanicize the established French tradition, so can *Ausführliche Redekunst* be seen as an effort to do for German students, although on a much larger scale, what Rollin's essay on rhetoric was meant to do for the French.

Mayans

Gregorio Mayans y Siscar (1699–1782), after completing his education at the Jesuit college at Cordelles, in Spain, went on to become the director of the

Biblioteca Real and professor of jurisprudence at Valencia during the reigns of Ferdinand VI and Charles III. He was active as a writer in a period of Spanish history that saw attempts by enlightened despots to reverse a hundred years of steady political and educational decline. An important part of their efforts consisted in the resuscitation and reform of universities along lines parallel to what was occurring in the rest of Europe. In conjunction with these reforms, the Crown encouraged cultural ties with England, Italy, and France. A French cultural presence had already begun to establish itself as a result of the availability in Spain of the Jesuit *Mémoires des Trévoux*; but by mid-century, the Spanish reading public was being exposed to French culture by such books as Ignacio de Luzán's *Memorias literarias de Paris*, by the network of literary academies established by royal decree, even by the French architectural style endorsed by the court at Madrid. Mayans' situation in Spain, in short, was much like Gottsched's in Germany.

Mayans was a man of enormous learning, the result no doubt of the access to books his position as director of the Royal Library afforded him. His *Retórica**, published first in 1757 and again in 1786, bears ample witness to his erudition, as it is a virtual compendium of all the rhetorical lore that was available to him. It is that very quality that has led some critics to regard the book as a mere recapitulation of Classical—especially Ciceronian—rhetoric. But Mayans' *Retórica* was more than that, for it is also a masterful adaptation of the Classical doctrines to prevailing cultural and political conditions; and as far as the history of specifically Spanish rhetorics is concerned, it was a watershed.

The Ciceronian traits of the *Retórica* emerge clearly in its organization and treatment of the parts of the art.[16] In five parts, or books, over 800 pages in the work's first edition, Mayans discusses invention, arrangement, elocution, and delivery, adding in Book 5 (as was not uncommon) treatments of genres whose ends were not precisely persuasive. In true Ciceronian fashion, and in a way reminiscent of Soares (whom Mayans never mentions, but whom he must have read with his Jesuit teachers), Mayans begins his section on invention with a consideration of *status*, adding (like Vossius, whom he does mention) the *status* of quantity to the other four standard questions. And in true Ciceronian fashion, he devotes considerable space to the *loci* of rhetorical arguments (1.11–23, pp. 92–160) and concludes that all the special genres of rhetoric should be reduced to the three basic *causae*: panegyric, deliberative, and juridical (1.41ff., pp. 216ff.). The importance Mayans ascribes to *status* and to *loci* sets it apart from other eighteenth-century rhetorics—and may explain in part why some think of it as a mere compendium—for, as will be recalled, those subjects all but drop out of the art. *Status* is viewed in the other rhetorics we have seen in this chapter, if it is viewed at all, as indicative of genre; and topics are dismissed by all as useless. Mayans makes it clear in his prologue (see pp. 64ff.), however, that it is necessary to know those things, partly because they are modes of reasoning, but mainly because all writers employ them.

His discussion of arrangement in Book 2 is, similarly, quite Ciceronian. There are six parts (including the partition) to a speech, each of which has "places" (*lugares*) appropriate to it. Two interesting embellishments of the standard discussion of arrangement here may be seen in Mayans' inclusion of an epitome of the discussion of exordia in Hermogenes' *On Invention* (see ch. 6, pp. 246f.) and a long chapter (pp. 258–286) on fictional narratives, in which Mayans distinguishes 10 types, each with its own moral end.

Book 3, on elocution, is by far the longest in the *Retórica*, over 250 pages long. Here, too, the basic conceptions are Ciceronian. Eloquence has three parts: clarity, dignity (which subsumes his long treatment of figures), and composition. Mayans' discussion of the last (pp. 523ff.) grafts onto the Ciceronian doctrine of three styles (here, *magnífico, bajo,* and *mediano*) some material from *On Style* by Demetrius and considerations based on Hermogenes' *On Qualities of Style* regarding stylistic "gravity" (*la gravedad*: see pp. 552ff.). One notable feature of Mayans' discussion is his insistence on the vital connection between *ornatus* and modes of thought and arrangement, a Ciceronian notion that the Ramists, for instance, had scrapped—to their detriment, in Mayans' view.

Book 4, the title of which is "Del decir agraciado," "On Genteel Speaking," is only 15 pages long (569–584). Here Mayans rounds out the parts of the art by treating of proper pronunciation and the difficulties many have with it; memory and its importance; and delivery, *la ación*. "Genteel" pronunciation requires, on the one hand, cadence and nobility (*cantidad* and *calidad*), without which the soul cannot be moved (p. 572); and clarity and elegance (*claridad* and *suavidad*), The necessity of these qualities not only stands to reason but is attested by Cicero, who is the chief authority in this discussion.

Book 5 demonstrates the rhetorical origin and nature of a variety of genres not normally seen as precisely persuasive. Thus petition and reply, conversation, letters of merit, dialogue, memorial inscriptions, and history all contain elements of rhetoric. A student who has mastered the general principles of the art should have no trouble understanding the special principles of these genres, but practice in them by means of elementary exercises (as in the progymnasmata of Hermogenes, whom Mayans cites specifically) is still necessary.

Mayans' work, therefore, seems quite thoroughly Classical in both conception and execution. There are, to be sure, a few occasions when Mayans looks to non-Classical authorities. His discussion of tropes at 3.4 (pp. 332ff.), for instance, is organized along the same lines as that of Talon; and no doubt Talon's discussion, with which Mayans was familiar by way of works by Sánchez de las Brozas and Pedro Nuñez that he cites, is in the background. Aside from that, however, there is little evidence of any Ramism worth mentioning in the *Retórica*. In addition, while Mayans' division of the arts in his prologue (see p. 66) may be an echo of Bacon, with whom Mayans may have been familiar through his reading of Benito Feijoo, as some have suggested,[17] it is interesting that neither Bacon nor Feijoo is mentioned by Mayans. Mayans, in short, does not seem to have been interested in recasting rhetoric in the image of the New Philosophy.

Mayans' rhetoric is, nonetheless, much more than a mere compendium of Classical rhetoric. It is as modern as Gottsched's or Rollin's, and in fact aims to achieve the same goals as the rhetorics of his French and German counterparts. It is obvious, for instance, that Mayans' frequent and extensive citation of Spanish authors, of Spanish proverbs, indeed of the Spanish version of Holy Scripture (which was illegal in Spain before 1782) is meant to do the same for Spanish as Gottsched's anthology of good German prose was meant to do for German. This becomes unmistakably clear when one consults Mayans' application for permission to publish the book, where his justifications are exactly the same as the arguments Rollin and Gottsched make in the prefaces to their works. If we take this view of Mayans *Retórica*, it is easy to see the work as a rhetoric designed to meet the needs created by the arrival of Enlightenment social and political norms in Spain. It is in that sense, and not because it somehow functions as a vehicle for the introduction of the New Philosophy into Spain, that Mayans' rhetoric is modern.

The new Philosophy did eventually make its way into Spain, but not until the educational ideas of Gaspar Jovellanos (1744–1810) became widely circulated and the *Filosofia de la eloquencia* of Antonio de Capmany was published, in 1777. Ironically, however, neither Jovellanos nor Capmany would exercise the most significant influence on rhetoric in Spain in subsequent decades. That distinction belonged to another authority on rhetoric from a place far from Spain, both geographically and culturally, Hugh Blair.

The examples of eighteenth-century treatises we have seen suggest that Continental writers on rhetoric were only marginally influenced by the New Philosophy. The chief concern of all seems to have been with the training of skilled speakers able to take a part in public life and operate in "polite company"—that is, of Rollin's *honnêtes hommes*. Rather than trying to read those rhetorics as applications of philosophical doctrine, then, we need to recognize their social (and perhaps political) functions. In societies where social mobility became possible, and indeed mandated, such rhetorics as Buffier's *Traité*, Gottsched's *Redekunst*, and Mayans' *Retórica* could be seen as not only interesting but important. Given the wide circulation of such books, it is clear that they actually were seen that way.

What is true of rhetorics composed on the Continent proves to be true in the British Isles as well, despite important differences in cultural and political traditions prevailing there. French influence not only pervaded all of Europe; it crossed the Channel as well. And so it is that so many French rhetorics came into circulation, both in French and in English translations, in eighteenth-century England, Scotland, and Ireland. In the next section, accordingly, we will turn to discussion of developments in rhetoric in those countries.

EIGHTEENTH-CENTURY BRITISH RHETORICS

The political situation in England in eighteenth century was rather different from that which prevailed in most states on the Continent. There was, for one thing, no "despotism" comparable to that in France or Prussia, where a ruler could say, as Frederick I did:

> One must serve the king with life and limb, with goods and chattels, with honor and conscience, and surrender all save salvation. That is reserved for God. The rest belongs to me.[18]

England had rejected the claim of the Stuarts to divine right and asserted the importance of the advice and consent of the Houses of Parliament. The administration of laws and services was not nearly as centralized as that in Prussia or France. Indeed, a professional politician or administrator would have struck an eighteenth-century British observer as an aberration. Government in England was the business not of professionals but of amateurs. The Master of the Mint appointed in 1699, for one example, was no expert in currency policy, but a theologian and mathematician, Isaac Newton.

Yet, in some respects, the social situation in England was not unlike that in many countries on the Continent. As was the case with France with Spain, for instance, colonial expansion had powerful effects on the distribution of wealth and social status. "Trade in England," Defoe observed, "has peopled this nation with gentlemen." Wealth, more frequently than had previously been the case, catapulted commoners into the peerage. At the same time, of course, this did not mean equal opportunity for all. Even in the best scenarios for social mobility, power in England, as in France, was limited to less than 10 percent of the population. While English society was by no means caste-bound, neither was it exactly egalitarian.

The Glorious Revolution of 1688 had restored a monarch to the throne of England, but the English were not inclined to accord much real power to that monarch. For one thing, William I and the Georges who succeeded him were not English but German, from the House of Hanover. Indeed, George I came to the throne without knowing, or desiring to learn, the language of the country he ruled. For another, the gains made by Parliament during the previous century were not easily reversed. The true seat of power was maintained by the House of Commons, where seats were obtained by election. Power flowed not from the throne but from the dispensers of political patronage. This became a highly developed system as the century wore on, creating vast reservoirs of influence for politicians like Robert Walpole (1676–1745) and increasing opportunities for the ambitious.

A young man of means who elected a political career—assuming he had the right connections—would likely start out with an education of sorts, schooling at Eton or Westminster followed by a few terms at Oxford or Cambridge. An actual university degree was not a requirement. Rather, this aspiring politician would be expected, if the advice of someone like Lord Chesterfield were taken seriously, to learn the facts and learn to think—but above all, learn to manipulate. Without well-mannered manipulation, he tells his son in one of his famous letters, learning and thinking are profitless. After such schooling as would teach him "to shift for himself and bustle in the world, and...a tolerable share of classical learning," he would then secure some local office or seat in Parliament, and learn "on the job," ideally, with the help of an experienced secretary.[19]

Educational institutions in England were geared to just such a preparation for careers in public life. As a partial consequence, they were neither very rigorous nor, as time went on, very well attended. Although the curriculum at Oxford and Cambridge remained Classical, the fact that students were expected to read Cicero and Xenophon was evidently no guarantee that they would read them well. Because a degree was not a necessary credential, enrollments declined steadily. Average enrollments in Oxford's 12 full colleges went down from 485 in 1710 to 111 in 1760 to only 67 by 1795. Those who did enroll in universities tended more and more to come from the upper class and gentry, aristocrats and "gentelmen-commoners" who seem to have been more interested in drinking claret and betting on cockfights than in learning for its own sake. If Edward Gibbon is to be believed, Oxford was full of dissipated undergraduates failing to be taught by college fellows sunk in port and prejudice, a sluggish stream meandering between overgrown meadows, in sharp contrast to the torrent of intellectual activity on the Continent.[20]

As we shall see, this was not the case in Scotland. While England, which led Europe in economic and technological development by mid-century, showed itself almost immune to Continental thought, Scottish thinkers were deeply affected by it. Common to both England and Scotland during this period, however, was an interest in rhetoric; and the reason for that interest, if it is not already clear, is well put—again—by Lord Chesterfield, who wrote to his son in 1739:

> A man can make no figure without it, in Parliament or in the Church, or in the law; and even in common conversation, a man that has acquired an easy and habitual eloquence, who speaks properly and accurately, will have a great advantage over those who speak incorrectly or inelegantly.... You must then, consequently, be sensible how advantageous it is for a man who speaks in public, whether it be in Parliament, or in the pulpit, or at the bar (that is, in the courts of Law), to please his hearers.[21]

Indeed, the essence of being a gentleman, Chesterfield wrote on another occasion, was to be pleasing: "Manner is all, in everything; it is by manner only that you can please, and consequently rise."[22]

Perhaps Chesterfield's advice is not exactly typical of the way every Englishman and Scot felt about rhetoric, but it is arguable that it is not far from typical. It is against a background of social aspiration such as we have sketched that the persistence of rhetoric as part of the curricula of schools and universities alike can best be understood. More specifically, it is against such a background that two rather distinctive developments in rhetoric in the British Isles—the so-called "Elocutionary Movement" and the transformation of rhetoric into the study of *belles lettres*—can be explained.

THE ELOCUTIONARY MOVEMENT

Lord Chesterfield's letter points up the necessity of being well-spoken. Inability to express oneself in correct English is a definite hindrance to one trying to forge a career in public life, as many North Countrymen and Scots, in particular, had discovered. Chesterfield's advice concerns effectiveness in pleasing an audience, as well. Oratory is performance, and one must know how to perform well if one hopes to affect the hearer. In most of the rhetorics we have seen thus far, very little attention is paid to the performance aspect of rhetoric; although many are careful to include a section on "delivery," the amount of attention paid to it is proportionately very little. The need for instruction in the arts of delivery was deeply felt by those in England who aspired to careers in Parliament, the Church, or the courts, and that need explains in great part the popularity of various works that appeared in Britain in the eighteenth century on "Elocution"—that is, pronunciation and gesture.

There had, of course, been a few attempts, both in France and in England, to codify these matters, most of them amplifying on what Quintilian had written about them in Book 11 of his *Institutes*. The *Vacationes autumnales, sive de perfecta oratoris actione et pronuntiatione libri III* of Louis de Cressolles, S. J., had appeared in Paris in 1620. This book treated at great length the lore concerning gesture and movement and the management of the voice. John Bulwer's *Chirologia* appeared in England in 1644, but concerned only gesture. Michel Le Faucheur's *Traité de l'action de l'orateur, ou de la Prononciation et de geste* came out in two separate editions, the first in 1657, the second in 1686. For obvious reasons, none of these works quite fits the bill, since they had little to teach anyone about polite English, although they could be consulted on matters of gesture.[23]

Le Faucheur's Traité came out in an English version in 1727 as *The Art of Speaking in Publick: or an Essay on The Action of an Orator; as to his Pronunciation and Gesture*,[24] a work generally acknowledged to mark the beginning of the Elocutionary Movement in England. The advertisement by the English editor is revealing:

> The Subject is new, and the novelty is worth any Gentleman's Perusal in the Kingdom; and especially, if he lays under the happy Temptation of being captivated or allur'd with the Air, Gallantry, and Grace of a good Pronunciation and Gesture, either for the Church, the Court, or the Camp (p. xiv).

He adds, a little later, "This Manual will not be thought unworthy of any young Gentleman's Pocket or Library who has any the least Value for the Graces of Action and the attracting Charms of Eloquence" (p. xx). It seems quite clear that the book was expected to do well precisely because it could help form the sort of gentleman Chesterfield had in mind.

Like Quintilian's treatment before it, and like various works written after it, *The Art of Speaking in Publick* is concerned chiefly with what can be conveyed by the inflection and cadences of the voice and by gestures: what tones to adopt when being sarcastic, how the eyes should be used to convey horror, or how the hand can be used to emphasize points. This concern with the communicative aspects of physiognomy and "the language of the body" is one that rhetoricians shared with philosophers who speculated on such matters as whether there is a universal sign language that, unlike verbal language, is natural and not conventional. Such interests are evident in the works of Descartes' successor Condillac, as well as in the curious work published anonymously in London in 1698, *Digiti lingua; or the most compendious, copious, facile, and secret way of silent Converse ever yet discovered. By a Person who has conversed no otherwise in above nine years.*[25] While *The Art of Speaking in Publick* has much to teach about the resources available to an orator who knows how to alter his voice and use his body, it does not say much that will help the aspiring gentleman who wishes to speak polite English. This *Art*, and others like it—for instance, James Burgh's *Essay on the Art of Speaking* (1762)—give us, in short, only one side of the Elocutionary Movement, albeit an important one.

A fuller picture can be gathered from a look at the work done by Thomas Sheridan (1719–88), the famous Irish actor and education reformer, who is commonly recognized as the "second founder" of the Elocutionary Movement. Sheridan's acting career occupied him for 15 years or so, from his completion of studies at Trinity College, Dublin, in 1743 to 1759, when he decided to channel his energies toward a different goal, establishing the art of oratory as the core of the educational system. This, he felt, would correct the chief defect he saw in Irish and English education alike, "the Want of proper Places to finish the Education of a Gentleman," as he put it in the oration announcing his project in 1757.[26]

A year before, Sheridan had published in London a long essay in which he laid down the broad outlines of his project "to revive the long lost art of oratory and to correct, ascertain, and fix the English language" (*British Education*, p. vi). But in the oration he gave in 1757, he tells us that this idea originated long before. "That which chiefly gave my mind this Turn," he says,

was a Conversation which I once had with Dr. Swift, soon after my Entrance into the College: He asked me what they taught there? When I told him the Course of Reading I was put into, he asked me, Do they teach you English? No. Do they teach you how to speak? No. Then, said he, they teach you Nothing.[27]

Jonathan Swift was an old friend of Sheridan's father and a continuing influence on Sheridan for life. Another supporter of Sheridan's project, it might be added, was none other than Lord Chesterfield, with whom he had become acquainted in 1746 while Chesterfield was serving as Lord Lieutenant of Ireland.

The nature of Sheridan's program of study can be gathered from a look at his main work, *A Course of Lectures on Elocution*, published in London in 1762, but bringing together lectures he had been giving at Oxford and Cambridge, Dublin, Belfast, London, and Edinburgh since 1757. The eight lectures in this volume make it clear that, when Sheridan spoke of "oratory" or "rhetoric," he meant only the traditional fifth part of the art, delivery. In the introductory lecture, he points out that this part of eloquence is regularly slighted in the normal course of education, although it is clearly the most important part. There is more to rhetoric than the mere communication of abstract ideas, he argues, and "some of our greatest men have been trying to do that with the pen, which can only be performed by the tongue; to produce effects by the dead letter, which can never be produced but by the living voice, with its accompaniments" (*Course*, p. xii).

The lectures that follow define elocution as "the just and graceful management of the voice, countenance, and gesture in speaking." Its two chief parts are voice and gesture. Sheridan devotes six lectures to voice, discussing articulation, pronunciation, accent emphasis, pauses, pitches, and tones. Good articulation is to the ear what good handwriting is to the eye. While it is not necessary for a gentleman to have good handwriting (whereas even a lowly clerk must), it would be disgraceful for a gentleman to omit syllables or run his words together so as to be unintelligible. Good pronunciation is fashionable pronunciation—namely, the dialect of the court. All other dialects are "sure marks either of a provincial, rustic, pedantic, or mechanical education; and therefore have some degree of disgrace annexed to them" (p. 30). Accent is important, too, because it serves as an indication of one's status and of what company one keeps. As for emphasis, it is necessary to attend to it in order to convey one's meaning clearly: different emphasis on words in a sentence will convey different meanings. Tones and gesture, the subjects of the last two lectures, are important because "upon [them], all that is pleasurable, or affecting in elocution, chiefly depend" (p. 93).

Thus, in addition to the obvious communicative aspects of voice and gesture—they are, so to speak, the languages of passion and imagination—Sheridan seeks to attach great importance to "the manner of sounding our words" (p. 29) in a proper and gracious manner. Anyone who aspires to a successful career, particularly the Irish, Scots, or Americans who find themselves hindered by an inability to speak polite English, will have to master that manner. And manner, we recall from Lord Chesterfield, is all.

Sheridan's proposals came at a time when the teaching of English was still a novelty in Britain and when there was a lack of a standardized English pronunciation. Members of the aristocracy and of the newly affluent middle class alike recognized the need for both, as is clear from, among other things, the huge success of Samuel Johnson's new dictionary, which came out in London in 1755, and of another important contribution to the elocutionary cause, John Walker's *Elements of Elocution*, which came out in 1781.[28] But above all, many in the British Isles obviously perceived a strong incentive to speak proper English for the purposes of self-advancement. Sheridan's project, then, could not have been proposed at a better time; and the extent of interest in what his *Course of Lectures* could provide to the socially ambitious can be measured by the continuing success of his book for a century to come, not only in Britain but in America as well.

Having had a glance at the Elocutionary Movement, we shall now turn to other developments in rhetoric in England, chiefly those in Scotland in the second half of the century. The discussion that follows will round off our survey of the eighteenth century by addressing an issue we examined earlier in this chapter, the relations between rhetoric and philosophy, as it pertains to the major treatises on rhetoric after 1750.

RHETORICS FROM THE HINTERLANDS

Rhetorics in English after 1750 did not emanate from the centers of cultured society but from its fringes. John Lawson's lectures on rhetoric were given at Trinity College, Dublin, and first published there in 1758. Joseph Priestley's *Course of Lectures on Oratory and Criticism* was published in 1777 in London but was based on his teaching of those subjects at the Warrington Academy, a Dissenters' (non-Anglican) school in the north of England, between Liverpool and Manchester. The more famous and influential works of this period, by Lord Kames, Campbell, and Blair, were all conceived and developed in Scotland, which had not even been an official part of Britain until the Act of Union in 1707 and where the vast majority of people spoke English, if they did not speak Gaelic, with an accent that Londoners found almost unintelligible and completely provincial.

All of these men, therefore, taught students who had serious cultural handicaps disabling them from pursuing professional careers or keeping "polite company." Chesterfield might have said they had no manners. The curricula at Trinity and Edinburgh and Marischal College in Aberdeen were designed precisely to help students to overcome those handicaps; and in accordance with that aim, rhetoric held an important position in the schools in the hinterlands. Because association with provincials was a potential source of cultural distrust on the part of the sophisticates in London, the teachers of rhetoric in the provinces were particularly careful to invest their rhetorics with a sort of rigor and range that was almost unprecedented in such works. Thus, Lawson made sure to mention not only Cicero and Quintilian, whom everyone included, but Aristotle and DuBos, whom we find mentioned else-where hardly at all. Priestley attempted to ground his conception of rhetoric on the most recent advances in philosophical psychology, as they had been articulated in David Hartley's *Observations on Man*; and George Campbell sought to base his work on the refutation by his colleague Thomas Reid of the insidious teachings of yet a third Scot, David Hume. As before, however, we need to keep those debts to philosophers in perspective. While Campbell, Priestley, and Blair were deeply and honestly interested in producing ideas as sound and as current as possible, their chief desire was to produce graduates who would not be sneered at by the likes of Lord Chesterfield.

In what follows, we shall pretty much restrict our attention to Campbell and Blair, although we shall have occasion to refer to the others in the course of discussing those two. As there is no lack of literature on this area of the history of rhetoric, moreover, our discussions will be brief.[29] If justification is required for limiting ourselves to Campbell and Blair, the fact that they exercised immeasurably more influence than the others on succeeding generations of teachers and students of rhetoric in Europe and America seems justification enough. And the brevity will help us bring an already long chapter finally to an end.

Campbell

George Campbell (1719–96) was born in Aberdeen, received his early education there, and eventually became principal (in 1759) and professor of divinity (in 1771) at Marischal College in Aberdeen. On the face of it, Aberdeen seems an unlikely place for the sort of intellectual activity that went on there. In the eighteenth century, the situation in Aberdeenshire was quite feudal, with small farmers absolutely dependent on landlords who occupied castles with gardens in the French style, set down in the middle of a barren land-scape. It was the common practice of the farmers to pay their rents not in cash but in service, as well as in oats, mutton, salmon, or peats. But Aberdeen had a long reputation for having a high rate of literacy going back to the sixteenth century, the result of an energetic Kirk whose elders were careful to insure that the young people in the shire should be able to read Scripture. By 1745, Aberdeenshire was the cultural equal, in fact, of Edinburgh and enjoyed a good reputation even in London as a center of learning.

Campbell's literary accomplishments are impressive. The majority of his published works, including his prestigious *Dissertation on Miracles* (1762), are mainly theological. He himself saw his *Philosophy of Rhetoric* as an ancillary to his main vocation, to teach young students how to defend the faith against the attacks of the skeptics—David Hume in particular—who were attacking it. But the *Philosophy of Rhetoric* (1776)* is nevertheless the book he is most remembered for.[30] It was reprinted at least 42 times in the course of the nineteenth century in Scotland and England, and many times in America.

By his account, Campbell had begun to work up the ideas presented in the *Philosophy of Rhetoric* as early as 1750, and developed them between 1758 and 1773, mainly in connection with his active membership in the Aberdeen Philosophical Society, where he met regularly with such colleagues as Thomas Reid, John Beattie, and John Stewart. At their meetings, members discussed papers on such subjects as the analysis of sense perception (by Reid, in 1758 and 1760), whether eloquence is useful or pernicious (Alexander Gerard, Campbell's predecessor as professor of divinity, in 1764), and the relation of eloquence to logic (among other papers, by Campbell himself in 1761). In view of the strong professional and social ties that Campbell formed with those others during the period in which the society was active, it is not difficult to understand why Campbell exhibits so much interest in specifically philosophical issues in what he consciously put forth as his *philosophy* of rhetoric.[31]

The goal of the *Philosophy of Rhetoric*, Campbell explains in the preface, is "to ascertain with greater precision, the radical principles of that art, whose object it is, by the use of language, to operate on the soul of the hearer, in the way of informing, convincing, pleasing, moving, or persuading (p. xliii). In pursuit of this, Campbell divides the book into three parts: Book One, "On the Nature and Foundations of Eloquence" (pp. 1–138); Book Two, "The Foundations and Essential Properties of Elocution" (pp. 139–284); and Book Three, "The Discriminating Properties of Elocution" (pp. 285–415).

Book One consists in the main of material he had put together for his meetings with the Philosophical Society, and accordingly it shows the most influence of the philosophical speculations that occupied the members of the group. The notion that practical knowledge (art) must be grounded in "scientific" truth—in a sense of "science" that includes theology and ethics—is clearly a byproduct of those meetings. Likewise, the idea that the time was ripe for continuing the progress shown in the history of rhetoric and moving up to the stage in which scientific explanations can be given for the phenomena that, until then, had only been observed and organized (see pp. l–li in the preface) is a commonplace of Enlightenment philosophy. Campbell's division of the kinds of rhetoric at the beginning of Book One (pp. 2–3) is quite Baconian, as he himself points out. His discussion of "evidence" (1.5, pp. 35ff.) is obviously based on his intimate familiarity with the ideas of his colleague Reid, as is his apology for "common sense," which includes also an acknowledgment of Father Buffier's contribution on that subject and an approving citation of Buffier's observation that the denial of the evidence of common sense is "not a sign of contradiction, but of insanity" (p. 42). Campbell takes issue with Hobbes on wit (pp. 27ff.) and with Priestley's attacks on Reid (pp. 38f.) as part of his general development of a conception of rhetoric grounded in the self-evidence of common sense that occupies the bulk of Book One.

The commonsense philosophy of mind serves as the basic justification, and guarantee for a number of Campbell's pronouncements on rhetoric. For instance, it is reasonable for rhetoricians to divide discourse into classes because the faculties of the mind are divided into specialized functions, each with its own verbal mode (compare Bacon and Buffier). Rhetoric will be effective if it is responsive to the promptings of the "sense" (compare Buffier's *sentiment*) of truth and goodness because the mind has a natural tendency to act in accordance with those promptings, not to doubt them (1.5.3ff.). Rhetorical "proof" ("moral reasoning" in Campbell; compare what Buffier said about "proof") should be conducted in accordance with the mind's natural movement from experience to conclusions (1.6). The natural association among passions, one passion being likely to occur in the company of certain others, must be our guide when explaining how they need to be treated by speakers (1.7.5–7). Rhetorical usage must conform to usage that is reputable in current national custom because the human mind has a tendency to accept as correct only those usages authorized by convention (2.1ff.). Only by remaining faithful to accepted usage, to conventional proper meanings, can rhetoric achieve perspicuity (2.7.2ff.). It would be possible to go on at great length detailing Campbell's reliance on common sense. What can be seen even from these few examples is that philosophy is used by Campbell in the service of rhetoric; rhetoric is not deduced from Bacon's or Reid's or anyone else's philosophy.

There are, therefore, many things Campbell is able to say about rhetoric with authority because Reid and Buffier were available to him, so to speak. The matters he treats in Book One, however, are quite general in nature and do not provide the sort of "precision" Campbell called for in his preface. Book One, obviously, is meant as a "Foundation" for Books Two and Three. We will not go into any detail about the contents of these two books—fully two-thirds of the *Philosophy*—as a glance at the table of contents provides a fairly clear picture of the subjects treated there. All of them, we cannot not fail to see, have to do with good elocution. Thus it would seem that the principles of good—that is, effective and tasteful—elocution are Campbell's chief concern. If this is the case, then the *Philosophy of Rhetoric* as a whole is rather less a philosophy of rhetoric as such than a rhetoric that happens to coopt the philosophical notion of common sense but that is, at base, a rhetoric very much like the others we have seen in this chapter. This is by no means to disparage Campbell's attempts to "ascertain. . .the radical principles of the art," for Campbell succeeds in doing that, whereas the others—for instance, Rollin, Gottsched, or Mayans—did not.

On this reading, Campbell's *Philosophy of Rhetoric* might be better understood by putting it into the context of the other eighteenth-century rhetorics than by attempting to reconstruct his philosophical "sources." While there is no doubt that Campbell took philosophy seriously, it is also clear that he was interested in philosophy primarily as it impinged upon his mission to train students to defend the faith and enter into polite society. The line of thinking that extended from Locke to Hume threatened the faith and made the rhetoric that could defend it impossible. That line of thinking, Campbell was convinced, had been refuted by the commonsense philosophy of Buffier and Reid; and so it was that he set himself the task of constructing a rhetoric that would be impervious to the attacks of the skeptics. Campbell's main concerns, however, were not much different from those of the Continental rhetoricians we have seen—indeed, not much different from those of Sheridan and the other elocutionists. Nor were they much different from those of another of his fellow Aberdeen philosophers, Hugh Blair. It is to Blair that we must now turn.

Blair

David Hume once described Hugh Blair (1718–1800) as "a vain, timid, fussy, kind-hearted little man that everybody liked," but these qualities hardly sum the man up. Born in Edinburgh, Blair went on to take a degree at the university there in 1739, get ordained as a Presbyterian minister in 1742, and eventually to become Regius Professor of Rhetoric and Belles Lettres at Edinburgh in 1762. Blair became famous as an editor of Shakespeare's plays, of a collection of works of British poets (in 44 volumes, 1773), and of the spurious *Works of Ossian*, purported by their original editor, James Macpherson (1736–96), to have been translated from the original Gaelic but actually written in large part by Macpherson himself. Blair was also one of the most famous preachers in Britain, which may explain why in 1783 he was offered 1,500 pounds sterling by the London publishing house of Creek and Strahan to allow them to publish his *Lectures on Rhetoric and Belles Lettres*.[32]

This soon became the book "which half the educated English-speaking world studied," along with Dr. Johnson's *Dictionary*. By 1873, it had gone into over 50 editions in England and America and appeared on the Continent in German (Leipzig, 1785–89), French (first in 1797), Spanish (1798), Italian (1811), and Russian (1837). In America, just to give an idea of how popular it was there, there were over 50 abridged or annotated editions published for use in schools and universities during the nineteenth century. Blair was highly valued in Germany, where there had been a long tradition of anglophilia (Swift and Defoe were particularly liked); his popularity in Spain is a little harder to understand, but true nevertheless.[33]

Lectures on Rhetoric and Belles Lettres contains 47 lectures, distributed as follows: an introductory lecture; 4 on taste; 4 on language; 15 on style; 10 on eloquence; and 13 on criticism, covering all major literary genres. Blair throughout rejects, on the one hand, any explanations of these matters based on "the mechanical operation of the spirit" model familiar from Hobbes and Locke; and, on the other, the "rules" in Continental rhetorics that he saw as "artificial and scholastic." His chief sources are, in fact, Cicero and Quintilian, although he does not hesitate to call on Rollin and Fénelon, for instance, when the occasion is right. His emphasis is ever on the natural foundations of eloquence. In that respect, Blair seems to share a common belief with other eighteenth-century rhetoricians. But a closer look at his lectures shows that Blair shares much more with rhetorics we have seen than the odd commonplace.

Blair conceived his task as "the initiation of youth into the study of Belles Lettres and of Composition. . .to cultivate their taste, to form their style. . . to prepare themselves for public Speaking or Composition" (pp. iv–v, in preface). While such cultivation would ideally result in a sound mind and a measure of self-knowledge, "studies of this kind, it is not to be doubted, will appear to derive part of their importance from the use to which they may be applied in furnishing materials for those fashionable topics of discourse, and thereby enabling us to support a proper rank in life" (Lecture I, p. 9). The echoes of Rollin (see above, pp. 201f) are clear, as are echoes of Chesterfield and Sheridan.

Lectures II–V concern taste. Good taste, Blair argues, is a composite of "delicacy," which is inborn and natural, and "correctness," which is learned. The foundation of taste is the same in all human minds. Taste is built upon "the sentiments and perceptions which belong to our nature." On the other hand, it is true that ignorance and prejudice can pervert this natural faculty, and it must then be rectified by reason, which, although it cannot substitute for innate "genius," can enlighten and assist it by pointing out "proper models and the chief things to avoid" (see Lecture II, p. 20ff.). It has been suggested that most of what Blair has to say about taste he got from Lord Kames, who had originally encouraged him to put together this course of lectures. That may be the case; but when Blair refers to taste as a faculty, he doesn't have quite the same thing in mind as Kames, who was convinced by the explanations of mental acts provided by the faculty psychology. Blair's "faculty" is, rather, something like *talent* in Buffier. Moreover, in his accounts of beauty and sublimity, those qualities apprehended by taste (see Lecture V), Blair seems to have Boileau's preface to his translation of Longinus before him. To be sure, he had in mind as a model of sublimity *The Works of Ossian*, which he believed (wrongly) to be the genuine utterances of a primitive close enough to Nature's wild beauties to convey them without art or artifice. But the basic idea here goes back to Blair's French predecessors.

Blair's "primitivism" also informs his lectures on language (VI–IX, pp. 77–141). Like many who speculated in his time about the origins and development of language among human beings, Blair believed that language began with "cries of passion" (Lecture VI, p. 101) and eventually developed as humanity progressed into an elaborate system of nouns and verbs. First these were of the most "imaginative" sort, but then, "as the imagination cools and the understanding ripens," language progressed further "from fire and enthusiasm, to coolness and precision" (Lecture VI, pp. 114ff.). English, in Blair's view, is a particularly rich language because of the "studious and reflective genius of [English-speaking] people" and its historically demonstrated ability to absorb the riches of other languages (Lecture VIII, pp. 146ff.).

Having established the natural capacity to apprehend beauty and its opposite and the richness of the English language, Blair devotes the next 15 lectures (X–XXIV) to style, searching for its roots and for a way of classifying the components of "the peculiar manner in which a man expresses his conceptions" by means of language (Lecture X, p. 183). Blair rejects the traditional division of styles into the high, low, and mean while nevertheless depending heavily on Cicero and Quintilian in his comments on perspicuity, climax, euphony, and figures. In place of the three traditional *genera dicendi*, Blair offers as criteria for identifying particular styles how a passage expresses an author's meaning; the degree of ornament "employed to beautify" that meaning; and the degree to which the writing is natural or affected. Like Rollin and Bouhours, Blair explains his system by a show-and-tell procedure, holding up as models passages from both Classical and reputable "modern" (English) authors.

Once he has determined the basic principles of style, Blair moves on to a consideration of "elocution," public speaking (Lectures XXV–XXXIV). The greater part of this section is taken up with a review of Classical lore on delivery, invention, and arrangement and of the importance of "ethical" and "pathetic" proof. Blair's reading of Classical rhetoric is, however, very much colored by the view of many of his post-Cartesian contemporaries that "conviction" must be separated from "persuasion," and that a speaker must first secure conviction and then, arousing desire by appealing to the passions, achieve persuasion. Lectures XXXI and XXXII, accordingly, have the following form:

XXXI	{	1. Exordium
		2. Partition
		3. Narrative or explication
XXXII	{	4. Reasoning or arguments
		a. Invention
		b. Arrangement
		c. Expression
		5. Emotional appeal
		6. Peroration

For support in this reading of Quintilian and Cicero, Blair appeals to Fénelon and Rollin, specifically; but it should be clear from what we have seen that this format is a common one in eighteenth-century rhetorics.

Finally, in the last group of lectures (XXXV–XLVII), Blair presents to his students a survey of "the most distinguished kinds of composition, both in prose and verse," indicating for each the pertinent points of criticism. The canon here is typical of eighteenth-century rhetorics broadly viewed, and quite conservative. The guiding principles behind his selection, in fact, are by and large not drawn from his considerations of style or from his observations on elocution, but from the general opinion of reputable and refined critics he and his students were familiar with. In appending the examples at the end of the "course," it will be noted, Blair follows the practice of Gottsched and Mayans (who were unknown to him) as well as that of Buffier and Rollin (whom he did know).

Quite apart from his clearly stated intentions, then, Blair's entire course of lectures is consistent with, and very similar to, the Continental rhetorics we saw earlier in this chapter. This similarity suggests quite strongly not only that Blair shared their ends but also that he saw his means as identical to theirs. Blair has sometimes been criticized for having failed to add anything significantly new to the rhetorical tradition. In view of the social goals of his *Lectures on Rhetoric and Belles Lettres*, however, it would be surprising if he had tried to do that.

Both Campbell and Blair, then, stood solidly in the tradition of rhetorics designed to transform students into gentlemen—and ladies, we must hasten to add—if not in Parliament, the pulpit, or bar, then certainly in polite conversation, as the novels of Jane Austen make abundantly clear.[34] If both were intent on incorporating recent advances in philosophy into their conceptions of what rhetoric was and of how rhetorics ought to be composed, both were nevertheless mainly concerned with initiating the youth of Scotland into the *beau monde* of *belles lettres*, as it were. In that respect, Campbell and Blair were after the same general result as Sheridan and the other representatives of the Elocutionary Movement. The same intention, it is also clear, informed the lectures and essays of men like Joseph Priestley (1733–1804) and Henry Home, Lord Kames (1696–1782). Priestley's *Course of Lectures on Oratory and Criticism* (1777) made explicit use of Hartley's new teaching on the association of ideas.[35] But what Priestley says in his dedication of the printed version of those lectures to Viscount Fitzmaurice is revealing:

> ...I was ambitious to dedicate the work to you; as a mark of my attachment, and of my earnest wish to contribute whatever may be in my power, towards your improvement in every thing that is useful or ornamental, and thereby to the distinguished figure that, I flatter myself, your Lordship will one day make in this country...[Y]our Lordship cannot but be fully apprized, that the only foundations for a respectable figure in life, are good principles and good dispositions, joined to a cultivated understanding.

It is also revealing that far more attention is paid to criticism than to rhetoric in Priestley's lectures. As for Lord Kames' *Elements of Criticism*, it is clear that Kames would not have written much of what he did if he had not come under the influence of some version of the doctrine of the association of ideas. But his book is, after all, meant to sharpen the critical faculties of its readers in order that they might consequently exhibit good taste and an easy familiarity with the best the literary world had to offer. In other words, to draw this discussion to a conclusion, all the rhetorics and related works we can point to in eighteenth-century Britain seem to fit into the same social context and represent, in the last analysis, no significant departure from their counterparts on the Continent.

SUMMARY

Our survey in this chapter suggests that the central concerns animating eighteenth-century rhetorics were social rather than philosophical. This is not to say that the New Philosophy had no influence at all. One thing it was able to provide some of the rhetoricians with was a psychological model that could be appealed to in order to show how rhetoric works. But the New Philosophy had to be adjusted and revised in order for it to be used because, in itself, it made rhetoric virtually impossible or, if possible, then disreputable. In any event, the evidence seems to show that the majority of rhetorics in the period subsume philosophy to social goals.

There are tentative efforts, starting with Lamy, to construct philosophical rhetorics on the Continent. But these give way to the rhetorics of Rollin, Gottsched, and Mayans. The attempt made by Priestley to ground a rhetoric on the principles of association laid out by David Hartley was overshadowed by the appeal of Blair's *Lectures on Rhetoric and Belles Lettres*. Thus it might be argued that, while the tendency of the New Philosophy would have been to deinstitutionalize rhetoric, the response of the new rhetorics was to reinstitutionalize it. What is new, in this respect, is that rhetoric moves from the public assembly and the courts of law into the realm of polite company and the courts of Europe.

All over Europe, between 1700 and 1800, we see in the rhetorics a concern with the production of *honnêtes hommes* in different national guises. The reasons for this are connected with the rise of absolutism and economic transformations in European society, particularly the rise of a wealthy nonaristocratic class. As rhetoricians sought to adapt to these new conditions, rhetoric became at the same time narrower and broader than it had been. It was no longer considered a method of inquiry, as it had been even in the seventeenth century (Keckermann, Vossius), but was restricted to elocution and delivery. Where *elocutio* had always been an important part of rhetoric, as it provided *copia* of expression, it became in the eighteenth century a matter rather of elegance of appearance, of "looking good"—an expression quite clearly connected with the emergence in France of an *ésthétique du paraître*, "an aesthetic of appearances." But rhetoric became broader, too. It had always been the traditional place to study eloquence systematically, the natural place in a curriculum that included study of Cicero's *Orator*, Quintilian's *Institutes*, Longinus, and Hermogenes' *On Qualities of Style*. In the interests of producing people fit for polite society, norms for eloquence in the various vernacular languages were developed and "eloquence" was broadened to include all sorts of discourse, the whole range of *belles lettres*.

Finally, it will be noted that these rhetorics are all, basically, what we have called unilateral "operational" rhetorics. The "controversial" rhetorics of Cicero and Quintilian were transformed by writers like Rollin and Mayans into techniques for managing appearances, not for coming to reasonable decisions on complex matters. The "operational" mode will continue to be dominant for some time to come after the period we have considered in this chapter.

FURTHER READING

Very useful for background reading on the eighteenth century is M. Anderson's *Europe in the Eighteenth Century: 1713–1783* (London/New York, 1987). Anderson's book should be supplemented by W. Willcox, *The Age of Aristocracy: 1688–1830* for developments in Britain. Both of these books contain substantial bibliographies. On rhetoric in Britain, W. S. Howell's *Eighteenth Century British Logic and Rhetoric* (Princeton, 1971) is still the most valuable resource book. Also useful is A. Scaglione, *The Classical Theory of Composition* (Chapel Hill, 1972), pp. 159–336.

D. Donoghue's *Jonathan Swift: A Critical Introduction* (Cambridge, 1969) contains a wealth of information about Swift's relationship with contemporary philosophical issues as they bear on rhetoric. On Locke generally, see D. O'Connor, *John Locke: A Critical Introduction* (New York, 1967). Some interesting observations on Locke's attitudes toward rhetoric and the implications of his theories for rhetoric are to be found in G. Bennington's "The Perfect Cheat: Locke and Empiricism's Rhetoric," in *The Figural and the Literal* (cited in Further Reading for Chapter 6). See also N. Struever's "The Conversable World: Eighteenth Century Transformations of the Relations of Rhetoric and Truth," in *Rhetoric and the Pursuit of Truth* (also cited in Chapter 6).

There is very little in English that can be consulted on French and German rhetorics. K. Wilkins' *A Study of the Works of Claude Buffier* (Studies on Voltaire and the Eighteenth Century, no. 66 [Geneva, 1969]) is useful, as are also the introduction to S. Bokil's translation of Buffier's *Éléments de Métaphysique* (*Indian Philosophical Quarterly* 2 [Poona, 1980]) and J. McCormick, "A Forerunner of the Scottish School," *The New Scholasticism* 15 (1941), pp. 299–317. B. Warnick, "Charles Rollin's *Traité* and the Rhetorical Theories of Smith, Campbell, and Blair," *Rhetorica* 3 (1985), pp. 45–65, provides numerous references to material on French rhetorics. On the concept of the *honnête homme*, see E. Kern, "*L'honnête homme*: Postscript to a Battle of the Scholars," *Romanic Review* 44 (1963), pp. 113–120, and, more recently, J-P. Dens, "L'honnête homme et l'esthétique du paraître," *Papers on French Seventeenth Century Literature* 6 (1976/77), pp.69–82. For German, the most useful introduction is to be found in E. Blackall, *The Emergence of German as a Literary Language, 1700–1775* (Cambridge, 1959). See also the essays in *Rhetorik: Beiträge zu ihrer Geschichte in Deutschland vom 16–20. Jahrhundert*, ed. H. Schanze (Frankfurt, 1974), and the extensive bibliography there, pp. 221–337. Biographical information will be found in *ADB*.

On educational reforms in the eighteenth century and the state of universities, see, for instance, the papers in *Facets of Education in the Eighteenth*

Century, ed. J. Leith (Studies on Voltaire and the Eighteenth Century, no. 167 [Oxford, 1977]) and the essays in *The University in Society*, ed. L. Stone, 2 vols. (Princeton, 1974). C. McClelland's "The Aristocracy and University Reform in Eighteenth Century Germany," in *Schooling and Society*, ed. L. Stone (Baltimore/London, 1976), pp. 146–176, is very informative. See also M. Wallbank, "Eighteenth Century Public Schools and the Education of the Governing Elite," *History of Education* 8 (1979), pp. 1–19. For the state of Oxford during this period, see *The History of Oxford University*, V: *The Eighteenth Century*, ed. L. Sutherland and L. Mitchell (Oxford, 1986).

Volume XII of Gottsched's *Ausgewählte Werke*, ed. P. Mitchell (Berlin/New York, 1987) contains an exhaustive bibliography on his life and works. On Mayans, see the introduction to *Obras completas*, III: *Retórica* (Valencia, 1984) by J. Gutiérrez. N. Glendinning's *A Literary History of Spain: The Eighteenth Century* (London, 1972) is invaluable as background reading on Spain. See also D. Abbott, "Mayans and the Emergence of Modern Rhetoric," *Dieciocho* 4 (1981), pp. 155–163; and "Antonio de Capmany and the New Rhetoric," 7 (1984), pp. 146–159. Both are informative, but Abbott overstates the "modernity" of Mayans.

On the Elocutionary Movement, see Howell, *Eighteenth Century*, pp. 145–256. F. Haberman, "The Elocutionary Movement in England 1750–1850" (Ph.D. diss., Cornell University, 1947) is still useful; as is W. Bacon's "The Elocutionary Career of Thomas Sheridan (1719–1788)," *SM* 31 (1964), pp. 1–54.

On developments in Scotland, J. McCosh's *The Scottish Philosophy* (London, 1875; rpt. Hildesheim, 1966) is necessary reading; and there are a number of good essays on milieu and influence in *Aberdeen and the Enlightenment*, ed. J. Carter and J. Pittock (Aberdeen, 1987). Also useful are the introductions to the Southern Illinois University editions of Priestley (by V. Bevilacqua), Campbell (L. Bitzer), and Blair (H. Harding). There is much to commend in D. Bormann's "Some Common Sense about Campbell, Hume, and Reid: The Extrinsic Evidence," *QJS* 71 (1985), pp. 395–421. R. Schmitz's *Hugh Blair* (New York, 1948) can still be read with profit.

NOTES

1. From "The Mechanical Operation of the Spirit," in *The Writings of Jonathan Swift*, ed. R. Greenberg and W. Piper (New York/London, 1973), p. 407.
2. Ibid., p. 408.
3. See the discussion in Donoghue (cited in Further Readings), pp. 109ff.
4. From *The Travels of Lemuel Gulliver*, III., ch. 4, in *Writings*, p. 158.
5. For instance, in Matthew Prior's 1721 "Dialogue between Mr. John Lock and Seigneur de Montaigne," "Montaigne" says at one point, "You, and Your understanding are the *Personae Dramatis*, and the whole amounts to no more than a Dialogue between John and Lock." See *Matthew Prior: Literary Works*, ed. H. Wright and M. Spears (Oxford, 1971), p. 620.

6. On the meaning of *sentiment*, see note 21 in Chapter 6.
7. For Buffier's works, see Sommervogel I, 145ff., described under "Buffier" (see note 1 in Chapter 6). I have used the texts as published in Buffier's *Cours de Science* (1732), a facsimile edition of which came out in Paris in 1971. Page references are to that edition.
8. I have used the 1984 Paris reprint of the 1818 Paris edition, which includes the notes and commentary by Fontanier.
9. See the opening of Gerard Genette's preface to the edition cited above.
10. The phrase is Chaim Perelman's, but that is the way tropes are studied in the grammar course in France even today.
11. An abridged text of Vico's *Institutiones* can be found in *Scrittori d'Italia* 183 (= G. B. Vico Opere VIII) (Bari, 1941), pp. 159–196. To my knowledge, Ward's book never went into a second edition. He is quoted extensively, however, in John Walker's *Rhetorical Grammar* (1785), which went into many editions.
12. *Les entretiens* was republished in 1962 in Paris, ed. F. Brunot, on the basis of the original 1671 edition. I have used the 1705 Amsterdam edition. I have also consulted the 1728 London edition of Oldmixon's version of *La manière*.
13. Page references are to the 1751 Halle edition, in 4 volumes.
14. Eighteenth-century editions of Quintilian have been noted by J. Cousin in *Recherches sur Quintilien* II (Paris, 1975), pp. 175ff.
15. I have used the text of *Ausführliche Redekunst* in the *Ausgewählte Werke*, ed. P. Mitchell, 12 vols. (New York/Berlin, 1968–1984), vol. VII (1975), parts 1–4.
16. Page references are to the text available in *Obras completas*, III: *Retórica*, ed. A. Mestre Sanchis and J. Gutiérrez (Valencia, 1984).
17. See the Abbott articles cited in Further Reading.
18. Cited by Anderson (see Further Reading), p. 145.
19. On the importance of manipulation, see Letter 112 (October 1746), vol. 1, pp. 151ff., and 289 (September 1752), vol. 2, pp. 268f., in the Strachey and Calthrop edition of Chesterfield's letters (2 vols., London, 1901). On how much learning the aspiring gentleman ought to have, see, for instance, Letters 69 (1740), vol. 1, p. 87f.; Letter 152 (May 1748), vol. 1, pp. 229f.
20. This characterization is that of Mitchell in *The History of Oxford University* (cited in Further Reading), p. 1, based on Gibbon's recollections in his *Memoirs* (London, 1891), pp. 64ff.
21. Chesterfield, Letter 45 (November 1739), Serachey and Calthorp ed., vol. 1, p. 56. His son was only eight years old when Chesterfield wrote this letter to him.
22. Letter 247 (March 1751), vol 2, p. 131.
23. Cressoles' *Vacationes* seems never to have seen a second printing. Bulwer's *Chironomia* is available in a 1974 Southern Illinois University edition, ed. J. Cleary (Carbondale, 1974).
24. I have used the 1727 London edition. Howell (cited in Further Reading), 165f., surmises that this is a second edition, but no trace of the first has been found.
25. On this general subject, see, for instance, J. Knowlson, "The Idea of Gesture as a Universal Language in the XVII and XVIII Centuries," *JHI* 26 (1965) pp. 495–508, and J. Seigel, "The Enlightenment and the Evolution of a Language of Signs in France and Germany," *JHI* 30 (1969), pp. 96–115. An interesting approach to this subject is taken by N. Lamedica, *Oratori, Filosofi, Maestri di Sordomuti* (Naples, 1984).
26. The full title of the oration referred to is *An Oration, Pronounced before a Numerous Body of the Nobilty and Gentry, Assembled at the Musick-Hall in Fishamble-*

street, On Tuesday the 6th of this instant December, And now first Published at their unanimous Desire. I have used a copy of a 1758 edition. *British Education* is available in a facsimile edition put out by the Scolar Press (Menston, 1971). The *Course of Lectures* was reprinted by the same press in 1968, based on the 1762 edition.

27. *An Oration*, p. 19.
28. Walker's *Elements of Elocution* is available in facsimile, 2 vols. (Menston, 1969).
29. See the bibliographies in the Southern Illinois University editions of Campbell and Blair, notes 30 and 32; and the essays in *Aberdeen and the Enlightenment* and the Bormann paper, both cited in Further Reading.
30. References are to book, chapter, and section from the Southern Illinois University edition of *The Philosophy of Rhetoric* (Carbondale, 1963), ed. L. Bitzer. A new edition, with a revised introduction by Bitzer, was published in 1988.
31. On the activities of the Aberdeen Philosophical Society, see McCosh (cited in Further Reading).
32. I have used the Southern Illinois University edition, ed. H. Harding, (Carbondale, 1965). References are to lecture and page.
33. On Blair's influence in Germany, see K. Dockhorn, *Macht and Wirkung der Rhetorik* (Berlin/Zürich, 1968), pp. 9ff. (with bibliography). A Spanish translation and compendium of Blair's *Lectures* by Munárriz went into eight editions between 1802 and 1824.
34. For an interesting view of this subject, see N. Struever, "The Conversable World" (cited in Further Reading), pp. 79–119, especially pp. 94ff., where Austen is discussed.
35. See V. Bevilacqua's introduction to the Southern Illinois University edition of Priestley's *Course of Lectures* (Carbondale, 1965).

G. B. VICO, *INSTITUTIONES ORATORIAE*

(Section numbers are from *G. B. Vico Opere* VIII, ed. Nicolini (Bari, 1941) (= *Scrittori d'Italia* 183.)

I. Ch. 1–7: On the nature, offices, and sources of eloquence
II. Ch. 8–21: On invention
  1. (9–10) Nature of invention
  2. (11–15) On topical invention, with examples
  3. (16) Arguments from emotion
  4. (17–21) Places proper to demonstrative, deliberative, and judicial rhetoric
III. Ch. 22–31: On arrangement
  1. (22) Artistic and "prudential" arrangement
  2. (23) The exordium
  3. (24) The narration
  4. (25) The digression
  5. (26–27) The proposition and partition
  6. (28) The confirmation: forms of argument
  7. (29) On amplification
  8. (30) The lines of argument for refutation
  9. (31) The peroration

CLAUDE BUFFIER, S. J., *TRAITÉ DE L'ÉLOQUENCE*

(References are to the version in *Cours de sciences* [Paris, 1732].)

[Examples of Eloquence in Different Types]*
    Prosecution and Defense (183–215)
    The speeches and essays of Patru (216–239)
    Sermons (240–257)
    Epideictic speeches (258–281)
    Harangues (286–306)
[Critical Observations]
    Aristotle (307–319)
    Cicero (319–331)
    Quintilian (331–419)

CHARLES ROLLIN, *TRAITÉ DES ÉTUDES: DE LA MANIÈRE D'ENSEIGNER ET D'ÉTUDIER LES BELLES-LETTRES*

(Page references are to the 1751 Halle edition, vol. 2.)

Preface.   On rhetoric generally (pp. 1–3)
Chapter 1. Precepts and examples (4–18)
Chapter 2. The method of composition
        1. General principles (19–26)
        2. On teaching composition (27–51)
Chapter 3. Reading and explication of texts
        A. On the different types of speaking (52–58)
           1. The simple style (58–70)
           2. The sublime style (70–80)
           3. The temperate style (81–89)
           4. General reflections (90–98)
        B. What to look for in different writers
           1. Reasoning and arguments (100–113)
           2. Ideas, clever thoughts (114–150)
           3. Choice of words (151–160)
           4. Arrangement (161–173)
           5. Figures (174–210)
           6. Rhetorical prudence (211–219)
           7. On emotion (220–235)
        C. The eloquence of the bar
           1. Models of eloquence (236–292)
           2. How to prepare the young to plead cases (293–314)
           3. The customs and bearing of advocates (315–326)
        D. The eloquence of the pulpit
           1. The tasks of the preacher
               a. To be clear (327–336)
               b. To please (337–353)

---

* Note how the "theory" section is far shorter than the section providing examples.

J. C. GOTTSCHED, *AUSFÜHRLICHE REDEKUNST*

(Page references are to the 1975 edition, ed. P. Mitchell, *Ausgewählte Werke*, vol. VII.)

GREGORIO MAYANS Y SISCAR, *RETÓRICA*

(References are to *Obras completas*, vol. III, ed. A. Mestre Sanchis and J. Gutiérrez [Valencia, 1984].)

GEORGE CAMPBELL, *PHILOSOPHY OF RHETORIC*

(Page references are to the 1850 London edition, reprinted 1988.)

CHAPTER 8

Rhetoric in the Nineteenth Century

Early in Jane Austen's *Northanger Abbey*, Catherine Morland and Henry Tinley discover that they both admire Ann Radcliff's gothic novel *The Mysteries of Udolpho.* Catherine is surprised, for she assumes that such novels are generally despised by young men. When Catherine asks him if he would go so far as to say that *Udolpho* is "the nicest book in the world," however, Henry cavils: "The nicest; by which I suppose you mean the neatest. That must depend on the binding." At this point, Henry's sister, Eleanor, intervenes:

> "Henry...you are very impertinent. Miss Morland, he is treating you exactly as he does his sister. He is forever finding fault with me for some incorrectness of language, and now he is taking the same liberty with you. The word 'nicest,' as you used it, did not suit him; and you had better change it as soon as you can, or we shall be overpowered with Johnson and Blair all the rest of the way." (p. 109)[1]

A little later, it is Eleanor who needs to be enlightened. Henry and Catherine have been talking about the impending publication of a new novel, of which Catherine says, "[S]omething very shocking indeed will soon come out in London...more horrible than anything we have met with yet.... I shall expect murder and everything of the kind"(p. 112). Eleanor thinks they are talking about an impending crisis or riot, an impression fostered by her brother. But Henry finally explains, "My dear Eleanor, the riot is only in your own brain.... And you, Miss Morland

> —my stupid sister has mistaken all your clearest expressions. You talked of expected horrors in London...and she immediately pictured to herself a

235

mob of three thousand men assembling in St. George's Fields; the Bank attacked, the Tower threatened, the streets of London flowing with blood, a detachment of the 12th Light Dragoons...called up from Northampton to quell the insurgents.... (p. 113).

These two passages say a great deal about Austen's time. In the background, we have, on the one hand, the world of polite conversation and learning—the world of Blair, in fact—and on the other, the disturbances and repression of insurgents, the strife that overtook all of Europe in the aftermath of the French Revolution. The lurid details of the "riot" Henry envisions had their real counterparts in incidents roughly contemporary with the first drafts of the novel. Austen's polite world, a world created by the imagination of the Enlightenment, was all but shattered during the next century by political and social revolutions. Yet only partly. Bourgeois and industrial Europe in the course of the nineteenth century largely succeeded in consigning the *ancien régime* to the ash heap of history but, paradoxically, continued to be haunted by the cultural standards of political absolutism and social caste. Novels like *Northanger Abbey*, in other words, were both nostalgic and prophetic, both backward- and forward-looking, just as the nineteenth century was.

In order to understand the many different fortunes of rhetoric in the nineteenth century—and, as we shall see, there were many—we need to look briefly at its historical setting, at its political and social context. Of course, we should always do that; but in this case, it is particularly important. There are at least four strands to nineteenth-century rhetoric: a powerful continuing presence of Classical influences, the ongoing interest in the arts of elocution, the *belles lettres* tradition, and an emerging scientific perspective on communication. The latter two can be explained in part by the persistence of commonsense philosophy; the former two cannot. All, it will be argued in this chapter, can be explained, at least in large part, by the curiously irrelevant character of rhetorical education in this period. To understand that "irrelevance," we need to understand what rhetoric was "irrelevant" to.

POLITICAL AND SOCIAL TRANSFORMATIONS

The nineteenth century was a period of rapid and violent change—political, social, technological, and intellectual. It was a century that saw revolutions in virtually every European country and in the New World colonies of those countries; a watershed between the old society of hierarchy and caste and the new culture of industrialism. It was the century of Manchester Liberalism and of the *Communist Manifesto*, of Beethoven and Wagner, Hegel and Nietzsche, Darwinian and paternalistic by turns. The political revolutions are easy enough to explain. Absolute monarchs were not on the whole a very inspiring lot—fickle in their exercise of power, loose in their morals often insane, reflecting the worst traits of the age, and frequently deposed, if not beheaded. The examples of the revolt of England's North American colonies against the deranged George III and the French Revolution, which brought Louis XVI to the guillotine, inspired many.

Concurrent with revolution came the rise of power politics as expressed in imperialism and war, the one designed to fuel industry and the other fueled by it, creating new and complex relations between industry and government. With that other revolution, the Industrial Revolution, came the shift in the center of power from privilege to wealth. Populations shifted, too, from the countryside to the centers of production. The agricultural population shrank in France from three-fourths of the total population to one-third; in Germany, from four-fifths to one-fifth. Parallel with the social and technological changes were successions of aesthetic movements—Romanticism, realism, naturalism, and symbolism—all of which questioned entrenched cultural canons, just as the social movements of the age had questioned the presumptions of private property and the "iron law of wages," and all of which were characterized by antagonism to bourgeois society.

Not so the educators and intellectuals. Few among them made any effort to shape social development. Most of them followed, working within the standards set by the old absolutism on the one hand and those promoted by the bourgeois believers in the mysteries of property on the other. Aside from such visionaries as Johann Heinrich Pestalozzi (1746–1827) and Johann Gottlieb Fichte (1762–1814), few saw education as a way of transforming society. It was, rather, a way of tapping the abilities of the masses in the effort to maintain the basis of wealth. Companies needed clerks who could write and workers who could read directions. At higher levels of education, social prejudice and the preservation of class distinctions prevented any meaningful adjustments in the curriculum. In the final analysis, higher education remained elitist.

It is against such a background as we have been able to glimpse here that the history of rhetoric in the nineteenth century must be seen. In many ways, the social "reading" we suggested in the last chapter is even more revealing for the nineteenth century than it was for the eighteenth. In what follows, we shall look briefly at developments during this period, working from country to country, so to speak, and attempt to discover the basic pattern, if there is one, of those developments, beginning where we left off in the last chapter, in Britain.

ENGLAND, SCOTLAND, AND IRELAND

The Industrial Revolution first took hold in Scotland and in the North of England. Concentration of activity around mills and mines resulted in the movement of many to towns and cities and in the increase of occupations requiring literacy, which became a vehicle of social mobility for some. Hence it makes sense that support for public elementary education becomes increasingly evident in the north during the early decades of the century, resulting in levels of school attendance of up to 25 percent (high, for the time) of the young.

Part of this education consisted of lessons in reading and elocution, lessons designed to teach children how to speak "proper English." In response to the increased school population, we find a proliferation of school manuals containing the basic rules of reading for sense and correct pronunciation and, frequently, sample passages of prose and poetry for recitation. Among them are, for instance, John Walker's *Academic Speaker*, which went into six editions in the first decade of the century; Thomas Ewing's *Principles of Elocution*, which was reprinted 36 times between 1815 and 1861; and A. M. Hartley's *The Oratorical Class-Book*, reprinted 15 times between 1824 and 1854. Most of these books were published in Glasgow, Edinburgh, Manchester, and Leeds, all centers of intense industrialization. Their general tone may be well summarized in the preface to Thomas Carpenter's *The School Speaker* (1813): to "introduce as much matter as possible, at a cheap rate, for the instruction of the rising generation, unmixed with any sentiment of an *immoral* tendency" (emphasis in the original).[2]

Proper elocution was not, of course, the concern only of elementary-school teachers. Sheridan's program, after all, was meant to be realized at higher levels, too; and, as we have seen, the Elocutionary Movement spread quickly throughout Britain. Yet that movement concentrated largely on accent and diction, giving little attention to the other component of delivery, gesture. It was this deficiency that Gilbert Austin's *Chironomia: or a Treatise on Rhetorical Delivery* (1806) was meant to make up for.[3] In it Austin sought to provide rules to the public—in fact, he specifically refers to the members of the clergy, members of Parliament, lawyers, and actors—that would improve oratory in Britain. *Chironomia* draws upon numerous Classical sources, Quintilian in particular, toward that end, organized, he says, on scientific grounds. Perhaps the most original feature of Austin's book is the elaborate system of notation in which all possible gestures were assigned a symbol and by which an orator could "score" a speech, much as a cellist might annotate a piece to indicate different fingerings. Certainly the most impressive feature of the book is the set of steel engravings illustrating his system.

Rhetorical instruction more broadly considered continued to be dominated by the recently developed *belles lettres* conception of the nature and end of the art, as is clear from the appearance of such school texts as Alexander Jamieson's *Grammar of Rhetoric and Polite Literature* in 1818 or Larret Langley's *Manual of the Figures of Rhetoric* in 1835. Interest in Classical authors, however, did not abate. Quite to the contrary, the Classical curriculum continued to prevail, on the assumption that mental discipline had to be added to good taste if students were expected to become leaders in their chosen professions. The continued importance attached to Classical learning evidently filtered down to those who did not actually have it, moreover. This seems clear from the appearance of numerous "popular" treatments of the works and career of Cicero during the period, for instance. It also explains why interest in Aristotle's *Rhetoric* was revived, both in university circles and in the popular press. Thomas Gaisford's 1805 critical edition of the *Rhetoric* was reissued three times by 1833; and separate translations by Thomas Taylor, Daniel Crimmin, and Theodore Buckley (in the Bohn Classical Library series) all went into multiple editions.[4]

The renewed interest in Aristotle, in turn, may explain why Richard Whately's *Elements of Rhetoric** could have achieved the success it did, and may even explain how Whately came to write it. Since this book became influential, more perhaps in America than in the British Isles, in the decades following its publication, we need here to look at it briefly.[5]

The book falls into four parts. In Part One, by far the longest part, Whately discussed the methods of establishing conviction in oneself of the correctness of a given thesis and of constructing arguments that will establish the truth of that thesis to the satisfaction of another. Rhetoric, he says (echoing Aristotle), is an offshoot of logic whose "only province" is "the art of inventing and arranging Arguments." The heart of Whately's theory of argument is the syllogism, which he had discussed at length in his earlier *Elements of Logic*, but it is far from a mere formal system. Whately is acutely aware of the argumentative situation; hence his long discussion on the nature of argumentative presumption and of the burden of proof (pp. 112–132).

Part Two analyzes the various forms of persuasion, "the art of influencing the Will" (p. 256), concentrating on the role of emotions, both those expressed by the speaker and those felt by the audience. Whately stresses that emotion must in some situations supplement reason but should always be kept within the control of reason. Here again Whately has in mind not simply description of psychological states, but the practical effects of the perceived character of the speaker and of the speaker's opponent as well as the character of those addressed.

Part Three treats of style, whose virtues he defines as perspicuity, energy, and elegance, echoing here not so much Aristotle as his eighteenth-century British predecessors. It is these qualities of style, Whately explains, that affect an orator's ability to communicate a message. On the first, he cites Aristotle: "[A]s Aristotle observes, language which is not intelligible, or not clearly and readily intelligible, fails, in the same proportion, of the purpose for which language is employed" (p. 258). "Energy," he explains, is used in a sense wider than the *energeia* of Aristotle and "nearly corresponding with what Dr. Campbell calls Vivacity" (p. 275). "Elegance" is not merely a stylistic quality but is closely related to energy, as the devices that contribute to energy will for the most part contribute to its more "aesthetic" counterpart. Whately's treatment of style, in short, is quite functional, directed mainly at the goal of successful communication.

The last part, Part Four, is on elocution—that is, delivery. Whately here rejects the precepts of the elocutionists, which he saw as leading to a mechanical delivery, and advocates a natural delivery achieved by "feeling the thought." Practice recitation at school is injurious, as is the acting of plays by students (see pp. 379ff.), since they make for little more than "a sorry display" (p. 384). Gesture, to which Austin had devoted some 600 pages, is dealt with in 3 by Whately.

Whately wrote *Elements of Rhetoric* while a tutor at Oriel College, Oxford, half a decade before he was named archbishop of Dublin and ex officio member of the House of Lords. In some ways, the lessons of *Elements* prefigure aspects of his career after it was published. On the one side, Whately practiced in his own public speaking what he preached in his book. Unfortunately, his precepts did not win for him favorable reviews from his contemporaries, one of whom characterized him as "preeminently a man of major premises" and his delivery as "natural even to a fault."[6] On the other side, reminding ourselves that Whately was not just an Oxford don but, like many dons of the day, a man of the cloth forces us to notice the ecclesiastical context of *Elements of Rhetoric*. That context includes a half-century of disputes between the theologians and the Humean skeptics—recall the educational aims of Campbell and Blair—over the general criteria of belief and, in particular, over the problem of miracles. In this context, Whately's dominant scenario for argumentation—that of debate, not demonstration—and his careful analysis of presumption and the burden of proof can be seen to be both concrete and specific. And indeed, as archbishop of Dublin, Whately was able to put his teaching into practice with rather more success that he had as a member of Parliament.

The *Elements of Rhetoric* went into several editions in England and even more in North America, where it was widely used in the United States and Canada. The precepts from *Elements* most influential on later rhetoric texts were not those on argument as such, but those on the proper method of teaching composition found in the revised version of the introduction to the book. There Whately explains that the first step in the process is to find an appropriate and engaging theme. After finding a subject, the student is to state the proposition(s) to be treated clearly. After making an outline, the student will develop the proposition in a unified and coherent fashion, writing in a "free, natural, and simple style" (p. 23), using only proper and correct diction and syntax, possibly imitating the manner of some approved author. A glance at almost any manual of composition from the past century and a half will be sufficient proof of Whately's enduring influence in that field.

By the large, rhetoric in England continued to be backward-looking and tied to the cultural values of the eighteenth century. This is true even of the contributions made by Herbert Spencer and Alexander Bain, which can fairly be said to amount to little more (as we shall see later) than old wine in new bottles, supplying a new scientific idiom but not adding much of substance. And it seems clear also in another body of material bearing on the subject. The entry for "Rhetoric" in the sixth edition of the *Encyclopaedia Britannica* (1822) says only, "See ORATORY." The long article on "Oratory" (vol. 15, pp. 301–400) is basically a recapitulation of eighteenth-century lore, recommending almost as an afterthought Ward's *System of Oratory*. The article on rhetoric in the eighth edition (1859) is a careful exposition of the subject by William Spalding (1809–59), professor of rhetoric and logic at St. Andrew's after taking his degree at Marischal College. Spalding's version is also deeply dependent on his predecessors at Edinburgh and Marischal. In the ninth edition, we find a long article on the subject by R. C. Jebb, the noted author of *The Attic Orators*, which is Classical—almost antiquarian—to the core. At the end, Jebb recommends for further study of the subject Whately's *Elements*, the only modern treatment Jebb mentions. In short, by 1886, the year the ninth edition came out, "Rhetoric" was indeed a thing of the past— in more ways than one.

FRANCE AND GERMANY

Meanwhile, the same sort of thing could be said about rhetoric on the Continent. France and Germany, like England, saw increasing industrialization and the social changes that went with it during the nineteenth century. The needs and opportunities of the system resulted in educational reform designed to make elementary education available even to the poor, on the one hand, and to maintain rigor in the higher education available to the rich, particularly the newly rich. As in England, the notion of proper and correct use of the national language caught hold, and steps were taken to insure that the speech and writing of the young should be cleansed of class and dialectal differences. The Classical curriculum, designed to produce men (not women) of Classical *Bildung* or *culture générale*, continued to prevail in higher educational institutions, private, public, and parochial. If it is true that educational reform offered an alternative modern curriculum, as in the French *école polytechnique* or the German *Realschulen*, it is also true that the alternative was not non-Classical but simply less Classical. And in all three countries, social mobility was carefully monitored: the funnel to the top, as one historian has put it, was very narrow.[7]

In France, the basic plan of education, even after the Revolution of 1789–92, was in all essentials the one laid out by Charles Rollin's *Traité*. Cultural standards were far from "revolutionary." One of the utopian dreams of the Revolution was to make all of France's citizens literate. Yet, despite repeated decrees requiring schools in every community and teachers' colleges (*écoles normales*) in every province, an 1832 census of young men drafted into the army shows almost half of them to be unable to read and write. The vast majority of children left school after only two or three years. Secondary education in the *collèges* and *lycées* continued to be accessible only to those families with money, and seldom enrolled more than 15 percent of the potential student population. The percentage of the total population of school-age children completing the *baccalauréat* necessary for admission to a university was, throughout the century, not more than 1 percent. Between 1876 and 1880, only 155 French university students took degrees in the arts that would make them eligible to teach secondary school students language, literature, and history. Education, in short, remained a privilege limited to a very few.[8]

Some idea of the prevailing attitude of university teachers of rhetoric may be gathered from two lectures by Abel-François Villemain (1790–1870), professor of rhetoric at the Sorbonne from 1816 to 1830 and twice appointed after that to the post of minister of education.[9] Both are lectures given at the beginning of his course on eloquence, designed to orient the students and explain the contents of the course. His course, he says, will consist of readings from the great orators and writers of the seventeenth century, the century of Louis XIV, chiefly Bossuet, Fénelon, and Pascal. Why the seventeenth century? Because that is the age of "good taste" (*bon goût*, p. 198); the others are "uncultivated and gross" (*incultes et grossiers*, p. 223). At the end of the 1822 lecture, he exhorts his students thus:

> Come, gentlemen.... Instead of contenting yourselves with a cold and solitary reading, come to this gathering and hear the immortal voices which will manifest themselves as so sonorous and alive.... Nourish now your souls with these great thoughts.... This eloquence has become the last resort of our political system (*institution politique*). (p. 216)

Villemain takes for granted that his students are already familiar with the Classical orators—Demosthenes and Cicero—and with the great speakers of the early Church—Chrysostom and Gregory Nazianzus. But now that they have reached the Sorbonne, they are to study French eloquence, which, he explains at some length (226ff.), surpasses that of all other nations. Contemporary society, he observes at the end of the 1824 lecture, is unstable and vague—"what a wonderful opportunity for eloquence!"

Villemain was of course not alone, nor the last to think this way; a fact that explains perhaps why no new important rhetorical work—certainly not anything comparable to Whately's *Elements*—appeared in France between 1789 and 1914.[10] France did not lack for eloquent speakers, to be sure, but their eloquence was (and in some ways still is) the eloquence of a past epoch. Such relatively popular textbooks as Louis Domarion's *Rhétorique français* (four editions between 1804 and 1826) or A. Baron's *Manuél abrégé de Rhétorique ou de composition oratoire* (three editions, 1850–68) added nothing to the curriculum. J. C. Leclerc's *Nouvelle rhétorique, extraite des meilleurs écrivains anciens et modernes* went into 23 editions between 1827 and 1891. By *écrivains...modernes* ("modern writers"), he means Bossuet and Fénelon. And perhaps the most important university-level text continued to be DuMarsais's treatise on tropes in the annotated version by Fontanier (1818 and after).

Such cultural conservatism was not peculiar to France, of course. The history of rhetoric in Germany during the nineteenth century exhibits many of the same traits, although the literature reveals a rather different set of emphases. We can see there, on the one hand, a preoccupation with the place of rhetoric in relation to the aesthetic realm and, on the other, a more or less constant stream of criticism of rhetoric by philosophers. In short, there is in Germany a sense of insecurity about the status of rhetoric as a legitimate enterprise that we do not see very much of in England or France. Yet because the classics continued to dominate the curricula of *Gymnasien* and universities alike, rhetoric remained highly visible and important in the schooling of German youth.

France's cultural domination over Germany began to wane in the nineteenth century, but English influence grew. Blair's *Lectures* were translated into German within two years of their publication in London; Sheridan's *Lectures on the Art of Reading* (1775) appeared in German in 1793; and Austin's *Chironomia* came out in an 1818 Leipzig edition, translated by the great German educator Johann Friedrich Michaelis. These works did not determine the course of rhetoric, however; they merely supplemented it. With the emergence of a strong strain of nationalism and the growth of carefully regulated bureaucracies set up to administer the modernization of Germany, a large body of quite peculiarly German manuals of rhetoric began to appear. In fact, the most frequently published rhetorical handbooks by mid-century were those of J. Rumpf, designed for use by Prussian bureaucrats.[11]

It is significant, moreover, that it was not Blair's *Lectures* that most excited German readers but his *Critical Dissertation on the Poems of Ossian* (1763), a work that was seen as a monumental contribution to literary criticism. Even after *The Works of Ossian* were known to have been fabrications, Romantic critics saw in Blair's *Dissertation* an important statement about the struggle between progress and primitivism, between intellect and poetic imagination. Rhetoric in Germany, like the reception of Blair's *Dissertation*, was strongly colored by the concerns of the new Romantic aestheticism that arose after A. G. Baumgarten's *Aesthetica* (1750) and was developed by the great German writers Goethe and Schiller. For such writers, the truly artistic is to be contrasted in the strongest possible terms with the mechanical. True poetry does not "go by the book" but is "organic," flowing directly from the deepest wellsprings of creativity within the poet and taking shape not according to the rules of any genre but according to the unity of poetic vision.[12]

If rhetoric is an art (*Kunst*), traditional approaches to the subject are, in the Romantic view, not legitimate as art but (shades of Plato!) are simply rulebooks for a pseudo-art. The response to this position by German authors was twofold. On the one hand, many of the standard texts composed in the shadow of the poets change their formats. The study of rhetoric—in German, "*Redekunst*," we recall—begins in such works as W. Wackernagel's *Poetik, Rhetorik und Stilistik* (1873) with the study of poetics. This book, it should be noted, was made up out of Wackernagel's course of lectures on the subject going back to 1836. The famous set of lectures by the renowned German critic Adam Müller, *Zwolf Reden über die Beredsamkeit* (1812), calls for a German eloquence that would complement the achievements of the great German poets.

On the other hand, we see in the years between 1750 and 1850 an enor-

mous outpouring of handbooks of declamation and elocution. One bibliography lists over 200 such books, including, for instance, D. Beifeld's *Über
Declamation als Wissenschaft* (On Declamation as a Science) (1801) and
J. Edwald's *Über Deklamation und Kanzelvortrag* (1809). The first is
interesting in that it attempts to link the effects of literary readings with the
psychological effects of sound and timbre; the second in that it connects
practice in declamation with mastery of the sort of delivery appropriate in
governmental discourse (*Kanzelvortrage*). The one, that is to say, seems to
justify the study of declamation on scientific grounds; the other, on practical,
perhaps careerist, grounds.[13]

The responses we have just mentioned illustrate the Scylla and Charybdis
German rhetoricians thought they had to negotiate, between the claims of
poetry, on the one hand, and the claims of science (*Wissenschaft*) on the
other. The challenge to rhetoric in Germany was strongly made by Immanuel
Kant in his third *Critique*, in 1790. Kant, who had turned down the chair of
poetry at Königsberg before accepting that of philosophy, put poetry in the
highest rank among the arts. "Poetry," he writes,

> plays with illusion, which it produces at will, and yet without using illusion
> to deceive us, for poetry tells us itself that its pursuit is mere play, though
> this play can still be used purposefully by the understanding for its business.
> Oratory (*Beredsamkeit*) [on the other hand] insofar as this is taken to mean
> the art of persuasion (*die Kunst zu überreden*)...i.e., of deceiving by means
> of a beautiful illusion...is a dialectic that borrows from poetry only as
> much as the speaker needs in order to win over people's minds for his own
> advantage before they judge for themselves, and so make their judgment
> unfree.[14]

In a note on the next page, Kant makes a distinction between the rhetorical
power and excellence of speech that belong to fine art and that which is used
simply to exploit others' weaknesses, "the *ars oratoria*" (pp. 327–328). This
latter, he says, is worthy of no respect whatsoever. Moreover, in Kant's
scheme of things, there cannot be either an "elementology" (*Elementarlehre*)
or a rigorous "methodology" for the fine arts. There is for them only a
"manner" (*Manier*), not a method (*Lehrart*) (p. 355). Hence to speak of a
"science" of rhetoric is to speak nonsense. Thus all those who claim for
rhetoric true "artistic" status or any sort of "scientific" status are defending
an untenable position.

Kant's attitude was shared by many, including Hegel and, indeed, Adam
Müller, two writers whose ideas had powerful effects on German education.
Hence the reassuring titles of so many treatises that promise an "art" of
rhetoric or a *wissenschaftlich* treatment of the subject. But the most serious
charge implicit in the philosopher's critiques of rhetoric was not its
epistemological failures but its moral failures. To this charge Franz Theremin
responded in his *Die Beredsamkeit eine Tugend, oder Grundlinien einer
systematischen Rhetorik* (1814; 2nd ed., 1837) (*Eloquence a Virtue: or,*

Outlines of a Systematic Rhetoric).[15] Theremin (1780–1846) taught homiletics at the University of Berlin and was known as a theologian and a distinguished orator. Rhetoric, he notes early in the book,

> is but the science of form, or, to use Milton's phrase, an "organic"—i.e., instrumental—Art. . . . Dissevered from Logic, or the necessary laws of Thought, it has become dissevered from the seat of life, and has degenerated into a mere collection of rules.[16]

In order to justify rhetoric. Theremin argued, we must base it on synthetic *a priori* principles (as in Kant) of practical action. These are to be provided by ethics, a subject that establishes "the laws according to which a free being may exert influence upon other free beings" (p. 69). True eloquence demands that "the particular Idea which the orator wishes to realize is. . . carried back to the necessary Ideas of the hearer" (p. 73). Having established this sort of foundation for rhetoric—an obvious response to Kant—he goes on to outline a "system" of rhetoric that is in all other respects Classical. Thus, aside from the philosophical concerns treated early in the book, *Die Beredsamkeit* is hardly what one would call a "new" rhetoric, but looks backward to Cicero—and to Gottsched, it appears.

We can thus see that many nineteenth-century German rhetorics were conceived in the context of recent poetics and philosophy but stayed well within the confines of eighteenth-century thinking about the nature and end of the art. At the same time, there appear two rather different manifestations of interest in rhetoric, one "ancient" and the other "modern." The "ancient" interest was philological. Immanuel Bekker's critical edition of Aristotle's *Rhetoric* came out in Berlin in 1837; Christian Walz's nine-volume *Rhetores graeci* was published in Tübingen in the mid-1830s; Leonhard Spengel's commentary on the *Rhetoric* was published in 1867 in Leipzig; and Richard Volkmann's synoptic *Rhetorik der Griechen und Römer* went into three editions in the last quarter of the century. The "modern" interest was psychological, emerging with the rise of experimental physiological psychology as practiced by Lotze, von Helmholtz, and Wilhelm Wundt. The basic goal of all three was to discover by some empirical means the underlying system binding mental and physiological events together. In many ways, their research was inspired by Scottish associationism, but they rejected the introspective methods of Hartley and Priestley. Their influence is perhaps most pronounced in the work of Alexander Bain in faraway Aberdeen, later in the century; but more nearly contemporary influence of their empirical orientation can be seen in such books as Ludwig Aurbacher's *Grundlinien der Psychologie, als Propädeutik zum Unterricht in der Rhetorik und Poetik* (1824) and Maximilian Langenschwartz's *Die Arithmetik der Sprache oder: der Redner durch sicht selbst, physiologisch-rhetorisches Lehrgebäude* (1837).[17]

The works we have mentioned here should provide some idea of the range of rhetorical theorizing in Germany. We should not, however, lose sight of the fact that the overwhelming majority of the books on rhetoric from this period were classicizing extensions of the rhetorics of the previous century. Cicero and Quintilian (whose *Institutes* saw at least 15 editions between 1805 and 1895) were still the backbone of rhetorical instruction, supplemented by examples of the best German prose and poetry. Concerns with contemporary philosophical issues and psychologizing tendencies did begin to emerge during this time. But, on the whole, German rhetoric in the nineteenth century continued to be dominated by the social and cultural ideals of the *ancien régime*.

THE UNITED STATES AND CANADA

The history of rhetoric in North America can be roughly divided into three periods: the colonial period, up to 1789; the years between 1789 and the end of the Civil War in the United States; and the latter part of the century, from 1865 to 1910 or so. In what follows, we shall proceed to sketch some of the more important intellectual currents and prominent books in each of these periods.

The late seventeenth and early eighteenth centuries saw the foundation of a number of colleges in the United States—Harvard, Yale, King's College (Columbia), and the College of New Jersey (Princeton), among them. All were quite sectarian in nature, their chief aim being the production of ministers of Congregationalist and Presbyterian churches. From what we can tell, a great deal of time was spent in those schools teaching homiletics. Ramism seems to have been the dominant cast of mind, as the popularity of William Dugard's *Rhetorices elementa* (1650), a digest of Ramus and Talon, suggests. At the same time, it is recorded that Farnaby's *Index rhetoricus* was used at Harvard in the 1720s; and Vossius' *Elementa rhetoricae* was recommended reading for Yale upperclassmen in the 1740s. Toward the end of the eighteenth century, the influences of the likes of Sheridan, Blair, and Campbell began to be felt, the latter two probably because their "commonsense" approach and their evangelical concerns sat well with the religious commitments of the faculties of American colleges.

John Witherspoon (1723–94) was one of those responsible for the influence wielded by the Scottish rhetoricians. Born in Scotland himself and educated at Edinburgh, Witherspoon emigrated to the colonies and taught his course on eloquence at the College of New Jersey from 1768 until the year of his death. Witherspoon's *Lectures on Eloquence*, published after his death, are interesting as a blend of Classical and Scottish schools of rhetoric.[18] On the one hand, his lectures cover the traditional five parts of rhetoric, the three levels of style, three subjects (pulpit, bar, and senate)—all in a rather Ciceronian spirit. But on the other, they show a typical eighteenth-century approach to the nature of language, the sources of the sublime, and the principles of taste. Indeed, at the very beginning (p. 475), he announces, "We are now to enter on the study of eloquence, or as perhaps it ought to be called, from the manner in which you will find it treated, Composition, Taste, and Criticism"—an eighteenth-century "manner" if there ever was one. Witherspoon and his colleagues at other schools were teachers of their time in other respects, too. We find in their lectures, and in the lectures and textbooks of the succeeding period, an enormous importance attached to good taste, propriety, and duty—that is, to the social and cultural ideals of the European *ancien régime*. So it is perhaps that we find among the models of eloquence appended to E. G. Welles' *The Orator's Guide* a disquisition on education in which we read that children

> cannot become rude and disorderly without violating all sense of decorum and gratitude; and breaking through, besides, all their early habits. The common sense of mankind is in accordance with all this. A rough, surly ungovernable boy, there is nothing more common than to call an *unnatural child*. Thus are children, by the very condition of their being, made fit subjects for *order* which "is Heaven's first law."[19]

The Classical curriculum dominated the colleges in the United States as it did on the Continent and in England. At Harvard, for instance, the lectures of the first Boylston Professors of Rhetoric and Oratory, John Quincy Adams (from 1806 to 1816) and Edward Channing (1819–52), show this clearly.[20] A similar situation existed at, for instance, King's College, Toronto, where both Cicero and Quintilian were required reading between 1856 and 1880. As in Europe, colleges were for those who could afford to send their sons to them, even the colleges whose main purpose was the production of ministers. Thus, it would seem, the widespread popularity of Blair's *Lectures* in the first half of the nineteenth century and thus almost certainly the appearance of such authorities on pronunciation and meaning as Noah Webster's *Dictionary of the English Language* and such widely used anthologies as Chauncey Goodrich's *Select British Eloquence*—all designed to produce men of "polite learning."

Scottish influence was quite pervasive, as a glance at such textbooks as that by Welles or at Samuel Newman's *A Practical System of Rhetoric*, which went into seven editions between 1827 and 1839, will show.[21] The catalogue for Amherst College for 1839 lists the following readings for the rhetoric course:

- First Year: E. Porter's *Analysis of the Principles of Rhetorical Delivery*; weekly compositions and declamations
- Second Year: S. Newman, *Practical System of Rhetoric*; Cicero, *De oratore*
- Third Year: Whately, *Elements of Rhetoric* and *Elements of Logic*; selections from Campbell, *Philosophy of Rhetoric*
- Fourth Year: Kames, *Elements of Criticism*

This list remained virtually unchanged until the 1880s. Examination statutes for Dartmouth College for 1856–60 show that all students were expected to master Whately's *Logic* and Blair's *Lectures*, along with selected orations of

Demosthenes and Richard Trench's *The English Language: Past and Present*. Similar requirements can be found in the syllabi for Brown in 1824 and McGill University in 1856.

Another side of rhetorical education in the United States is evident in the attention paid to rhetorical delivery and elocution. Inspired by both Sheridan and Austin, American teachers of eloquence carried on that tradition until well after the Civil War. Just how widespread such training was can be gathered from the circulation of the books on the subject by Ebenezer Porter (1772–1834), for many years a professor of homiletics at the Andover Theological Seminary. Porter's *Analysis of the Principles of Rhetorical Delivery*, intended for preachers, went into many editions between 1827 and 1841. His *The Rhetorical Reader*, a version of that work intended for high-school and academy students, went into 75 editions by 1841. Porter's books were used at Amherst, as we have seen, as well as at Brown, Dartmouth, Wesleyan, and the University of Georgia. As time went on, the theoretical basis for elocutionary training shifted from that underlying Sheridan and Austin to, on the one hand, the pseudo-scientific "system" of François Delsartre or, on the other, the more respectable psychological foundations of works like Thomas and William Hydes *A Natural System of Elocution and Oratory* (1886).[22]

The competing claims of the champions of *belles lettres* and those of elocution lie behind Matthew Boyd Hope's *Princeton Textbook of Rhetoric* (1859), where Hope explicitly limits rhetoric to the study of literary works and consigns persuasion to the realm of ethics (as in Theremin, whose book had been translated into English in 1844), and John Mitchell Bonnell's *Manual of the Art of Composition* (1867). Bonnell argues strenuously for the separation of composition and delivery, with only the art of composition laying legitimate claim to the title "Rhetoric."

Bonnell's argument seems to have been taken seriously, for "rhetoric," after 1867, becomes increasingly identified with composition and increasingly differentiated from "elocution" or even "public speaking." James DeMille's *Elements of Rhetoric* (1882) and John Franklin Genung's *Practical Principles of Rhetoric* (1886) are exclusively concerned with composition. It is not easy to pinpoint the reasons why Bonnell's argument should have been taken as seriously as it was; but, clearly, Bonnell was in some way saying the right thing at the right time. The most likely explanations concern two changes that occurred in education in the United States, a demographic change and an attendant change in educational philosophy.

The American college went through many transformations after the Civil War. It became more secularized and reached out to more people. A college education, it was argued, should not be restricted to the elite or to those preparing for the pulpit and should have as its goal not the initiation of the young into polite society but their preparation for a fruitful occupation and individual self-realization. The years after the war, after all, were to be thought of as a commercial and industrial golden age—these are the years

Mark Twain called the "Gilded Age"—offering unlimited opportunity for middle-class success. Those years also saw the emergence of the state university, which, unlike the older elite institutions like Harvard or Princeton, was practical in its orientation, designed to serve the industrial and agricultural interests of a growing population.

The ability to write clearly and correctly was one skill everyone agreed was essential to success: hence the emergence of required courses in composition and of the conviction that oratorical performance was important only for the pulpit or for an evening's entertainment. *Belles lettres* were seen as a frill, and the study of polite letters declined accordingly. If the old manner of teaching good writing by exposing students to exemplary literature was no longer appropriate, the question arises as to what the new manner of teaching good writing ought to be. Moreover, as one would expect in an age preoccupied with economic growth, how can good writing be taught *efficiently*?

Attempts to answer such questions took an increasingly scientific turn in the postwar decades. The formats of many rhetorics of the day reveal an abrupt departure from the matters of taste and propriety that determined the shape of antebellum textbooks and a new commitment to the psychological conditions of successful communication. The psychology in question, curiously, was not much more than a refined version of the faculty psychology behind Campbell and Blair. The specific refinements were to be found in the works of two noted scientists, Herbert Spencer and Alexander Bain, both of whom had a great deal to say about good writing and both of whom were extraordinarily influential in the United States.

We shall look at their contributions in the next section, but at this point we can draw our brief survey of rhetoric in North America to a close and say something about a more widely distributed pattern that emerges in the nineteenth century in both the Old and the New Worlds. What we see on looking over the material is that American rhetoric develops—or fails to develop—in much the same way as rhetoric in Europe did, preserving for the most part the cultural ideals of the *ancien régime*. This preservation continues to hold true in Europe well into the twentieth century. Indeed, it would not be too much to say that rhetoric in European countries stagnated. It is remarkable that a large bibliography and a set of studies on rhetoric put out in France in 1970 should stop, respectively, at 1701 and at the speeches of Henry IV of France, but it is true.[23] Largely because of the changes in American education we noted before, however, rhetoric takes a different sort of turn, moving in a scientific direction that to this day still defines a large sector of rhetorical study, whether it be the study of effective communication in general or of the composition process more narrowly. On the whole, however, rhetoric in the nineteenth century continues throughout the period, in both Europe and America, to be peripheral, limited to a cultural elite, often antiquarian and, when it has not been reduced to matters of composition merely, complacent.

SPENCER AND BAIN

No history of rhetoric in the nineteenth century would be complete without some mention of the contributions of Herbert Spencer (1820–1903) and Alexander Bain (1818–1903). Neither was interested primarily in rhetoric, but both are well–remembered for their work on the subject. Both were powerful influences on the scientific turn the study of rhetoric took in the latter part of the century, which promised a break from the traditions of the century before. Neither, however, was completely free of those traditions.

Spencer

Herbert Spencer was a self-educated polymath: an engineer, inventor, student of natural history, one of the founders of what is today sociology, and an avid dabbler in phrenology—a rather extraordinary man, in short. His study of Lyell's work in geology and Lamarck's in biology inspired his first major work, *Social Statics*, which elaborated a view of social institutions rooted in the concept of evolution nine years before the appearance of Darwin's *On the Origin of Species*, in 1859. His importance to rhetoric is due to a short piece he wrote originally as a part of his projected *Principles of Sociology* and first published in the *Popular Science Monthly* in 1852, "The Philosophy of Style."[24]

This essay was published separately in 1872 and was frequently printed and very widely appreciated, particularly in the United States. Its argument is, basically, that all excellence of composition may be traced to two principles: economy of the attention and economy of the sensibility of the recipient—that is, the reader or listener. Assuming that a reader can have at his (so Spencer) command only a definite amount of power of attention, it is clear that whatever part of that power is employed on the form of a composition must be subtracted, thus leaving less power to be applied to the matter of the composition. An obscure style, after all, absorbs an inordinate amount of the reader's attention; a tedious one simply exhausts our energy and leaves us deficient in the mental vigor that ought to be occupied with what the author has to say.

Spencer applies his principles broadly. Thinking of languages as the "vehicle" of communication, he observes that

> there seems reason to think that in all cases the friction and inertia of the vehicle deduct from its efficiency; and that in composition, the chief, if not the sole thing to be done, is, to reduce this friction and inertia to the smallest possible amount. (p. 4)

Thus, with regard to word choice, Anglo-Saxon words are to be preferred to Latinate words, for they are more familiar and generally shorter, and therefore use up less energy on the recipient's part. Tropes and figures, far from being mere ornaments, are ways of economizing on both expression and attention spent on understanding what is said. Likewise, the whole matter of sentence composition is reduced to what might be called "the economics of expression," an economy based on efficiency. "The general principle," Spencer tells us, "is that, other things being equal, the force of a verbal form or arrangement is great in proportion as the mental effort demanded from the recipient is small" (p. 28). And so, too, the use of imagery, if it is skillfully managed, can be very efficient; otherwise, "the attention would be...frittered away" (p. 29).

The mark of a good writer is not conformity to stylistic exemplars, nor is it mastery of a particular style. "To have a specific style," Spencer says, "is to be poor in speech." Rather, it is the ability to adjust modes of expression to states of feeling that marks the ideal writer. From such adjustment "there will flow from his pen a composition changing to the same degree that the aspect of his subject changes. He will thus without effort conform to what we have seen to be the laws of effect" (p. 43). Writers who are unable to do this, he warns in Darwinian terms, will fall by the wayside, while good writers survive.

Spencer thus succeeds in liberating his principles from the canons of the *belles lettres* tradition and, consequently, from the social structures that gave rise to that tradition. Spencer's vision is, we might say, more individualistic and egalitarian, assuming that all individuals have roughly the same intellectual apparatus and powers of adaptation and adjustment. The standards he sets up are, moreover, as objective and immutable as the laws of friction and inertia, rooted in the very psychological constitution, the fusion of specialized organic functions peculiar to human beings. In such ways, Spencer's philosophy of style may be said to be progressive, both socially and scientifically.

In other ways, however, Spencer may be said to be regressive. His psychological model is, after all, quite Hobbesian. What Spencer has that Hobbes did not is a technical vocabulary derived from scientific mechanics. But LaMettrie had that also as far back as 1740. In practice, moreover, Spencer's "force" is merely Campbell's "vivacity" expressed in brute physical instead of biological terms: both are forms of "energy." Thus, while leaving behind the social apparatus of the eighteenth century, Spencer clings to its psychological apparatus. Very likely, Spencer does this unwittingly. Never an avid reader—he is notorious among classicists for his assertion that he would rather give a large sum of money than read a word of Homer—Spencer had probably never read a word of Hobbes or Campbell. So in at least one respect, Spencer was a man of his age, both forward- and backward-looking, whether he knew it or not.

Bain

Alexander Bain is also an interesting character. The son of a weaver who toiled 15 hours a day to insure his son's education, Bain became one of the most famous psychologists of the century and was perhaps equally famous for his *English Composition and Rhetoric*.[25]* Bain taught a number of subjects at various schools between 1840 and 1860, when he was appointed to the chair of logic at the University of Aberdeen, newly formed in the merger of King's College and Marischal College, where Bain had taken his degree. His appointment was no doubt due to the success of his *The Senses and the Intellect* (1855) and *The Emotions and the Will* (1859). In 1880, he retired from teaching and was thereafter twice elected rector of Aberdeen, in 1881 and in 1884, when his opponent for the position was Lord Randolph Churchill, the father of Sir Winston Churchill of twentieth-century fame. A sickly man all his life, he lived to the age of 85, an achievement he attributed to his distrust of doctors and his fondness for hydropathy ("taking the waters").

The goal of his psychological works was to carry out the implications of Hartley's version of associationism for explaining mental events—which for him included taste and ethical values—in terms of the juxtaposition of sensory impressions. To Hartley's introspective speculations, Bain added the latest empirical research by the German physiological psychologists active at the time, particularly Wilhelm Wundt, as well as the contributions Spencer had made to the field. He was especially interested in the origins of complex attitudes and sentiments involved in the formation of aesthetic, moral, and religious values.

Bain's notion of rhetoric and his philosophy of composition are direct extensions of his psychological work. Rhetoric, for Bain, was the means by which language is rendered effective. Effective discourse can be differentiated according to the particular mental power it addresses. Hence—the three basic functions of discourse—to inform, persuade, and please—are determined by the three basic mental functions, thinking, willing, and feeling. The study of style, which is the sole concern of rhetoric, is the study of the stylistic means of provoking and combining associations according to the mental laws uncovered by psychology. The effect of a given stylistic device is directly proportional to the strength of the impression it makes. One way of achieving increased impact on the minds of one's hearers or readers is by the use of figures, which can be organized according to the various kinds of association the mind makes: comparison, contiguity, and contrast. These impressions may be distributed along the lines of intellectual and emotional qualities, which, in turn, are defined in terms of the modes of association and the classification of the emotions. It is clear, that is to say, that for Bain the basic understanding of the processes of composition is rooted in his psychological theories, especially as they had been articulated in *The Emotions and the Will*. It is also clear that Bain-is marching down a well-trodden path.

Bain's *English Composition*, like Spencer's "Philosophy of Style," was very popular and remains influential to this day. He is often granted the honor of having conceived of the notion of the organic paragraph, which remains a central tenet of composition theory. His dedication to the same spirit of scientism that made Spencer so attractive in America probably explains why he has continued to exercise such authority. And like Spencer, Bain can also be credited with helping to liberate teachers and students alike from what I. A. Richards has since called the "Club Spirit" of the eighteenth-century writers.

Bain's chief novelty was his introduction of the vocabulary of psychology into the English composition classroom in a systematic way. Aside from this, there is little else. His associationism is indeed Hartley's. The pronounced operational side of his notion of rhetoric is also nothing new. In the eighteenth-century rhetorics we saw in the last chapter, one made a "good impression" by affecting one's hearer's mental impressions. In Bain, the importance of making a "good impression" is played down in favor of effectiveness in communication, with psychology giving hints as to the best technologies for achieving that end. Deprived of its context of social decorum, Bain's notion of rhetoric becomes not only unilateral and individualistic but competitive as well, as each writer will seek to maximize success in having effects on his or her readers in a quiet battle for control of the mental events taking place inside them. In the next chapter, we shall examine some of the responses to this sort of scenario by generations after Spencer and Bain.

SUMMARY

There are at least four strands to nineteenth-century rhetoric: the continuing presence of Classical influence, the spread of the Elocutionary Movement, the *belles lettres* tradition, and the emerging scientism of communication and composition theory. The latter two can be explained by the persistence of the commonsense school: on the one hand, we see the continued influence of Blair's *Lectures* and, on the other, the extensions of eighteenth-century associationism, as in Spencer and Bain. The psychologizing of rhetoric brought into high relief the implicit managerial side of eighteenth-century rhetoric as more emphasis was placed on rhetoric's ability to control "mental events" in readers and hearers. The former two are also hangovers from the eighteenth century, although elocution, too, takes a scientific turn later in the nineteenth. As we examine the broad picture of the development of rhetoric both in Europe and in America, the most salient feature seems to be the Janus-like characteristic of looking both backward and forward at the same time. The cultural standards of the *ancien régime* persist to the end of the century, but there is much in the latter half that in a sense foreshadows twentieth-century communication and composition studies. The other salient feature is the increasing peripheralization of rhetoric as it had been traditionally understood. Although the nineteenth was a century of great orators—Disraeli, Gladstone, Webster, and Lincoln—the importance of rhetoric in education declined as it became detached from the formation of able citizens and the conduct of affairs. While not the wasteland it is often thought to have been, the nineteenth century marks a low point in the history of rhetoric.

FURTHER READING

For general background on the nineteenth century, one might profitably consult E. Anderson's *Nineteenth Century Europe: Crisis and Contribution* (Washington, DC, 1964) and A. Mayer, *The Persistence of the Old Regime* (New York, 1981). There is no comprehensive study of rhetoric in the period;

but on England and America, see the essays in Parts One and Two of *History of Speech Education in America*, ed. K. Wallace (New York, 1954) (hereafter, *History*), and the papers by W. Guthrie, "The Development of Rhetorical Theory in America: 1635–1850," *SM* 13 (1946), pp. 14–22; 14 (1947), pp. 38–54; 15 (1948), pp. 61–71; 16 (1949), pp. 98–113; and 18 (1951), pp. 17–30.

On Jane Austen, see Warren Roberts, *Jane Austen and the French Revolution* (New York, 1979). For the Elocutionary Movement, F. Haberman's 1947 Cornell dissertation, cited in Chapter 7, is still the most complete account. See also his essay "English Sources of American Elocution," in *History*, pp. 105–126. For education and social conditions, see M. Sanderson, "Literacy and Social Mobility in the Industrial Revolution in England," *Past and Present* 56 (1972), pp. 75–104. On the influence of Cicero, see M. Rosner, "Cicero in Nineteenth-Century England and America," *Rhetorica* 4 (1986), pp. 178–189. On Whately, see D. Akenson, *A Protestant in Purgatory: Richard Whately* (Hamden, CT, 1981).

For France, see V. Karady, "De Napoléon à Duruy: Les origines et la naissance de l'université contemporaine," in *Histoire des universités en France*, ed. J. Verger (Toulouse, 1986), pp. 261–322; and J. Lough, *Writer and Public in France* (Oxford, 1978), pp. 275–370. D. Breuer's "Schulrhetorik im 19. Jahrhundert" in the Schanze volume, pp. 145–179, cited in Further Reading for Chapter 7, is most useful. See also the extensive bibliography in Schanze, pp. 293–337; C. Winkler, *Elemente der Rede* (Halle, 1931), especially the bibliography at pp. 169–198; and M. Linn, *Studien zur deutschen Rhetorik und Stilistik im 19. Jahrhundert* (Marburg, 1963). The Winkler book is discussed by E. Cain in *WJS* 27 (1963), pp. 222–226. On Theremin, See J. Ray, "The Moral Rhetoric of Franz Theremin," *Southern States Communication Journal* 40 (1974), pp. 33–49.

The revival of interest in Aristotle's *Rhetoric* is touched on by R. Pfeiffer, *History* (cited in Further Reading in Chapter 5), p. 138ff. A good survey of developments in psychology in the nineteenth century can be found in G. Murphy, *Historical Introduction to Modern Psychology* (New York, 1949), pp. 137–173.

On John Witherspoon, see W. Howell, *Eighteenth Century British Logic and Rhetoric* (cited in Chapter 7), pp. 671–691. The general picture is clear from the Guthrie studies cited above. A different aspect of rhetoric in nineteenth-century America is taken up by C. Oravec in "The Democratic Critics: An Alternative American Rhetorical Tradition in the Nineteenth Century," *Rhetorica* 4 (1986), 395–421. On the development of composition theory, see J. Berlin, *Writing Instruction in Nineteenth-Century American Colleges* (Carbondale, 1984). Bain's idea of the organic paragraph is discussed by N. Shearer in "Alexander Bain and the Genesis of Paragraph Theory," *QJS* 68 (1972), pp. 408–417. Most of the good information about both Spencer and Bain can be found in their autobiographies, both published in New York in 1904.

NOTES

1. Austen references are to the Chapman edition of *The Novels of Jane Austen*, Vol. 5 (London, 1969).
2. For an account of these school texts, see Haberman (cited in Further Reading), p. 324ff.
3. *Chironomia*, with an introduction by M. Robb and L. Thonsen, was reissued by the Southern Illinois University Press in 1966.
4. See on this Rosner (cited in Further Reading).
5. Whately's *Elements of Rhetoric*, ed. D. Ehninger, is available in a Southern Illinois University Press edition (Carbondale, 1963). Page references are to that edition.
6. See, in addition to Akenson (cited in Further Reading), L. Einhorn, "Richard Whately's Public Persuasion: The Relationship between His Rhetorical Theory and His Rhetorical Practice," *Rhetorica* 4 (1986), pp. 51–65. The information about Whately's "reviews" is cited on pp. 60f.
7. See Mayer (cited in Further Reading), p. 253.
8. My figures are from Mayer, pp. 259–271, and Lough, pp. 276–283 (see Further Reading).
9. References are to A.-F. Villemain, *Discours et mélanges littéraires* (Paris, 1888): "Discours prononcé à l'ouverture du cours d'éloquence française de 1822" (pp. 195–216) and "Discours prononcé . . . 1824" (pp. 217–239).
10. Citing the year 1914 is a bit arbitrary. In fact, it is arguable that the first significant work on rhetoric in French since the eighteenth century was Chaim Perelman and L. Olbrechts-Tyteca, *Traité de l'argumentation* (Paris, 1958)!
11. The bibliography in Schanze (cited in Further Reading for Chapter 7) is invaluable.
12. A good example of the sort of criticism that grew out of these convictions about poetry would be Coleridge's "Essay on Method."
13. Winkler (cited in Further Reading) supplies a bibliography with more than 200 relevant titles of works on elocution in Germany between 1750 and 1850. The subject is still largely unexplored territory.
14. References are to the page numbers in the margins of the edition by W. Pluhar, *Immanuel Kant: Critique of Judgment* (Indianapolis, 1987).
15. I have consulted the translation by W. Shedd (New York, 1850).
16. Theremin, p. 12.
17. On these developments in philology and psychology, see Pfeiffer and Murphy (cited in Further Reading).
18. Witherspoon's *Lectures* can be found in volume 3 of the four-volume edition of his works (Philadelphia, 1802), pp. 475–592.
19. E. G. Welles, *The Orator's Guide* (Philadelphia, 1822), p. 88. The excerpt is quoted by Welles, with approval, from "On Education" by Dr. Mason, president of Dickinson College.
20. Both of these sets of lectures are available in Southern Illinois University Press editions.
21. I have used the 1860 New York edition—the sixtieth edition, according to the title page.
22. The pseudo-scientific "system" of Delsartre became quite popular late in the century. See, for instance C. Shaver, "Steel MacKaye and the Delsartrian Tradition" in *History*, pp. 202–218. *A Natural System of Elocution and Oratory*

(New York, 1886), was written by Thomas and William Hyde (both taught at Harvard).

23. *Cahiers du CRAL* (Centre de recherches et d'applications linguistiques); *Études de rhétorique*, Vol. 1 (Nancy, 1969); Vol. 2 (Nancy, 1970).

24. I have used the 1895 Boston edition, ed. Fred Newton Scott, who did much to promote Spencer's ideas in the United States.

25. There were two versions of *English Composition and Rhetoric*, the original 1866 version and the revised and expanded two-volume version of 1886–87. I have appended an outline of the latter to this chapter.

RICHARD WHATELY, *ELEMENTS OF RHETORIC*

(Page references are to the 1846 London edition., rpt. Carbondale, 1963)

Introduction (pp. 1–34)
Part One.   Of the Address to the Understanding, with a View to Produce Conviction (Including Instruction)
  A. Of propositions to be maintained (35–39)
  B. Of arguments (39–108)
      1. General considerations (35–45)
      2. Of different kinds of arguments (46–52)
      3. Signs (53–57)
      4. Testimony (58–76)
      5. Calculation of chances (76–81)
      6. Progressive approach (81–85)
      7. Example and analogy (85–103)
      8. Real and invented examples (103–108)
  C. Of the various use and order of the several kinds of propositions and of arguments in different cases (108–168)
      1. Arguments suitable to different cases (108–112)
      2. Presumptions and burden of proof (112–132)
      3. Matters of fact and opinion (132–137)
      4. Precedence (137–138)
      5. Arrangement (139–146)
      6. Establishing and accounting facts (146)
      7. Refutation (146–161)
      8. Excess of proof (161–167)
  D. Of introductions and conclusions (168–174)
Part Two.   Of the Address to the Will, or Persuasion
  A. Introductory considerations (175–188)
  B. Of the conduct of any address to the feelings (189–203)
      1. Exhortation (189–192)
      2. Description (192–195)
      3. Indirect description (195–197)
      4. Comparison (197–199)
      5. Exaggeration (199–202)
      6. Diversion of feelings (202–203)

C. Of the favorable or unfavorable disposition of the hearer or reader towards the speaker (203–256)
   1. Character of the persons addressed (203–210)
   2. Disadvantage of being thought eloquent (210–215)
   3. The character to be established (215–219)
   4. Personality (219–221)
   5. Authority (221–227)
   6. Allaying of unfavorable impressions (227–230)
   [7. Influences of the Professions (230–256)]

Part Three. Of Style
   A. Of perspicuity (257–275)
   B. Of energy, or vivacity (275–328)
      1. Choice of words (275–299)
      2. Number of words (299–312)
      3. Arrangement of words (312–328)
   C. Of elegance, or beauty (328–338)

Part Four. Of Elocution, or Delivery
   A. General considerations (339–347)
   B. The artificial and natural modes of elocution (347–360)
   C. The differences between reading and speaking (360–376)
   D. Practical deductions from the foregoing (376–390)

ALEXANDER BAIN, *ENGLISH COMPOSITION AND RHETORIC*

Part One: Intellectual Elements of Style
(Page references are to the 1887 New York edition.)

   I. Order of Words: Proximity and Priority (pp. 1–26)
   II. Number of Words: Brevity, Pleonasm, Circumlocution (27–54)
   III. The Sentence (55–90)
      A. The Period and the Loose Sentence (55–65)
      B. The Balanced Structure (66–73)
      C. Distribution of Emphasis (74–83)
      D. Length of the Sentence (84–85)
      E. Unity (85–90)
   IV. The Paragraph (91–134)
      A. Distribution into Sentences (91–93)
      B. Explicit Reference (94–104)
      C. Parallel Construction (105–108)
      D. Indication of the Theme (108–113)
      E. Unity (112–113)
      F. Consecutive Argument (114–120)
      G. Marking of Subordination (120–134)
   V. Figures of Speech (135–232)
      A. Figures Founded on Similarity
         1. General Considerations

CHAPTER 9

Rhetoric after the Great War

The twentieth century, in truth, began on the day the Archduke Ferdinand was assassinated in Sarajevo. That is, it began with what was then, and for 25 years after, called the Great War, World War I. Itself a conflict of unprecedented political scope and human destruction, the Great War brought about social and economic changes whose effects are felt to this day. Among the most subtle and troubling of those consequences were changes in collective attitudes toward language, changes that set the themes for much of what we find in the renaissance of interest in rhetoric after Versailles.

A shift in the stance toward language is obvious to anyone familiar with developments in philosophy after 1920, and we shall have a few things to say about some of those in due course. But the evidence of that shift in postwar literature is perhaps more telling, as it reflects awareness ouside the common rooms of Oxford and Cambridge of something that was occurring in our experience of language. In the poetry of Wilfred Owen, Siegfried Sassoon, and Edmund Blunden, for instance, we see the recontextualization, if not the subversion, of poetry and its commonplaces. A poem Blunden wrote while serving in Flanders begins this way:

> O rosy red, O torrent splendour
>   Staining all the orient gloom,
> O celestial work of wonder—
>   A million mornings in one bloom[1]

These lines seem hardly extraordinary when read against the background of the yards of poetic verse declaiming the beauties of the dawn that were composed in the decades before the war, the sort of poetry Blunden had read as a young man in school. As we read on, however, it becomes clear that

Blunden's dawn is no idyllic gift of beauty bestowed by Nature. This dawn is the time of attack, of charging "over the top" toward the enemy's trenches. And before long, in Blunden's poem, the "rosy red" of the rising sun is put in a very different context from its conventional one:

> The dawn that hangs behind the goal,
> What is that artist's joy to me?
> Here limps poor Jock with a gash in the poll,
> His red blood now is the red I see....

The beauties of Nature—and of poetry—are deceptions; only the unnatural and unspeakable horrors of war are real. Instead of "glorious dawn," the beginning of a peaceful day in the garden or the countryside, this time of day is, rather, as Blunden put it in the opening lines of another poem of his ("The Zonnebeke Road"):

> Morning, if this late withered light can claim
> Some kindred with that merry flame
> Which the young day was wont to fling through space!
> Agony stares from each grey face.
> And yet the day is come....[2]

In quite another area, too, intense concentration was turned in the years after the Great War to a different aspect of language, to language as it was used by the competing nations on an unprecedented scale and with unprecedented effectiveness in propaganda, a word "which has come," as Harold Lasswell observed in 1927, "to have an ominous clang in many minds." There was, after the war, a flood of speculation about and investigation of this new use of language on both sides of the Atlantic by scholars who, Lasswell tells us, "probe the mysteries of propaganda with that compound of admiration and chagrin with which the victims of a new gambling trick demand to have the thing explained....Fooled by propaganda? If so, they writhe in the knowledge that they were the blind pawns in plans which they did not incubate, and which they neither devised nor comprehended nor approved."[3] The conditions and methods of propaganda needed to be mapped and tracked in order to find out why it had the effects it had on large populations, how it fed and fed on the willingness of the masses to view the enemy as bestial and satanic and the conviction that only total victory would rid the world of "them," and how the wise could guard against that happening again. In more ways than one, the Great War was seen as "the war to end all wars"; and if it was not that, those looking back on it were convinced, it had to be made to be.

On the one hand, then, we see the collapse of conventional understandings, the elimination of an entire body of poetic commonplaces about the world we live in, and a consequent mistrust of poetry's ability to tell us anything about that world. We see growing mistrust of anything that might appear in the mass media, an emerging conviction that language is no longer a means of conveying information but the powerful tool used by clever men in quiet offices for the shaping and motivating of attitudes and actions. Moreover, those actions were to be performed in the best interests not of the actors but of politicians and members of the boards of international corporations. Many of these, after all, had bought newspapers in foreign countries where they did business to ensure the integrity of their image. Cynicism, the primary emotion of the so-called Lost Generation of the 1920s, seemed the only defense.

On the other hand, however, we note that Blunden and Sassoon and (although he did not survive the war) Owen did not consign poetry to the ash heap of history but wrote poems and sent them back to London to be published and read by those at home. Poetry was, in spite of everything, their way of dealing with the horrors around them; and it was obviously thought to be a good thing for readers to hear and understand. We note, too, that Lasswell and many others in Europe and America did not despair in the face of the proven successes of the propagandists on all sides, but committed themselves to the study of those successes, and the failures, convinced that understanding would provide a remedy for the abuses of power and meaning implicit in the manipulations of the public relations operatives. The other side of the period, in short, shows a determined optimism.

The crisis of confidence in language as used in the past that we see in the poets and the political scientists, and their determination to gain new confidence through analysis, understanding, and innovation, provide, together, a perspective from which to view the resurgence of interest in rhetoric in the earlier decades of the twentieth century. Language, as it was used in poetry and politics, becomes a matter of paramount importance for the authors we will take up in the present chapter: I. A. Richards, Kenneth Burke, and Richard Weaver. Of course, language became very important to philosophers and scientists during this period, too: Bertrand Russell, G. E. Moore, and Gilbert Ryle in Britain, Rudolf Carnap and Alfred Tarski on the Continent. But our eyes will be turned on writers who proclaimed the cure to the world's ills to be in the successful investigation of language as it is used in the world at large, not just in the study or the laboratory, and on their works, all of which center on what they saw as "rhetoric."

RICHARDS' "RHETORIC"

I. A. Richards (1893–1979) was, and remains, one of the most influential educators and literary critics of this century. His active career spanned almost 60 years, during which he taught at Cambridge, at the Tsing Hua University in Beijing, and, from 1939 until his death, at Harvard. Richards' publications include some four dozen books on criticism, semantics, and language as well as numerous articles in journals on both sides of the Atlantic. The most important books for our purposes have all attained a status as virtual classics in language studies and criticism: *The Meaning of Meaning* (co-authored with C.

K. Ogden in 1923), _Principles of Literary Criticism_ (1924), _Practical Criticism_ (1929), and _The Philosophy of Rhetoric_ (1936).[4] In what follows, we shall be concerned to explain the positions Richards took in those books, particularly the last, and to gauge Richards' contributions to the study and teaching· of rhetoric.

(3) _The Philosophy of Rhetoric_ was originally a series of lectures Richards gave at Bryn Mawr College in 1935 to an audience that must have been familiar with his leading ideas about meaning and the importance of communication from his earlier books and short papers, which had been quite widely read. The basic argument of _PR_ runs along classic lines: the recognition and diagnosis of an ill, the proposal of a remedy, and an assessment of the good results promised. In many ways, _PR_ may be read as a compendium of previous versions of the same case made earlier in _The Meaning of Meaning_, _Principles of Literary Criticism_, and _Practical Criticism_. So we shall occasionally have to refer to those books at places where Richards leaves important assumptions based on them lingering in the background.

(4) Conflict arises from misunderstanding, and misunderstanding arises in large part from misplaced expectations and less than conscious presumptions about language, Richards argues. What is required is a "new rhetoric." Unlike the "old rhetoric"—"the theory of the battle of words...dominated by the combative impulse" (p. 24)—the new rhetoric will be "a study of misunderstanding and its remedies" (p. 3), one that explores the conditions of understanding discourse by studying how language does what it does, based on "what may be called policeman doctrines...designed not to make us do anything, but to prevent others from interfering unduly with our lawful activities" (p. 38)

Misunderstanding is an old concern of Richards', going back to his collaboration with Ogden just after the Great War on _The Meaning of Meaning_. In the preface to that book, Ogden and Richards explain that their new "science of Symbolism" will be of assistance to "practical people...convinced of the urgency of a stricter examination of language." The view that language works well enough as it is, they say,

> can only be held by those who use it merely in such affairs as could be conducted without it—the business of the paper-boy or the butcher, for instance, where all that needs to be referred to can equally well be pointed at. None of those who close their eyes to the hasty readaptation to totally new circumstances which the human race has during the last century been blindly endeavouring to achieve, can pretend that there is no need to examine critically the most important of all the instruments of civilization.[5]

The same conviction lies behind what Richards proposes at the end of the last lecture in _PR_ when he says,

> It seems modest and reasonable...to hope that a patient persistence with the problems of Rhetoric may, while exposing the causes and modes of the

misinterpretation of words, also throw light upon and suggest a remedial discipline for deeper and more grievous disorders; that...their study may also show us more about how these large-scale disasters may be avoided. (p. 136f.)

The villains in Richards' piece are the likes of Kames, Campbell, and Whately—as well as Locke, although he is not explicitly attacked—who have for centuries continued to exercise an insidious influence on our notions of language. Two common "superstitions" have above all led us to where we are now in our abilities to cope with misunderstanding. The first is the "Proper Meaning Superstition," the belief that each word has a meaning, ideally, a single meaning, of its own, "independent of and controlling its use and the purpose for which it should be uttered" (p. 11). The second is the "Proper Usage Superstition," the doctrine that there is a correct or commendable use for every word and that "literary virtue consists in making that good use of it...a doctrine which can be found in most of the Manuals of Rhetoric and Composition which have affected the schools—American schools especially" (p. 51). Related to these is another problem, the pervasive tendency to fail to grasp metaphors that results from the eighteenth-century assumption that "metaphor is something special and exceptional in the use of language, a deviation from its normal mode of working" (p. 90). The basic problem with the superstitions, in short, is that they bear no real relation to how language actually works. More serious is the fact that it is just those supersititions and failures that create the problems of misunderstanding Richards' philosophy of rhetoric is meant to solve.

The cure Richards proposes is his Context Theorem of Meaning, which he claims will "prevent our making hundreds of baseless and disabling assumptions that we commonly make about meanings" (p. 38) and which, as it helps us develop our skills in comprehension, will bring about "a new era of human understanding and cooperation in thinking" (p. 73). "Context" is the name for a "cluster of events that recur together" in our minds and in the world to constitute the governing conditions of meaning. What a word means is "the missing parts of the contexts from which it draws its delegated efficacy" (p. 35). The initial terms for this theorem, Richards cautions, are not impressions but "sortings, laws of response, recurrences of like behavior" (p. 36).

To understand what Richards is talking about, we need to back up a bit and refer to his earlier discussion of meaning in *The Meaning of Meaning*, for the Context Theorem of *The Philosophy of Rhetoric* is little more than an abbreviated version of the conclusions Richards and Ogden reached in that earlier book. Richards and Ogden observe first that the explanation of "meaning" must begin with the consideration that, as human beings, we respond to sensory data in our environment. Every stimulus we receive through the senses leaves a trace or impression, what they call in *Meaning* an "engram." In every perception, a context is formed made up of the sensations experienced and stored in the memory. Whenever any part of a context is experienced, the missing parts of that context are recalled; so when part of the context is experienced, that part affects us as though the entire context were present (*MM* 53ff.; see also *PR* 14f.). Words derive meaning from having been associated with a context that once affected us as a whole cluster of perceived events and serve as substitutes for the parts of that context that are not currently present (*MM* 174ff.).

The capacity of words to stand for the missing parts of their contexts is what Richards calls in *The Philosophy of Rhetoric* their "delegated efficacy" (p. 32). For example, the word *fish* stands for—means—the clusters of recurring perceptions associated with the word in our experience. What *fish* stands for is not what it putatively refers to (a gilled and finny creature of the genus *Ichthys*) but those associations. Meaning is, in short, not simply a matter of matching a word to thing, but comprises the relations between the word, its referent, and the cluster of perceptions we associate with both. Since there is no determined or *a priori* determinable set of associations that *fish* may stand for in the absence of the objects of the associated perceptions, what *fish* means to one person will not be the same as what it means to another. The word is, therefore, radically ambiguous—quite precisely, "open to interpretation."

The interpretation of a single word in isolation is impossible, since there are any number of meanings it might have in a given utterance of it, and so also is a judgment as to its correct or incorrect, good or bad usage (pp. 51f.). On the other hand, we can usually make an intelligent guess as to what a word *cannot* mean based on our knowledge of how the word is customarily used or, even more, on the basis of the words it is used in conjunction with in a sentence. Words in conjunction "interinanimate" one another and thus exercise a sort of "mutual control" (p. 57) over the interpretative possibilities of an utterance as the "overlap" of their respective contexts sets limits to the sense they might be construed to have when isolated from their controlled neighbors. Interpretative possibilities are also defined when we consider the influences of other words that are not actually uttered but are only "in the background"—words, for instance, that are phonemically or morphemically cognate as well as other words that "we might have used instead" or parallel usages (*PR*, pp. 63f.). A word's force comes from all these various contexts and more:

> As the movement of my hand uses nearly the whole skeletal system of the muscles and is supported by them, so a phrase may take its powers from an immense system of supporting uses of other words in other contexts. (p. 65)

Sensitivity to these ways in which language actually operates—not how it should work or how some critics would like it to work—is indispensable to any effort to comprehend meanings, to keep oneself from being hobbled, if not knackered, by the Proper Meaning Superstition and the Proper Usage Superstition, which have proven to be so specious and groundlessly elitist. It also allows us to grasp the profound importance of a particular kind of "interinanimation" metaphor. Metaphor is the use of one reference to a group of objects of perception that are related in a particular way in order to discover a similar relation in another group: "two thoughts of different things active together and supported by a single word, or phrase, whose meaning is a resultant of their interaction" (p. 93). Given the Context Theorem, it is easy to see that metaphor is not just a special or deviant use of language but the very essence of language, which continually calls up borrowed and related missing contexts. Metaphor is, in fact, the essence of thought itself, since thought is also a transaction between contexts as thought works about its activities of sorting, comparing, and abstracting. Command of metaphor is essential in the interpretation (the apprehension of the meaning) of all discourse, and of poetry in particular. But it can do more, Richards argues, for can help us understand how our minds work and thus help us "control...the world that we make for ourselves to live in" (p. 135) and "restore life itself to order" (p. 134).

Such, in brief, is the argument of *The Philosophy of Rhetoric*. Two important questions arise at this point about Richards' claims there. The first question is, precisely how can conflicts be resolved through the elimination of misunderstanding? In one sense, it seems obvious that if misunderstandings produce conflict, removing misunderstanding will resolve it. Richards seems to be drawing upon the same presumption that underlay, for instance, the eighteenth-century belief that if all philosophical conflict was just a matter of words, so were most other conflicts, the sorts of conflicts Samuel Werenfels worried about in his *Logomachys* ["Word wars"] in 1732, for instance. In another sense, Richards' claim regarding the relation between conflict and misunderstanding is quite remarkable. History is full of tragic instances where parties in conflict understand one another very well indeed or deliberately refuse to "understand" the other's position—Catholics and Protestants in the North of Ireland, for instance. The second question is perhaps more vexing because more elementary: What has Richards' argument to do with rhetoric? He calls the discipline required for the restoration of order to life a "new rhetoric"; but against the background of a more traditional understanding of the term, Richards' "new rhetoric" seems hardly recognizable as a rhetoric at all. It is apparently to be understood as the study of the cooperation of words with one another in their contexts; but that is exactly the definition Richards gives, not of rhetoric, but of grammar in a book he wrote in 1938, *Interpretation In Teaching* (see p. 16).

To answer the first question, we need to refer to Richards' *Principles of Literary Criticism*. He makes various claims there about the value of poetry that bear on the issue of how elimination of misunderstanding might obviate conflict and, as he put it in *Philosophy of Rhetoric*, "restore life to order." Richards applies to literary theory the same treatment he applied in *Meaning of Meaning* to meaning in general, and that application yields a defense of poetry as a worthwhile activity as well as a criterion according to which good poetry may be distinguished from bad. What a poem is, Richards says, is essentially what it does (see *PR*, p. 5). For the poet, poetry is at base an ordering of impulses, of processes "in the course of which a mental event may occur...apparently beginning in a stimulus and ending in an act" (*PLC*,

p. 86). The poet's ordered impulses, in Richards' scenario, are communicated to a reader who properly understands the poem in such a way as to order the reader's impulses in turn.

Hence teaching good poetry serves an important social function, for as it contributes to the satisfaction of individuals' impulses it will eventually lead to a collective ordering of impulses and therefore to a general condition of the emotional equilibrium that comprises happiness. As Richards puts it, the value of poetry has as its ground "humane, sympathetic, and friendly relations between individuals" (*PLC*, p. 53). The impulses art satisfies, however, are not just "aesthetic," but enter into nonartistic activities as well: "We pass *as a rule* from a chaotic to a better organized state...typically through the influence of other minds" (p. 57). Literature and the arts are the chief, but by no means sole, vehicles by which those influences are diffused. In *Philosophy of Rhetoric*, Richards generalizes these ameliorative aspects of poetry to all communication.

Our second question was, What does Richards mean by "rhetoric"? It is clear, to begin with, that he is concerned in *Philosophy of Rhetoric* to distinguish his "new" rhetoric from the "old" (p. 24). But Richards never defines what he means by "rhetoric" in that book; he only tells us what he does not mean. The only place he offers a definition of the word is in *Interpretation in Teaching*, in which he cites George Campbell's definition—"the art by which discourse is adapted to its end"—with approval (p. 12). This definition, together with remarks he makes in *Philosophy of Rhetoric*, suggests that his "new rhetoric" has little, if anything, to do with persuasion, which he associates with "the combative impulse" that makes us "take another man's words in the ways in which we can down him with least trouble" (*PR*, p. 25). Indeed, persuasion is never recognized by Richards as a legitimate function of language. Apart from the "symbolizing" function of language, or "sense" as Richards called it in *Meaning of Meaning* (see also the appendix in *PC*, p. 355ff.), only three other functions of language are distinguished in his books. These are the expression of the writer's attitude toward the reader (Tone); the expression of the attitude toward the subject (Feeling); and the expression of purpose (Intention). Richards' attention is consistently directed toward the reader's attempts to interpret a text rather than toward the use of language by the writer. There is no mention in Richards of *arousing* an attitude in an audience. What Richards means by "rhetoric" is, then, something like "the study of prose" or, more precisely, "the interpretation of prose." Just so, what he means by "a rhetoric" is a rule book for composition of discourse distinguished on the one side from poetry and on the other from scientific discourse—that is, purely referential discourse.

In short, Richards' notion of "rhetoric" is the notion of rhetoric that became current after Blair, Bain, and Spencer, as we saw in the last chapter. But Richards' notion is unlike those writers' to the extent that, in his view at least, "rhetoric" should avoid the prescriptive stance found in the earlier works. Learning the art of rhetoric amounts to acquiring the ability to understand prose. This, in turn, presumably may result in the ability to adapt one's discourse to its end; but Richards leaves that side of rhetoric quite undeveloped in his works.

Richards' impact was nevertheless both broad and deep. "Rhetoric"—discourse in prose and the study of it—was in effect reintegrated into a larger picture of verbal expression generally conceived. "Good prose" could no longer be seen as a form of discourse that obeyed a special set of rules that distinguishes it from other uses of language. Effective communication, like good poetry, could be seen as an instrument for the betterment of other minds and of society itself as it contributed to the elimination of misunderstanding. Above all, Richards' notion of rhetoric was based as no other before it had been on observation and on a psychological model that, in principle, could actually be tested empirically.

That promise was probably the most significant contribution Richards made to the study of rhetoric, for a number of writers after him, whether inspired by or displeased with his theories, sought to subject communication to empirical scrutiny. In doing this, they both answered Richard's repeated calls for such investigation (see, for example, PR, pp. 34f., 134) and followed up on his speculations about "engrams," his equation of attitudes with motor "sets" of emotions, and the great importance he attached to the idea of the "innervation of the musculature." As the physiological basis of Richards' theory about how both poetry and prose "work" cannot be ignored, so the comfortable fit of that theory with behaviorist psychology cannot be avoided. Much twentieth-century communication research by psychologists—Osgood, Woolbert, and Skinner—has been conducted with Richards' "philosophy of rhetoric" as a backdrop.[6] We cannot concern ourselves here with that corpus of research, but it ought to be noted that very little of its relevance to the study of rhetoric can be understood without reference to I. A. Richards.

LITERATURE AND REFORM: THE EARLY BURKE

Richards' theory of meaning and its corresponding theory of literature was, we have seen, developed in an atmosphere of anxiety about the role of language in conflict and of its resolution. Particularly noteworthy is the sense Richards was able to convey of the central importance of good literature to a stable and harmonious society. While it was an important and influential contribution, Richards' theory of literature was by no means the only one being promoted in the decades after the Great War, nor even the only one linking, however tenuously or closely, literature and politics.

In 1921, Kenneth Burke (1897–) gained steady employment as a reviewer, music critic, translator, contributor, and eventually co-editor of *The Dial*, a "little magazine" published in Greenwich Village and dedicated to the dissemination of new ideas in literature, music, and the arts. *The Dial* allied itself with the avant-garde in both the arts and progressive politics. In its pages Americans read for the first time the works of T. S. Eliot, of André Gide, and Thomas Mann (in a translation by Burke, as it happens); and could follow the fortunes of modern art and new composers such as Béla Bartók and Paul Hindemith. While working at *The Dial*, Burke became involved in progressive politics, an active participant in literary debates on the relevance of writing to society—"Is there such a thing as proletarian literature?" was one hotly argued question—and wrote, among many other things, a number of essays that were later to be gathered together to comprise his first book, *Counterstatement*.

In what follows, we shall examine the development of Burke's vision of the role of communication in human relation from the early 1920s to the mid-1950s. It is not that work done since then by Burke is of no interest or importance, but the argument he made for a "new rhetoric" was pretty much fully articulated by the publication of his *Rhetoric of Motives*, in 1950. We shall pay particular attention, moreover, to his earlier works, since it is in them that the social dimension of his thinking emerges most clearly. *Counterstatement* (1931) is seminal, because in it he lays out the basic themes he was to pursue in *Permanence and Change* (1936) and *Attitudes toward History* (1937), and develop even further in two of his later books, *A Grammar of Motives* (1945) and *A Rhetoric of Motives*. No summary can do justice to the richness and variety of Burke's thought, but there is one theme that runs through it, "Towards a Better Life," which serves to unify his many writings and can consequently serve also as a focal point for our examination of them.[7]

Burke's *Counterstatement*

Burke did not set out to write *Counterstatement* as a book. It is, rather, a collection of essays he had published during the 1920s in *The Dial* and elsewhere, along with a few important additions. When he did publish it, after the demise of *The Dial*, he intended it to be just what the title states it is, a response to much of the "received wisdom" about literature and politics current at the time. The time, of course, covers both the Roaring Twenties, which, among other things, saw the introduction of surrealism and avant-garde literature to the New York intellectual scene, and the Great Depression after the Crash of 1929, seen by some as the fulfillment of Marx's prophecies about the end of capitalism. Both aesthetically and politically, in short, the 1920s was a period of creative turmoil and the gospel of the new.

On the one hand, then, Burke attacks the myth of "art for Art's sake" in the first chapter, "Three Adepts of 'Pure' Literature" (pp. 1–28), and in the fourth, "The Status of Art" (pp. 63–91), the popular notion that art is "ineffective," a notion that could be traced back to Kant's definition of the aesthetic as the realm of "purposiveness without purpose" and had lately been reinforced by Oswald Spengler's dismal *Decline of the West*. In "Three Adepts," Burke argues that a purely aesthetic theory of literature could not sustain itself in the present circumstances; in "Status," that "effectiveness," particularly when defined in political and economic terms (as "efficiency"), is beside the point. This idea emerges, he argues, with particular clarity in the recent works of Mann and Gide, which he takes up in the fifth chapter (pp. 92–106). The lesson they teach is that

> society might well be served by the corrective of a disintegrating art, which converts each simplicity into a complexity, which ruins the possibility of ready hierarchies, which concerns itself with the problematical, the experimental, and thus by implication works corrosively upon these expansionistic certainties preparing the way for our social cataclysms. An art may be of value purely through preventing a society from becoming too assertively, too hopelessly, itself. (p. 105)

This is the sort of message Burke had been trying to send since 1922, but it took on new significance in the years of the Depression.[8]

Thus, on the other hand, Burke lays out a "new" aesthetic, based on his conception of "form" and his notion of the "poetic process," an aesthetic which had, in his view, important political implications. "Psychology and Form" (pp. 29–44) comes immediately after his observations on "art for Art's sake." Here Burke makes a distinction between a "psychology of information" and a "psychology of form." It is the latter that is operative in art. Using the opening scenes from *Hamlet*, he generates a notion of form as "the creation of an appetite in the mind of the auditor, and the adequate satisfying of that appetite" (p. 31). Thus form is a function not of the subject matter but of the psychology of the audience, of "those curves of emotion which, because they are natural, can bear repetition without loss" (p. 36). The methods of maintaining interest most natural to the psychology of information, he says, are surprise and suspense, whereas "the method most natural to the psychology of form is eloquence" (p. 37). So, for Burke, "psychology," "form," and "eloquence" are virtually synonymous, and "eloquence...becomes the essence of art" (p. 40).

"The Poetic Process" (pp. 45–62) emphasizes the relation between the poet's "original emotion" and the "individuation" of it in a symbol. The mechanism invented to reproduce the original mood of the artist can be considered to take both an emotional form, in the symbol, and a "technical form," the sort he discussed in "Psychology and Form" and analyzes in detail later, in the inventory of basic movements of experience that can be exploited by art, "Lexicon Rhetoricae" (pp. 123–183).

> We can discuss the basic forms of the human mind under such concepts as crescendo, contrast, comparison, and so forth. But to experience them emotionally, we must have them singularized into an example, an example which will be chosen by the artist from among his emotional and environmental experiences. (p. 49)

What is important to bear in mind is that the self-expression of the artist is not distinguished by the utterance of an emotion but by the evocation of an emotion: "If, as humans, we cry out that we are Napoleon, as artists we seek to create an army" (p. 53). Art, then, is rhetorical in nature, as Burke makes explicitly clear at the end of the book (p. 210). And rhetoric, far from being mere artifice of language, is the most constant and most natural feature of literature.

No poem, in short, is purely aesthetic or purely utilitarian; every poem is both. There is in the aesthetic of *Counterstatement* no room for the sort of "either/or" choice presented, on the one hand, by the "adepts of 'pure' literature" and, on the other, by the likes of Spengler. Art uses "technical forms," but the use of technical form is not the only end of art. Every poem, Burke tells us, equips its author better for life, makes him more at home in the "jungles of society" (p. viii), in the "wilderness of social forces" (p. 105). Art is, thus, a corrective bearing on the problems of living (p. 154f.). Art is "eternal" in that it deals with the constants of human nature. But art is also historical in that it is "a particular mode of adjustment to a particular cluster of [historical] conditions" (p. 107), which, since they are constantly shifting, call for changes of emphasis on "which emotions and attitudes should be stressed, and which slighted, in the aesthetic adjustment to the particular conditions of today." Burke's aesthetic, then, is one that stresses not an "either/or," but a "both/and"; and it is an aesthetic that, because it concerns literature as "equipment for life," has ethical and political implications.

These implications are identified and discussed in the chapter Burke entitled "Program," in which he proposes tracing the possible political and economic implications of his aesthetic and the attitude it calls for. What, in other words, "could be the practical results of his particular 'aesthetic'" (p. ix)? The dominant factor in contemporary (in 1931) American society is industrialism, characterized by dedication to "efficiency, prosperity, material acquisitions, increased consumption, 'new needs,' expansion, higher standards of living, progressive rather than regressive evolution, in short, ubiquitous optimism" (p. 111). The emphasis on efficiency in such a system projects society on the model of a well-run factory, a model that is in fact redolent of "ideal Fascism" (p. 114). Instead of embracing the current enthusiasm for a contrary system, the one summed up in the anti-industrialist manifesto of the Southern Agrarians, Burke argues, we ought to ally ourselves with "a modernized version of the . . . bourgeois-Bohemian conflict" (p. 111). This fundamentally aesthetic stance "would seek to discourage the most stimulating values of the practical" and "throw into confusion the code which underlies commercial enterprise" (p. 115). The aesthetic ("Bohemian") stands for "inefficiency, indolence, dissipation, vacillation, mockery, distrust, hypochondria, non-conformity, bad sportsmanship, in short, negativism" (p. 111). This "program," Burke recognizes, will have few defenders; but as art is a mode of survival, and survival is threatened by the current "philosophy" of ambition, the aesthetic must be made to subsume a system of politics. "Let us," Burke says, "reaffirm democracy (government by interference, by distrust) over against Fascism" (p. 119). "When in Rome, do as the Greeks."

Burke's insistence on the notion of the art as a mode of survival; his equation of form, psychology, and eloquence; his consequent determination that rhetoric is the essence of literature; and his call for a "Bohemian revolt" were not very well received by his critics. Some of the most severe among those were, curiously, fellow antifascists on the Left—Granville Hicks and Harold Rosenberg, for instance.[9] But Burke persevered and continued to develop those ideas in his next two books, *Permanence and Change* and *Attitudes toward History*. In these two books, Burke expanded his literary observations to cover all communication.

Like *Counterstatement, Permanence and Change* was written "in the early days of the Great Depression, at a time when there was a general feeling that our traditional ways were headed for a tremendous change, maybe even a permanent collapse."[10] The world we live in is marked by faction and change, and the problem is how to survive. We need, Burke argues, to sort out what is temporary—the changing conditions of historical situation—from what is permanent—that is, universal in human nature—in order to find the key. His analysis of poetry in *Counterstatement* isolated some of those universals in the psychological grounding of the forms of appeal. Burke makes the bearing of his literary observations on the larger questions of survival in a world marked by tension quite clear: as poetry is at base a "problem of appeal," so in fact is all social life. The study of poetry can give us invaluable hints for describing modes of practical action

> too often measured by simple tests of utility and too seldom with reference to the communicative, sympathetic, propitiatory factors that are clearly present in the procedures of formal art and must be as truly present in those informal arts of living we do not happen to call arts. (*Permanence and Change*, 339f.)

What stands immediately in the way of any effort to exploit the resources of eloquence in grappling with "a world of movement and countermovement forces within and forces without" (p. 30) are assumptions about meaning, value, and truth that amount in the final analysis to "trained incapacities," indeed, in the present age, a sort of "occupational psychosis" (p. 69ff.). We need to alter our "orientation," that is, consciousness, which always "occurs in situations marked by conflict" (p. 30). What is required, if we are to escape "logomachies," is the recognition that all interpretive schemes are but shorthand and that such schemes are of necessity finite and various. After setting out ways by which "orders of rationalization" may be perceived as no more than "weighted vocabularies" (pp. 95ff.), Burke casts about for some way of resolving the conflicts they engender. The procedure to be followed here is that of "perspective by incongruity," by which categories generally believed to be mutually exclusive may be merged. Burke calls for an emphasis on "men as communicants" (see p. 343), an orientation similar to the poetic in which peace, not war, is the ideal; action not competition, the goal; and a complete, not partial, account of man the principle. Man's patterns of purpose and choice might be characterized by "borrowings from the terminology of rhetoric, 'the art of appeal'" as the relation between individual and group can be "greatly illuminated by reference to the corresponding relation between writer and audience" (see p. 341). Thus rhetoric becomes the object of our attention not only in our efforts to individuate an original emotion, as in *Counterstatement*, but in the conduct of life itself in the movement "towards a better life."

Burke continues to seek an adequate and comprehensive exposition of his insight into the relations between aesthetic appeal and social being in *Attitudes toward History*, taking a somewhat different tack. *Attitudes* begins with "Acceptance and Rejection" (vol. 1, pp. 1–40), in which he examines various literary genres in order to show how "each of the great poetic forms stresses its own peculiar way of building the mental equipment (meanings, attitudes, character) by which one handles the significant factors of his time" (p. 34). Thus such genres as epic, tragedy, and comedy are different ways of dealing with the imperfections perceived in one's relation to conditions ("the problem of evil") and dictate various "attitudes" that are formed, both psychologically and aesthetically, to avoid emotional devastation. In the second section, "Curve of History" (vol. 1, pp. 141–226), Burke extends such principles to account not only for literary genres but to periods of Western culture, pointing out that each epoch "features" different "key terms" as "permanent"; however, they are displaced in the processes of historical changes. Cultures are "collective poems," in fact; and history itself can be projected on the scheme of a five-act play, in which successive periods (roughly equivalent to the "orders of rationalization" in *Permanence and Change*) consolidate clusters of key terms that they exploit and exhaust, the "plot" of which culminates in the present, characterized by "emergent collectivism." The first part of Section Three, "The General Nature of Ritual" (vol. 2, pp. 1–52), inquires into "the ways routines become rituals and rituals become routines." "Collective strategies" for survival are shaped into socially integrative interpretive schemes. An inventory of such schemes, indicative of attitudes and principles of social "self-analyses" (among them, "alienation," "identification," and "transcendence"), makes up the last large section of the book (vol. 2, pp. 52–249).[11]

What we see in these first three books of Burke verges on an obsession with the abilities of language to overcome faction instead of contributing to it, to equip us better for "the good life." Burke's focus shifts somewhat from the "individualism" of the aesthetics of *Counterstatement* to concern with collective aspects of meaning. *Permanence and Change* attempts to establish a notion of communication as ideal cooperation; *Attitudes*, to characterize tactics and patterns of conflict typical of actual human associations. All three are marked by a sense of urgency, a notion that collapse was not far distant and that some way had to be found to avoid it. And all three are premised on the idea that the true way of understanding human nature is through examination of how words, as vehicles of artistic and social appeal, make possible the introduction of attitude and value into the emotionally barren universe dictated by technology and science. The study of those possibilities is, in a word, "rhetoric."

AD BELLUM PURIFICANDUM

Burke's earlier work set the agenda for what follows, as can be seen from the fact that the "key terms" he had isolated by 1937 continue to inform his *Grammar of Motives* (1945) and *Rhetoric of Motives* (1950). Nor does the ethical imperative driving those earlier works—"Towards a Better Life"—change. If anything, it becomes more pronounced, as the crisis of the Great Depression was superseded by the rise and spread of fascism in Germany, Italy, and Spain and by the prospect of another global war. Burke's own response to that imperative was to become more systematic in the "study of human relations *via* a methodological inquiry into cycles or clusters of terms and their functions." This study he named "dramatism."[12] It was also to inquire more deeply into the grounds of disagreement and agreement among social beings.

Thus the *Motives* books both resume and develop the earlier formulations of his position. *Grammar* is a long meditation on the dialectics of interacting systems and clusters of terms that offers an analysis both of the basic forms that "talk about experience" will inevitably take and of a process by which conflicting accounts of human action may be resolved. Burke begins with the observation that any account of action, if it is "rounded," will encompass five issues: who, what, where, how, and why. The paradigm here, as in the opening of "Psychology and Form," is drama. These five terms comprise a "pentad," and the various relations (ratios) among them define different interpretations of action. Hence, for instance, it makes a great deal of difference whether one "explains" an action (Act) by reference to the "where" (Scene) or by reference to the "why" (Purpose) (see pp. 3–20).

Moreover, it must be recognized that whenever we talk about anything, we define it, and in doing that we say something both about what it is and what it is not. In this sense, every act of naming channels our thinking in one direction instead of another. Whenever there is "meaning," then, there is "persuasion." Every act of naming, furthermore, involves us in what Burke calls the "paradox of substance": there are no two things, however different the classifications their definitions imply, that cannot be seen from another perspective as standing on some common, underlying ground (*substans*, whence "substance"). Alternative "namings," therefore, are in principle equivalent: no one account of action is privileged over another.

When we consider philosophical accounts of human action, we are struck by the way in which each of the major "schools" of philosophy can be characterized as "featuring" one term of the pentad as prior to, or even exclusive of, others. Hence, Materialism "features" Scene; Pragmatism, Agency and Purpose; Idealism, Agent; and Realism, Act. Philosophers, like poets, try to forge interpretive vocabularies to "rationalize" their accounts of experience—both to render intelligible and to justify those accounts—and therefore these efforts can be characterized as "casuistries." The conflicting claims and rationalizations can be mapped and brought into opposition with one another by consideration of the "ratios" at work in their formation. The pentad thus becomes a tool for locating agreements and disagreements among conflicting accounts, an indispensable tool, in fact, if we have hopes of resolving basic questions about how life should be led.

Put to proper use, the pentad can show the way toward "creative conflict," a paradigm case of which Burke locates in the dialectical process by which the U.S. Constitution came into being. Only by mutual recognition by the participants at the Constitutional Convention of the nature of their differences and agreements could such a document—indeed, more than a mere document: a nation—have been forged. The Constitution stands as a model, but it is far from perfect, as Burke goes on to argue (pp. 349ff.), for, in the final analysis, it was not so much agreement as compromise that brought it about. In this, it is like so many other agreements. Indeed, dialectic itself is less than perfect, as it is, ultimately, incomplete; yet we cannot afford to overlook its resources as an intrument of overcoming division.

If the *Grammar* deals with "a level of motivation which even wholly rival doctrines of motives must share in common," the *Rhetoric* will go a step further in studying "the competitive use of the cooperative" in order to transcend the limitations of mere compromise, the realm of "the Human Barnyard, with its addiction to the Scramble," as Burke puts it at the end of the *Grammar* (p. 422). And if the *Grammar* may be characterized as a meditation on the basically horizontal interaction of conflicting accounts, the *Rhetoric* can be characterized as one on the problems of communication within the inevitable hierarchies of social, economic, and political organization. In very broad terms, it could be said that *A Rhetoric of Motives* is a "catalogue" of the ingenious modes of formal appeal created by symbol-using animals in the processes of adaptation to historical conditions wherein changing arrangements create new challenges to avoid breakdowns in communication. In that respect, its links with *Counterstatement* and *Attitudes*, in particular, are clear. But *Rhetoric* does more than simply rehearse the ideas of those older books, as the following brief sketch of its argument should make apparent.

The opening sections of *A Rhetoric of Motives* function as a sort of overture, delineating the main themes of what is to follow. The "anecdotes" from Milton's *Samson Agonistes* and Matthew Arnold's "Sohrab and Rustum" are in the order of killing, enmity, and suicide; but even in them we can, by adopting Burke's "perspective by incongruity" stance, find elements of the benign underlying the apparently malign implications of those poems. The very imagery of killing, Burke argues, suggests patterns of identification through transformation. In fact, in every instance of division, or faction, there is a compensatory element of identification. Further, death, as an ultimate term, hints at the element of hierarchy implicit in identification. The two concepts of identification and hierarchy are central to the argument of *Rhetoric*.

The introduction of the principle of *identification* suggests ways in which rhetoric as traditionally understood may be extended. Burke shows this in principle in the section entitled "Realistic Function of Rhetoric" (pp. 43ff.), but spends some time after that detailing the ways in which, for every case of division implicit in rhetoric, there is an element of identification. Thus, considering imagination as a suasive device, Burke is moved to inquire into the persuasive function of the poet's symbols. Poetic symbolism is ordinarily thought of as antithetical to "reason" or "ideas"; but Burke tries to show how such antitheses collapse under scrutiny and are replaced by an emphasis on what binds them together (pp. 78ff.). With the extension of rhetoric, Bentham's "legal fictions," for instance—principles of social order, not just poets' symbols—can be seen as "latent images" (pp. 90ff.); and Marx's "ideologies"—principles of dominance and class conflict—can likewise be seen as "images" (pp. 101ff.). Burke finds corroboration in Carlyle's observations on the social function of fashion and the element of "mystery" in it —"mystery," rather than the "mystifications" behind Marx's "ideology"— and in William Empson's analysis of pastoral poetry, which can be seen as a mode of resolving divisive social hierarchies through the principle of identification (pp. 114ff.). A whole range of things not normally associated with rhetoric can thus be considered "rhetorically," stressing the benign, in a way not possible in the social sciences, for instance.

The second key term is hierarchy, which is built-in, indigenous to all systematic thinking, and the key to rhetorical appeal, which is, at base, identification, as all identification is "in terms of something" that transcends the level of conflict and division. All persuasion occurs in a context that is beyond reduction to "positive" terms and explanations—that is, to scientific analysis. Hence we see the vital importance of the study of the patterns of formal appeal that seek identification. This sort of "persuasion" is, of course, to be differentiated from "mere persuasion," "winning the day," or "the Kill" (pp. 176ff.).

To overcome the limitations inherent in the view of conflict resolution offered by the "pentadic" analysis of Grammar, we need to recognized that persuasion involves ultimate terms, the opposite of "positive terms" (p. 189). The model here is that of courtship, as in pastoral or Shakespeare's Venus and Adonis (pp. 212ff.); and a paradigm of the mixing of rhetorical and social hierarchy, within which we all struggle for perfection, can be found in Castiglione's Book of the Courtier (pp. 231ff.). Caricatures and bizarre versions of these hierarchical/symbolic motifs can be seen in Kierkegaard and Kafka.

We need, then, to keep clear on the scope and purpose of rhetoric and the study of it. We are not just mapping out forms of appeal (as in Counterstatement); we are examining the totality of modes by which identification and its malign counterparts ("the Kill")—in short, the totality of human relationships—operate (pp. 264ff.). The prime "motive" is the impulse to perfection, which in rhetorical terms would eventuate in Pure Persuasion, something that, paradoxically, is not something one seeks actually to achieve (for then there would be no division, hence no rhetoric), but that explains why one can and does seek "perfect" identification (pp. 273ff.). It is in this context of the "goadings of mystery" that rhetoric needs to be apprehended if we ever hope to get a glimpse of Beyond the Barnyard Scramble, of the way Towards a Better Life. Burke ends by enjoining his readers: "Let us," he says, "as students of rhetoric, scrutinize its range of entrancements, both with dismay and in delight" (p. 333).

A Rhetoric of Motives thus puts us very much in mind of the themes of Burke's early work: his discovery of "salvation" in poetry, the principles by which communication (often in Burke a kind of "communion") is achieved by formal modes of appeal, all of which fall under the general rubric of "eloquence." What Burke encourages throughout is the study of the patterns of *rhetorica utens*, "the use of language as a symbolic means of inducing cooperation in beings that by nature respond to symbols" (*A Rhetoric of Motives* p. 43), to be recapitulated in a *rhetorica docens*, at base, a "linguistic skepticism [that], in being quizzical, provides the surest ground for the discernment of linguisitic resources" (*A Grammar of Motives*, p. 443). To be sure, the tone changes somewhat, as Burke's earlier defiant "Program" is transformed into a plea for sanity in the face of what he describes in a 1943 essay ("Tactics of Motivation")[13] as "dissipation" (opportunism) and "technological hysteria." But the issues remain the same.

Burke's later pleas, like his earlier pronouncements, were heard by some—notably, his colleague Stanley Edgar Hyman and the sociologist Hugh Duncan—but largely dismissed—by his old nemeses Sidney Hook and Harold Rosenberg, among others—as eccentric and irrelevant. One gets the impression that the lessons of two world wars, of the Cold War that brought out the very dissipation and hysteria Burke had predicted, and of the hideous perversion of the highest technological achievement to that time—the atomic bomb—were carried away by a tide of political dogmatism too powerful to control by words alone. Recent scholarship has begun to recognize not only how great his contribution to the revival of rhetoric was but also how prophetic Burke really was. But even Burke, in the years just after *A Rhetoric of Motives* was published, seemed to give up the fight.

Thus far, we have seen, in the work of Richards and Burke, two responses to political and intellectual crisis. Both rediscover "rhetoric" as a salutary resource in their different accounts of how division and conflict might be overcome. Their rhetorics, it should be clear, are quite different from one another. The one focuses on "misunderstanding and its remedies"; the other on "formal appeal." Richards' rhetoric is radically individualistic in its orientation, Burke's is radically social. Richards draws on the latest advances in cognitive psychology; Burke is mistrustful of all the "-ologies" and draws on a recovery and analysis of principles implicit in traditional rhetoric. These two rhetorics make up only a part of the picture of the history of the art in the first half of the twentieth century, however. We must turn now to a third, that of Richard Weaver, to get another important part.

WEAVER'S REVOLT AGAINST THE MASSES

Richard M. Weaver (1910–63) was born in Asheville, North Carolina, where his father owned a livery stable. After his father's death in 1915, he was brought by his mother to Lexington, Kentucky. When he completed high school, he enrolled at the University of Kentucky, where he received a bachelor's degree in English in 1932. America was, of course, in the depths of the Great Depression. Like many other young people, Weaver joined Normal Thomas' American Socialist Party. He soon left it, however, disappointed with the shallow objectives of his comrades, and a little shocked, he tells us, that one of his group suggested having a "hillbilly band" play at one of the party's rallies.[14]

In 1933, he began graduate study at Vanderbilt University, in Nashville, where he became familiar with the Southern Agrarian movement, came into contact with some of its leading proponents, and was strongly influenced by one of its leaders, John Crowe Ransom. This is the same movement Burke disparaged in "Program" as irrelevant to contemporary problems in its celebration of the agrarian economy of the South, "in harmony with the rhythms of nature," as a response to the ills of industrialism. Weaver's association with this movement and with such men as Robert Penn Warren, Allen Tate, Cleanth Brooks, and Ransom—all of whom would later join in the literary movement known as the "New Criticism"—left an indelible mark on him.

By 1940, he tells us in "Up from Liberalism," he found himself disgusted by the "philistinism" of those around him and distrustful of the "concept of a man-dominated universe" and entered on a course of study that he felt would liberate him from the "essentially sinful" aspects of "contemporary radicalism." This course of study did that, but it also resulted in a dissertation he completed at Louisiana State University in 1943, "The Confederate South, 1865–1910: A Study in the Survival of a Mind and Culture," in which he argued that the South had "an ethical claim which can be described only in terms of the mandate of civilization."

This dissertation, more an apologia than a historical study, reveals a Richard Weaver who had become a devoted Southern Agrarian. Written while war raged all over the world, it establishes four distinctive features of antebellum Southern tradition: a feudal theory and social organization, a code of chivalry, the concept of a gentleman, and a certain "unintellectual" religiosity. Such features, Weaver argued, made the South morally superior to the North, which by virtue of its material superiority, had defeated the Confederacy in the Civil War. The culture of the South was a "rooted culture," unlike that of the anonymous and socially indifferent North; the persistence of that culture explains why the South, for instance, never fell under the spell of that "false messiah," science. Indeed, that persistence shows the South to be "the last non-materialist civilization in the Western world."[15]

This is not a mere provincialism speaking, but a deep conviction about the state of Weaver's contemporary situation, which he saw as bent on violating "the deep-laid order of things." On the one hand, he saw the ideals of Left "radicals" as amounting to "one of the greatest of heresies," "the denial of substance," lacking "a respect for the tragedy of existence"; and on the other, the fact of persistent evil underlined by the events of World War II, particularly by what he saw as the betrayal by the Great Powers—England and the United States—of Finland to the Russians at the Yalta Conference.

The South, for him, was a symbol of the culture of order that could offer escape from the insidious relativism of "man is the measure of all things."[16] Like the man in the storm of dust and sleet in Plato's *Republic*, Weaver took refuge behind "The South," trying to keep himself free from iniquity.

Weaver elaborated his diagnosis of the ills of the world in a book he originally wanted to call *The Fearful Descent* but was persuaded to change to *Ideas Have Consequences* (1948). This book is part jeremiad, part a program or radical reform. Thus he begins by tracing the origins of the deterioration of culture to the "evil decision" by William of Occam (d. 1349) to abandon belief in universals and replace it with his new philosophy of nominalism, which taught that only individual things exist. The "stark and disastrous" consequences of this decision were compounded by the rise of empiricism, which drove a wedge between facts and values, replaced belief in original sin with the dogma of man's innate goodness, and demolished the hierarchies and distinctions that make civilization possible. Thus, he says, we have lost sight of the "metaphysical dream" that integrates all.[17]

What he calls for is an attitude of piety toward nature, other human beings, and the past. The right of private property—"the last metaphysical right remaining to us" (*Ideas*, p. 131)—must be defended so that we might find refuge from the encroachments of "modern barbarism." And perhaps most important, language must be purified. There is a causal link between the corruption of language by the "impulse to dissolve everything into sensation" (p. 148), rhetorical illiteracy, and the errors of our times. Thus we have in this first book of Weaver's, a book hailed by one reviewer as "the *fons et origo* [source and origin] of the contemporary American conservative movement,"[18] both a manifesto and an agenda, an agenda in which rhetoric plays a conspicuous role.

That role is elaborated in Weaver's next book, *The Ethics of Rhetoric* (1953). In *Ideas*, Weaver had laid down a tripartite analysis of knowledge and a general theory of culture consistent with that analysis. There are three levels of "conscious reflection" at which we perceive, order, and evaluate our world: ideas, which are thoughts about particular empirical things; beliefs, or concepts that order the world of facts; and the "metaphysical dream," an "intuitive feeling about the immanent nature of reality" (18f.).[19] Truth resides at the level of the metaphysical dream and is determined by the degree to which facts and ideas conform to their archetypal essences (p. 136ff.). Every culture revolves around some metaphysical dream embodied in a "tyrannizing image" that acts as the principle of coherence society imposes on the morass of things. Accordingly, a developed culture is

> a way of looking at things through an aggregation of symbols, so that empirical facts take on significance, and man feels that he is acting in a drama, in which the cruxes of decision sustain interest and maintain the tone of his being. (p. 19)

Weaver builds on these basic principles in *Ethics*, observing that, as an expression of a culture's "tyrannizing image," rhetoric mediates between speaker and audience and becomes the means by which the members of a culture achieve emotional and ethical participation in it. Rhetoric is central to the achievement and maintenance of social order. It is an expression of a culture's "logic of belief." In it, the metaphysical basis for union, without which society would be a mere aggregation of individuals, is visible: "The major premises tell us how [one] is thinking about the world" (p. 15). Seen in the perspective of its function in society, rhetoric is "an art of emphasis embodying an order of desire," and has the office of "advising men with reference to an independent order of goods" (p. 17f.).

But, Weaver cautions, there is no "honest rhetoric" without a "preceding dialectic." Rhetoric without dialectic will fail to ensure that a speaker's argument is founded on the principle consistent with "the order of things." Dialectic is a method of inquiry whose object is "the establishment of truth about doubtful propositions" on the basis of categorization, definition, implication, and exposure of contradictions. But dialectic, since it is concerned only with the meaning of propositions in discourse, cannot establish truth or compel belief by itself. It cannot *move* individuals to action or attitude (p. 28). Thus dialectic must be supplemented by rhetoric in the world of action.

It should come as no surprise that such ideas bear a strong resemblance to those of an author we discussed earlier—namely, Plato—for they are laid out in the lead essay of *Ethics*, "The *Phaedrus* and the Nature of Rhetoric." This essay leaves no doubt as to the main inspiration behind Weaver's theory of rhetoric, and the rest of the book is hardly any less unequivocal. His Platonic conviction that the "noble rhetorician's" arguments will be rooted in dialectic allows him to construct a hierarchy of argumentative modes by which it can be seen, for instance, that Lincoln's arguments in his debates with Stephen Douglas are superior to those of Edmund Burke in *Reflections on the Revolution in France*. They are superior because they are arguments "from definition" and not, like Burke's, "from circumstance," a rather debased form of argument in Weaver's view.[20]

This conviction also gives Weaver a way to provide a grounding for rhetoric that will guarantee its legitimacy. That grounding, like Plato's in the *Phaedrus*, is to be found "in the ideal, which only the intellect can apprehend and only the soul can have affection for." Indeed, "when we finally divest rhetoric of all the notions of artifice which have grown up around it, we are left with something very much like Spinoza's "intellectual love of God" (p. 25). And toward the end of the book, we read that "rhetorical force must be conceived as a power transmitted through the links of a chain that extends upward toward some ultimate source" (p. 211).

Thus the comparison we made between Weaver and Plato's man in the storm is hardly coincidental. Deeply troubled by the world around him, a world in which "[we are] confronted not only by evil practicioners, but also, and probably to an unprecedented degree, by men who are conditioned by the evil of others" (p. 231), Weaver revived the idealism of Plato in his search for social and personal salvation. This orientation toward "the universe as a paradigm of essences" is, moreover, not just a philosophical one but a political one as well, as it characterizes what he understood to be "true conservatism" and provides a systematic basis for his critiques of the radical Left, of radical egalitarianism, "progressive education," cultural relativism, materialism, and degenerate forms of art and music. All of these were, in his view, the work of "the cult of the mass" (see *Ideas*, pp. 35f.), aided and abetted by the alarming proliferation of "thoughtless rhetoric" (*Ethics*, p. 231).

Nor is it coincidental that Weaver's Southern Agrarianism should have thus transformed itself into a new Platonism. The social order represented by the Old South, which he consistently invoked throughout his life as a sort of norm, stood as an approximation of the logical order of Plato's universe. As the culture of the South was a "rooted culture," the rhetoric that can allow us to order "our own minds and our own passions" (*Ethics*, p. 231) is a rhetoric "rooted" by its links with the ultimate. If the South was "the last non-materialist civilization in the Western world," a rhetoric grounded in dialectic might point the way to the new one Weaver so ardently desired.[21]

Like both Richards and Burke, then, Richard Weaver was moved by the conflicts of his age to find some cure, and the cure he found he called a "rhetoric." But Weaver's "rhetoric" is clearly not that of I. A. Richards, nor is it that of Kenneth Burke. While all three appeal to "rhetoric" as a salutary art, they develop quite distinct versions of it. What was the "study of misunderstanding and its remedies" in Richards became in Burke "the use of language as a symbolic means of inducing cooperation in beings that by nature respond to symbols" and in Weaver "something very much like Spinoza's 'intellectual love of God.'" The revival of interest in rhetoric represented in the works of these three writers is a phenomenon that few would expect in an age more frequently characterized by its technological and scientific advances than by a turn to "mere rhetoric" in the search for solutions.

SUMMARY

Given the signs evident after the Great War of anxiety over language, perhaps it is not strange, after all, that rhetoric should be revived. If there is a single theme binding Richards, Burke, and Weaver together, it is the sense of crisis they shared. All of them saw the world "going to hell in a handbasket," and for good reasons. Richards saw a solution in the training of students in the detection of the causes of misunderstanding. If language was at the heart of the world's problems, its users must be reformed. Burke and Weaver, from very different perspectives, saw rhetoric as central to social cohesion, with Burke tracking the vectors of formal appeal as they determine modes of communication and Weaver setting the metaphysical conditions for a "noble rhetoric" that would fulfill its traditional advisory function.

A second striking aspect of these "new rhetorics" is their comprehensive scope. Rhetoric is seen not as a special use of language that could in special circumstances win approbation on aesthetic or social grounds, as in the older bellelettristic tradition of the *ancien régime*. It is, rather, the study of all communication. If Richards' explicit definition seems to restrict "rhetoric" to the realm of prose, we must remember that the ways in which prose can improve us are the same as the ways poetry can. Burke and Weaver, of course, offer massive documentation of their contentions as to the centrality of rhetoric—in plays, poems, scholarly articles and books, and indeed the popular press, as well as in discourse normally seen as "rhetorical." Rhetoric, in short, becomes for these men not a minor discipline to be taught to the upwardly mobile, but an "architectonic" art around which culture itself can be ordered.

Finally, a reader of the works we have discussed in this chapter cannot help being struck by the similarity between the array of conceptions of rhetoric generated between 1920 and 1950 or so and the array of rhetorics we saw in the first chapter of this book. Richards' philosophy of rhetoric can be traced back, via Hobbes, perhaps, to the Gorgianic rhetoric of the late fifth century BC. This possibility becomes quite clear when we see the applications of his theory of meaning in empirical communication research. Burke, with his accent on eloquence and his skeptical stance, recalls the rhetoric of the Protagorean sophists. In fact, Burke's broad vision of "the entrancements" of rhetoric might be more specifically described as Isocratean; for what is "identification" if not an update of Isocrates' *homonoia*? Finally, in Weaver, as we have noted, we see a response that is not only similar to Plato's response to the shambles Athens had become but explicitly linked with it. The "new rhetorics" of Richards, Burke, and Weaver, in other words, are hardly new at all at base, for they represent anew the range of rhetorics evident in antiquity. Perhaps this is what Burke had in mind when he wrote in one of his poems, "The Dialectician's Hymn":

> . . .may we have neither the mania of the One
> nor the delirium of the Many—
> But both the Unity and the Diversity—
> The Title and the manifold details that arise
> As that Title is restated
> In the narrative of History.

In any event, it is no exaggeration to say that what we see happening with rhetoric in our own time recapitulates what happened with it long ago.

FURTHER READING

Good introductions to the work of Richards and Weaver can be found in S. Foss et al., *Contemporary Perspectives on Rhetoric* (Prospect Heights, IL, 1985); the treatment of Burke there is less satisfactory. On all three, the extensive bibliographies, pp. 260ff., are extremely useful.

On the cultural atmosphere in postwar Europe, see P. Fussell's excellent

The Great War and Modern Memory (New York, 1976). The milieu Burke worked in is nicely sketched in the various memoirs of his friend Malcolm Cowley, in, among others, *Think Back on Us...* (Carbondale, IL, 1967) and—*And I Worked at the Writer's Trade* (New York, 1978); and in R. Pells, *Radical Visions and American Dreams* (New York, 1973). For an account of the post-World War II cultural milieu, see W. Barrett, *The Truants* (Garden City, NY, 1982). The setting for Weaver's work is covered in G. Nash, *The Conservative Intellectual Movement in America since 1945* (New York, 1976).

Much can be learned about I. A. Richards' life and work from the essays printed in *I. A. Richards: Essays in His Honor*, ed. R. Brower (New York/Oxford, 1973) and even more from J. P. Russo, *I. A. Richards: His Life and Work* (Baltimore, 1988). There is an excellent full-length study by W. Hotopf, *Language, Thought, and Comprehension* (London, 1965). Hotopf's reading is both sensitive and incisive.

The best book to date on Burke is W. Rueckert's *Kenneth Burke and the Drama of Human Relations* (first ed., Minneapolis, 1963; second, rev. ed., Berkeley, 1982). Burke's impact on sociology can be seen in H. Duncan's *Communication and Social Order* (New York/London, 1962). Burke has received attention abroad, as well, for his contributions to both social and literary theory. See C. Roig, *Symboles et société* (Berne, 1977) and the special number of the annual review *Recherches anglaises et américains* (Strasbourg), no. 12 (1979). Rueckert's collection of reviews of Burke in *Kenneth Burke: The Critical Response, 1924–66* (Minneapolis, 1969) is invaluable.

On Weaver, see Nash, cited above. An issue of *Modern Age* (14 [1970]), a conservative periodical to which Weaver contributed, contains two interesting pieces: F. Meyer's "Richard Weaver: An Appreciation" (pp. 243–248) and M. Bradford's "The Agrarianism of Richard Weaver: Beginnings and Completions" (pp. 249–256).

NOTES

1. Edmund Blunden, "Come On, My Lucky Lads," in *Undertones of War* (London, 1924; rpt. New York, 1965), p. 219. This poem was printed again with the title "Zero" in *Masks of Time* (London, 1945), p. 41.
2. See *Undertones of War*, p. 221; *Masks of Time*, p. 44.
3. H. Lasswell, *Propaganda Technique in the World War* (London, 1927; rpt. Cambridge, MA, 1971), p. 2.
4. Hereafter, *Meaning of Meaning* (London/New York, 1923) = *MM; Principles of Literary Criticism* (London, 1924) = *PLC; Practical Criticism* (London 1929) = *PC; Philosophy of Rhetoric* (London, New York, 1936) = *PR; Interpretation in Teaching* (New York, 1938) = *IT*.
5. *MM*, preface, p. ixf. (in the 1937 London edition).
6. I have in mind C. Osgood's *The Measurement of Meaning* (Urbana, IL, 1957), as well as a large number of studies on "semantic interaction," "language intensity," and "attitude change"—for instance, C. Vick and R. Wood, "Similarities of Past Experience and Communication of Meeting," *SM* 36 (1969), pp. 159–162.

7. *Towards a Better Life* is in fact the title of the novel Burke published in 1932. On this, see the essay by D. Donohue, "When in Rome, Do as the Greeks," in *Critical Response* (cited in Further Reading), pp. 479–491. Unless otherwise noted, all references in this section on Burke are to first editions: *Counterstatement* (New York, 1931); *Permanence and Change* (New York, 1935); *Attitudes Toward History*, 2 Vols. (New York, 1937); *A Grammar of Motives* (New York, 1945); and *A Rhetoric of Motives* (New York, 1950). All of these books are available in more recent editions put out by the University of California Press.

8. See on this R. Heath, "Kenneth Burke's Break with Formalism," *QJS* 70 (1984), pp. 132–143.

9. For the response of Granville Hicks, see *Critical Responses*, pp. 18ff.; for Rosenberg's response, see pp. 26ff. of that work.

10. From the "Prologue" to the second (1954) edition.

11. In view of the fact that it is hard to come by a first edition of *Attitudes Toward History*, page references to the more accessible 1954 edition—in one volume— (rpt. Berkeley, 1985) may be helpful: "Acceptance and Rejection," pp. 3–107; "Curve of History," pp. 111–175; "General Nature of Ritual," pp. 179–215; and the last large section, "Dictionary of Pivotal Terms," pp. 216–338.

12. Burke explains "dramatism" in the article he wrote on it for the *International Encyclopedia of the Social Sciences*, Vol. 7 (New York, 1968), pp. 442–452. See also his *Dramatism and Development* (Barre, MA, 1972), two lectures he gave at Clark University.

13. "The Tactics of Motivation" was published in two parts in a short-lived magazine, *Chimera: A Rough Beast*, 1 (1943), pp. 21–33, 37–49.

14. Most of this information can be found in Weaver's autobiographical "Up from Liberalism," *Modern Age* 3 (1958–59), pp. 23–42. See also Nash (in Further Reading), pp. 40ff.

15. The dissertation was published in 1968 as *The Southern Tradition at Bay: A History of Postbellum Thought* (New Rochelle, NY). For the characterization of the South as "the last non-materialist civilization," see p. 391.

16. *Ideas Have Consequences* (Chicago, 1948), p. 4.

17. These notions can be found in *Ideas Have Consequences*, pp. 133ff., but are repeated in *Visions of Order* and *Language Is Sermonic* (Baton Rouge, 1964, 1970), both published posthumously.

18. See Meyer, "An Appreciation" (in Further Reading), p. 243.

19. This three-way analysis of knowledge bears an interesting resemblance to the distinctions drawn by his friend Cleanth Brooks of three kinds of poetry: sensuous, "platonic," and (synthesizing the best of both) "metaphysical." See the opening chapter of *The Well-Wrought Urn* (New York, 1947). Weaver constantly reminded his readers that his view of the world was, at base, "poetic."

20. See "Abraham Lincoln and the Argument from Definition," *Ethics of Rhetoric* (Chicago, 1953) pp. 85–114; "Edmund Burke and the Argument from Circumstance," pp. 55–84.

21. On Weaver's politics and his association with conservative intellectuals in the 1940s and 1950s, see Nash (in Further Reading) for a complete account.

CHAPTER 10

Philosophers Turn to Rhetoric

Despite the efforts of such writers as Richards and Burke to establish rhetoric as a critical instrument, "rhetoric" continued to denote in ordinary academic parlance "composition." The study of public speaking, virtually peculiar to American schools, was called "speech." This was to change, as philosophers in various countries, almost in spite of their original intentions, had recourse to rhetoric in the face of their loss of confidence in the ability of formal philosophy to solve problems of decision and action. In what follows, we shall attempt to trace the development of this philosophical resurgence of rhetoric as it has occurred during and since World War II in Chicago; Cambridge, England; Brussels; and Frankfurt, focusing on the contributions to this philosophical turn by Richard McKeon, Stephen Toulmin, Chaim Perelman, and Jürgen Habermas.

RICHARD MCKEON

The University of Chicago, during and after World War II, was the scene of a dispute important in the formation of attitudes toward rhetoric in our time. At Chicago, such political thinkers as Leo Strauss and Hans Morgenthau had found a base from which to carry on their critiques of leftist politics after they had fled Nazi Germany. One of their fellow travelers at Chicago was Richard Weaver, who taught humanities and composition there from 1944 until he died, in 1963. Under the president of the university at the time, Robert Hutchins, the Department of Philosophy had attracted a number of internationally famous thinkers. Rudolf Carnap, one of the most illustrious philosophers of science and language, came in 1935 after leaving Germany. Bertrand Russell visited in 1939. Charles Morris, one of the founders of modern-day semiotics, was a professor there for decades. Before Carnap's arrival, in 1930, Hutchins had invited Mortimer Adler, perhaps best known today as the founder of the Great Books program and as editor of the *Encyclopaedia Britannica*, but famous then for his recently published *Dialectic*. In 1934, Adler persuaded Hutchins to appoint to the Chicago faculty one of his old friends from Columbia University, Richard McKeon (1900–85).[1]

But a quarrel arose between McKeon and Adler. This surprised many, in view of their long friendship. An argument with Carnap or even with Morris would not have been surprising; but one with Adler was almost unthinkable. Adler, however, had undergone a change of position from the one he had laid out in *Dialectic*. There, he had argued for a radically undogmatic view of philosophy, in which the history of philosophy must be seen as merely a "documentary record" of the development of different ideas and methods, all of which could be absorbed into the matrix of dialectical conversation that "in the essential inconclusiveness of its process...avoids ever resting in belief or in the assertion of truth" (243). The highest form of intellectual freedom, he asserted, is "the independence of thinking from any belief whatsoever" (p. 246). One of the most fervent "converts" to that position was his friend McKeon.

What caused Adler's move away from his earlier position was his reading of the *Summa Theologica* of Thomas Aquinas, which, paradoxically, had been recommended to him by none other than McKeon himself. Adler describes the effect it had on him in his autobiography as "cataclysmic."[2] As Adler worked at making a Thomist of himself, his relations with McKeon cooled. "My inclination was now," Adler wrote in his *Philosopher at Large*, "to come down flatly in favor of certain propositions as true, rejecting their contraries or contradictories as false. McKeon, on the other hand, now appeared to me to be taking the approach I had recommended in *Dialectic*" (p. 175). For taking that position, which he described in a letter to Hutchins as "nothing but clever sophistry," Adler could not then, and never did, forgive him. McKeon, rejecting Adler's new dogma, remained steadfastly pluralistic, determined to legitimate the "sophistry" Adler had charged him with.

Born at Union Hill, New Jersey, in 1900 of a Catholic father and a Jewish mother, McKeon attended Columbia University, where he studied with John Dewey. He later went on to take up the study of medieval philosophy both at Columbia and, for a time, at the University of Paris under Étienne Gilson. After his return from Paris, his interests shifted to Spinoza, whose philosophy he examined in his 1928 dissertation; and from Spinoza, under Adler's influence, to what he came to call "historical semantics" and to the formulation of a schematism for describing philosophical methods and their interconnections. This schematism, as we shall see, provided the framework for his eventual shift of focus from dialectic to rhetoric.

McKeon never wrote a book elaborating his views. Indeed, his only full-length work was a version of his dissertation, *The Philosophy of Spinoza*, which was published the same year the thesis was approved. His position was laid out in a number of penetrating articles written over a long span of time on various subjects, and thus needs to be reconstructed from various sources.

McKeon tells us in an autobiographical essay published in 1952, "A Philosopher Meditates on Discovery,"[3] that in 1921 he had been jolted by his reading of a passage in Cicero's *De finibus* to the "recognition...that there is a sense in which truth, though one, has no single expression." The events of the years after World War I, and those after World War II perhaps even more, led him to see that philosophy had entered into a new importance, but had become so blurred by ambiguities that the relevance for action of principles and arguments was thrown into doubt. Since there is no single statement of the single truth and since any statement of the truth is subject to "degradation, misinterpretation, and misapplication," McKeon writes, "it becomes important to distinguish the aspects by which the forms of expression and proof may be differentiated and by which the criteria of continuing validity and value may be applied" (p. 118). This approach, of course, involves the study of an enormous range of philosophic problems before commitment to action or to grounds of action.

McKeon's determination to pursue that study resulted in, among other actions he was to take, the formation in 1944 at the University of Chicago of an interdepartmental unit called the Committee on the Analysis of Ideas and the Study of Methods. The program of "Ideas and Methods," as it was called, was devoted to the examination of philosophical positions and the methods of discovery and justification devised in their elaboration and defense. The view taken of the activity of philosophizing was to be broad, including inquiry, presentation, apologetic, and reflection. The study of the history of philosophy from this multidimensional perspective reveals a recurrence of themes and configurations of "places" by means of which philosophical views are established, defined, and transformed in the constitution of new facts, beliefs, and attitudes.

The picture one gets from such a systematic survey of ideas and methods is that of a constant "oneness of mind in the truth" sustained by the virtues of faith and honesty. Yet the dominant motif in this view of philosophical inquiry is not continuity or genetic evolution but discontinuity and dispute, controversy. Accordingly, the pedagogical goal was to train students to see the patterns and modes of philosophical discourse and to make of the students philosophically minded individuals capable of articulating, arguing, and applying claims, to engage them in cooperative disputation in inquiry centered on points at issue. This is not just a matter of producing "experts" in philosophical disputation. The dialectical exercises, if they are to be of any real worth, must contribute as well to the formation of character, to habits and virtues of sensitivity, originality, coherence, and moral purpose. McKeon's aim was not so much to elevate philosophy to an exalted position as it was to "bring philosophy down from the heavens," as Cicero once put it (in speaking of Socrates), "and give it a place in the cities and habitations of men."[4]

This hope that philosophy could be turned to some humane practical purpose benefiting the world community perhaps explains the role McKeon took in the passing of a resolution at the Interamerican Congress of Philosophy held in Mexico City in 1950 under the auspices of UNESCO. This resolution proposed a cooperative project aimed at improving international communication that would produce, among other things, a dictionary of fundamental terms of philosophical and political thought. Such a work, it was believed, would contribute to the clarification of the meanings attached to terms of political and moral thought that are, as McKeon put it, "subject to ambiguity and misinterpretation in a political debate and therefore a source of danger in international understanding and peace." It was to be a dictionary of "opinions grounded on philosophical traditions, as expounded by philosophical schools, as held by national and cultural groups, and as reflected in political discussion and propaganda"—of *opinions*, it should be stressed, rather than of truths "grounded in the nature of things."[5]

In the initial phase of this immense project, it was proposed that a short list—on the order of 150 items!—be covered by sets of five articles on each term, setting forth their meanings in English, French, German, Italian, and Spanish traditions. The list of terms would include both methodological and metaphysical terms such as *dialectic, history,* and *order*, and properly political terms—*peace, law, property,* and the like. Out of this list, four terms were chosen to begin with: *freedom, right, democracy* and *dialectic*. At that time, the conference's Central Committee recognized the need to include also, as soon as possible, other traditions and cultures, including Arabic, Hindu, and Japanese.

This project was not intended solely for philosophers but was meant to cultivate sensitivity and creativity among diplomats, executives, and heads of state as well. As a contribution of philosophy to practical discussion, it aimed to "reinforce the possibility of coming to agreement." Predictably, there were significant obstacles to be overcome. While it was thought, for instance, that there would be little trouble finding collaborators in the project from the Near, Middle, and Far East, few, in fact, stepped forth. While it was recognized that there would be a problem treating the terms "in the meanings they have assumed in Communist Countries," since it would be difficult to establish either historical origins or specific cultural ramifications, the intellectual recalcitrance brought about by the Cold War in both Communist and non-Communist countries was underestimated. As McKeon observed in 1951, the chief problem of contemporary misunderstanding, misinterpretation, and misrepresentation lay in the confrontation between the traditions "now opposed, in propaganda statements, as 'The Free World' and 'Mass Democracy.' "

If philosophy had been brought down from the heavens, few seemed to notice. A number of articles connected with the project appeared in scholarly journals such as *Ethics*, many—if not most—of them by McKeon himself. Almost 10 years after the 1950 meeting, a thick volume called *The Idea of Freedom* was published by the International Institute of Philosophy under the direction of Mortimer Adler. Cooperative inquiry and debate were fostered by the Center for the Study of Democratic Institutions, founded by

Robert Hutchins. But while these events were taking place, the Korean war broke out, McCarthy was destroying reputations, Hungarians revolted and were crushed by Russian tanks, U.S. Marines were sent to prop up a failing government in Lebanon, and the world became, if anything, a more mistrustful place. The dictionary never came out.[6]

Nevertheless, stung, perhaps, by his experiences while he was involved with UNESCO and struck, as he explains, by "the uneasy similarities of our own philosophic preoccupations to those of the Roman, the Carolingian, and the Renaissance periods,"[7] McKeon persisted. A long series of publications was to comprise a project aimed at a philosophy that could be called upon "to illuminate human problems of freedom and its absence, of life and death."

Such a project, McKeon repeatedly explained for decades, involves the assimilation of philosophy to rhetoric, or at least to rhetoric as it once was— namely, the sort of rhetoric that assimilated itself to philosophy. The model for this sort of philosophy is, of course, Cicero's method of *controversia*, in which, as we saw in our discussion of Cicero, there is a merger of the uses of philosophical discourse and rhetorical method. To call for such a merger is to insinuate a revolutionary change by virtue of which philosophizing becomes an activity in which "places" (*topoi* or *loci*), and not intuitions or sense verification, are the primary means by which modes and meanings in nature and art are illuminated. Our concern, in this sort of philosophizing, must no longer be restricted to self-conscious questions of validity or eternal verities but turned to the discovery of interpretations or new combinations within the body of *loci* that constitute our common store of "facts" and "evidence" that will allow us to discover new "facts" and relations. That is, philosophizing becomes an enterprise of "invention" proceeding from the *sedes argumentorum*.[8]

In some of his later papers, McKeon is even more specific about the importance of rhetoric. Given the complexity of problems in a world community characterized at once by conflict and interdependence, and in which discussion of those problems is betrayed by "abstract and fantastic formulations," he wrote in 1966,

> the method of a new rhetoric, transformed to philosophic uses, is needed to bring invention to bear on innovation of insights rather than on repetition of verbal forms and to bring judgment to bear on issues of causes rather than on adjustments to formed habits, characters, and prejudices.[9]

By 1971, he was to go beyond his call for the restoration of the study of rhetoric to the school curriculum to a call for the elevation of rhetoric to the status of "architectonic." Rhetoric, then, would become "a universal art,"

> an art of producing things and arts, and not merely one of producing words and arguments....Rhetoricians and philosophers might today make rhetoric an architectonic art which relates all things by means of science and the experiences of men. Rhetoric in all its applications is focused on the particular, not the universal—particular questions or constitutions in law,

particular works or compositions in art, or particular facts or data in experience and existence. In an age of technology the diremption to be removed is the separation of theory and practice by the constitution of a
technology which is theory applied. . . . We seek to produce it in concrete
experience and existence by rejoining reason and sense, cognition and
emotion, universal law and concrete occurrence.[10]

Only with such an art can we "eliminate oppositions and segregations based
on past competitions for scarce means."[11]

The direction of McKeon's thinking leads, then, from dialectic to rhetoric. In the process, his early discovery of a "schematism" by which all
philosophical methods might be described underwent a subtle transformation. As he described it in "A Philosopher Meditates on Discovery," the
schematism was conceived as a neutral and objective way of comparing
methods without distortion. By considering the subject matters, applications,
assumptions, and ends of different philosophies as they are elaborated by
their proponents, McKeon was able to generate four fundamental methods
of discovery and explanation, each coherent in its own right and irreducible
to the others. Once we understand these, we can determine the sources and
implications of misunderstanding and disagreement, discover what there is
to be said within different frameworks of assumptions, and present those
"sayables" in a coherent fashion. What we are seeing here, it will be noted,
is something very like the analysis of the "schools" of philosophy in Burke's
Grammar.[12]

The general study of philosophical methods uncovers "places" both
within each method and shared by all. But in light of the problems faced by
the world community, some way has to be found to apply the insights gained,
not simply in the determination of meanings but in the activities of demonstration, deliberation, and decision regarding particular problems. The traditional art designed to deal with particulars is of course rhetoric, and Ciceronian
rhetoric, as we have seen, is a sort of model. But the problems faced in an age of
conflict and interdependence go far beyond the problems Ciceronian method
was meant to resolve. Hence what is needed is a new schematism of commonplaces. The examination of the history of philosophy since Cicero's time and of
the factors differentiating the methods characteristic of those philosophies
turns up "places" that both supplement and replace the Ciceronian ones, which
were primarily adapted to questions arising in forensic settings. In addition,
therefore, to the intrinsic and extrinsic places of a work like Cicero's *Topics*, we
discover as places common to all methods consideration of, for instance, the
relation of means to end, of history to theory, of theory to practice, and of
sequence to structure. What we have, then, is the basis for a "new rhetoric"
suitable for the discussion and resolution of problems peculiar to the age of
international conflict and cooperation, technological innovation, and rapid
change. It is a rhetoric of invention, as it provides the possibility for perceiving new connections and implication between objects, events, thoughts, and
actions through the creative implementation of commonplaces.

No summary of McKeon's recovery of the resources of rhetoric can adequately convey the richness, subtlety, and erudition of his thought. What should be evident, however, is that McKeon, in the search for principled applications of philosophical thinking to the problems of the contemporary world led him from dialectic to rhetoric—as indeed it had also led an old friend and erstwhile colleague of his at Chicago, Kenneth Burke. It is also clear that McKeon moved, over the years, from a remarkably consistent pluralism bordering on relativism that was inspired by his reading of Cicero to a clear philosophical position, also inspired by his old Roman predecessor, summed up, perhaps, as a joining of wisdom and eloquence. While McKeon is most frequently associated with the so-called neo-Aristotelian Chicago School, it was not Aristotle, but Cicero, who loomed largest in his philosophical imagination.

STEPHEN TOULMIN

England was at war when Stephen Toulmin (1922–   ) took his bachelor's degree in natural science and mathematics at King's College, Cambridge, in 1942. Like many other graduates, he entered wartime civil service and served as a junior scientific officer in the Ministry of Aircraft, first employed at the Malvern Radar Research Center and later as an intelligence officer at the Supreme Headquarters, Allied Expeditionary Force (SHAEF) in Germany. Toulmin received a master of arts at Cambridge on his return from duty and went on to prepare for a doctoral degree in philosophy, which he received in 1948. Since those years, he has taught at many universities, including Oxford, Columbia, and the University of Chicago; and published extensively on ethics, the philosophy of science, and the history of ideas.[13]

In the years before World War II, Cambridge had been one of the foremost centers for philosophy in the world and home to such great thinkers as Bertrand Russell, G. E. Moore, and Ludwig Wittgenstein. Philosophy after World War I had taken a linguistic turn or, rather, two quite different linguistic turns, partly as a consequence of a revolt from philosophical idealism that had begun in the late nineteenth century, more immediately because of the intellectual upheavals after the Great War. On one side were the reformers of language itself in an effort to purge it of ambiguity. Russell's *Principia* broke the ground, and Carnap in Germany cultivated it in his investigations into the logical basis of syntax aimed at producing a formally consistent symbolic system for philosophical analysis. On the other side were philosophers determined to reform not language itself but the users of it. These "ordinary language philosophers"—Moore, Ryle, Austin, and the later Wittgenstein—sought to uncover the sources of philosophical delusion in everyday usage. Both groups of reformers are usually referred to as "analytic" philosophers. And it is with philosophers like these that Toulmin studied while at Cambridge.[14]

It is difficult to state briefly the essence of analytic philosophy—indeed, some would say it is impossible, so great is the variety of positions held by its various proponents. But there are two sets of conclusions about the properly philosophical use of language that are of interest, since they serve to contextualize Toulmin's work, which may be broadly characterized as a reaction to them. First, analysis shows that the surface features of a proposition are not necessarily adequate representations of its deeper logical structure. Any proposition that cannot, on analysis, be reduced to a logically coherent form must be deemed nonsense. Thus, for example, a sentence such as "Blueness entails extension" is in itself nonsensical, since analysis reveals its true structure to be paraphrased as "There is an x such that x is blue AND x is extended." The conjunction here is not equivalent to entailment, as logicians understand it. The implications of such analysis are quite devastating, for many propositions customarily taken as meaningful in descriptions of reality, predictions, and statements of value can be seen, under analysis, to be nonsense.

Second, and not unconnected with the previous matters, judgments of value are not judgments at all but merely expressions of feeling or desire. An assertion of value may be taken as a true or false report of one's feelings, but in the end it is only an interjection or ejaculation like "Bah!" or "Aha!" The "emotive theory of value" deprives ethics of any possibility of rational analysis. It is in this view technically impossible to say that one expression of value can actually contradict another: two feelings are merely different and bear no logical relation to one another. On this account, there is no such thing as a rational standard of right or wrong, and there is nothing good or evil in the world until someone adopts an attitude toward it—and that, of course, has nothing to do with the actual nature of the thing.

The philosophers, at Cambridge and elsewhere, were not very happy about these matters, it should be added. Russell, for one, decided that there was no reason why the irrationality of ethics should prevent him from doing things he thought—or rather, felt—"good," both noble acts like his conscientious objection during the Great War and his antinuclear activities after World War II; and other acts that most would not think very noble. Moore devoted some 30 years of his life to resolving the apparent contradictions between philosophy and common sense. And young Stephen Toulmin, just lately back from SHAEF headquarters, set about to reexamine the relations between rationality and ethics in the thesis he wrote in 1948 for his doctorate, later to be published as *An Examination of the Place of Reason in Ethics.*[15]

In retrospect, the issues Toulmin raised in *Reason in Ethics* can be seen as the issues that inform his entire output since that time. Questions about the nature and proper function of reason explain his forays into the history of science and his long interest in what it means to talk of human understanding. Questions about the connection between reason and right conduct explain the eventual shift in his work from the focus on theoretical philosophy to one on practical philosophy. That interest in practical philosophy, in turn, has been expressed most recently as a call for the renewed study of rhetoric as the means by which practical philosophy might be recovered from the rubble of intellectual history.

Reason in Ethics begins with a critical examination of current philosophical thinking about ethics. Toulmin takes up, in turn, the theories of Moore, the positivist critique of ethics by A. J. Ayer, and the emotive theory of value as analyzed by the American philosopher Charles Stevenson. All of these, he concludes, are hopelessly useless, "vague beyond redemption" (p. 62). Part Two consists of a meditation on "reason," a reassessment of science as a paradigm of reasoning, and an argument for the independence of different modes of reasoning. In the third section, Toulmin turns to the "logic" of ethical reasoning and the function of ethics. The real problems, he concludes are not problems of abstract philosophy but problems of life and human relations. It is, moreover, possible to provide "good reasons" in ethical issues. In the last part, Toulmin sets out the criteria for deciding which ethical arguments should be accepted and how far one can rely on reason in coming to moral decisions.

It is unnecessary for our purposes to go into detail in describing Toulmin's arguments. What is important about *Reason in Ethics* is that he makes a cogent case for ethics as a field of rational inquiry, taking exception to the dogmas current at Cambridge and Oxford at the time. But Toulmin's quarrel with his masters was not just an intellectual one. Toulmin is quite clear about the importance of his project. It is nothing less than a matter of survival:

> At times of crisis, when problems of particular complexity and importance are to be considered, the volume increases and the arguments offered become more wild and confused; until finally, when war or tyranny comes, reason is driven out into the wilderness, and the open discussion of general moral problems, even when completely abstract, is paralysed by the dangers of lapsing into bad taste or treason.[16]

Considering when this was written, when war and tyranny were just recently brutal facts of life, the restoration of reason to ethics was a matter of particular urgency.

A similar sense of urgency can be detected beneath the surface of the essays that comprise Toulmin's next major work, *The Uses of Argument* (1958). This book was written because Toulmin had become convinced that a radical reordering of logical theory is needed in order to bring it more nearly in line with critical practice. If it was true that the ethical theories of Ayer and the rest had "nothing to offer Everyman in his everyday problems but confusion" (*Ethics*, p. 222), it is equally true that the relevance of current assumptions about what constitutes logical validity to our everyday disputes remains unclear. How do the laws of logic "apply in practice," Toulmin asks, "when in everyday life we actually assess the soundness, strength and conclusiveness of arguments"?

Toulmin begins by drawing a distinction between arguments and proofs, pointing out that arguments are not inferences but justifications. Hence the "geometric" model is irrelevant, as are the "frozen forms" of Carnap's "logical syntax." He then goes on to dispute the traditional view that only an argument that is "analytic"—that can be formally expressed as a tautology—can be a good argument. The determination of whether or not an argument is sound cannot be reduced to a matter of calculation. Moreover, the formal structure of an argument insisted on by the logicians conceals some vital ambiguities that prove to be fatal to the ideal of "analyticity." In other words, the logicians, like the ethical theorists in *Reason in Ethics*, cannot much illumine what goes on in everyday life.

Toulmin's demonstration of this last point is developed in the chapter entitled "The Layout of Argument," probably the best-known part of the book to most of his adherents. Here he traces out the organic form of an argument. Arguments begin when one party makes a claim and another disagrees with or disbelieves it. It then becomes necessary for the claimant to show the grounds for the claim, to answer the question "What have you got to go on?" In the event the connection between the claim and the support offered for it is unclear, the claimant must explain what "warrants" the connection. The resulting "layout," then, looks like this:

Further elements may come into play. If the factuality of the grounds or the force of the warrant are doubted, it may be necessary to supply support. If the connections are not completely clear, one needs to qualify with a *possibly* or *probably*. And if there is a distinct contrary probability, one needs to introduce a qualification or disclaimer.[17]

The truly revolutionary element in this "layout" analysis, however, is not its redefinition of argument as justificatory rather than inferential, but Toulmin's observation that arguments in different "fields," which address different kinds of problems, are not all reducible to the same criterion of "soundness." Disputants in different fields accept different modes of warranting connections between claims and the support offered for them. Hence the determination of whether an argument is sound will vary materially from field to field, although all arguments may be "laid out" in much the same way. Toulmin, in other words, finds a middle ground between the absolute standards of the formal logicians and the position that the logicians saw as the only alternative: relativism, or subjectivity on the order of the "Bah!" indicating "bad" in ethics.

Perhaps predictably, *The Uses of Argument* failed to win many converts at Cambridge and Oxford. The reaction was, in fact, quite brutal. One perceptive critic, however, saw what Toulmin's detractors failed to see: the similarity between Toulmin's "warrants" and the *topoi* of traditional dialectic and rhetoric. This may in part explain the success of the book outside England, in the United States. Toulmin was puzzled, he explained later, by the fact that the book was selling well. But "when I visited the United States," he wrote.

> I found out who was buying it. Then, I met people from Departments of Speech and Communication up and down the country, who told me that they used it as a text on rhetoric and argumentation. So, the study of practical reasoning was kept alive after all; but this was done only *outside* the Departments of Philosophy, under the wing of Speech or English, or at Schools of Law.[18]

Over the years, *The Uses of Argument* came to dominate the literature on debate and argumentation almost completely. Toulmin's contacts with the teachers of argumentation matured into collaborations. But most significantly, Toulmin became increasingly conscious of his deep-seated Aristotelianism, not that of Aristotle's *Analytics* but that of the *Topics* and *Rhetoric*. In 1982, he was prepared to admit that

> by the time I wrote *The Uses of Argument*, in the mid-1950s, then, logic had become completely identified with "analytics," and Aristotle's *Topics* was totally forgotten: so much so that, when I wrote the book, nobody realized that it bore the same relation to the *Topics* that Russell and Frege's work bore to the traditional "analytic" and "syllogistic." Only in retrospect is it apparent that—even though sleepwalkingly—I had rediscovered the topics of the *Topics*.[19]

And in an article published even more recently in *American Scholar*, "The Recovery of Practical Philosophy," he goes even further. There he is quite clear (see p. 345f.) that by "practical philosophy" he means "rhetoric."[20]

In McKeon and Toulmin we see two philosophers whose careers may be characterized by a turn from philosophy to rhetoric. McKeon's rhetoric, based as it is on considerations of genre, stasis, and commonplaces, is the rhetoric of Cicero, and is a rhetoric of invention. Toulmin, with his notion of fields of argumentation and the warrants that will vary with them, is in the tradition of Aristotle; and his is a rhetoric of judgment that eventually becomes, in principle, a rhetoric of invention as well. It is not without significance, however, that, in the 1982 lecture quoted above, Toulmin also invokes the name and accomplishments of Hermagoras; and that, in the 1988 article, he cites Cicero's *De officiis*. Do we see, then, in the concerns of McKeon and Toulmin with the problem of how to make philosophy relevant to everyday life, an emerging "new Ciceronianism" in this century's resurgence of rhetoric? We will return to this question after we have looked at two other philosophers who have turned to rhetoric, Perelman and Habermas.

CHAIM PERELMAN

Shortly after the German invasion and occupation of Belgium, the rector of the Free University of Brussels called into his office four Jewish professors and asked for their resignations, in lieu of dismissing them outright. They refused on the grounds that to resign would be to ratify Nazi policy. A compromise was achieved, however: they would simply not conduct their lectures while keeping their positions. One of those professors was Chaim Perelman (1912–84).[21]

Perelman was born in Warsaw in 1912 and came with his parents to Belgium in 1925. Something of a prodigy, he received a doctorate in jurisprudence in 1934 and another in philosophy in 1938, both from the Free University. He then served as professor of logic, ethics, and law at the university until his death. During that time, he was frequently invited to teach elsewhere, chiefly at the Hebrew University in Jerusalem.

During the years of the German occupation, Perelman once explained, he "had to stay home, for good reasons."[22] This modest version of his activities between 1940 and 1944 fails to mention that he also became an important figure in the Belgian Resistance. And it does not tell what he did while at home—namely, to complete an essay on the idea of justice that was to mark the beginning of his turn from philosophy to rhetoric.

"De la Justice" ("On Justice")[23] was an attempt at an analysis of the notion of justice in a philosophically rigorous way in the fashion of Gottlob Frege, the German logician who was the subject of Perelman's philosophy dissertation. Frege, one of the founders of positivism, believed it to be impossible to treat values rationally or scientifically, since they are nothing but subjective expressions of emotion or feeling. Perelman tried to generate a notion of formal justice that would satisfy a Fregian requirement of objectivity. His analysis of various formal principles of justice—such as "To each according to needs" or "Equal treatment of equals"—led him to conclude that, while such formal principles do not contain value judgments, neither does that fact explain how one can rationally compare situations in appealing to judicial precedent. In a systematic application of the formal principle of justice, as he put it once, one has no problem with the major premiss; the problem is always with the minor. In other words, it is impossible to proceed from formal justice to concrete ("material") justice without some value judgments. At this point—at the end of the essay—he asks, "How then *does* one reason about values?" and ruefully decides that the sort of analysis he had performed cannot answer that question.

The implication was grave. If it were true that no decision as to the justice or injustice of an act can be free of value judgements, then no such decision can be rational. Nothing in the philosophical literature he read seemed to offer a way out of this impasse, so he set about to find an answer on his own by exploring all sorts of domains in which value judgments were made: aesthetics, politics, and philosophy in general, as well as in law. Eventually, his reading led him to see that the way out could be found in the study of the old dialectic of *controversia* and the rhetoric associated with it. This was truly a surprise, he tells us. After all,

> while still enrolled in high school, I had the privilege of taking the last course in rhetoric offered in Belgium. In 1929, rhetoric was removed from the curriculum both in high schools and in the universities.
> What did I learn in this final course on rhetoric? Something on the theory of syllogisms and something on the figures of speech. When I came to the university and studied logic, I always asked myself: "What has formal logic in common with figures of speech?" Thus, I believed, the people who gave me this course on rhetoric did not know what they were speaking about. Consequently, it became meaningless. Not surprisingly, therefore, rhetoric, in my opinion, was dead.[24-]

Yet Perelman, along with his associate Lucie Olbrechts-Tyteca, devoted a decade to the study of specific examples of argumentation concerning questions of value, examples of "informal reasoning" which constituted rhetoric.

The result of this study came out in 1958 as *Traité de l'Argumentation** (*Treatise on Argumentation*), recognized today as a landmark in the renaissance of rhetoric in this century. The book had an immediate impact on the Continent, where it was reviewed favorably in almost every journal devoted to philosophy. Surprisingly, it was praised even in Britain, in a review by Peter Strawson in *Mind*, a journal dominated by the "ordinary language philosophy" current at Cambridge and Oxford. But the most enthusiastic welcome was offered in the United States, where, Perelman was to say later, he least expected it.[25]

Traité de l'Argumentation, or *The New Rhetoric*, as it has come to be known in English, is a comprehensive book, full of insight, and elegantly written (a feature that does not emerge in the English version). It consists of three main sections.[26]

In the first, "Les cadres de l'argumentation" ("The Framework of Argumentation") (pp. 17–83/11–62), a distinction between argumentation and formal proof is drawn, the main difference being that argumentation is always addressed to an audience. *Argumentation* is defined as the discursive means by which an audience is led to adhere to a given thesis, or by which its adherence is reinforced.

Section Two, "Le point de départ de l'argumentation" ("The Starting Point of Argumentation") (pp. 87–248/63–183), treats of the premises concerning facts, truths, and values that are basic to agreement; the choice of data and their adaptation to the speaker's purposes; and the modes of presentation in discourse. Here the essential connection between argumentative forms and figures of speech and thought is established. Figures not only contribute to vividness and variety but themselves establish connections between things—synecdoche and metonymy, for instance, say something about part-whole relationships. It becomes clear, then, that Perelman and Olbrechts-Tyteca are talking about the entire range of discursive means of argumentation, not just the "logical" forms.

In this section, Perelman discusses at some length the "places" (*loci*) out of which arguments are derived. A *locus* is "a premiss of a general nature"; the sum of all *loci* constitutes a storehouse or arsenal (*magasin*) "on which a person wishing to persuade another will have to draw, whether he likes it or not" (pp. 113/84). There are two sets of *loci*: *loci* of the preferable (amplifying on those of Aristotle's *Rhetoric* 1.7) and *loci* that enable one to establish connections (*liaisons*) between facts. *Loci* on the preferable (quality, quantity, order, the existing, essence, and the person) break down into two large sets: those centering on "quantity"—such as "the whole is preferable to the part" or "the normal is preferable to the unique"—and those centering on "quality"—for example, "the unique is preferable to the normal."

Loci for establishing *liaisons* between facts are identified and exemplified in Section Three, "Les techniques argumentatives" ("Argumentative Techniques") (pp. 251–674/187–508). Perelman divides these *loci* into associative *loci* and dissociative *loci*. Associative *loci* include what he calls quasi-logical schemes (tautology, transitivity, etc.) and another class of associations centering on, for instance, cause and effect, contraries, complements, comparisons, or act and person. Dissociative *loci* turn on stipulations as to the character of facts as real or apparent, as latent or manifest, as constructed or given, and so on, which enable one to counter or transcend arguments founded on associative *loci*, much as *loci* of quality can be employed to counter or transcend arguments based on quantity. Association and dissociation are always mutually interactive.

Such, in a severely abridged form, are the contents of the *Traité*. The book has elicited an enormous body of critical response, some admiring and some quizzical. Most critics agree on the elegance of the critique it constitutes of Cartesian formalism and of the repositioning of the question of what is "reasonable." On the other hand, there are some who have had trouble with the notion of "the universal audience," or indeed with the radical audience orientation of the book: "facts are what are generally agreed to be facts," for instance. Putting aside these responses, there are a few points that need to be made about the book.

First, the primary subjects of the *Traité* are invention and expression. That is, the book is a compendium of methods of securing adherence, both argumentative schemes and stylistic resources, that extend far beyond the "perfectly unjustified and unwarranted limitation of the domain of action of our faculty of reasoning and proving" imposed by logic (p. 4/3). A parallel may be seen between the project here and Renaissance rhetorics—Agricola's, for instance—that lay out the *copia* of "things and words" that an orator must control. In view of what Perelman says in the introduction to the *Traité* —that the book is "mostly related to the concerns (*préoccupations*) of the Renaissance" (p. 6/5)—drawing such a parallel seems more than justified.

Second, the discoverable *liaisons* among facts or statements are much more subtle, much more flexible, and much more in the realm of particulars than the *liaisons* recognized as legitimate by logicians. Since Perelman calls his *loci* "premisses" and "argumentative schemes," one might be tempted to equate them, respectively, with "premisses" in syllogisms or enthymemes (or perhaps with Toulmin's "warrants") and with something like the inferential schemes of formal logic. No doubt, a *locus* of preference that one might express as "the whole is preferable to the part" could be construed that way, and it would be easy to fabricate a syllogism using that *locus* as a major premiss. But that is not what Perelman and Olbrechts-Tyteca are up to. Perelman has little if any interest in syllogisms. At best, they might be seen as a subset of his "quasi-logical" argumentative schemes. In reality, a syllogism or enthymeme is just one way among many of arranging an argument. In any event, it is difficult to see how arguments from analogy, comparison, example, or division, for example, could be transformed into syllogisms without doing great violence to what Perelman does in the *Traité*.

Finally, the *Traité de l'Argumentation* is, in spite of its size and system, a passionate book. If that seems an overstatement, a careful reading of the conclusion is in order. Here we will settle for just two brief quotations from the last pages of the book:

> We combat uncompromising and irreducible philosophic oppositions presented by all kinds of absolutism: dualisms of reason and imagination, of knowledge and opinion, of irrefutable self-evidence and deceptive will, of a universally accepted objectivity and an uncommunicable subjectivity, of a reality binding on everybody and values that are purely individual. (p. 676/510)

The theory—and practice—of argumentation allow us to transcend such dualities, particularly that opposing reality and values. And in the very last paragraph of the book, we read:

> Only the existence of an argumentation that is neither compelling (*contraignant*) nor arbitrary can give meaning to human freedom, a state in which a reasonable choice can be exercised....The theory of argumentation will help to develop...the justification of the possibility of a human community in the sphere of action. (p. 682/514)

When the *Traité* is read against the background of the experiences that gave rise to it, there can be no mistaking the tone of urgency in this concluding statement.

JÜRGEN HABERMAS

One of the central themes of Günter Grass' powerful novel *Dog Years* (*Hundejahre*) is that the horrors of the Nazi regime were in part made possible by a predisposition of the German people to avoid the stark truth of their situation by casting it in language that blinded them to it. Thus Grass imagines the German army issuing communiqués such as "The Nothing attuned to distantiality (*Fernsinn*) is acknowledged as the Nothing in the Steiner Group sector" or,

First and foremost, modes of encounter between Nothing attuned to distantiality and Twelfth Army will be investigated for their encounter-structure (*Begegnisstimmten*).... The digressiveness of the not-at-hand (*Unzuhandenen*) will provisionally be passed over with a view toward establishing authentic at-handedness (*probehaltiger Zuhandenheit*).[27]

This sort of language also pervades—and perverts—the thinking of one of the main characters in the book, Walter Matern, described toward the end of the book as leaving a POW camp with a copy of the book that made such language current in German, Heidegger's *Being and Time*. In fact, so obsessed is Matern with Heidegger that he journeys to the Black Forest to visit him. His visit is in vain, however, for he arrives to find a shuttered house surrounded by a wrought iron fence. The response to his shouting—"Open up, Stockingcap! Matern is here, manifesting himself as the call of care!" he says—is silence, nothing.[28]

Grass is clearly arguing in *Dog Years* that Heidegger's writings had reinforced such mindlessness as Matern's, a total lack of personal thought, by supplying a set of preconceived ideas and a jargon to go with it. Another member of Grass' generation, Jürgen Habermas (1929–), shares his distaste and dislike of Heidegger. But in the view of Habermas, it is not only the fact that Heidegger collaborated with the Nazis that condemns him, but the very project embodied in *Being and Time*, the *Destruktion* of the European metaphysical tradition and the ensuing irrationalism it engendered.[29] Hence, as Grass hoped to "bring the German people to their senses" with his fiction, Habermas has devoted himself, in the wake of the disaster of National Socialism, to the restoration of rationality to society.

Habermas was born in Düsseldorf in 1929.[30] Like many others in the generation that grew up in Nazi Germany, he was a member of Hitler Youth. At the end of the war, however, when the results of Hitler's policies were all too visible in the ruined cities of Germany, and, perhaps above all, when the fact of the Holocaust became known to the German people, he saw that "we had been living in a politically criminal system."[31] This recognition led him to embrace the most systematic form of antifascism—namely, Marxism—and to begin a course of philosophical study that took him from Göttingen to Zürich to Bonn. There he received a doctorate in 1954 for a dissertation on Schelling's philosophy of history, and from there, he moved to Frankfort, where he became an assistant to the head of the Institute for Social Research, Theodor Adorno. Since that time, Habermas has written prolifically on social and economic theory and has become one of Germany's most illustrious—and perhaps most visible—philosophers.

The influences on Habermas are many and various, but add up nevertheless to a coherent line of thinking. Marx, or perhaps the version of Marx developed by the "Critical Theory" of Adorno and his associates at Frankfurt, is far and away the most important. Not only is the Marxist critique of society central to his work; but the distinctively "dialectical" character of his thought is Marxist in nature. From the critique of society comes the analysis of social life based on production and exchange—in Habermas, exchange not just of material goods but of symbols. The "dialectical" approach led him to conclude that no particular exchange of symbols (communication) can be understood without developing first a universal model of all communication. This, in turn, led him to explore the work of Hans-Georg Gadamer, the writings of Freud, and the ideas of some of the "ordinary language philosophers" active in England—in particular, Wittgenstein and J. L. Austin.

Habermas' program is directed toward the development of a model that will show how rationality—and irrationality—are manifest in ordinary social interaction—that is, ordinary communication between "speaking and acting subjects." Gadamer's contribution to this program was his discussion of the hermeneutical realities of communication. Meaning and validity are internally connected and arise together in the process of interpretation. That is, there are no "presuppositionless" criteria for establishing meaning. The problems with Gadamer's position are, first, that it too easily falls into a sort of relativism and, second, that it fails to take account of the phenomenon of "systematically distorted communication" that results in self-deception or deception of others. Here is where Freud comes in, with his analysis of the relation between distorted communication and neurosis. As neuroses impede the individual's progress toward self-fulfillment, socially distorted communication, "ideology," impedes progress toward full emancipation, which is the goal of the just society. Both Gadamer and Freud, however, fail to offer a systematic analysis of communicative behavior. For this, Habermas turns to Austin's extension of Wittgenstein's notion of "language games," the so-called speech-acts theory. All these elements are combined in Habermas' notion of "communicative rationality," two aspects of which are important for our purposes: the "consensus theory of truth" and the "ideal speech situation."[32]

Habermas rejects traditional approaches that attempt to define truth in terms of objective experience, drawing a sharp distinction between problems of the objectivity of experience and problems of truth. Even the correspondence theory of truth of the positivists (for instance, Ayer) must be conceived in discursive terms. Since the supposed correspondence between statements and facts can be ascertained only through statements, the correspondence theory attempts "in vain" to break out of the sphere of language.[33] Further, "facts" are not "things" or events in the world, but are, rather, "derived from states of affairs; and states of affairs are the propositional content of assertions." Assertions, therefore, are the locus of truth, and the problem of truth centers on the validation of claims made in discourse. The question of truth arises first when people call into question and examine in discourse the truth claims they take for granted in everyday communicative transactions.

The validation of truth claims, then, is a function of consensus, but not any consensus will do. What is needed is a "grounded," or "rationally motivated," consensus, one that derives exclusively from the dynamics of the discourse itself, from the force of the better argument, and that excludes any external constraints and biases. At this point, Habermas turns to Toulmin's "jurisprudential" model of argumentation, which requires that anyone whose claims are called into question must offer evidence (data, "warrants,") and defend them against objections. This will ensure freedom from bias or distortion provided that there is complete freedom to move between levels of discourse so that no aspect of the evidence is excluded from scrutiny.

The scenario that would make such communicative interaction possible is Habermas' ideal speech situation. To ensure that whatever consensus arrived at is rationally grounded, all participants in the discourse must have a symmetrical and equal distribution of chances to select and perform speech acts, to contribute, in other words, to the argumentative assessment of truth claims. Ideally, the speech situation should be able to be extended indefinitely through time so as to guarantee that no participant is denied a place in the debate and no relevant opinion denied expression because of contingent historical conditions. Admittedly, such a speech situation is indeed ideal, perhaps even "utopian"; but anticipation of a consensus arrived at under the conditions laid down by the ideal is a necessary presupposition of "rationally grounded" communication, especially communication aimed at assessing truth claims.[34]

The goals Habermas sets down and the scenario he creates in his ideal speech situation will be familiar to anyone who knows about the history of rhetorical inquiry. The criteria and operational shape of "communicative rationality" Habermas describes bear a close resemblance to the classic idea of *controversia* properly conducted. And indeed, Habermas' work has attracted an enormous amount of attention among scholars interested in argumentation theory, particularly in the United States.[35] Moreover, it is possible to draw out of Habermas' work some parallels with other philosophers we have seen in this chapter. We have already seen that Habermas draws on Toulmin for his account of a logic of argumentative discourse. Habermas and Perelman both reject positivism on the grounds that it is, in the final analysis, dehumanizing; and both project an antidogmatic setting for the rational solution of problems by way of argumentation. And so one could go on, as in fact a number of his American critics have done in an effort to assimilate his theory into their own work. In this respect, the reception of Habermas by scholars in the United States is like their reception of Toulmin and Perelman.

Yet nowhere does Habermas express any interest in "rhetoric," unlike McKeon, Toulmin, or Perelman. One can only guess why this is the case, of course. But one obvious reason is that Habermas has, over the years, expressed deep fears about the essential corruptness of language itself. How can we ever be sure, he wonders, that we ourselves are not involved in yet another episode of "systematically distorted communication"? In an essay on Hannah Arendt,[36] he brings out a related concern, which he characterizes as the problem of illusionary and nonillusionary conviction. In systematically restricted communication, the participants form convictions that are free of compulsion from a subjective point of view, but they are in fact illusionary. In forming those convictions, they thereby engender a power that, as soon as it is institutionalized, can also be turned against them. The reference here is.

clearly, to the experience of Germany in the years before and during the Second World War; and the implication is that there is a need for some objective critical standard by which we can discriminate between illusion and nonillusion. As a consequence, Habermas' concerns are oriented toward the development of a universal principle of rationality that will supply new integrating structures that can never be accused of being accomplices of the old order they are meant to overcome. As we have seen, "rhetoric" in German history was an important element in that old order. And as we have also seen, there were good reasons, in post-World War II Germany, to consider rhetoric suspect. So for reasons of historical circumstance, if nothing else, it is not surprising that Habermas should avoid "rhetoric" as a part of his critical project. But at the same time, it is not without reason that rhetoricians these days should make Habermas a part of theirs.

Thus we see that rhetoric has begun to emerge as an important element in Continental thought. Perelman and Habermas were both deeply affected by the events of 1939–45, perhaps even more by the hardships of the postwar years and by the hardening of ideological positions during the Cold War years. Their philosophical concerns arose from a keen awareness of the bankruptcy of current philosophy as a reservoir of solutions for problems of practice. Their respective inquiries led them to see that real problems of judgment and action require particular solutions arrived at by real people, not by the application of abstractions. The relevant notion of rhetoric that emerges from those inquiries, it is by now clear, is not the Platonic variety, for Plato's Truth had been removed from the picture. In any event, that sort of Truth petrifies into dogma, and dogma spawns ideology, the social neurosis that impedes society's progress toward human freedom. Nor is the sophistic rhetoric of affective manipulation acceptable, as pervasive as it is in modern mass media, for it is both unprincipled and unanswerable. What is relevant, in the views of Perelman and Habermas, is the model of *controversia* grounded dialectically in the exchange of arguments.

Perhaps remarkably, these are precisely the concerns and conclusions reached by McKeon (who knew Perelman and his work) and, before him, by Burke, whose social analyses are at times strikingly similar to those of Habermas. The consensus among these thinkers seems to indicate that, indeed, there is an emerging "new Ciceronianism" that characterizes the important contributions they have made to rhetoric since World War II.

CONCLUSION AND SUMMARY

Our history ends here, as all histories must, in the present. McKeon and Perelman are dead, but Toulmin and Habermas are, at this writing, still active. The recently available work of others, too—Wayne Booth and Ernesto Grassi, for example—suggests that the rhetorical tradition is still healthy and the resurgence of interest in rhetoric still gaining momentum. Even more indicative of the persistence of interest in rhetoric is the growing volume of publication in the field of debate and argumentation and the increase in international scholarly cooperation in rhetorical studies sponsored by such organizations as the International Society for the History of Rhetoric. So the present in rhetorical studies is prelude to an encouraging future.

In this chapter, we have discussed four philosophers whom we have characterized as turning to rhetoric in response to the crises they perceived in philosophy and in the world around them. In this regard, they are like virtually all the writers on rhetoric we have seen in our survey of rhetoric in the European tradition. But these four—McKeon, Toulmin, Perelman, and Habermas—also share something more specific, and perhaps more profound and important: a determination to combat dogma, to relate philosophy to everyday life, and to ground that philosophy in *controversia*.

Critical responses to the crises of language and life in the earlier decades of this century seem to replicate, or so we have argued, the responses evident in ancient Greece, and may be distributed accordingly. Thus we were able to pair Weaver with Plato, Burke with Isocrates, and rhetorics influenced by Richards with the Gorgianic tradition. The more recent work that has been the subject of the present chapter suggests the emergence of a consensus that amounts to a "new Ciceronianism," reminding us of the "uneasy similarities" McKeon perceived between our times and those of Cicero and of Alcuin.

This new Ciceronianism represents both a revival of the ideals of *controversia* and the modes of inquiry and presentation it suggests and a departure from the old. In the generations after Cicero, his successors, from Quintilian to Gottsched, made him a model and assigned him to a place in educational systems designed to preserve the existing social structures. The goals of the rhetorics of the present century, especially those conceived by Burke, Weaver, and the four philosophers we have just looked at, involve education in rhetoric as a means, rather, of transforming society.

In this respect, the history of rhetoric in the European tradition and its current revival, if we have read it rightly, plays out John Dewey's distinction between education as a function of society and society as a function of education. Then again, this distinction, like so much in the rhetorics that have characterized themselves as "new," may not be so new after all. Dewey's distinction is by no means peculiarly modern. The difference between Plato and Isocrates, after all, lay in the fact that Plato wanted to construct a perfect *polis* and educate its citizens in accordance with its structure; and Isocrates wanted to educate the citizens to eliminate strife and enmity by teaching them how to achieve *homonoia*, "oneness of mind" or, indeed, "consensus." In a sense, then, our history ends in the present, but it is a present, one hopes, informed and enlightened by the past.

FURTHER READING

Contemporary Perspectives on Rhetoric (cited in Further Reading for Chapter 9) contains useful sections on Toulmin, Perelman, and Habermas, as well as extensive bibliographies for each. Unfortunately, the bibliographies for

Perelman and Habermas include only the literature in English. R. Pells' *The Liberal Mind in a Conservative Age* (New York, 1985) is a good background work on the intellectual traffic between Europe and the United States after World War II.

There is very little useful secondary literature on McKeon's work. A collection of some of his important essays can be found in *Rhetoric: Essays in Invention and Discovery*, ed. and with an introduction by M. Backman (Woodbridge, CT, 1987). The University of Chicago Press has recently announced plans to publish all of McKeon's papers. The general editor of this project is Zahava McKeon, Richard McKeon's widow. On the milieu at Chicago, see M. Gardner's *Order and Surprise* (Buffalo, 1983), as well as Adler's *Philosopher at Large* (Chicago, 1977).

A large number of articles on Toulmin are listed by Foss *et al.* in *Contemporary Perspectives*, pp. 276–280. Oddly, the selection does not include O. Bird's "The Rediscovery of the Topics," *Mind* 70 (1961), 534–540. The general outlines of analytic philosophy are neatly summarized by B. Blanchard in "The Philosophy of Analysis," *Proceedings of the British Academy* 38 (1952), pp. 39–70.

The secondary literature in English on Perelman can be found in *Contemporary Perspectives*, too, pp. 282ff. P. Strawson's review of *Traité*, however, is missing. It can be found in *Mind* 68 (1959), pp. 420f.

T. McCarthy's *The Critical Theory of Jürgen Habermas* (Cambridge, MA, 1978) is still the best introduction in English, although a very short but useful book on him by M. Pusey, *Jürgen Habermas* (London/New York, 1987) has appeared. The essays in *Habermas: Critical Debates*, ed. J. Thompson and D. Held (Cambridge, MA, 1982) are supplemented by Habermas' "A Reply to My Critics," pp. 219–283.

Ernesto Grassi's work is just lately available in English. See "Rhetoric and Philosophy," in *Philosophy and Rhetoric* 9 (1976), pp. 200–216; rpt. in his *Rhetoric as Philosophy: The Humanist Tradition* (University Park, PA, 1980). Wayne Booth is perhaps most famous for his *Rhetoric of Fiction* (Chicago, 1963); his *Modern Dogma and the Rhetoric of Assent* (Notre Dame, 1972) is necessary reading. The International Society for the History of Rhetoric continues to promote high-quality research, the results of which appear in the journal *Rhetorica*, which we have had frequent opportunities to cite in this book.

NOTES

1. On the milieu at Chicago, see "The Strange Case of Robert Maynard Hutchins" and the postscript to "Art, Propaganda, and Propaganda Art" in Gardner (see Further Reading), pp. 13–28, 39–44. Carnap briefly describes his experiences there in his "Intellectual Autobiography," published in *The Philosophy of Rudolf Carnap*, ed. P. Schilpp (LaSalle, IL, 1963), pp. 32 ff. See also Adler's *Philosopher at Large* (Chicago, 1977), pp. 173ff. (=" Adler").

2. See Adler, p. 83. The quotations from Adler's *Dialectic* (London, 1927) are found on pp. 241f. This book, incidentally, was published in the series International Library of Psychology, Philosophy, and Scientific Method, ed. C. K. Ogden. Among other books published in that series are Richards' *Principles of Literary Criticism* and Wittgenstein's *Tractatus Logico-Philosophicus*.

3. In *Moments of Personal Discovery*, ed. R. MacIver (New York/London, 1952), pp. 105–132. This essay also appears in the Backman collection (see Further Reading), pp. 194–220.

4. Cicero, *Tusculan Disputations* 5.4.10; and see McKeon's "Character and the Arts and Disciplines," *Ethics* 78 (1967–68), pp. 109–123. Some of the material in this section appeared in T. M. Conley, "The Virtues of Controversy: *In memoriam* R. P. McKeon," *QJS* 71 (1985), pp. 470–475.

5. McKeon describes this project in a long note appended to his "Dialectic and Political Thought and Action," *Ethics* 65 (1954–55), pp. 28ff. See also *Democracy in a World of Tensions*, ed. R. McKeon (Chicago, 1951), Appendix III: "Report of the Committee on the Philosophical Analysis of Fundamental Concepts," pp. 527ff.

6. McKeon's articles in *Ethics* include "Philosophical Differences and the Issues of Freedom," 61 (1950–51), pp. 105–135; "Philosophy and Action," 62 (1951–52), pp. 79–105; "Communication, Truth, and Society," 67 (1956–57), pp. 88–108; "The Ethics of International Influence," 70 (1959–60), pp. 197–203; and "Mankind: The Relation of Reason to Action," 74 (1963–64), pp. 174–185.

7. "A Philosopher Meditates on Discovery," pp. 113, 123 (in Backman, pp. 202, 212).

8. These matters are discussed by McKeon in "Creativity and the Commonplace," *Philosophy and Rhetoric* 6 (1973), pp. 199–210 (in Backman, pp. 25–36); and "The Methods of Rhetoric and Philosophy: Invention and Judgment," in *The Classical Tradition: Literary and Historical Studies in Honor of Harry Caplan*, ed. L. Wallach (Ithaca, NY, 1966), pp. 365–373 (in Backman, pp. 56–65).

9. "Methods of Rhetoric," p. 72 (Backman, p. 64).

10. See "The Uses of Rhetoric in a Technological Age: Architectonic Productive Arts" in *The Prospect of Rhetoric*, ed. L. Bitzer and E. Black (Englewood Cliffs, NJ, 1971), p. 62 (Backman, p. 24).

11. Ibid.

12. Burke and McKeon were old friends from their days at Columbia. Burke was in residence for a term at Chicago in 1941.

13. Biographical information on Toulmin can be found in *Contemporary Authors*, ed. A. Avory (Detroit, 1982) and Foss et al., pp. 78f.

14. The general outlines of "analysis" are sketched by Blanchard (cited in Further Reading). Information about the various philosophers mentioned here can be found in the *Encyclopedia of Philosophy*.

15. The dissertation was published by the Cambridge University Press in 1950. Citations are to that edition.

16. *Reason in Ethics*, p. 2.

17. *The Uses of Argument* (Cambridge, England, 1958; rpt. 1969), pp. 94–107.

18. See "Logic and the Criticism of Argument," a lecture given at Michigan in 1982, printed in J. Golden et al., *The Rhetoric of Western Thought*, 3rd ed. (Dubuque, 1978), pp. 391–401. This quotation is from p. 395.

19. Ibid.

20. The article appears in *The American Scholar*, Summer 1988, pp. 337–352.

21. This story is related by J. Gerard-Libois and J. Gotovitch in *L'an 40: La Belgique occupée* (Brussels, 1971), p. 462. Other biographical information may be found in Foss et al., pp. 102f.

22. As related by Perelman in a talk he gave at Ohio State University in 1982, printed in J. Golden and J. Pilotta, *Practical Reasoning in Human Nature* (Dordrecht/Boston, 1986), p. 3.

23. Originally published in Brussels in 1945; rpt., trans. J. Petrie as "Concerning Justice" in *The Idea of Justice and the Problem of Argument* (London, 1963), pp. 1–60.

24. Golden and Pilotta, p. 2f.

25. See Perelman's account in "The New Rhetoric and the Rhetoricians," in *QJS* 70 (1984), pp. 188–196. This article was published after his death in January 1984.

26. Originally published in Paris, 1958; rpt. Brussels, 1970; English trans., *The New Rhetoric: A Treatise on argumentation* (Notre Dame, 1969). Citations are to both the French and the English versions, respectively.

27. *Hundejahre* (Neuwied am Rhein, 1963), pp. 345f.; text in English, *Dog Years* (New York, 1965), pp. 417f.

28. Ibid, p. 393/475.

29. This theme is developed at length in Habermas' *Der philosophische Diskurs der Moderne* (Frankfurt, 1985); see also his *Nachmetaphysisches Denken* (Frankfurt, 1988), pp. 45ff.

30. For biographical information and bibliography (only English), see Foss et al., pp. 214f., 311ff.

31. See A. Honneth et al., "The Dialectics of Rationalization: An Interview with Jürgen Habermas," *Telos* 49 (1981), p. 5.

32. This summary is based on Habermas' "Towards a Theory of Communicative Competence," *Inquiry* 13 (1970) pp. 360–375; "A Postscript to *Knowledge and Human Interests*," *Philosophy of the Social Sciences* 3 (1973), pp. 157–189; and "Wahrheitstheorien," in *Wirklichkeit und Reflexion*, ed. H. Fahrenbach (Pfullingen, 1973), pp. 211–265. See also McCarthy (cited in Further Reading), Chapter 4.

33. "Wahrheitstheorien," p. 216.

34. Ibid., p. 257ff.

35. The bibliography in Foss et al. bears ample testimony to this.

36. "Hannah Arendt: On the Concept of Power," in *Philosophical-Political Profiles* (Cambridge, MA/London, 1983), pp. 171–188.

CHAIM PERELMAN AND LUCIE OLBRECHTS-TYTECA, *THE NEW RHETORIC: A TREATISE ON ARGUMENTATION*

(Page references are to the English version, trans. J. Wilkinson and P. Weaver, [Notre Dame, 1969].)

Chronological Tables

Authors and Works		Important Events	
	Common Era		
c. 50	"Longinus" active	54–68	Reign of Nero
93	Quintilian, *Institutes*	69–79	Reign of Vespasian
	Tacitus, *Dialogue*		
100	Pliny, *Panegyric*		
155–225	Hermogenes		
		330	Constantinople founded
	Gregory of Nazianzus (d. 389)		
		395	Official division of Roman Empire
	John Chrysostom (d. 407)		
354–430	Augustine	410	Fall of Rome to Vandals
426	Completion of *De doctrina christiana*		
475–524	Boethius		
			Sixth to ninth centuries: Dark Ages
		800	Coronation of Charlemagne
c. 802	Alcuin, *Disputatio*		
c. 817	Hrabanus Maurus, *De institutione*		
940–1003	Gerbert of Reims		
950–1022	Notker Labeo		Ninth to thirteenth centuries: Revival of Byzantine Empire
c. 1120	Thierry of Chartres		
1210	Geoffrey of Vinsauf, *Poetria nova*		
		1321	Death of Dante
c. 1320	Robert de Basevorn, *Forma praedicandi*		
1333–45	Petrarch's discoveries of important speeches and letters of Cicero		
1416	Bracciolini's discovery of Quintilian's *Institutes*; Trebizond arrives in Venice		

Authors and Works	*Important Events*
c. 1440 Trebizond, *Rhetoricorum libri quinque*	
	1453 Fall of Constantinople
1444–85 Rudolf Agricola	
	1492 Columbus lands in America

1466   Birth of Erasmus
        1509 *Praise of Folly*
        1521–25 Disputes with Luther
	Beginning of Reformation

1521 Melanchthon, *Elements of Rhetoric*	
1531 Cox, *Arte*	
	1540 Society of Jesus chartered
1550 Sherry, *A Treatise on Schemes and Tropes*	
1553 Wilson, *The Arte of Rhetorique*	
1555 Ramus, *Dialectique*	
1560 Soares, *De arte rhetorica*	
1577 Peacham, *Garden of Eloquence*	
1584 Talon, *Rhetorica* Fenner, *The Artes of Logicke and Rethorike*	
1588 Fraunce, *The Arcadian Rhetoricke*	1588 Defeat of Spanish Armada
	1603 Death of Elizabeth I
1605 Bacon, *On the Advancement of Learning*	
1607 Keckermann, *Systema rhetorica*	
	1610 Assassination of Henri IV
	1618–48 Thirty Years' War
1619 Caussin, *De eloquentia sacra et humana*	
1621 Vossius, *Rhetorices contractae*	
1637 Descartes, *Discourse on Method*	

Authors and Works		Important Events	
		1638–1715	Louis XIV
		1660	Royal Society founded
1675	Lamy, *Art de parler*		
		1688	Glorious Revolution in England
1687	Bouhours, *La manière de bien penser*		
1711	Vico, *Institutiones oratoriae*		
1726–28	Rollin, *De la manière d'enseigner et d'étudier*		
1728	Buffier, *Traité de l'éloquence*		
1729	DuMarsais, *Des Tropes*		
1736	Gottsched, *Ausführliche Redekunst*		
1757	Mayans, *Retórica*		
1762	Sheridan, *A Course of Lectures on Elocution*		
1776	Campbell, *Philosophy of Rhetoric*	1776	Declaration of Independence
1783	Blair, *Lectures on Rhetoric and Belles Lettres*		
		1789–92	French Revolution
1806	Austin, *Chironomia: or a Treatise on Rhetorical Delivery*		
1828	Whately, *Elements of Rhetoric*		
		1861–65	U.S. Civil War
1866	First ed. of Bain, *English Composition and Rhetoric*		
1872	Spencer, *Philosophy of Style*		
		1914–18	World War I
1931	Burke, *Counterstatement*		
1934–85	McKeon at Chicago		
1936	Richards, *Philosophy of Rhetoric*		
		1939–45	World War II
1945	Burke, *Grammar of Motives*		

Authors and Works	*Important Events*
1948 Weaver, *Ideas Have Consequences*	
Toulmin, *An Examination of the Place of Reason in Ethics*	
1950 Burke, *Rhetoric of Motives*	
1953 Weaver, *The Ethics of Rhetoric*	
1958 Toulmin, *The Uses of Argument*	
Perelman, *Traité de l'Argumentation*	
1968 Habermas, *Knowledge and Human Interests*	

Glossary

Actio. (Lat.) Gesture in delivery.

Argumentatio. (Lat.) Argumentation—i.e., the expression of the *argumentum*, or argument.

Arrangement. (Lat., *dispositio*; Gk., *taxis*) That part of rhetoric concerned with the ordering of arguments in a speech.

Attic. Of or pertaining to Athens, with particular reference to dialect or style.

Causa. (Lat.) A question for debate involving particular circumstances, from which comes the English "case."

Cento. (It.) Patchwork composition (usually poetic) made up of snippets of other works to produce a new work.

Chreia. (Gk.) In **progymnasmata**, an exercise consisting of the amplification of a moral saying or proverb.

Confirmatio. (Lat.) Proof, or the argumentative part of a speech.

Controversia. (Lat.) Debate in which both sides of an issue (*in utramque partem*) are argued; in Cicero and Erasmus, the only reasonable way to resolve issues.

Copia. (Lat.) Abundance of expression and/or subjects of discourse.

Dicanic. (> Gk.) Of the sort of rhetoric practiced in the courtroom (compare Lat. *genus iudicale*, "forensic").

Diaeresis. (Gk.) Division, sometimes binary, sometimes less specific.

Diegesis. (Gk.) Narration of pertinent facts in a speech (compare Lat., *narratio*).

Doxa. (Gk.) Opinion.

Eikos. (Gk.) Variously, image (as in Plato); probability (Aristotle).

Ekphrasis. (Gk.) In **progymnasmata**, description; in Agricola, the method of running a term through the "places".

Elocutio. (Lat.) Variously, expression and style; to be distinguished from pronuntiatio, the actual speaking.

Enkyklios paideia. (Gk.) Rounded education; in **Hellenistic** times, consisted of curriculum that included grammar, rhetoric, and dialectic, arithmetic, geometry, music, and astronomy; in Lat. tradition, *artes liberales*, "liberal arts."

Enthymeme. (Gk.) Popularly, a truncated syllogism; properly a rhetorical syllogism. In some texts, a figure that works on the principle of antithesis.

Epicheireme. (Gk.) Generally, an expanded and amplified syllogism.

Epideictic. (> Gk.) Commonly, rhetoric of praise and blame; later, of both and of didactic rhetoric as well (Lat., *genus demonstrativa*, demonstrative rhetoric).

Episteme. (Gk.) Loosely, "knowledge"; more often, "exact knowledge," "knowledge of universals."

Ergasia. (Gk.) Working up, or amplifying discursively.

Eristic. (> Gk. *eris*, "strife") Disputation, sometimes for its own sake.

Ethos. (Gk.) Character; in Aristotle, the character of the speaker as it comes out in the speech; hence, a **pistis**.

Expeditio. (Lat.) Argument from residuals; also recognised as a **schema**.

Figura. (Lat.) Figure, see **schema**.

Florilegium. (Lat.) An anthology or collection of brief extracts.

Hellenistic. Referring to Greek cosmopolitan culture that developed out of Alexander's conquests and passed into Rome in first century BC.

Idea. (Gk.) Variously, "idea," "type," "quality of style."

Invention. (> Lat. *inventio*) That part of rhetoric concerned with the discovery of arguments or, more loosely, of things to say about a given subject (compare Gk., *heuresis*).

Logographos. (Gk.) Speechwriter.

Logos. (Gk.) Variously, depending on the context, "rational thought," "reason," "speech," "word."

Orthography. (Gk.) Correct spelling, or the standards of correct spelling.

Paideia. (Gk.) Education or training; specifically, the education designed to initiate youth into the Greek cultural heritage.

Pathos. (Gk.) Feeling, emotion; in Aristotle, of the disposition of the audience toward the speaker or subject, hence, like **ethos**, a **pistis**.

Periodic composition. (> Gk. *periodos*) A form of composition stressing coherence and working on the principle of expectation and fulfillment.

Peroration. (> Lat. *peroratio*) The final section of a speech (compare Gk., *epilogos*.)

Pistis. (Gk.) Conviction; in Aristotle, a mode of producing or reinforcing conviction.

Probabilitas. (Lat.) Usually translated "probability"; but the term refers more precisely to the "provability" of a claim by means of **argumentatio**.

Progymnasmata. (Gk.) Elementary rhetorical exercises.

Prooimion. (Gk.) The prologue of a speech (compare Lat., *exordium*).

Protagorean antilogic. The procedure whereby disputes are resolved by examining the arguments on both sides of an issue (see **controversia**).

Protasis. (Gk.) Usually, a premiss; in Aristotle, often equivalent to a **topos**.

Quadrivium. (Lat.) In the Middle Ages and Renaissance, the name of the set of curricula in arithmetic, geometry, music, and astronomy.

Reprehensio. (Lat.) Rebuttal of opponent's **confirmatio**.

Schema. (Gk.) A figure of thought or of speech (compare Lat., *figura*).

Sentiment. (Fr.) Apprehension, at once intellectual and emotional, of an idea, thought, and so on.

Sophist. (> Gk. *sophos*, "wise") From the fifth century BC, an itinerant teacher of, among other things, rhetoric; later, a generic name for a professional speaker.

Stasis. (Gk.) Commonly, "strife" and "immobility"; technical term in Hellenistic rhetorics for the point at issue in a debate (compare Lat., *constitutio, status*).

Syllogism. (> Gk.) Usually, a form of argument in which the claim ('conclusion') is supported explicitly by two coherent premisses.

Symbouleutic. (> Gk.) Of the sort of rhetoric appropriate in public deliberations (compare Lat., *genus deliberativum*, deliberative rhetoric).

Technē. (Gk.) Art, as in "technique": also, the term for a handbook (a *technē* on rhetoric).

Trivium. (Lat.) In the Middle Ages and Renaissance, the name for the three liberal arts of grammar, rhetoric, and dialectic.

Topos. (Gk.) Litcrally, "place", variously, depending on author, "line of argument," "commonplace," "warrant."

Trope. (> Gk.) A strategic substitution of an unexpected expression for the normal one.

Warrant. In Toulmin, a statement that explicates the connection between a claim and its support.

Index

808
C75 218   LINCOLN CHRISTIAN UNIVERSITY

130067

Made in the USA
Middletown, DE
16 March 2015